THE MISSION AND DEATH OF JESUS IN ISLAM AND CHRISTIANITY

FAITH MEETS FAITH

An Orbis Series in Interreligious Dialogue
William R. Burrows, General Editor
Editorial Advisors
John Berthrong
Diana Eck
Karl-Josef Kuschel
Lamin Sanneh
George E. Tinker
Felix Wilfred

In the contemporary world, the many religions and spiritualities stand in need of greater communication and cooperation. More than ever before, they must speak to, learn from, and work with each other in order to maintain their vital identities and to contribute to fashioning a better world.

The FAITH MEETS FAITH Series seeks to promote interreligious dialogue by providing an open forum for exchange among followers of different religious paths. While the Series wants to encourage creative and bold responses to questions arising from contemporary appreciations of religious plurality, it also recognizes the multiplicity of basic perspectives concerning the methods and content of interreligious dialogue.

Although rooted in a Christian theological perspective, the Series does not limit itself to endorsing any single school of thought or approach. By making available to both the scholarly community and the general public works that represent a variety of religious and methodological viewpoints, FAITH MEETS FAITH seeks to foster an encounter among followers of the religions of the world on matters of common concern.

FAITH MEETS FAITH SERIES

THE MISSION AND DEATH OF JESUS IN ISLAM AND CHRISTIANITY

A. H. Mathias Zahniser

ORBIS BOOKS
Maryknoll, New York 10545

Founded in 1970, Orbis Books endeavors to publish works that enlighten the mind, nourish the spirit, and challenge the conscience. The publishing arm of the Maryknoll Fathers and Brothers, Orbis seeks to explore the global dimensions of the Christian faith and mission, to invite dialogue with diverse cultures and religious traditions, and to serve the cause of reconciliation and peace. The books published reflect the opinions of their authors and are not meant to represent the official position of the Maryknoll Society. To obtain more information about Maryknoll and Orbis Books, please visit our website at www.maryknollsociety.org.

Manufactured in the United States of America.

Library of Congress Cataloging in Publication Data

Zahniser, A. H. Mathias, 1938-
The mission and death of Jesus in Islam and Christianity / A.H. Mathias Zahniser.
p. cm. — (Faith meets faith)
Includes bibliographical references and index.
ISBN 978-1-57075-807-2
1. Jesus Christ—Islamic interpretations. 2. Jesus Christ—Crucifixion. 3. Islam—Relations—Christianity. 4. Christianity and other religions—Islam. I. Title.
BP172.Z25 2008
297.2'465—dc22
2008019678

This book is dedicated
to the memory of Ali Kurdieh,

my first Muslim dialogue partner

Contents

Arabic, Greek, and Hebrew Transliteration Tables xi

Preface and Acknowledgments xiii

1. **From Common Ground to the End of Jesus' Mission** 1
   - Dialogue from Common Ground 1
   - Muslims and Christians Worship the Same God 3
   - Scriptures: The Qurʾān and the Gospels 4
   - Reverence for Jesus 7
   - Respect for the Apostles 8
   - Some Principles for a Dialogical and Common-Ground Apologetic 10
   - An Overview 12

2. **The Final Days of Jesus' Mission in the Qurʾān** 15
   - The Denial Verse: "They Killed Him Not Nor Crucified Him" 15
   - The Denial Verse in the Context of Its *Sūrah* 21
   - The Affirmation Verse: "I Will Cause You to Die and Raise You to Myself" 23
   - The Affirmation Verse in Context 28
   - God Triumphs 31

3. **"Someone Was Made to Look Like Him"** 32
   The Final Days of Jesus' Mission in Classical Qurʾān Commentary
   - The Occasion for Revelation of the Affirmation Verse 33
   - Classical Commentary on the Affirmation Verse 34
   - Classical Interpretation of the Denial Verse 37
   - Al-Rāzī's Objections to the Substitutionist Interpretation of the Denial Verse 42
   - Shīʿīte Commentators Opt for the Substitutionist Interpretation 44

4. **"Before the Hour, Jesus Will Descend"** 45
   The Final Days of Jesus in the Prophet's Sunnah
   - The Sciences of Tradition 45
   - The Descent of ʿĪsā Tradition in *Ṣaḥīḥ* Muslim 47
   - Ṭabarī's Argument Revisited 50
   - The Descent of Jesus Traditions in Major Ḥadīth Collections 52
   - Questions about the Authenticity of Ṭabarī's Eschatological Tradition 55

5. "Would God Have Let His Messenger Be Killed?" **59**
The Final Days of Jesus' Mission in Modern Qur'ān Commentary
The Commentary of Qāsimī 63
The Gospels Reveal Confusion about the Last Days of Jesus 64
The Gospel Narratives Support the Qur'ānic Interpretation 64
Claims and Counterclaims of Christians 69
Further Gospel Contradictions and Irrational Claims 72
A Wavering Christian's Case 73
The Gospels and the Crucifixion 76
Christians Exhibit No Consensus on the Crucifixion 77
For the Apostle Paul, Crucifixion Is Metaphorical 78

6. Judas Crucified in Jesus' Place **79**
The Final Days of Jesus' Mission in the Gospel of Barnabas
Qāsimī and the Gospel of Barnabas 82
The Gospel of Barnabas on the Last Days of Jesus' Mission 83
Evaluation of the Gospel of Barnabas 86
Silence on Barnabas in the *Sunnah* of the Prophet 93

7. Did Early Christians in Egypt and Syria Deny the Crucifixion of Jesus? **95**
A Look at the Christians Cited by Qāsimī and Riḍā 96
Believers in the Cross at Centers of Christianity before Paul 106

8. Sent Down or Raised Up? **115**
A Comparison of Islamic and Christian Scriptures
The Canonization and Composition of the Gospels 117
Disciplines of Gospel Research 120

9. "The Days Will Come When the Bridegroom Is Taken Away" **130**
Jesus' Final Days in the Context of His Life
"When the Bridegroom Is Taken Away" 130
"When Jesus Heard This, He Withdrew to a Deserted Place" 131
"Are You Able to Be Baptized with My Baptism?" 132
"Are You Able to Drink the Cup That I Drink?" 134
"She Has Anointed My Body Beforehand for Its Burial" 136
"It Is Impossible for a Prophet to Be Killed Outside of Jerusalem" 137
"I Will Never Again Drink of the Fruit of the Vine until That Day When I Drink It New in the Kingdom of God" 138
"The Hour Has Come!" 141
"This Is the Heir; Come, Let Us Kill Him" 144

10. "The Son of Humanity Must Be Killed" **148**
Jesus Predicts the End of His Mission
The Caesarean Prediction Following Peter's Confession 149

The Galilean Prediction Following the Transfiguration 157
The Judean Prediction of Jesus' Passion and Resurrection 161
Are the Predictions Too Explicit? 166

11. "Let This Cup Pass from Me" 170
The Transfiguration, the Last Supper, and the Garden of Gethsemane
The Transfiguration 170
The Last Supper 177
The Garden of Gethsemane 181

12. "The Son of Humanity Will Be Handed Over to Be Crucified" 185
The Arrest, Trial, Crucifixion, and Burial of Jesus
Betrayal and Arrest 185
Trial 193
Crucifixion 195

13. "And after Three Days Rise Again" 206
The Resurrection of Jesus
Did Jesus Really Die on the Cross? 206
The Resurrection of Jesus 210
The Historicity of the Resurrection: The Empty Tomb, the Appearances of Jesus, and the Experience of the Resurrected Lord 218
The Problem of Women Witnesses 225

14. "The Son of Humanity Came . . . to Give His Life a Ransom for Many" 227
The End of Jesus' Mission and the Forgiveness of Sins
Original Sin: A Closer Look and a Wider Perspective 227
Atonement and the Cross: A Closer Look and a Wider Perspective 234
The Cross and the Message of Jesus 239

15. "In Plain Sight They See the Return of the Lord to Zion" 245
The End of Jesus' Mission and the Nature of God
Common Ground in the Beautiful Names of God 245
Divine Intimacy in the Qurʾān 246
The Cross and the Involvement of God 248
Christian Scripture and Divine Engagement 255

Index 259

Arabic, Greek, and Hebrew Transliteration Tables

The Library of Congress system for transliteration has been followed throughout except in direct quotations. In book and article titles the system of the author has been retained. The tables indicate the transliteration scheme.

Arabic

ء = ʾ	خ = kh	ش = sh	غ = gh	ن = n	*fatḥah* = a
ب = b	د = d	ص = ṣ	ف = f	ه = h	*kasrah* = i
ت = t	ذ = dh	ض = ḍ	ق = q	و = w	*ḍummah* = u
ث = th	ر = r	ط = ṭ	ك = k	ى = y	with ا = ā
ج = j	ز = z	ظ = ẓ	ل = l	ة = h or t	with ى = ī
ح = ḥ	س = s	ع = ʿ	م = m		with و = ū

Greek

α = a	θ = th	ο = o	φ = ph	αυ = au
β = b	ι = i	π = p	χ = ch	ευ = eu
γ = g	κ = k	ρ = r	ψ = ps	ου = ou
δ = d	λ = l	ς = s	ω = ō	υι = ui
ε = e	μ = m	σ = s	ʿ = h	
ζ = z	ν = n	τ = t	γξ = nx	
η = ē	ξ = x	υ = y	γγ = ng	

Hebrew

א = ʾ	ד = dh	י = y	ס = s	ר = r	*pathaḥ* = a	*ṣerê* = e
בּ = b	ה = h	כּ = k	ע = ʿ	שׂ = ś	*seghôl* = e	long *ḥîreq* = î
ב = bh	ו = w	כ = kh	פּ = p	שׁ = sh	short *ḥîreq* = i	*shûreq* = û
גּ = g	ז = z	ל = l	פ = ph	תּ = t	*qibbûṣ* = u	*ḥôlem* = ô
ג = j	ח = ḥ	מ = m	צ = ṣ	ת = th	*qāmeṣ-ḥāṭûph* = o	
דּ = d	ט = ṭ	נ = n	ק = q		*qāmeṣ* = ā	

Preface and Acknowledgments

My interest in Islam and the Qurʾān goes back to the spring of 1958. To complete the requirements for a class on ethics at Greenville College (Illinois), I wrote a term paper on Islam. Since the curriculum of the college at that time offered no course on world religions, our instructor, Walter Johnson, said we could write our term paper on a world religion. When I arrived at my home in Maryland for spring break, I found a whole shelf of books on Islam, most of them acquired by my father from the main mosque in Washington, DC. That shelf determined the topic of my paper and—as it turned out—contributed to the direction of my life.

The book that interested me the most was a two-volume edition of the Qurʾān with the translation and commentary of A. Yusuf Ali. The publication of this edition of the Qurʾān was undertaken by the Murray Printing Company of Cambridge, Massachusetts, for Khalil al-Rawaf in commemoration of the visit of a delegation from Saudi Arabia in 1946. It stood on a shelf with other books given to my father by the imam at the mosque on Massachusetts Avenue near where my father worked. The first edition of Ali's translation appeared in the Indian subcontinent in 1934, the third edition in the year of my birth, 1938. The edition given to my father was a copy of the third edition. Although I did not start to learn Arabic until 1960, it was the calligraphy of that edition of the Qurʾān by Pīr ʿAbdul Ḥamīd that attracted me to the Arabic language and to the religion and culture of Islam. I wrote the paper, and my mother typed it and sent it to me after I had returned to college. In a sense, then, it was my father and mother, along with Walter Johnson, who launched me on my vocation. Now, almost fifty years later, I am still working from this fascination and love of things Arabic and Islamic.

My understanding of the tensions and possibilities inherent in dialogue with Muslims also started in college. I participated in student government with a classmate and close friend, Ali Kurdieh, from Jerusalem. Our friendship found us engaged in many conversations similar to the conversation represented by this book. Ali, by then an entrepreneur in Jerusalem, lost his life in an accident in the early 1990s. Mourning his loss, I have dedicated this book to his memory.

It was my mentor, James A. Reinhard, whose passion for the Muslim world tipped the scale in my sense of vocation toward giving my life to the interpretation of Christianity among Muslims and the interpretation of Islam among Christians. In the process of more than forty years of preparation for, and work in, this area, I have come to the conclusion that the most important dimension of this task is the interaction of ordinary Christians with ordinary Muslims. By "ordinary" I only mean Christians whose vocation is something other than the vocation of people like myself whose primary focus is on Islamic studies and the interpretation of Islam to Christians or—less frequently—Christianity to Muslims.

Christians who reach out to their Muslim neighbors, colleagues, and friends in hospitality and engage them in conversation, willing to grapple with matters of faith and life as understood by Muslims, are by no means ordinary. And Muslims, such as Ali Kurdieh, who grapple with the convictions, beauties, and blemishes of Christianity in friendship and sincerity cannot be counted as ordinary either. But it would be a dream come true if such conversations did in fact become ordinary—and an alternative to the interactions that get the attention of the world these days, dominated as they are by conflict and violence from both sides.

When conversations between Muslims and Christians occur, whether they become ordinary or not, they inevitably get to the question of the end of Jesus' mission. According to Christian scripture and its dominant tradition, Jesus' mission ended in the ignominy of crucifixion and the victory of resurrection. From the dominant Muslim perspective, the mission (*risālah*) of Jesus ended in divine rescue from the plot of those who would have destroyed him. Thus, he did not die, nor was he crucified, but was taken up to God.

By using the term "mission," I imply what can be found resident in the word "end" as well, namely, the *telos* or *purpose* for which Jesus was "sent." For Christians believe it was Jesus' *telos* to die and be raised, something he took great pains to prepare his followers for. For many Muslims, the end of Jesus' mission, that is, his purpose, like that of Muḥammad and other divine messengers, was to bear witness to the truth of divine unity and to provide divine guidance for God's people.

Lest Christians and Muslims despair over the impasse posed by their differences over the mission of Jesus and its purpose, let us be reminded that we do have this Jesus in common, along with many other features of our worldviews. It is possible to work from common ground toward mutual understanding. But if we focus only on our common ground, we will miss some of the motivating force of our traditions because that force derives not only from what we hold in common but also from those convictions holding us with uncommon tenacity.

In this book, I have grappled with the end of Jesus' mission as taught in Christian scripture and by the dominant Christian tradition as a response to what in my experience has been the dominant Muslim view of the end of Jesus' mission. While the final days of Jesus' earthly life are not deeply significant for Islam, they are fundamental to Christianity—or shall we say crucial! A strictly common-ground approach, then, to the meeting of the two faiths would exclude the discussion this book undertakes. Nevertheless, I have tried to undertake it in the spirit of common ground and mutual understanding, eschewing double standards, attempting the difficult task of objectivity, while admitting its illusive nature.

Many have contributed to the fruition of this writing project. I want to thank William R. Burrows and Catherine Costello of Orbis Books for their substantial help. Bill provided wise guidance and skillful editing. Catherine pleasantly and patiently led in preparing the text for publication.

Marston Speight, Arabist, Islamicist, and expert on Christian-Muslim relations, read the whole manuscript, critiquing it from the perspective of his long and intensive engagement with Arabic and Islamic civilization. Suleiman Darrat, director of Arabic and Islamic Studies at the University of Kentucky, examined the whole book carefully from the point of view of the Muslim reader and offered significant advice. New Testament scholar and exegete Joel B. Green evaluated my treatment of the Bible. My colleague and office mate at Asbury Theological Seminary, Dale Walker, spent long hours reading drafts of the book and making valuable suggestions. John Parks read the manuscript at one point, which resulted in a helpful interaction. Karen Strand Winslow read the theological chapters carefully and gave detailed feedback. Kiluba Nkulu helped me with the chapter on the Gospel of Barnabas. Phil Matanick contributed his practical experience in intensive interactions in life situations with Muslims by evaluating the whole book. Harold E. Read read a draft; James Demaray made a suggestion about the opening chapter; and James Zahniser made a suggestion for the closing chapter.

Howard A. Snyder, Kenneth E. Nolin, and Chris Van Gorder supported and encouraged me over the life of this project. Jerry Walls, Frank Thompson, and Darrell Whiteman have been of indispensable encouragement. My wife, Ann H. Zahniser, in addition to providing me with the solitude and work time this task required, read the manuscript. I alone am responsible for the book in its final form. Portions of the book have been given in lectures at Greenville College and Asbury Theological Seminary, as well as in a number of other institutional settings.

The secretarial assistance of Pat Richmond, Julee Bellar, Korrie Harper, and Pat Ferguson at Asbury Theological Seminary was rendered with enthusiasm and skill; I am deeply grateful. The support of Ronald Crandall, retired dean of the E. Stanley Jones School of World Mission and Evangelism at Asbury Theological Seminary, Randy Bergen, Greenville College provost, and Brian Hartley, chair of the Department of Philosophy and Religion at Greenville College, supported my efforts with resources and advocacy. I am grateful for the accommodations, library collection, and the staff of Tyndale House, Cambridge, England—especially Bruce Winter, Elizabeth Magba, David Instone-Brewer, David Baker, Peter Head, Fiona Craig, and Tonia Raiola. Residence at Tyndale House in parts of three years gave me access to other libraries at Cambridge University; I am thankful for their collections as well. My sister, Esther Zahniser Gillies, and her husband, Duncan Gillies, opened their home to Ann and me during several months-long periods. We will always be grateful for their substantial support and untrammeled confidence. Their hospitality made it possible for me to use the ideal facilities of the British Library. I thank God for the collection of that great library, especially for its division of Oriental and African Studies, which, along with the resources of the W. T. Young Library at the University of Kentucky and the B. L. Fisher Library at Asbury Theological Seminary, made this project possible. Diane Hoffman and others from the staff of the Ruby E. Dare Library at Greenville College assisted me with obtaining books through interlibrary loan.

1

From Common Ground to the End of Jesus' Mission

In the autumn of 2003, I was privileged to attend a lecture by Sheikh Fawzī al-Zafzāf, president of al-Azhār University's Permanent Committee for Dialogue with the Monotheistic Religions and representative of the grand imam of al-Azhār to International Interfaith Organizations. Al-Azhār al-Sharīf in Cairo, Egypt, founded in 969 CE,[1] is the principal Sunnī Islamic university and the oldest active university in the world. The lecture was sponsored by Ridley Hall, an Anglican Theological College in Cambridge, England. Sheikh Fawzī was touring with an interpreter, the Rt. Rev. Dr. Mouneer H. Anis, Episcopal bishop of Egypt.

Dialogue from Common Ground

The sheikh offered a gracious and optimistic program for dialogue between Christianity and Islam. He laid out carefully for this audience of mainly Christian seminarians the vast common ground Muslims and Christians share. The prophets of the Christian Bible and the Prophet of the Qurʾān, Sheikh Fawzī assured us, were sent to bring people back to the true path—God's path; to recognize the presence of God, the unity of God, and the worship of the one God; and to the recognition of prophets, angels, and eternity, or the next world. He stressed that the specific commands of the scriptures revealed to the Heavenly Religions were different because of the differences in the times and locations of their revelation; but their core messages essentially agree. In fact, he explained, the Holy Qurʾān says one of the purposes of the variety of peoples God has placed on the earth is mutual understanding:

> O mankind! We created you from a single (pair) of a male and a female, and made you into nations and tribes, that ye may know each other. Verily the most honoured of you in the sight of Allah is (he who is) the most righteous of you. And Allah has full Knowledge and is well-acquainted (with all things). (*Chambers* [49]:13)[2]

1. From here on, only dates BCE will be designated as such. If dates are not designated BCE, it is assumed that they are during the Common Era (CE).

2. Unless otherwise noted, the English quotations from the Qurʾān in this book will be from the translation of A. Yusuf Ali. I sometimes omit parenthetical clarifications added by Ali.

The sheikh stressed that Heavenly Religions differ from other religions in that they come from one Source, they have one aim, and one goal. According to a saying of Muḥammad, connecting the one Source to the many cultural contexts of prophethood, "The Prophets are brothers of one father, their mothers are each different but their religion is one."[3] In the sheikh's view, our strife is owing to our lack of mutual understanding. The purpose of dialogue, then, is to strive for mutual understanding by focusing on the larger area of agreement between the two faiths and to call forth obedience, goodness, and cooperation. Sheikh Fawzī saw the obligation of both partners in the ongoing dialogue as working toward solutions to problems common to both Muslims and Christians, problems that grow out of extremism, fanaticism, and terrorism, along with promoting forgiveness, love, and peace among all peoples.

In the context of extremism and fanaticism it sometimes appears as if no common ground exists between our two faiths. But the truth is that significant agreement does exist between Christianity and Islam. Solving common problems and fostering forgiveness, love, and peace among all peoples seems in itself a worthy goal for any endeavor, and the sheikh and his university find it worthwhile enough to send him out on a mission to encourage it.

Yet, why should dialogue be limited to an exploration of only common ground? Will dialogue achieve mutual understanding if partners in dialogue ignore areas of disagreement between the two faiths? I think not. The Qurʾān invites Christians to participate in such a dialogue (*Family of Imran* [3]:64). In fact, one area of disagreement provides the central subject of this book: the final events of the mission of Jesus son of Mary, the Messiah, in general and his crucifixion in particular. While the cross represents the central symbol of faith for most Christians, most Muslims believe Jesus was spared crucifixion.[4] Can common-ground dialogue realize adequate mutual understanding without exploring these contrasting positions? In fact, I believe our pilgrimage together will reveal that the force of differences will appear less by looking more closely at normative sources rather than at later interpretations. While I am making a case in this book for the historical reality of the death of Jesus and its meaning, I am trying to do so by identifying and exploring several major areas of common conviction, noting in each case certain contrasts.[5] The first is our common belief in the one God.

---

3. Aḥmad ibn Muḥammad Ibn Ḥanbal (d. 855), *Musnad* 6 vols. (no place: no pub., n.d.), 2:406.

4. As a matter of fact, the death of Jesus, while of central importance to Christians, is much more marginal for Muslims. Were we to explore inductively what the Qur'ān has to say about Jesus, we would discover much more urgent denial of the Christian conviction that Jesus is the Son of God. In this book I am not treating this point of difference directly. I believe, however, that Christians can discover common ground with Muslims even on the humanity of Jesus—a discovery not incompatible with what we mean by Jesus as God's son.

5. Mahmoud A. Ayoub identifies four types of dialogue: the dialogue of life; the theological dialogue; the dialogue of witnessing to one's faith; and the dialogue of faith. This book fits into his third category, though my purpose is not disguised evangelism. I do, however, hope to show the roots in Islam and the meaning for Christians of the convictions I hold deeply regarding the event of Jesus'

Muslims and Christians Worship the Same God

It is almost embarrassing to have to make the case for the fact that Christians and Muslims worship the same God, but the case has to be made. I have given lectures in churches in several parts of the United States and have taught Islam to Christian students for many years. In both of these contexts, some member of my audience insists that Allah and the God of the Bible are not the same being.

When in 1985 I first encountered this position in a church setting, it rendered me shaken. I was not prepared for it. I had not encountered it since I began studying Islam and Christianity in 1958! But since 1985, I have gotten used to it. Going over the evidence for this essential and crucial common ground will be worth our while.

Badru D. Kateregga, a Muslim, and David W. Shenk, a Christian, have co-authored a book composed of their dialogue on common topics. As they interact, it becomes clear that the territory they share is considerable. Kateregga, in his initial presentation, stresses that God is one, creator, merciful, all-powerful, wise, all-knowing, and eternal. In his response, Shenk agrees that Christians and Muslims worship the same God and that but one true God exists, "the righteous and transcendent Creator of all things in heaven and earth." He affirms as a Christian Islam's ninety-nine names of God, including Allah. He goes so far as to say, "The profound Muslim appreciation of the sovereignty and transcendence of God is a witness . . . Christians need to hear."[6]

Kateregga challenges the Christian understanding of the one God by asserting that the oneness of God excludes his having a son (*Purity* [112]). Shenk, however, believes that the Christian understanding of the sonship of Jesus does not violate God's oneness. In this case, Kateregga and Shenk agree on their subject, the one God, but they differ over some of *what is predicated or said about the one God.*[7]

Consider an analogy. Because my first name is Alison, I sometimes get mail from people who think I am a woman. Once I got a mailing announcing I had been nominated for woman of the year, offering me a wall plaque for £93 to display my nomination! I am the same person, however, regardless of the predicates that correspondents assume apply to me. Christians and Muslims surely do differ over some predicates ascribed to God, but we will not disagree that God is "the merciful, all-knowing, all-wise, all-powerful One who is Creator of all." After all, before Muḥammad's birth the name Allah showed up in Christian Arab names, and the Arabic translations of Christian scripture use Allah for God.

While the late Fazlur Rahman, seasoned student of the Qur᾽ān, maintains

---

death and resurrection (see Ayoub, *A Muslim View of Christianity: Essays on Dialogue*, ed. Irfan A. Omar, Faith Meets Faith [Maryknoll, NY: Orbis Books, 2007], 68).

6. Badru A. Kateregga and David W. Shenk, *A Muslim and a Christian in Dialogue* (Scottsdale, PA: Herald Press, 1997), 34.

7. Kenneth Cragg, *The Call of the Minaret*, 2nd ed. (Maryknoll, NY: Orbis Books, 1985), 30-31.

that humankind is its central focus,[8] God is certainly another major focus: "God is, God rules, God creates, God sends, God guides, God ordains, God has mercy, God judges."[9] The emphasis is clearly on God's exalted, sovereign rule and control. Few Muslims give much room for the vulnerability of God. Nevertheless, the Qur'ān provides attributes of God that "involve God and humanity in relationship,"[10] that suggest God's intimacy as well as ultimacy. Describing God as "Oft-forgiving, Most Ready to Appreciate" (*Ghafūr Shakūr*) (*Originator* [35]:30, 34; *Consultation* [42]:23), for example, suggests "a delight in human thankfulness, a reflexive joy in man's capacity for religious response. . . ."[11]

Both the ultimacy and intimacy of God find a place in the Christian Gospels. Jesus' affirmation of the fruitfulness of persistence in prayer (Luke 18:1-9), his analogy suggesting that God is an awesome judge who needs to be reverently feared in life's walk (Luke 12:57-59), and his parable likening God to a father who runs to meet his prodigal son returning in shame and remorse (Luke 15:11-32) can be seen to affirm and elucidate Qur'ānic and Islamic convictions about God (*Opening* [1] and the beginning of all *sūrah*s but one). Christians can likewise enhance their appreciation of God by careful meditation on Qur'ānic passages saturated with the divine (*Light* [24]:35-38). Kenneth Cragg insists that "in listening to the Qur'ān" Christians can grasp "the profound 'association' between God and man on which it proceeds."[12]

Scriptures: The Qur'ān and the Gospels

Another area of common ground between Heavenly Religions such as Christianity and Islam is scripture. Indeed the Qur'ān refers to Jews and Christians as "People of the Book" (*ahl al-kitāb*). For example, see *Table* [5]:59, where common belief in scriptures is affirmed, and *Table* [5]:45, which addresses Christians as "People of the Gospel." The Qur'ān acknowledges the now-lost pages (*ṣuḥuf*) of Abraham, the Torah (*tawrāh*) of Moses, the Psalms (*zabūr*) of David, the Gospel (*injīl*) revealed to Jesus, as well as the Qur'ān revealed to Muḥammad. The Qur'ān evidences a genuine respect for these scriptures, a respect shared by many Muslims I have known. According to Kateregga, "All the previous Books revealed by God must be accepted as true. However, the Qur'ān is the final revelation, which confirms earlier scriptures and perfects the truth."[13]

Shenk appreciates the fact that both Christians and Muslims "have an exceedingly high regard for the Word of God." The Qur'ān affirms Christian scrip-

8. Fazlur Rahman, *Major Themes of the Qur'an* (Chicago/Minneapolis: Bibliotheca Islamica, 1980), 1.

9. Kenneth Cragg, *Muhammad and the Christian: A Question of Response* (London: Darton, Longman & Todd/Maryknoll, NY: Orbis Books, 1984), 101.

10. Ibid., 110.

11. Ibid.

12. Ibid., 111.

13. Kateregga and Shenk, *A Muslim and a Christian*, 60.

ture and warns Christians and Jews not to conceal their sacred books, but to provide them openly to humankind (*Family of Imran* [3]:71).[14] We will come back to this below. Shenk urges Muslims and Christians to "reflect carefully together on the nature and meaning of revelation."[15]

As is the case with our mutual belief in God, our mutual respect for scripture will lead to an awareness of distinctive differences in our scriptures. On one occasion I showed the Gospels to a group of Muslim men. After examining a passage carefully, one of them exclaimed, "This is not scripture; it's narrative." To these Muslims the Gospels did not look or sound like the Qur᾿ān. Suleiman Darrat, director of the Arabic and Islamics Studies program at the University of Kentucky, points out that the Gospels incorporate both God's word as sent down and raised up. And, if one adds the *Ḥadīth* or Muslim Tradition to the Qur᾿ān, the Muslims too have authoritative documents that are both sent down and raised up.[16] One could say, contrasting our scriptures, that God sent the Qur᾿ān down to the Prophet Muḥammad for the Muslim community, while God raised the Gospels up from the Christian community through the Apostles and their interpreters.

The scriptures of Christianity do not come down from God. Although God speaks in them (e.g., Mark 9:7), they are not the very words of God; they are not preserved on a tablet in heaven. Christian scriptures arise out of communities of faith in the living God, a product of God's involvement in those communities after the ascension of Jesus. Initially, the authoritative scriptures of Christianity consisted of the Hebrew and the Greek scriptures of Judaism. The most important of these Christians now call the Old Testament. It corresponds in content to the Hebrew scriptures, but with the prophetic books placed last because they point to the coming of Jesus.[17] In God's providence communities of believers in Jesus as God's Messiah recognized Christian writings and compositions from oral reports as authoritative scripture. They discerned that these scriptures shared in the divine inspiration of the Hebrew Bible. In other words, God sent down Jesus and raised up documents composed by inspired humans—letters, Gospels, and other treatises—to bear witness to who Jesus is and what his mission means for all humankind.

Many Muslims find our four Gospels puzzling for another reason: the Qur᾿ān refers to Christian scripture as "the Gospel" (*al-injīl*) in the singular. But the fact that more than one scriptural story of Jesus has been preserved—and in many ancient manuscripts—supports the authenticity of their stories of Jesus. Kenneth Cragg puts it succinctly, "The gospels bring a cumulative witness to a central figure without conspiring to eliminate secondary divergences."[18] That is, the very

---

14. It seems the People of the Book referred to here are Christians, but they could also have been Jews, or the term could refer to both Jews and Christians.

15. Kateregga and Shenk, *A Muslim and a Christian*, 61.

16. Personal communication, January 2007.

17. H. D. Beeby, *Canon and Mission* (Harrisburg, PA: Trinity Press International, 1999), 32.

18. Cragg, *Call of the Minaret*, 248.

existence of some differences in the stories points to the fact that Gospel writers and their sources did not conspire to forge the story of Jesus, who remains the central figure in their narratives. This feature of the Christian Gospels finds a parallel in the Muslim *Ḥadīth* also.

Although the Qurʾān does not refer to the four Gospels or the other books of the New Testament, it has only positive things to say about the Gospel given to Jesus. It implies that this is the scripture currently in the possession of the Christians whom it addresses. And it nowhere insists that these scriptures exist in a corrupt form. This shows the Qurʾān's positive attitude toward Christian scripture.

> We sent Jesus the son of Mary, confirming the Law that had come before him: We sent him the Gospel: therein was guidance and light, and confirmation of the Law that had come before him: a guidance and an admonition to those who fear God. (*Table* [5]:46)

In another passage Jesus himself says, "I am the servant of God: He has given me the Book and made me a prophet" (*Mary* [19]:30).[19] Although in these passages, the Gospel—or the Book—is given to Jesus, other passages equate it as revelation with the Qurʾān and the Torah by referring to it as "sent down" by God: "God! There is no god but He . . . sent down (*nazzala*) to thee [Muḥammad] in truth, the Book, confirming what went before it; and He sent down (*anzala*) the Law and the Gospel" (*Family of Imran* [3]:2-3). According to the Qurʾān, God gave Jesus "inspiration" (*waḥy*): "We sent inspiration to Abraham, Ishmael, Isaac, Jacob and the descendants, to Jesus, Job, Jonah, Aaron, and Solomon, and to David we gave the Psalms" (*Women* [4]:163). Because the verse mentions the Psalms in connection with David, the Gospel must be implied in connection with Jesus (cf. *Bee* [16]:43 and *Consultation* [42]:3).

The Qurʾān appears to value the Gospel positively as clear signs or proofs: "We gave Jesus, the son of Mary clear signs and strengthened him with the Holy Spirit" (*Cow* [2]:87). The Qurʾān, as we have already seen, says God sent Jesus "the Gospel," which contains "guidance and light," confirms the Torah, and represents "guidance and admonition" (*Table* [5]:46; cf. *Lines* [61]:6). The Gospel appears to be all these things for humankind in general: "God . . . sent down the Law and the Gospel . . . as a guide to mankind" (*Family of Imran* [3]:3, 4).

The scriptures that the Qurʾān confirms seem to be at hand for the people who first heard Muḥammad's message. If Christian scripture had been abrogated or seriously corrupted, would the Qurʾān urge Christians to make judgments based on it? In the Qurʾān, God tells Muḥammad, "Let the People of the Gospel judge by what Allah hath revealed therein. If any do fail to judge by what Allah hath revealed, they are those who rebel" (*Table* [5]:47). Furthermore, the Qurʾān

19. My translation.

exhorts Muḥammad to consult the scriptures of Christianity for interpreting his own revelation:

> If thou wert in doubt as to what We have revealed unto thee, then ask those who have been reading the Book from before thee: the Truth hath indeed come to thee from thy Lord: so be in no wise of those in doubt. (*Jonah* [10]:94)[20]

The Qur'ān does charge People of the Book (Jews and Christians) with corruption of scripture, but not with falsifying the scriptures themselves. First, the Qur'ān reprimands the People of the Book for concealing their scripture. They conceal the truth (*Cow* [2]:146). They hide the evidence and guidance revealed to them (*Cow* [2]:159). Muḥammad brings to light scriptures they have been concealing (*Table* [5]:15; see also *Family of Imran* [3]:71; and *Cattle* [6]:92). Second, the Qur'ān charges People of the Book with changing the scripture orally. "Can ye (O men of Faith) entertain the hope that they will believe in you?—seeing that a party of them heard the Word of Allah, and perverted it knowingly after they understood it?" (see also *Cow* [2]:58-59; *Table* [5]:41; and *Heights* [7]:161-62). Third, People of the Book apparently wrote false bits of scripture for sale to Muslims: "Then woe to those who write the Book with their own hand, and then say: 'This is from Allah,' to traffic with it for a miserable price!— Woe to them for what their hands write, and for the gain they make thereby" (*Cow* [2]:79; see also *Cow* [2]:174; *Family of Imran* [3]:187; and *Luqman* [31]:6). Within their contexts, these verses appear to be addressed to Jews. At any rate, the Qur'ān nowhere portrays the written scriptures possessed by Jews and Christians as corrupt and unreliable. Dare we say that the scripture sent down confirms the scripture raised up (see chapter 8 below)?

Reverence for Jesus

Another important area of common ground explored by Kateregga and Shenk is the Muslim reverence for Jesus, whom the Qur'ān calls ʿĪsā. In almost every dialogue I have engaged in with Muslims, their respect for Jesus has surfaced. Indeed the Qur'ān gives great attention to Jesus. It refers to him as the son of Mary because of his virgin birth, as the Messiah, as a messenger of God, as a prophet, as a word from God, and as a spirit from God. This selection from *Mary* [19]:27-33 offers a flavor of what the Qur'ān says about him.

> At length she brought the (babe) to her people, carrying him (in her arms). They said: "O Mary! Truly an amazing thing hast thou brought!

20. In *Prophets* [21]:7, 48, 50, the revelation is referred to as *al-dhikr*, a word related to the idea of remembering.

> O sister of Aaron! Thy father was not a man of evil, nor thy mother a woman unchaste!" But she pointed to the babe. They said: "How can we talk to one who is a child in the cradle?" He said: "I am indeed the servant of God: He hath given me the Book and made me a prophet;[21] and He hath made me blessed wheresoever I be, and hath enjoined on me Prayer and Charity as long as I live; (He) hath made me kind to my mother, and not overbearing or miserable; so Peace is on me the day I was born, the day that I die, and the day that I shall be raised up to life (again)"!

Muslims revere all the prophets who went before Muḥammad. I have heard many Muslims say that if they do not believe in all the prophets, they are not true Muslims. Some of the prophets are especially noteworthy. The prophet Ibrāhīm (Abraham) is known as the friend of God. The prophet Mūsā (Moses) is special for speaking directly to God. Jesus son of Mary is known for his miraculous acts of compassion.[22]

Kateregga starts his own discussion of Jesus in response to Shenk's initiative by stressing common ground: "Muslims have great respect and love for Jesus (Isa) the Messiah. He is one of the greatest prophets of Allah. . . . Muslims sincerely believe that Jesus (PBUH[23]) was born of a virgin mother, Maryam (Mary), by Allah's divine decree. . . . The Qur'an teaches that the coming of the Messiah was 'glad tidings'" (*Family of Imran* [3]:45).[24] Of course, the two partners in dialogue differ over Jesus' sonship and his relationship to God.

Respect for the Apostles

An area of common ground not mentioned in Kateregga and Shenk's dialogue is respect for the disciples, or Apostles, of Jesus. Although the New Testament designates others such as Paul (Galatians 1:1-2), Barnabas (Acts 14:14), Andronicus, Junia (Romans 16:7), and Apaphroditus (Philippians 2:25) as Apostles, the designation primarily refers to the group of men highly esteemed as the closest followers of Jesus (Matthew 10:2; Mark 6:30; Luke 6:13), "the ones sent" (Greek: *hoi apostoloi;* sing. *apostolos*) with the good news of the gospel (Matthew 28:16-20; Acts 5:17-21, 6:2-6), and to whom Jesus gave authority to heal. After Jesus' ascension, these, with Matthias replacing Judas (Acts 1:21-26) and Paul of Tarsus designated an apostle to the Gentiles (Romans 11:13), led the

---

21. I made some adjustments to A. Yusuf Ali's translation of verse 30 to adhere more closely to the Arabic text.

22. Kateregga and Shenk, *A Muslim and a Christian*, 65-66.

23. The blessing *ṣallā Allāhu ʿalay-hi wa-sallam* does not mean "Peace be upon him" (PBUH), but "may the prayers and peace of God be upon him." Muslims, however, use it as an English equivalent of the Arabic blessing. "Peace be upon him" (*ʿalay-hi al-salām*) is the epithet used in Arabic for Jesus and other prophets.

24. Kateregga and Shenk, *A Muslim and a Christian*, 165.

communities of faith that believed in Jesus as the Messiah (Acts 2:42-43; 5:2, 12; 6:2-6).

Although none of the four Gospels contains any direct reference to the identity of its author, church tradition has referred to them as "the Gospel according to Matthew," "the Gospel according to Mark," "the Gospel according to Luke," and "the Gospel according to John." The Gospels had the authority of contact with the Apostles. Matthew and John were among the original twelve Apostles; according to early church tradition, Mark's work reflects the eyewitness influence of Peter; Luke, the author of both the Gospel ascribed to him and the Acts of the Apostles, was closely associated with the Apostle Paul.

The Qurʾānic word for the Apostles of Jesus, *ḥawāriyūn*, occurs only four times, never in the singular (*Family of Imran* [3]:52; *Table* [5]:111-12; and *Lines* [61]:14). Commentators on these passages explain the meaning of *ḥawāriyūn* in various ways. They derive it from one of two verbs. If derived from *ḥāra*, "to return," a disciple would be one to whom one "turns" for help. If derived from *ḥawira*, "to be glistening white," or from the noun *ḥawar*, "intense whiteness," it could mean the followers of Jesus were fullers or that they wore pure white garments; or it could reflect the purity of the Apostles' hearts. Some interpreters understand *ḥawāriyūn* as synonymous with *mujāhidūn*, "strivers." Other interpreters note that the Apostles of Jesus are God's helpers (*anṣār Allāh*), being reminded of the helpers from Medina who supported the Muslim immigrants from Mecca after the Hijrah, according to the usage in the Qurʾān (*Lines* [61]:14). The fact that the word *ḥawāriyūn* does not occur in the Qurʾān in connection with any other person or group and that it is cognate with the word for Apostle in the Ethiopic New Testament, *ḥawārya*, suggests that the Qurʾān uses it to designate one of Jesus' twelve Apostles and shares in the Christian appreciation for the Apostles.

While the Qurʾān mentions only two events connected specifically with the disciples, or Apostles, of Jesus, a high level of respect is discernible where they are concerned. In one, the Apostles ask Jesus to request God to send down a table of food to assuage their hunger and to strengthen their faith. Jesus agrees, but warns them that having had such a confirmation of faith, no deviation on their part will ever be tolerated by God (*Table* [5]:112). In the other, at the end of his mission when Jesus anticipates coming under attack, he asks, "Who will help me in the way of God?" His Apostles answer, "We shall be the helpers of God. We believe in God; and you be our witness that we submit and obey" (*Family of Imran* [3]:52-53; see also *Lines* [61]:14). Another passage compliments Jesus' followers but does not specifically mention his Apostles or disciples: "We . . . put in the hearts of his followers compassion and kindness" (*Iron* [57]:27).[25] The verse goes on to chide them for how they later handled monasticism, a major feature of Arab Christianity at the time of Muḥammad.

Other areas of agreement abound. For example, we could look at the

---

25. The translation of these two verses is from *Al-Qurʾān: A Contemporary Translation*, trans. Ahmad Ali, 9th ed. (Princeton, NJ: Princeton University Press, 2001).

common ground in the Qurʾān and the Bible for a number of figures of significance to both traditions: Adam, Noah, Abraham, Joseph, Moses, David, Solomon, and (especially) Mary. We could find ample common ground for moral values precious to both spiritual traditions: knowledge, faith, loyalty, communal solidarity, confession, forgiveness, family loyalty, social justice, economic security, and political order.[26] All these areas and more are important for the kind of dialogue envisioned by Sheikh Fawzī al-Zafzāf. But I feel it is imperative to take a common-ground and dialogical approach to dealing with an important area of difference in the two traditions. While the last days of Jesus' mission are not of crucial significance to most Muslims, they are central to the message and mission of Christian followers of Jesus. But before we engage in examining Jesus' last days, I would like to lay out some important features of what I understand as a dialogical and common-ground approach to my task of making a case for a meaningful death of Jesus.

Some Principles for a Dialogical and Common-Ground Apologetic

This book makes a case for the crucifixion of Jesus that I trust will be helpful and meaningful to thoughtful Muslims and Christians who wish to participate in mutual engagement and understanding. I hope it will serve to enrich the faith of my readers as it has enriched mine. Following are some principles I espouse for a common-ground and dialogical apologetic.

Root Out Double Standards

A dialogical apologetic should be devoted to rooting out *double standards*. Hugh Goddard, lecturer in Islamic Theology at Nottingham University, has laid excellent groundwork for such devotion in his book *Christians and Muslims: From Double Standard to Mutual Understanding*.[27] Goddard deals with such topics as historical origins, scriptures, development of religious thought, law and ethics, spread and history, and modern developments of both Islam and Christianity in a profound effort to be completely fair to both sides. He demonstrates—with a high degree of sophistication and care—what it means to eschew double stan-

26. Recently a group of 138 Muslim leaders summoned Christians to conversations with Muslims on a common concern of the two faiths: love for God and love for neighbors. Designated "A Common Word Between Us and You" according to a Qurʾānic phrase (*Family of Imran* [3]:64), the Muslim statement was published in the *New York Times* (www.acommonword.com). The document recognizes differences between our two religious traditions, but offers a starting place for working together for peace. About three hundred Christians have responded positively to the initiative in a document, "Loving God and Neighbour Together" (www.yale.edu/faith/index.htm).

27. Hugh Goddard, *Christians and Muslims in Dialogue: From Double Standards to Mutual Understanding* (Richmond, Surrey, UK: Curzon, 1995).

dards and to work for mutual understanding. For example, Goddard's chapter 7, dealing with the "spread and history" of the two religions, will prevent Christian apologists from using a double standard in presenting how the two faiths have been spread. Islam was not, generally speaking, spread by coercion. And Christianity has not spread exclusively by persuasion.

Recognize the Primacy of Persons

Another principle that characterizes the dialogue for which this book is designed to supply material can be stated in the following motto: A Muslim is a person first and then a Muslim. Or, a Christian is a person first and then a Christian. I do not mean by this that persons do not have a Muslim or a Christian identity. I do not mean by this that Islam is not a total way of life or that Christianity does not lay claims on whole persons and their communities of faith. I mean that Christians or Muslims cannot assume that what they have learned about Islam or Christianity is true of the person they find themselves in conversation with. This book deals with Muslim and Christian positions on the end of Jesus' mission that I have experienced as pervasive and typical, or that I feel are constructive and true. But I have also encountered significant differences in actual cases. Here are a couple of examples from my engagement with Islam.

Mahmoud M. Ayoub, Professor and Scholar in Residence, Pacific School of Religion, Berkeley, California, a devout Muslim originally from Lebanon, a profound scholar of Christian-Muslim dialogue, and a person well versed in the general subject of this book, published in the *Newsletter of Christian-Muslim Concerns* a lecture he gave at the Muslim-Christian Colloquium on March 31, 1989, in Toronto. He treats the last actions and words of Jesus according to the Christian Gospels as evidence of the submission of Jesus, connecting them with the liberation of people. His presentation includes these sentences:

> Throughout the trial and subsequent crucifixion Jesus showed himself as an absolute Muslim, that is to say, as one who absolutely submitted his life and his will to the will of God. The Qur'an and earlier Scriptures tell us in so many words that God's mercy, sometimes called love, . . . transcends all our folly and tempers even God's justice, thus making it possible for us to be called children of God.[28]

In the fall of 2001, the Muslim Student Association at Cambridge University asked me to speak as a Christian for about ten minutes on the value to Christianity of dialogue with Muslims. My remarks were to precede those of the main speaker, Thomas McElwain, a Muslim professor from a Scandinavian university. I was

---

28. *Newsletter of Christian-Muslim Concerns* 43 (July 1990), 3. The *Newsletter* is published by Interfaith Relations of the National Council of Churches of Christ in the U.S.A, in cooperation with the Duncan Black Macdonald Center for the Study of Islam and Christian-Muslim Relations of Hartford Seminary.

eager to participate and so I agreed. It was my good fortune to have some time with him after his afternoon prayers and before we addressed the audience. I discovered that he was a former Baptist missionary to Russia from West Virginia; that he was one of the few remaining speakers of an American Indian dialect; that he was a professor of anthropology in Sweden; that he had gone to seminary in France; that his wife was from Finland; and that he had become a Muslim in Russia as a result of a relationship formed with a Muslim shopkeeper.

Since he asked me what I was doing, I told him I was working on a book on the end of Jesus' mission, especially his crucifixion. He told me that he believed the Gospel accounts of the end of Jesus' mission were true, but he did not believe in the death of Jesus as atonement for sins.

In any dialogue between Muslims and Christians the actual faith of the persons involved needs to be taken into consideration. Participants should be allowed to define their own faith. Getting to know the person is essential for effective communication, which starts from common ground and proceeds into sensitive subjects where differences are significant. In a book, however, the author cannot know readers personally. Nevertheless, I have tried to acknowledge as I proceed that not all Muslim and Christian readers will agree with my statements about Islam and Christianity. Frequently I use such terms as "most" or "some" when referring to positions I espouse or respond to. I am, thus, trying to honor my motto: A person is a person first and then a Muslim or a Christian.

Another dimension of this motto related to this book leads me to realize that not everything I include will be necessary for every reader to grasp my case or follow my argument. For example, in many chapters I give a lot of detail in supporting the reliability of passages from the Christian Gospels that are important in making a case for the death of Jesus as a fact of history. Many readers and dialogue partners may already have, like Thomas McElwain, a belief in the truthfulness of the Gospels. In such cases the details I include will not be needed.

Build Relationships

Finally, this book provides a starting point for satisfactory mutual understanding between Muslims and Christians over the matter of the end of Jesus' mission. Since building relationships represents the bedrock of mutual understanding, I hope that Muslim, Christian, and other readers of this book may derive from it motivation for engaging in discussions leading to mutual understanding over the issue of the end of Jesus' mission.

An Overview

Chapter 2 represents a Christian reading of the most important passages from the Qurʾān dealing with the end of Jesus' mission. In some of the paragraphs above, I have already justified to my satisfaction Christians reading the Qurʾān and interpreting it. It would be a double standard not to grant Muslims the same privilege. The interpretations that I and other Christians I cite in this chapter are not final; rather, they are offered for engagement and dialogue. Can the Qurʾān be read in a way that does not flatly contradict the Christian view of the end of Jesus' mission? I think it can.

Chapters 3 and 5 look into both classical and modern Qurʾān interpreters. Chapter 3 centers on the comprehensive commentary of Muḥammad ibn Jarīr al-Ṭabarī (d. 923). In case the relevance of this medieval commentary to the modern scene of Muslim belief and practice should be questioned, I include this story told by a prominent Western and Christian expert on the Qurʾān, Jane Dammen McAuliffe, President of Bryn Mawr College, Bryn Mawr, Pennsylvania, and editor of the recently completed *Encyclopaedia of the Qurʾān*:

> A few years ago I walked into the Safeway grocery store in Amman, Jordan one Saturday afternoon to do some shopping. By that time of my life, I had been studying the Qurʾānic commentary (*tafsīr*) tradition for a number of years. I had some sense of the scope, both chronological and linguistic, of the exegetical effort that had been expended on explaining and clarifying the Qurʾānic text for more than a millennium. I was also well aware of the enduring importance of that exercise and of its productions, both classical and contemporary, in Muslim intellectual life. Nevertheless the sight at the entrance to the Amman Safeway came as something of a surprise. A small book display of literature for children and adults had been set up in the supermarket foyer, and placed squarely in the center was a thirty-volume edition of the early tenth-century Qurʾān commentary by Abū Jaʿfar b. Jarīr al-Ṭabarī.[29]

McAuliffe reminds us of the contemporary relevance in much of the Muslim world of this commentary, which predates the entire "medieval Christian university system in the West." She makes clear that "Muslim scholars of the Qurʾān remain conceptually and methodologically connected to their ninth- or eleventh- or thirteenth-century counterparts."[30] The presence of the copy in the Amman Safeway also suggests the relevance of Ṭabarī's commentary to ordinary—though probably educated—Muslims in Amman.

This same Ṭabarī concludes in his commentary on *Family of Imran* [3]:55 and *Women* [4]:157 that Jesus was not crucified and did not die but was taken up to heaven only to descend again in the future to break the cross, kill the pigs, kill the Antichrist, and establish the pervasive rule of Islam and the prevalence of peace over the earth. Since Ṭabarī bases this interpretation on a tradition (*ḥadīth*) going back to the Prophet Muḥammad, I devote chapter 4 to discussing the whole issue of Prophetic Tradition in general and this tradition in particular. Chapter 5

---

29. Jane Dammen McAuliffe, "Legal Exegesis: Christians as a Case Study," *Islamic Interpretations of Christianity*, ed. Lloyd Ridgeon (Richmond, Surrey, UK: Curzon, 2001), 55.

30. Ibid.

then switches to modern commentaries that discuss not only the Islamic traditions about the end of Jesus' mission but also the Christian traditions about it. Since the Gospel of Barnabas figures prominently in these modern commentaries, I come to terms with this in chapter 6.

Chapter 7 focuses on some features of the early Christian churches, showing that even those not founded by the Apostle Paul believed in the crucifixion of Jesus. I have already mentioned that chapter 8 deals with the Christian and Muslim understanding of scripture. Because scripture has significant authority in both traditions, we have common ground on the necessity of taking scripture seriously. Since Christian scripture is raised up rather than sent down, some space is needed to explain what this means.

Chapters 9-13 consist of responses to the issues Qurʾān commentators have raised in support of the Muslim view of the end of Jesus' mission. Chapters 9 and 10, arguing that Jesus predicted his crucifixion and resurrection both implicitly and explicitly, lead to asking, "Is it reasonable that Jesus would have predicted his death and resurrection as part of his teaching about his role as Israel's Messiah only to petition God to free him from that role in the end?"

Chapters 11 and 12 respond to the treatment of such events as the Transfiguration, the Last Supper, the agony in Gethsemane, the arrest, and the trial of Jesus in the Muslim Qurʾān commentaries. Chapter 13 concludes that the resurrection requires the crucifixion as antecedent and that the Christian movement can hardly make any historical sense without both.

Chapter 14 wrestles with a number of Muslim theological and ethical objections to a very popular Christian doctrine of the atonement. It takes a closer look at the traditional doctrine of original sin and proposes a wider view based on the Bible. In a similar way, it reexamines the doctrine of atonement in light of a Muslim critique, proposing a wider view of it as well. Chapter 15 returns to the common ground of belief in one God and suggests connections between the end of Jesus' mission and the nature and purposes of God.

2

The Final Days of Jesus' Mission in the Qurān

According to the standard commentaries, the Qur'ān denies that Jesus was killed or crucified. Instead, God outsmarted those who would have done God's Messiah in, substituting someone else for him on the cross. In my view, not only does the Qur'ān exhibit a more ambiguous stance than these commentators allow; it barely touches on the subject and presents no discussion of the meanings Christians have attached to the death and resurrection of Jesus. So what does the Qur'ān have to say about the end of Jesus' mission? Two main verses must be considered: a denial verse and an affirmation verse.[1]

The Denial Verse: "They Killed Him Not Nor Crucified Him"

The Qur'ān denies emphatically that the Jews crucified Jesus:

> That they said, "We killed Christ Jesus the son of Mary, the Messenger of Allah"—but they killed him not, nor crucified him, but so it was made to appear to them. And those who differ therein are full of doubts, with no knowledge at all, but only conjecture to follow. For of a surety they killed him not. (*Women* [4]:157)

"They" in the verse refers to the People of the Book, mentioned at the outset of verse 153 of the same *sūrah*: "The People of the Book ask thee to cause a book to descend to them from heaven. . . ." Although "People of the Book" or "scriptuaries" (*ahl al-kitāb*) could be Jews or Christians, in this case the Jews are intended. In verse 153, Moses is addressed, and in verse 154 the People of the Book are commanded not to transgress the Sabbath. In verse 160 they are specified as *alladhīna hādū,* "those who are Jews."[2] Thus, the verse

1. The labels "denial verse" and "affirmation verse" come from Kenneth E. Nolin, "A Pilgrimage into Islam," unpublished manuscript, 1980.

2. *The Noble Qur'an: The First American Translation and Commentary*, trans. and ed. Thomas B. Irving (Brattleboro, VT: Amana Books, 1992).

clearly asserts that the Jews neither killed nor crucified "the Messiah Jesus, son of Mary, the Messenger of God." Nevertheless, some knowledgeable Christian commentators believe the verse does not deny the death of Jesus. We will first look at some moot points within the verse itself, then examine the verse more carefully in its immediate context (153-70).

Two Questions for Interpretation

One way to get at the interpretation of a passage is to address it with interpretive questions. In this passage one of the most important questions is, What does "but so it was made to appear to them" mean? The verse suggests that the Jews honestly thought they had crucified Jesus. It says, according to the translation we are following, "They killed him not, nor crucified him, *but so it was made to appear to them*." That is, something happened affecting their perception of an event to the extent that they thought they had crucified Jesus.

The words "but so it was made to appear to them" (*wa-lākin shubbiha lahum*) turn out to be ambiguous. Readers unaided by commentary cannot be sure *who* made *what* look to the Jews as though they had crucified and killed Jesus. The passive verb *shubbiha* is third person masculine singular and in the perfect (or past) tense. The active form of the verb, *shabbaha*, is derived from the noun *shibh*, meaning "a likeness," and means "he likened" or "he made (object 1) like (object 2)."[3] If we recast the sentence in the active voice, we have to supply an *object 1* and an *object 2*. We could say, "he made the event (object 1) look like a killing and crucifixion of Jesus (object 2)." But who is "he"? In the active voice we have to know the identity of the *making-like* agent. The Qur'ān leaves the agent of the making-like completely unknown. Since Arabic has no neuter gender, every noun being either masculine or feminine, the agent would not even have to be a person. We could say, for example, "The dim light caused the man they were crucifying to look like Jesus." Here the subject is "the dim light" and the two objects, "the man" and "Jesus." The passive construction hides both the agent and the object. We know the passive verb is in the masculine singular, so we know that one of the objects of the likeness was a masculine individual or a masculine event or process. Since the subject under discussion is Jesus, it is reasonable that he is either object 1 or object 2. Ali could have translated the passage, "They did not kill him, nor crucify him, but *someone* (object 1) was made to look like *him* (object 2) to them." But "killing/crucifying" is also a significant event in the discussion. Ali's translation takes object 2 to be crucifixion and death: "They did not kill him, nor crucify him, but so (= killing/crucifixion, object 2) it (= the event, object 1) was made to appear to them."

Joseph Cumming, of Yale University's Peace and Reconciliation Program, points out that grammatical analysis itself calls into question all the narratives that report that someone was made to look like Jesus and substituted for him in crucifixion.

---

3. Edward William Lane, *An Arabic-English Lexicon*, 8 vols. (Beirut: Librairie du Liban, 1968; reprint of 1872 edition), 4:189.

> The verb *shubbiha* must be an impersonal passive. If the subject of this passive verb were Jesus, then it would mean that Jesus was caused to resemble someone else. But that is the reverse of what the substitution stories relate: Jesus was not caused to resemble someone else; someone else is supposed to have been made to resemble Jesus. And the subject of the passive verb *shubbiha* cannot be the substitute who was killed . . . [in Jesus' place], because that person is not mentioned in the Qur'ān, so cannot serve grammatically as an antecedent subject.[4]

Was the event made to look like a crucifixion and killing of Jesus, while in fact he did not really die and was not really crucified? If so, who made it happen thus? Did the Jews think they were the instrumental cause of Jesus' crucifixion and death? Were they wrong about this? Did the Roman rulers actually bring it about? Maybe God was the one who caused Jesus to die through crucifixion. Was the person crucified made to look like Jesus? Did he just happen to look like Jesus? All these possibilities appear compatible with the passive construction here. The second question is, Who are "those who differ"? Did the Christian sects contemporary with the Qur'ān hold differing views on the death of Jesus? Do the differences referred to mean differences in the views of Jews and Christians—or maybe Jews, Christians, and Muslims up to the time of this revelation? The answer to this question remains obscure if we rely upon the Qur'ān itself.

The Qur'ān, however, does refer to differences among Christians and Jews. It warns Muslims against the same disunity that afflicted Jews and Christians (*Mary* [19]:37; and *Consultation* [42]:13). This may indicate that those who differ are the Jews, the Christians, and possibly even the Muslims.[5] If one of the parties that differ were the Muslims, would the Qur'ān specify that those who differ are full of doubts? It would seem, however, that the Christians would agree with the Jews that Jesus was crucified and killed. And the Jews who claim they killed and crucified Messiah Jesus seem to have been anything but uncertain and conjectural. Was it then the Christians whom the Qur'ān accuses of being devoid of knowledge and having to resort to conjecture? Are they the ones who differed among themselves? A. Yusuf Ali thinks so, although he admits that the whole issue is shrouded in mystery.[6] We can solve the mystery in part by examining the denial verse in its Qur'ānic contexts.

The Denial Verse in Its Immediate Context

The *sūrah* of *Women* can be divided into a number of distinct thematic units. One of these is clearly the thematic unit comprising verses 153-70. It begins

---

4. Joseph Cumming, "Did Jesus Die on the Cross? The History of Reflection on the End of His Earthly Life in Sunnī Tafsīr Literature," Yale University, 2001 (www.yale.edu/faith/reconciliation).

5. Richard Bell, *A Commentary on the Qur'ān*, ed. C. Edmond Bosworth and M. E. J. Richardson, 2 vols., Journal of Semitic Studies Monograph 14 (Manchester: University of Manchester Press, 1991), 1:139-40.

6. A. Yusuf Ali, trans., *The Meaning of the Holy Qur'ān*, New Edition with Arabic Text, Revised Translation, and Commentary (Beltsville, MD: Amana Publications, 1989), 236 n. 664.

with a challenge to Muḥammad from the People of the Book, who turn out to be the Jews. They challenge him to have a book sent down from heaven (153). The Qur᾽ān responds by identifying acts committed by the Jews that displeased God (153-61). A couple of verses assure the Prophet that there are bad Jews and good Jews (161-62). Then four verses assure him of the validity of this revelation and its relation to previous recipients of inspiration (163-66). Finally, the thematic unit closes, reminding all of the fate of those who disbelieve and exhorting all to respond positively to the Prophet's truthful message (verses 167-70). The last verse (170), directed to humankind, can also be connected to the following thematic unit because that unit ends with an appeal to humankind in general (174) and contains within it an appeal to Christians. So verse 170 serves as a kind of hinge or transition between the thematic unit related to the mistakes of the Jews (verses 153-69) and the thematic unit warning the Christians about exaggerated claims for the nature of the Messiah Jesus, son of Mary (verses 171-75).

Within verses 153-69, there are two groups of Jewish errors with a number of divine responses. The first is a group of two errors (153-54). The divine response here is rather elaborate (153-54). The second group of ten errors (155-61) concludes with a very brief statement of divine response. In between transgressions 7 and 8, a divine response is also mentioned (160). I have laid out these verses below.

Figure 2.1 Structural Presentation of *Women* [4]:155-62, Showing Charges against the Jews (Numbered in Square Brackets) and Remarks about These Charges (Set Off by { })

155.	a		In their breaking their Covenant [1];
	b	and	their rejection of the Signs of God [2];
	c	and	their killing the messengers in defiance of right [3];
	d	and	their saying, "Our minds are closed"[7] [4];
	e		{no, Allah hath set the seal on their hearts for their blasphemy,
	f		and little is it they believe;}
156.	a	and	in their unbelief [5];
	b	and	their making against Mary a grave false charge [6];
157.	a	and	their saying, "We killed Christ
	b		Jesus the son of Mary, the Apostle of God" [7];
	c		{they killed him not, nor crucified him,
	d		but so it was made to appear to them,
	e		and those who differ therein

7. From *The Qur'an*, trans. M. A. S. Abdel Haleem, Oxford World's Classics (Oxford/New York: Oxford University Press, 2005). Haleem notes that the phrase *qulūbu-nā ghulf* literally means "our hearts are covered," or "encased."

	f		are full of doubts,
	g		with no knowledge at all,
	h		but only conjecture to follow,
	i		for of a surety they killed him not.[8]
158.	a		Nay, God raised him up unto Himself;
	b		and God is Exalted in Power, Wise;—
159.	a	And	there is none of the People of the Book
	b		but must believe in him before his death;
	c	and	on the Day of Judgment he will be a witness against them;}
`160.	a		{For the iniquity of the Jews
	b		We made unlawful for them certain (foods) good and wholesome which had been lawful for them;}
	c	and	their hindering many from God's Way [8];
161.	a	and	their taking usury [9],
	b		{though they were forbidden;}
	c	and	their devouring men's substance wrongfully [10];
	d		{We have prepared for those among them who reject Faith a grievous punishment.
162.	a		But those among them who are well-grounded in knowledge,
	b	and	the Believers, believe in what hath been revealed before thee:
	c	and	those who establish regular prayer
	d	and	practice regular charity
	e	and	believe in God and in the Last Day:
	f		to them shall We soon give a great reward.}

Clearly the Jews are being reprimanded for an error they made in claiming they had killed and crucified Jesus. The Qur'ān does not upbraid them for killing Jesus in the way it upbraids them for slandering Mary and for "killing the messengers in defiance of right." It upbraids them for *claiming to have killed him*. Why would the Jews claim to have killed the Messiah, Jesus son of Mary? What could possibly have motivated them to make this claim? Were they claiming that Jesus could not have been the Messiah because they had crucified him?

Verse 158 says that, in contrast to the Jewish claim to have killed Jesus, God raised him up—not specifically in the sense of resurrection from the dead but in the general sense of exaltation, or ascension. Furthermore, verse 159 features an ambiguity not discernible from the English translation of A. Yusuf

8. An interpretive tradition going back to Ibn 'Abbās (d. 687/688) takes the object of "they did not kill" to be "their conjecture" (*ẓanna-hum*) in 157h, making an idiom, "they never confirmed their conjecture."

Ali, who renders it in accordance with the prevailing Muslim interpretation of these verses. It could also be understood to promise not that all People of the Book will believe in Jesus before Jesus dies, but before each one of the People of the Book dies.[9]

Based on its immediate context, some Christian interpreters have been able to read verse 157 not as a denial of the cross of Jesus per se, but strictly as a denial of a Jewish claim to have defeated him.

Christian Interpretation of the Denial Verse

E. E. Elder,[10] Geoffrey Parrinder,[11] and Kenneth Nolin believe *Women* [4]:157 means "[The Jews] could not make him dead once and for all"[12]—that Jesus got the victory over death according to God's plan. Their argument is also based on the immediate context of the verse under discussion. Nolin, who calls this verse "the denial verse," in an exploratory paragraph presents this perspective clearly, "Suppose God has accepted the very worst that mankind can bring to bear against Him, in Jesus Christ, but then turns it around into an ultimate triumph . . . one which meets and satisfies Islam's deep and very valid concern that God not be defeated or thwarted?"[13]

W. Montgomery Watt, one of the principal European interpreters of Islam, sums up what can clearly be said about this verse.

> [T]he primary denial is of something heretical, namely, the Jewish contention that the crucifixion had been a victory for them, and the same denial would of course be most vigorously affirmed by Christian orthodoxy. Unfortunately it is linked with a positive assertion which is unacceptable to orthodox Christians, contained in the rather vague phrase here translated "a semblance was made for them" (*shubbiha la-hum*). In the present context there is no need to speculate on the possible gnostic origin of the positive conception. The point to be insisted on here is that the Qurʾān is not attacking Christianity, but rather defending it against Jewish attacks.[14]

Women [4]:157 could be a defense of Islam as well; both Islam and Christianity consider Jesus to be the Messiah.[15]

---

9. Muḥammad ibn Jarīr al-Ṭabarī, *Tafsīr al-Ṭabarī* (*Jāmiʿ al-bayān ʿan taʾwīl āyyāt al-Qurʾān*), ed. Muḥammad Shākir and Aḥmad Muḥammad Shākir, 16 vols. Turāth al-Islām [Cairo: Dār al-Maʿārif, 1971], 9:382, e.g., #10809) has collected many traditions on the interpretation of this verse. A number of them interpret the "he" in "before he dies" to refer to the Person of the Book.

10. E. E. Elder, "The Crucifixion in the Koran," *The Muslim World* 13 (1923): 242-58.

11. Geoffrey Parrinder, *Jesus in the Qurʾān* (New York: Barnes & Noble, 1965), 105-21.

12. Elder, "Crucifixion," 257.

13. Kenneth E. Nolin, "A Pilgrimage into Islam," unpublished manuscript, 1980, 60.

14. W. M. Watt, "The Christianity Criticized in the Qur'ān," *The Muslim World* 57 (1967): 200-201.

15. The Qurʾān refers to the Messiah (Christ) eleven times: 3:45; 4:157, 171, 172; 5:12, 72, 75; 9:30, 31. All refer to Jesus.

The Denial Verse in the Context of Its *Sūrah*

What can we say about the denial verse in light of its position in *Women* [4] as a whole? Overall, the *sūrah* can be divided into five sections.[16] Section 1 (1-43) is distinguished by community guidance about women and related subjects. Section 5 (127-76) comprises three main divisions: verses 127-35; 136-75; and 176, a long verse. The first and third divisions of this section treat issues related to women similar to those treated in §1. I am convinced §5 balances §1, giving the *sūrah* a ring structure. This coheres also with the name of the *sūrah*, *Women*. Section 3 (71-104) at the center of the *sūrah* provides the Muslim community with guidance for fighting in the way of God. Sections 1, 3, and 5 turn out to be of approximately equal size, a factor reinforcing my conviction that the *sūrah* exhibits a ring structure. All three of these major sections of similar size provide guidance for the community on matters vital to its survival and well-being.

Section 2 (44-70) mainly engages the People of the Book. Section 4 (105-26) appears to be directed toward traditional Arabian religionists. Each of these sections features one of two virtually identical verses. Verses 48 in §2 and 116 in §4 have the following in common, "Allah forgiveth not that partners should be set up with Him; but He forgiveth anything else, to whom He pleaseth; the one who sets up partners with Allah. . . ." Only the last three words of the verses differ. Verse 48 ends, "devises a sin most heinous indeed," and verse 116 ends, "hath strayed far, far away."[17] The Qurʾān contains no other verses like these. Since oral discourse uses exact repetition to show relationships between passages, the presence of the doublet (48, 116) probably connects §2 and §4, suggesting a warning for the People of the Book that they too are in danger of polytheism, the one unforgivable sin.[18]

Toward its end, the *sūrah* contains a set of verses (171-73) addressed to People of the Book. I lay out these verses below along with verses before and after (fig. 2.2).

The structure of the passage, especially its being marked off by two instances of the form of address, "O humankind" (170 and 174), connecting it with the opening verse of the *sūrah*, suggests it has a prominent place in the *sūrah*'s message. Near the end of the *sūrah*, this eloquent plea, framed and connected with the opening of the *sūrah* by the formula of address "O humankind," urges the People of the Book not to exaggerate claims for Jesus and to desist in holding a trinitarian perspective.

---

16. A. H. Mathias Zahniser, "Sūra as Guidance and Exhortation: The Composition of *Sūrat al-Nisāʾ*," in Asma Afsaruddin and A. H. Mathias Zahniser, eds. *Humanism, Culture, and Language in the Near East: Studies in Honor of Georg Krotkoff* (Winona Lake, IN: Eisenbrauns, 1997), 71-85. The major formal features include formulas of address, verse structure, rhyme pattern, and concatenation, 74.

17. The identical parts of the verses deviate significantly from each other in Ali's translation, obscuring for the English reader this striking doublet. I have revised Ali's translation of the two verses somewhat so the parallels and differences show up more clearly.

18. This does not mean that no polytheist can forsake idols and turn to God, but that God will not overlook idolatry (*shirk*) on the part of someone who has not confessed and abandoned it.

Figure 2.2 A Structural Diagram of *Women* [4]:170-75, Showing Its Forceful Challenge to Christians

O humankind!
The Messenger has come to you with the truth from your Lord.
So believe! It is better for you.
But if you disbelieve,
so what? God owns everything in heaven and on earth.
God is all-knowing and wise. (170)
O People of the Book!
Do not go beyond the truth in your religion,
speak correctly about God.
The Messiah, Jesus son of Mary,
is strictly the Messenger of God
and God's word, which He delivered to Mary—
and a spirit from Him.
So believe in God and in His messengers.
And do not say "Three."
Desist! It is better for you.
God is strictly one God.
He is exalted well beyond having a child.
He owns everything in heaven and on earth;
God needs no deputy. (171)
The Messiah will never be too proud to be a servant of God,
nor will God's intimates, the angels.
Those too proud to be God's servants, who are haughty,
He will force to come to Him *en masse*. (172)
But to those who believe and do good deeds
He will give their full due,
and even more from His bounty.
But those who despise servanthood and exalt self,
those are the ones He will painfully punish;
and for them—other than God—there will be neither benefactor nor helper. (173)
O humankind!
a proof has come to you from your Lord,
and we have revealed to you clear light. (174)
Those who believe in God and cling to Him,
them He shall plunge into his own mercy and grace,
and lead them to Himself upon a straight path. (175)

So how does our analysis of the structure of the *sūrah* of *Women* contribute to our study of the end of Jesus' mission in the Qur᾿ān? Simply this: in spite of the obvious interest of the *sūrah* in a polemic with believers in Jesus, it gives little or no attention to a polemic or plea about the death of Jesus and its meaning. And this is the case in spite of the fact that the killing of Jesus by crucifixion appears to be flatly rejected in the verse we have been interpreting. In addition, no other passage in the Qur᾿ān deals with the issue of Jesus' death and the Christian convictions about its meaning. While this point shares in the weakness of all arguments from silence, it possesses some merit, given the fact that the denial verse occurs in a polemic directed at Jewish claims and not in a polemic directed at Christian claims, and given the prominence of a polemic directed at other Christian claims. It would seem that if the Qur᾿ān had any quarrel with Christian teaching about the death of Jesus, it would have shown up in this *sūrah*.

Following Nolin, I have referred to *Women* [4]:157 as "the denial verse." Nolin also designates *Family of Imran* [3]:55 as the "affirmation verse." We turn to this now, examining it in its immediate narrative context as well as in its place in *Family of Imran* as a whole.

The Affirmation Verse: "I Will Cause You to Die and Raise You to Myself"

One of the most important passages in the Qur᾿ān for understanding what Muslims believe about how Jesus' mission ended occurs in *Family of Imran* [3]:42-55. On the heels of the story of the angel's announcement to Mary of the birth of Jesus, Jesus bears witness to himself and clarifies his mission in a lengthy testimony. He comes with a sign from God by breathing life into a clay bird, healing the blind and leprous, and bringing the dead to life. He testifies also to his role as a messenger who guides the community, interprets the law, and proclaims the oneness of God.

Then the scene switches from first person narrative to a drama set toward the end of Jesus' prophetic mission on earth. Jesus, sensing unbelief among his followers, asks who among them will help him. His Apostles (*ḥawāriyūn*) assure him they are his helpers and assert that they are believers, submitters, and witnesses. A brief verse points to the plotting of God and of his enemies.[19] Then the verse affirming Jesus' death emerges as a promise of God to Jesus:

> Behold! God said: "O Jesus! I will take thee and raise thee to Myself and clear thee (of the falsehoods) of those who blaspheme; I will make those who follow thee superior to those who reject faith, to the Day of

19. Dale Walker points out that this verse (*Family of Imran* [3]:54) could be a reflex of the Gospel tradition that God did one better than the Jewish plotters, like Caiaphas making a prophecy in saying that "it was better to have one person die for the people" (John 18:14) (personal communication, 2004).

> Resurrection: Then shall ye all return unto me, and I will judge between you of the matters wherein ye dispute." (*Family of Imran* [3]:55)

Where in this verse, one may legitimately ask, is the affirmation of Jesus' death? Like all translations, this rendering by A. Yusuf Ali *interprets*. The phrase "I will take thee" translates the word *mutawaffī-ka*, an active participle from the verb *tawaffā* plus its object, a second person singular masculine pronoun, *-ka*. Ali takes the verb to mean "take." But what does *take* mean in this context?

The answer emerges in part from the following words, "and raise thee to Myself" (*wa-rāfiʿu-ka ilayya*). "Raise" here does not necessarily refer to resurrection. The word "resurrection" (*qiyāmah*) also occurs in the verse. Resurrection could be implied, however, if we understand the previous participle to mean "I will cause you to die." This is the sense of the verb *tawaffā* in other places in the Qurʾān, such as "Allah . . . will take your souls at death" (*yatawaffā-kum*) (*Jonah* [10]:104), and "those whose lives the angels take in a state of wrongdoing" (*yatawaffā-hum*) (*Bee* [16]:28).[20]

According to Islamic tradition, Ibn ʿAbbās (d. 687/688) and Wahb ibn Munabbih (d. 728 or 732), two early authorities on Qurʾān interpretation, held that *mutawaffī-ka* meant in this context "I shall cause thee to die."[21] But most Muslim Qurʾān commentators have found this interpretation unsatisfactory. Muḥammad ibn Jarīr al-Ṭabarī, whose massive commentary transmits this tradition, rejects it, concluding Jesus did not die:

> As for God's plot against them, . . . it is his casting a resemblance of Jesus on one of his followers so that those plotting against Jesus killed him, thinking he was Jesus. God . . . had already raised Jesus.[22]

Ṭabarī bases his conclusion on a saying (*ḥadīth*) of Muḥammad he considers reliable. According to this tradition, in the future God will send down Jesus son of Mary who will kill the Antichrist, then dwell on earth for a period of time. He will die a natural death and be buried; then God will raise him on the day of resurrection.[23] This tradition helps Muslim Qurʾān interpreters harmonize this affirmation verse with the denial verse examined above (*Women* [4]:157). The plain meaning of the affirmation verse, taken alone, would seem to be that God caused Jesus to die as part of his plan to foil the unbelievers' plot and then raised him.

Muslim interpreters of the Qurʾān, both Sunnī and Shīʿī, have generally found in the affirmation verse not only a *denial* of the humiliating crucifixion

---

20. See also *Pilgrimage* [22]:5; *Believer* [40]:67, and other references in Neal Robinson, *Christ in Islam and Christianity: The Representation of Jesus in the Qurʾān and the Classical Muslim Commentaries* (London: Macmillan, 1991), 117-24; and A. H. Mathias Zahniser, "The Forms of *Tawaffā* in the Qurʾān: A Contribution to Christian-Muslim Dialogue," *The Muslim World* 79 (1989): 14-24.

21. Ṭabarī, *Tafsīr,* 6:457 (#7141); Ismāʿīl ibn Kathīr, *Tafsīr*, 7 vols. (Beirut: Dār al-Andalūs, 1966), 2:44.

22. Ṭabarī, *Tafsīr,* 6:454.

23. Ibid., 6:458.

of Jesus but also a denial that he died. Some interpreters, in contrast, have discovered in the affirmation verse a Qur'ānic affirmation of the death of Jesus and even of his crucifixion.

Two Affirmative Interpretations of the Affirmation Verse

Now we will turn to two modern interpreters, both of whom conclude that *Family of Imran* [3]:55 affirms the death of Jesus. Both offer their analysis in the interest of better Christian-Muslim understanding about the end of Jesus' mission. Both analyses require dealing with the denial verses also. No interpreter of the final days of Jesus in the Qur'ān can ignore this passage.

A Christian Interpretation. As we have mentioned above, E. E. Elder,[24] Geoffrey Parrinder,[25] and Kenneth E. Nolin have presented a Christian interpretation of the denial verse. The affirmation verse naturally figures into their interpretation as well. Here we focus on Nolin's interpretation. He studied the Qur'ān in Egypt over a number of years with both Muslim experts and Christian pastors to see how it could be interpreted through the witness of the New Testament. Nolin firmly believes the Qur'ān and the New Testament read together yield a new understanding of Jesus' mission for both Muslims and Christians. According to him, Christians could consider the Qur'ān a word from God, if interpreted in the light of the New Testament.

Obviously, his proposal of New Testament interpretation requires an agonizing and difficult reconception for Muslims, even though—as we saw in chapter 1—the Qur'ān seems to require Muḥammad to consult the scriptures of Christianity for interpreting his own revelation (*Jonah* [10]:94-95 and *Prophets* [21]:7). Acceptance of the Qur'ān as a word from God requires an agonizing and difficult reconception for Christians as well. Nolin says, "Read in agreement with those earlier scriptures, . . . the Qur'ānic evidence is seen to point most naturally to the death of Jesus on the cross, *not* his rescue from it."[26] After all, Nolin points out the Qur'ān testifies to the death of Jesus in *Mary* [19]:33, a passage revealed before *Family of Imran* [3]:55.

The Nestorian patriarch Timothy I (d. 823), in a conversation with the Muslim caliph al-Mahdī (reigned 775-785) during the year 782-783, followed this same approach, combining the *Mary* passage with the *Family of Imran* passage.[27] In the *Mary* passage Jesus himself identifies three blessed events he

---

24. Elder, "Crucifixion," 242-58.

25. Parrinder, *Jesus in the Qur'ān*, 105-21.

26. Nolin, "Pilgrimage," 57.

27. Hans Putnam, *L'Église & l'Islam sous Timothée I (780-823): Études sur L'Église Nestorienne au temps des premiers ʿAbbāsides avec nouvelle édition et traduction du dialogue entre Timothée et Al-Mahdī*, Recherches publiées sous la direction de l'Institut de Lettres Orientales de Beyrouth, nouvelle série B. Orient Chrétien 3 (Beirut: Dar el-Machreq, 1986), 253 [Arabic text, 35-36]. Al-Mahdī (d. 785) was the third Abbasid caliph. An English summary of this discussion can be found in Robinson, *Christ in Islam*, 107-8; and a more detailed analysis in Mark N. Swanson, "Folly to the *Ḥunafā'*: The Crucifixion in Early Christian-Muslim Controversy," in David Thomas, Mark

has experienced or will experience: birth, death, and resurrection: "So Peace is on me the day I was born, the day that I die, and the day that I shall be raised up to life (again)!" The fact that the Qurʾān says the same of John, the son of Zechariah (*Mary* [19]:15), reinforces the natural sequence of these events.

Nolin also finds in *Cow* [2]:87 an implication that Jesus was killed:

> We gave Moses the Book and followed him up with a succession of Messengers; we gave Jesus, the son of Mary, clear (signs) and strengthened him with the Holy Spirit. Is it that whenever there comes to you a Messenger with what ye yourselves desire not, ye are puffed up with pride? Some you call imposters, and others ye slay!

Based on its order, the verse implies that the Jews called Moses an imposter and killed Jesus. Nolin contends that these Qurʾānic "affirmation" verses (*Family of Imran* [3]:55; *Mary* [19]:33; and *Cow* [2]:87) can be read in harmony with the Christian Gospels.[28] Not only that, but he harmonizes the denial verses with the affirmation verses and, in the final analysis, with the way Jesus' mission ended according to the Gospels. As we saw above, the denial verse denies only the Jews' claim to have defeated Jesus. Nolin insists that the qualifying phrase "it only appeared to them" (*Women* [4]:157) means the crucifixion was made to look to the Jews like an ultimate victory for them over Jesus—but of course it was not.[29]

Recognizing that Muslims reject the cross because they believe the God who sends prophets would not abandon Jesus to such a horrendous defeat, Nolin concludes:

> But what if the al-Nisāʾ verse [*Women* (4):157] is simply affirming that same victory . . . after the apparent defeat in Jesus' death? Suppose God has accepted the very worst that mankind can bring to bear against Him, in Jesus Christ, but then turns it around into an ultimate triumph . . . ?[30]

A Muslim Interpretation. Mahmoud M. Ayoub offers another interpretation designed for better Muslim-Christian understanding. It also gives evidence of flexibility in interpreting the last events of Jesus' mission. He concludes that *Family of Imran* [3]:55, "O Jesus! I will take thee/cause thee to die and raise thee to Myself," indicates Jesus did die.[31] He also examines carefully the views of Sunnī, Shīʿī, and Ṣūfī exegetes on the subject of the death, or the supposed death, of the Messiah Jesus from an interfaith perspective: "The ultimate aim of

---

Swanson, and Emmanouela Grypeou, eds., *The Encounter of Eastern Christianity with Early Islam* (Leiden: Brill, 2006), 248-55.

28. *Table* [5]:117 is also an affirmation verse, much like *Family of Imran* [3]:55.

29. Nolin, "Pilgrimage," 58.

30. Ibid., 60.

31. Mahmoud Ayoub, "Towards an Islamic Christology, II," *The Muslim World* 70 (1980): 91-121, reprinted in Irfan A. Omar, ed., *A Muslim View of Christianity: Essays on Dialogue by Mahmoud Ayoub*, Faith Meets Faith (Maryknoll, NY: Orbis Books, 2007), 156-83.

this study," he says, "is to promote constructive and meaningful dialogue among the men and women of faith in [the Muslim and the Christian] communities."[32]

First, Ayoub asserts that the very ambiguous and mysterious aspects of the verses we are discussing point to the human condition itself. Human beings are presented in these passages about the last days of Jesus as suffering, conjecturing, enduring ambiguity, and exercising arrogance. Thus "the Qur'ān presents Jesus as a challenge not only to human folly and unbelief (*kufr*) but equally to human ignorance and reliance on mere conjecture."[33]

Second, Ayoub rejects the view that someone was substituted for Jesus on the cross. Such a scenario does not cohere with divine justice and mocks, he says, the "primordial covenant of God with humanity to guide human history to its final fulfillment."[34] That is, God has covenanted to be consistent with humans. How could this consistency be assured if God were to make one person look like another? In consequence, he affirms the view of Fakhr al-Dīn al-Rāzī (d. 1209) that Jesus suffered in body, but not in his holy and exalted soul.[35] He says this position "goes a long way toward meeting the Qur'ānic challenge of Jesus . . . [and] provides a good starting point for Muslim-Christian understanding."[36]

Third, from other affirmation verses, Ayoub offers evidence that the Qur'ān does not deny Jesus' death.[37] He is convinced that *Table* [5]:117 and *Family of Imran* [3]:55 indicate that God brought about an end to Jesus' life on earth which was followed by a celestial life with God, and that these verses stress the "Oneness of God" (*tawḥīd*).[38]

Fourth, Ayoub adduces some Qur'ānic evidence for his conviction that Islam and the Qur'ān have a place for a positive view of the mystery of suffering. In addition to its portrayal of the distraught Jacob over the loss of his son, the suffering of Job, Abraham, Zechariah, and John the Baptist, the Qur'ān shows Muḥammad suffering agony and depression under the burden of his divine mission. In fear and loneliness, he had to be reassured by God's words, "Have we not expanded thee thy breast?" (*Expansion* [94]:1).[39]

Finally, Ayoub maintains that statements about Mary's being the sister of Aaron (*Mary* [19]:27-28), the statements about Jesus' death, or supposed

---

32. Ayoub, "Towards an Islamic Christology," 92; idem, *A Muslim View*, 157.

33. Ayoub, "Towards an Islamic Christology," 103, 104; idem, *A Muslim View*, 166.

34. Ayoub, "Towards an Islamic Christology," 104; idem, *A Muslim View*, 166.

35. Ayoub, "Towards an Islamic Christology," 105; 167. Rāzī's interpretation can be found in Fakhr al-Dīn al-Rāzī, *Al-tafsīr al-kabīr*, 16 vols. in 8 (Beirut: Dār al-kutub al-ʿilmīyah, 1990), 4:8.60-74 and 6:11.78-83. The volumes and pagination in the 1934-38 edition published in Cairo are 8.63-76 and 11.100-101. His argument is summarized in English by Mahmoud Ayoub, *The Qur'ān and Its Interpreters: The House of ʿImrān,* 2 vols. (Albany: SUNY Press, 1992), 2:175-78.

36. Ayoub, "Towards an Islamic Christology," 105; idem, *A Muslim View*, 167.

37. Ayoub, "Towards an Islamic Christology," 106; idem, *A Muslim View*, 168.

38. Ayoub, "Towards an Islamic Christology," 107; idem, *A Muslim View*, 168-69.

39. In Ayoub, "Towards an Islamic Christology," 116 n. 97; idem, *A Muslim View*, 176. The reference for this quotation is given incorrectly as 93:1. Ayoub has also published a thorough study of redemptive suffering in his *Redemptive Suffering in Islam: A Study of the Devotional Aspects of ʿAshūra in Twelver Shiʿism* (The Hague: Mouton, 1978).

death (and all other statements about him), have to be taken theologically in the broadest sense. Mary, the mother of Jesus, was not the sister of Aaron.[40] Their relationship, therefore, has to be interpreted theologically rather than literally in conjunction with the Qur'ānic dictum that all the prophets are descendants one of another (*Family of Imran* [3]:38). In other words, *Women* [4]:157 directs its reproach of the Jews not at their telling a historical lie but at their human arrogance, folly, and ignorance. It is not directed at the Jews alone, but at all humanity who think they can get the victory over a divine Word that will always triumph.[41] Ayoub's final theological response runs as follows:

> In their earnest striving for a true understanding of the sacred text, Muslim commentators did more than indulge in an exercise of textual analysis. The Qur'ān insists on "letting God be God," and this the Muslim community has taken with uncompromising seriousness. . . .
>
> Christianity has insisted, and with equal uncompromising seriousness, on "letting God be man" in order for man to be divine. . . . The final purpose for the two communities of faith is one: let God be God, not only in His vast creation, but in our little lives as well. . . .[42]

Both Nolin, a Christian, and Ayoub, a Muslim, offer an alternative to the dominant Muslim interpretation of the affirmation verse. Both look at it in relation to the denial verse. Both interpret the affirmation and the denial verses without primary allegiance to the Prophetic Tradition (*ḥadīth*) and traditional Qur'ān exegesis (*tafsīr*). Both believe the Qur'ān affirms Jesus' death. Both find in it divine triumph over human evil. Both offer their findings for Christian-Muslim dialogue. But neither looks at the verses in the context of the *sūrah* as a whole. What, we must ask, is the meaning of the affirmation and denial verses if we read them in the context of their *sūrah*s? We have looked at the contexts of the denial verse above; as this chapter ends, we examine the context of the affirmation verse.

The Affirmation Verse in Context

A couple of very popular modern Qur'ān exegetes give attention to the contexts of the verses under discussion here. According to Sayyid Quṭb (d. 1966), *sūrah* 3 centers on the fundamental issue of the singularity and unity of God, referred to in Arabic as *tawḥīd*. But he means this concept to include not only the singularity and unity of the Divine (*tawḥīd al-ilāhīyah*) but also the unity

40. It is common in Arabic to address people in metaphorical relations such as *yā akh al-ʿArab*! (O brother of the Arabs). Suleiman Darrat, personal communication, January 2007.

41. Ayoub, "Towards an Islamic Christology," 117; idem, *A Muslim View*, 176.

42. Ayoub, "Towards an Islamic Christology," 118; idem, *A Muslim View*, 177.

and order of the way we are to live (*tawḥīd al-qawāmah*) that results from this basic unity.[43]

Another modern interpreter, Maḥmūd Shaltūt (d. 1963), identifies two great issues dominating this *sūrah*: (1) the issue of the Divine and the establishing of the truth concerning the Divine through the revealing of books and revelation to prophets; and (2) the establishing of the fact that the deceitfulness of possessions and family causes people to deviate from seeking the truth and following a proper way of life.[44] Shaltūt's truth concerning God obviously amounts to something like Quṭb's divine unity and singularity. And the deceitfulness of possessions and family represents a principal threat to living according to the unity and singularity of God. We turn now to look at the affirmation verse within the overall structure of its *sūrah* and in the context of the narrative passage that gives it its name.

Overall Structure.[45] *Family of Imran* has four main sections: §1, a prologue (1-18); §2, a long section, including a narrative addressing primarily People of the Book (19-101), although the Prophet himself is addressed here also; §3, a long section addressing primarily Muslim believers (102-89); and §4, an epilogue (190-200).[46]

In §1 (1-18), the prologue, themes are developed as follows: first, *tawḥīd*, the singularity and oneness of God, is emphasized clearly (3, 5, 6, 18); a second theme is the giving of scriptures (3, 7); and a third theme combines "backsliding" and its antidote, "steadfastness" (4, 8, 13). Section 2 (19-101) focuses on the People of the Book, namely Jews and Christians, foreshadowing the themes of §3 (102-89). In verses 64-99 the phrase "People of the Book" occurs at the outset of six verses in three clusters of two (64-65, 70-71, and 98-99). Section 3 (102-89) is addressed to the community of Muslim believers. Although the phrase "O ye who believe" occurs frequently in the Qur'ān, its repetition in this section of *sūrah* 3 signals a community of address, supported by the contents of the section.

The Narrative Section. We turn now to the narrative (33-57) about the family of ʿImrān and the verses following it (58-63). This narrative traces Jesus' prophetic lineage back to Adam, telling the story of the births of Mary, John, and Jesus and closing with the end of Jesus' mission on earth. The narrative is

43. Sayyid Quṭb, *Fī ẓilāl al-Qur'ān*, 6 vols. (Beirut: Dār al-Shurūq, 1974), 3:390.

44. Maḥmūd Shaltūt, *Tafsīr al-Qur'ān al-karīm: al-ajzā' al-ʿasharah al-ūlā* (Cairo: Dār al-Qalam, 1966), 92.

45. I have given more thorough attention to the structure of this *sūrah* in "The Word of God and the Apostleship of ʿĪsā: A Narrative Analysis of Āl ʿImrān (3):33-62," *Journal of Semitic Studies* 37 (1991): 77-112.

46. The places where there is a transition from one section to another are difficult to determine precisely. This is because of the way the Qur'ān makes transitions. See my "Major Transitions and Thematic Borders in Two Long Suras: *al-Baqara* and *al-Nisā'*," in Issa J. Boullata, ed., *Literary Structures of Religious Meaning in the Qur'ān* (Richmond, Surrey, UK: Curzon, 2000), 26-55. My analysis of the structure of *sūrah* 3 in this article differs somewhat from my earlier analysis in "Word of God," 84-87. See n. 45 immediately above.

certified and defended in verse 62 as "the true narrative" just before the section ends with a declaration that no god exists but Allah and a warning that God is aware of what those do who turn away to corruption (63). Woven in among other threads of the narrative are ample testimonies to the oneness and sovereignty of God (e.g., 33, 36, 40, 42, 45, 47).

Angels announce to Mary the identity of Jesus: "a Word from Him: his name will be the Messiah Jesus, the son of Mary . . ." (45). God, who creates him in the womb of Mary, will teach him the Book and the Wisdom, the Torah and the Gospel (47-48). The Qurʾān sets out prominently his roles as "Messenger" and "Confirmer" at the beginning of the next two verses, while the content of these verses ties the first person narrative of Jesus to the sovereign activity of God:

> A messenger to the Children of Israel,
> I have come to you with a sign from your Lord,
> in that I make for you out of clay, as it were, the figure of a bird,
> and breathe into it, and it becomes a bird
> by Allah's leave,
> and I heal those born blind, and the lepers,
> and I quicken the dead,
> by Allah's leave. . . .
> To attest the Torah. . . .
> I have come to you with a sign from your Lord.
> So fear Allah and obey me. (49-50)[47]

The final statement Jesus makes as messenger drives the message of divine unity and singularity home: "It is Allah who is my Lord and your Lord; then worship Him. This is a Way that is straight" (51). Thematically it enunciates, in the words of Jesus, what the whole narrative supports: "Allah is my Lord and your Lord; then worship Him."

Next, the "unbelief" (*kufr*) Jesus senses among "them" (52) serves as a link with the following episode: the plot against Jesus and God's promised counterplot. Both the ambiguous "they" of verses 52 and 54 and the "unbelief" of verse 52 come together in verse 55, further emphasizing its content as a focal point and climax of the whole narrative section that gives the *sūrah* its name.

The narrative probably ends at verse 55 because verses 56 and 57 rehearse the fate of unbelievers (56) and the reward of those who believe (57). Verses 58 through 63 then confirm the validity of the whole revealed story. In other words, verse 55—the crucial affirmation verse of our study—stands out as the key and climactic verse of the narrative. Note its impact if we translate the first part of it literally:

> God said, "O Jesus, I will cause thee to die (*mutawaffī-ka*), raise thee (*rāfiʿu-ka*) to me, and purify thee (*muṭahhiru-ka*) from those who practice unbelief. . . ."

---

47. This is my translation, presented so as to reveal the structure of the verses.

The climactic verse of the narrative and the verses following deal with Jesus, the key figure for Christians, but these verses stress the sovereignty of God, not the death of Jesus or its meaning. God's plot and God's promise are presented as Jesus' hope of escape from the unbelievers scheming against him. Furthermore, the narrative affirms that the Apostles of Jesus volunteered under difficult circumstances to remain steadfast and to help him *because they were God's helpers*. They are exemplars of those who do not backslide under adversity and who will be victorious because—just as God will rescue Jesus from among the unbelievers—God will reward them in full (57).

God Triumphs

In the Qur'ān, we are looking at the event of Jesus' last days on earth from the divine side, in the sense that God triumphs over the unbelievers. In the process, *the words* of the Qur'ān dwarf *the details of the events* connected with the end of Jesus' mission. Indeed, one could argue from the structure and content of the narrative that the *sūrah*'s emphasis on God's word and sovereign action eclipses the significance of the final events of Jesus' mission—except as the affirmation verse announces that God got the best of the unbelievers who plotted against Jesus.

The *sūrah* and its narrative passage deal in their own way with the nature of God and of God's word. The prevalence in the Christian Gospels of the details of Jesus' last days also yields important insights into the nature of God. It is the biblically based Christian understanding of God that provides the foundation for the significance of the end of Jesus' earthly life for the transformation and final destiny of believers in him. Again, as we noted above in connection with the denial verse in its context, the Qur'ān remains virtually silent about the Christian meaning of the end of Jesus' mission.

Ironically, Christian interpreters at the time of Muḥammad appear to have been as silent about the atoning death of Jesus as the Qur'ān itself is. John Wansbrough, after examining the historical traditions about Muḥammad's life, concludes that the primitive disputation between Christians and Muslims reveals no real emphasis on the cross and the atonement—even from the Christian side![48]

The Qur'ān emphasizes the dominance of the word and plan of God when interpreting the confrontation between Jesus and human unbelief as his mission comes to an end. It does not, however, set itself unambiguously against a Christian interpretation of God's victory over human unbelief in the death and resurrection of Jesus, demonstrating graphically that God is both ultimate "in His vast creation" and intimate "in our little lives as well."[49]

---

48. John Wansbrough, *The Sectarian Milieu: Content and Composition of Islamic Salvation History*, London Oriental Series 34 (London: Oxford University Press, 1978), 102.

49. Ayoub, "Towards an Islamic Christology," 118; idem, *A Muslim View*, 177.

3

“Someone Was Made to Look Like Him”

The Final Days of Jesus’ Mission in Classical Qur’ān Commentary

In the previous chapter we have seen that, taken together, *sūrahs Family of Imran* [3] and *Women* [4] are not clear about what happened at the end of Jesus’ mission. What we have called the affirmation verse literally says, “I will cause you to die and raise you to myself” (*Family of Imran* [3]:55). The statement is limited in its scope, but clear. It is clear, that is, unless read along with what we have called the denial verse. The denial verse states unequivocally about the Jews, “They killed him not, nor crucified him, but so it was made to appear to them. . . . For of a surety they killed him not” (*Women* [4]:157). The next verse goes on to say, “Nay, Allah raised him up unto Himself . . .” (158). We also discovered that, whereas both *sūrahs* contain polemic directed at Christians, they say nothing about the Christian conviction that Jesus died for humanity. The Qur’ān says nothing about the Christian view of the end of Jesus’ mission in the sense of its purpose or meaning.

In other words, the Qur’ān itself is ambiguous about Jesus’ death and silent as to its meaning. Any ambiguity or apparent contradiction in scripture summons commentary and explanation. This certainly applies to the *sūrahs* dealing with the last days of Jesus’ mission. To take an example, an early twentieth-century commentator, Jamāl al-Dīn al-Qāsimī (d. 1914), devotes seventy-nine pages to *Women* [4]:157-59. He unequivocally holds that Jesus did not die, was not crucified, but ascended into heaven, escaping from those who plotted against him and that someone was then crucified in his place.

In this chapter we examine some of the classical commentators on the Qur’ānic passages dealing with the end of Jesus’ mission. By classical commentaries, I mean the major commentaries written before the wide distribution in 1908 of the Gospel of Barnabas, which will be discussed in chapter 6 below. Although an early Gnostic Gospel promulgated the idea that Judas was substituted for Jesus on the cross and an early Qur’ān commentary mentions that some early

Christians believed this,[1] it is the Gospel of Barnabas that has made this scenario popular among Sunnī Muslims. The Shīʿīs have another view, as we shall see. Except when quoting, I render the narratives and reports in the remainder of this chapter rather loosely, casting them in contemporary English narrative style, often substituting proper nouns for pronouns to reduce ambiguity. We look first at the occasion for the revelation of the narrative beginning of the *sūrah* of the *Family of Imran* and then at commentary on the affirmation and denial verses.

The Occasion for Revelation of the Affirmation Verse

Most commentators connect the revelation of at least the first eighty verses of *sūrah* 3 with the coming to Medina of a Christian delegation from Najrān, a town in southern Arabia. Al-Wāḥidī (d. 1076), who devotes a treatise to the occasions for Qurʾānic revelations, based his presentation on reports from commentators. According to them, a delegation consisting of sixty horsemen, including fourteen noblemen, came to Muḥammad at the time of the afternoon prayers. Three of them had special authority among the people of Najrān: two political and social leaders, one called the ʿAqīb and the other the Sayyid, and one religious leader and head of their religious school, called the Imām. The latter was a man of enormous learning respected even by the Byzantine king. The delegation was elegantly attired, which caused the Companions of the Prophet to marvel. The delegation was allowed to pray in the mosque, facing east.

According to Wāḥidī's report, after they had prayed, when the Messenger of God invites the Sayyid and the ʿAqīb to accept Islam, they reply, "We have been *muslims* long before you." Muḥammad quickly denies their assertion, "Your claim that God has a son, your worship of the cross, and your eating of swine prevent you from being *muslims*."

They shoot back, "If Jesus was not the Son of God, then who was his father?" From here on the Messenger appears to have the upper hand. Among the things he says is, "Do you not know that our Lord is living and will never die, while Jesus is subject to extinction?" When they agree, he goes on, "Do you not know that our Lord has control over all things which he alone preserves and sustains?" Responding again to their affirmation, Muḥammad continues his questioning, "Does Jesus possess the power to do any of these things?" They answer, "No."

So Muḥammad continues, "It is our Lord who formed Jesus in the womb as He willed. Our Lord, moreover, neither eats, drinks, nor does he void. Do you not know that the mother of Jesus bore him in the same manner as women bear their children, and delivered him as they do, and that he was then nurtured as any child would be; then he ate, drank, and voided?" They again say simply, "Yes."

---

1. Abdelmajid Charfi, "Christianity in the Qurʾān Commentary of Ṭabarī," *Islamochristiana* 6 (1980): 123 and n. 133.

When the Messenger of God concludes with a final question, "How could it then be as you say?" they say nothing.[2]

Muḥammad ibn Jarīr al-Ṭabarī (d. 923), in his massive commentary on the Qurʾān, says the delegation from Najrān debated with Muḥammad on the question of Jesus, and the delegation evidenced unbelief in God. On this basis, *Family of Imran* was "sent down." The delegation, however, did not respond even to this revelation in faith; this situation resulted in Muḥammad's prophetic challenge for both communities to submit their positions to God, letting God curse the party in the wrong (*Family of Imran* [3]:61). When the Christians request that Muḥammad charge them a tax (*jizyah*) instead, he agrees, and the Najrān delegation returns home.[3]

The delegation, according to Ṭabarī's treatment of the incident, never responds at all to the charges of Muḥammad except to condone his analysis. Nothing is said about the cross except that Christians worship it. Let us turn now to examining the way the early commentators expand on the succinct account in this *sūrah* of the end of Jesus' mission.

Classical Commentary on the Affirmation Verse

An early interpretation of *Family of Imran* [3]:55 paraphrases it, "I will cause you to die and raise you to myself." Ṭabarī records the following interpretation attributed to Ibn ʿAbbās, who uses the more literal "I will cause you to die" (*mumayyitu-ka*) for the more metaphorical *mutawaffī-ka*:[4] "Jesus died," he reports, "and his soul was received by God."[5] An early convert from Judaism, Wahb ibn Munabbih says, "God caused Jesus, son of Mary, to die for three hours during the day, then took him up to himself."[6] Ṭabarī and others also transmit from Ibn Isḥāq (d. 768), "God caused Jesus to die for seven hours."[7] Mahmoud M. Ayoub, a modern compiler and interpreter, says this was an idea interpreters later attributed to Christian reports.[8]

---

2. Abū al-Ḥasan al-Wāḥidī, *Asbāb nuzūl al-Qurʾān* (Cairo: Dār al-Kitāb al-Jadīd, 1969), 90-91. The quotations are taken from the translation by Mahmoud M. Ayoub in *The Qurʾān and Its Interpreters: The House of ʿImrān*, 2 vols. (Albany: SUNY Press, 1992), vol. 2.

3. Abū Jaʿfar Muḥammad ibn Jarīr al-Ṭabarī, *Tafsīr al-Ṭabarī* (*Jāmiʿ al-bayān ʿan taʾwīl āyy al-Qurʾān*), ed. Maḥmūd Muḥammad Shākir and Aḥmad Muḥammad Shākir, 16 vols., Turāth al-Islām (Cairo: Dār al-Maʿārif, 1971), 6:150-51; translated into English by Mahmoud M. Ayoub (*The Qurʾān and Its Interpreters: The House of ʿImrān*, 3). According to Ibn Kathīr (see Ismāʿīl ʿImād al-Dīn Abī al-Fidāʾ Ibn Kathīr al-Qurayshī al-Dimashqī, *Tafsīr al-Qurʾān al-ʿazīm*, 7 vols. [Beirut: Dar al-fikr, 1970], 2:3), this event took place in the year 9 of the Hijrah, about 631.

4. See the discussion of this phrase in chapter 2 above.

5. See Ibn Kathīr, *Tafsīr*, 2:44. English translation from Mahmoud M. Ayoub, "Towards an Islamic Christology, II," *The Muslim World* 70 (1980): 107.

6. Ṭabarī, *Tafsīr*, 6:457 (#7142); Ibn Kathīr, *Tafsīr*, 2:44. See also Michel Hayek, *Le Christ de l'Islam* (Paris: Editions du Seuil, 1959), 255. Compare Matthew 27:45.

7. Ṭabarī, *Tafsīr*, 6:458 (#7143); and Ibn Kathīr, *Tafsīr*, 1:366, 2:44.

8. Ayoub, "Towards an Islamic Christology," 108; reprinted in Irfan A. Omar, ed., *A Muslim*

Ṭabarī records other interpreters' taking the position that *mutawaffī-ka* means something other than "I will cause you to die." Some say that the word means "I will receive you."[9] The gloss employed is *qābiḍu-ka,* "I will grasp/seize/take you."[10] This tradition Ṭabarī and others transmit from Maṭar al-Warrāq (d. 742) and ʿAbd Allāh Ibn al-Zubayr (d. 692).[11] According to the classical commentator al-Rāzī, *mutawaffī-ka* means "completing the term (*ajal*) of your life" and "protecting you from the evil schemes of your enemies." The participle's verbal noun, *tawaffin*, includes death, but is not synonymous with it. The participle with pronoun *-ka* found in the following verse, *rāfiʿu-ka*, along with the preposition with pronoun, *ilayya*, means, "I will raise thee to myself." It specifies the type of *tawaffin* involved.[12]

Ṭabarī includes a variety of reports, evaluates them, and gives his own best judgment as to where the historical truth lies. He concludes, "As for God's plot against the Jews it is his casting a resemblance of ʿĪsā on one (*baʿḍ*) of his followers so that they killed him instead of ʿĪsā, God having raised ʿĪsā beforehand." He cites a tradition to this effect from Kaʿb al-Aḥbar (d. 652), a Jewish chief rabbi. Ṭabarī bases his preference for "I will take/receive you" over "I will cause you to die" on the soundness of an eschatological tradition attributed to the Prophet Muḥammad.

The tradition teaches that Jesus remains alive in heaven but will come back to earth in the future, marry, raise a family, and die a natural death. Then on the resurrection day he will, along with Muḥammad, participate in the final judgment. Obviously, Jesus could not experience two deaths. So he did not die at the hands of the Jews. Ṭabarī rejects the report that Jesus died also on the basis of its poor supporting chain of authorities (*isnād*).[13] Another version of this same tradition specifies that God took Jesus in his sleep so he would not be frightened at the experience of death.[14]

The following narrative from Ṭabarī on the authority of Qatādah (d. 735), reporting from Abū Hurayrah (d. 678), represents a version of what the Prophet said about this eschatology.

View of Christianity: Essays on Dialogue by Mahmoud Ayoub, Faith Meets Faith (Maryknoll, NY: Orbis Books, 2007), 169. Jesus was dead for three days, then was resurrected and taken up into heaven (see Muḥammad ibn ʿAlī ibn Muḥammad al-Shawkānī, *Fatḥ al-qadīr al-jāmiʿ bayn fannay al-riwāyah wa al-dirāyah min ʿilm al-tafsīr* [Cairo: Musṭafā al-Bābī al-Ḥalabī, n.d.], 1:346), cited in Ayoub, "Towards an Islamic Christology"; see 108 n. 66; and idem, *Muslim View,* 181 n. 43.

9. Ṭabarī, *Tafsīr*, 6:455; and Ibn Kathīr, *Tafsīr*, 1:366; 2:44.

10. In its root meaning, *qābaḍa* implies taking hold of something or someone with the whole of the hand (Edward William Lane, *Arabic-English Lexicon*, 8 vols. [Beirut: Librairie du Luban, 1968 (1885)], 7:2481).

11. Ṭabarī, *Tafsīr*, 6:455; Ibn Kathīr, *Tafsīr*, 2:44; and Muḥammad ʿAbd al-Munʿim al-Jammāl, *Al-tafsīr al-farīd li-al-Qurʾān al-majīd*, 4 vols. (Cairo: Dār al-kitāb al-jadīd, 1973), 1:353.

12. Fakhr al-Dīn Muḥammad ibn ʿUmar al-Rāzī, *Al-tafsīr al-kabīr*, 32 vols. (Cairo: al-Maṭbaʿah al-bāhiyah al-Miṣrīyah, 1934-1962), 7:72.

13. Ṭabarī, *Tafsīr*, 6:486-87; cited by Ayoub, "Towards an Islamic Christology," 107 with English translation; omitted in idem, *Muslim View*.

14. Ṭabarī, *Tafsīr*, 3:455; and Ibn Kathīr, *Tafsīr*, 2:44.

> Of all men, I have the most rightful claim to Jesus son of Mary because there was no prophet between him and me. He shall be my successor (*khalīfah*) over my community. He will surely descend. When you see him you will recognize him. He shall be a man of medium height, with hues of red and white color, and of straight hair. His hair will appear as though dripping, although no water had touched it. He will be clad with two yellow garments. He shall break the cross and kill the swine, dispense abundant wealth, and wage war on behalf of Islam against men until God causes all other religions to perish in his time. At his hand, God will also destroy the Messiah of error, the deceiver, al-Dajjāl. Security will then cover the earth, so that lions will graze with camels, tigers with cattle, and wolves with sheep. Youths will play with snakes, but they will not harm them. He shall dwell in the earth for forty years. Then he will die, and Muslims will pray over him.[15]

Classical Ṣūfī commentaries make the traditional interpretation of what we have been calling the affirmation verse analogous to the spiritual journey: Jesus was taken up to heaven and will "return to share in our human life more fully than he did during his first sojourn on earth." When he returns, he will purify the earth, kill the one-eyed liar, remove barriers between people, marry and beget children, die, be buried with Muḥammad, and they shall be resurrected together.[16]

The exegete Muḥammad ibn Aḥmad al-Qurṭubī (d. 1272) transmits a number of these eschatological traditions on the authority of Abū Hurayrah. For example, the Prophet said, "By God, the son of Mary will descend as a just judge. He shall break the cross and kill the swine. He shall abolish the *jizyah* poll tax. Young she camels will be left to graze, and no one will attempt to lead them away. All rancor, hatred and envy will cease. People will be invited to receive wealth, but no one will have any need of it."[17]

Some traditions show confidence in the more obvious meaning of *mutawaffīka* as "I will cause thee to die" but harmonize it with the eschatological tradition by saying that the order in *Family of Imran* [3]:55 does not reflect the chronology of events. God will cause Jesus to die in the more distant future, in accordance with the tradition. In the nearer future, God will raise Jesus, in accordance with the standard interpretation of this verse.[18]

---

15. Ṭabarī, *Tafsīr*, 6:459 (#7159). The passage is found translated by Ayoub in *The Qurʾān and Its Interpreters: The House of ʿImrān*, 171.

16. Ismāʿīl al-Ḥaqqī, *Tafsīr rūḥ al-bayān* (Istanbul: Al-Maṭbaʿah al-ʿUthmānīyah, 1718?[=1130 A.H.]), 2:318; and Sanāʾallāh al-ʿUthmānī al-Mazharī, *Tafsīr al-Mazharī* (Hyderabad, n.p., n.d.,), 2:57; cited in Ayoub, "Towards an Islamic Christology," 109; idem, *Muslim View*, 170.

17. Abū ʿAbdallah Muḥammad ibn Aḥmad al-Anṣārī al-Qurṭubī, *Al-jāmiʿ li-aḥkām al-Qurʾān*, 20 vols. (Cairo: Dār al-kitāb al-ʿArabī, 1967), 4:99-102; cited by Ayoub, *The Qurʾān and Its Interpreters: The House of ʿImrān*, 174-75 in English translation.

18. Abū Ṭāhir ibn Muḥammad al-Fīrūzabādī al-Shīrāzī, *Tanwīr al-miqbās min Tafsīr Ibn*

Classical Interpretation of the Denial Verse

For a taste of the typical interpretations of *Women* [4]:157 on the part of classical Qurʾān commentators, we can do no better than to examine Ṭabarī's discussion in summary form.

He starts by acknowledging the diversity of ways interpreters deal with the most ambiguous phrase of the denial verse, "making it appear that way to them" (*shubiha la-hum*).[19] "Them" refers to the Jews. Some interpreters report that when the Jews surround Jesus and his companions they are unable to determine for certain precisely which one is Jesus because all members of the group have been transformed into an image of Jesus. When one of the company who was with Jesus in the house comes out to them, the Jews kill him, thinking he is Jesus.[20] The various reports supplied by Ṭabarī elaborate on this basic perspective.

One such report handed down from Wahb ibn Munabbih, of Jewish origin and an early Muslim commentator on the Qurʾān,[21] has Jesus coming with seventeen of his Apostles into a house. While they are in the house the Jews surround them. When the Jews, however, enter in upon them, they say the Apostles have bewitched them because God has made every one of them look like Jesus. When the Jews threaten to kill them all unless they identify the real Jesus, Jesus asks for a volunteer to be sent out to the Jews who will in exchange for being killed in Jesus' place be guaranteed a place in paradise. A volunteer then goes out and identifies himself as Jesus, God having made him look like Jesus. So they take him and kill him and crucify him. The Jews as well as the Christians, therefore, think they have killed Jesus. Meanwhile, God has taken Jesus up.[22]

The same Ibn Munabbih transmits another traditional scenario, one closer to the narrative of the Christian Gospels.[23] When God tells Jesus he would be leaving this world, he becomes anxious and severely troubled by the prospect of death. So he calls his Apostles together, prepares food for them, and serves them. After supper he begins to wash their hands and to perform ablutions for them and to wipe their hands with his garment. That grieves them and they dislike it. So Jesus says, "Will no one render to me tonight anything of what I have done?"

When he and his Apostles have finished with their meal, Jesus says, "My serving you food and washing your hands tonight was to set an example for you.

ʿAbbās (Cairo: Dār Iḥyāʾ al-kutub al-ʿarabīyah, n.d.), 39; cited in Ayoub, "Towards an Islamic Christology,"107 in English translation; omitted in idem, *Muslim View*. See also Ṭabarī, *Tafsīr*, 3:456-59; and Ibn Kathīr, *Tafsīr*, 2:44.

19. See the discussion of this phrase in chapter 2 above.

20. Ṭabarī, *Tafsīr*, 9:367.

21. Gordon Darnell Newby, *A History of the Jews of Arabia*, ed. Frederick M. Denny, Studies in Comparative Religion (Columbia: University of South Carolina Press, 1988), 66, 67, 69, 143 n. 88.

22. Ṭabarī, *Tafsīr*, 9:368 (#10779).

23. According to Haim Z. Hirschberg, "Many of [Wahb's] tales give faithful biblical descriptions, and deviations and errors may be attributed to later authors" ("Wahb ibn Munabbih," in Cecil Roth and Geoffrey Wigoder, eds., *Encyclopaedia Judaica* [Jerusalem: Macmillan, 1972], 16:242).

Since you can see that I am the best of you, let none of you exalt himself above the others. Let each of you give of himself for the others as I have given myself to you."[24]

Jesus asks them to pray earnestly that God would extend his term of life in a scenario as much like the Gospel accounts of the Garden of Gethsemane as the narrative has so far been like the Gospel accounts of the Last Supper. After Jesus and his Apostles have been dispersed, the Jews look for Jesus and take Shamʿūn (Simon), one of his Apostles, and accuse him of being one of Jesus' companions. He denies the charge. The cock crows and Shamʿūn weeps and grieves.

When morning breaks, one of the Apostles comes to the Jews and asks what they would give him to guide them to Jesus. The Jews offer him thirty dirhams. The Apostle takes the money and guides the Jews to Jesus. Meanwhile, this Apostle has been made to look like Jesus. They take Jesus, secure themselves against him, and bind him with rope. As they lead him away they say to him, "You raised the dead to life, cast out Satan, and cleansed the possessed, can you not save yourself from this rope?" They spit on him and cast thorns on him until they bring him to the wood they want to crucify him on. Then God raises him, and they crucify the one who was made to look like Jesus for them.[25]

A report about Jesus, his mother, and the woman whom Jesus healed by cleansing her from the Jinn follows. As these women come weeping to the place where he had been crucified, Jesus comes to them and says, "Why are you weeping?" They say, "For you." He says, "God has raised me to himself and nothing but good has befallen me. Since this matter is confusing to them (*shubbiha la-hum*), command the Apostles to meet me in such and such a place." Then he meets the eleven in that place—the one having sold him and guided the Jews to him being missing. When Jesus asks his companions about the betrayer, they say, "He regretted what he had done and hanged himself." Jesus responds, "Had he repented, God would have relented." Then Jesus asks them about a young man following them called Yuḥannā (John) and says, "He is with you." They go away and indeed every man among them becomes able to speak the language of a particular ethnic group in order to warn them and summon them.[26]

According to Ṭabarī, Qatādah[27] and al-Qāsim ibn abī Bazzah (d. 742)[28] in separate traditions relate that when Jesus asks those with him in the house for a volunteer to have his likeness cast upon him a man responds. A likeness of Jesus is cast on him. He is killed and Jesus son of Mary is taken up.

In separate traditions, Qatādah[29] and al-Suddī (d. 745) have Jesus offering a

---

24. Ṭabarī, *Tafsīr*, 9:368 (#10780).

25. Ibid., 9:368-69 (#10780). Charfi provides an English translation for this report ("Christianity in Ṭabarī," 124).

26. Ibid., 9:369-70 (#10780). This little bit about Yuḥannā also shows up in the Gospel of Barnabas (222a) (Lonsdale Ragg and Laura Ragg, eds. and trans., *The Gospel of Barnabas* [Oxford: Clarendon Press, 1907], 473).

27. Ṭabarī, *Tafsīr*, 9:370 (#10781).

28. Ibid., 9:370 (#10784).

29. Ibid., 9:370 (#10782).

place in paradise to whoever volunteers. Suddī and others include a discussion of the number of disciples who were with Jesus.[30]

Ṭabarī records several reports from Ibn Isḥāq, an early biographer of Muḥammad. In one, Jesus' fear of death and his Gethsemane experience are reported. Here is the essence of the report. No servant from among the servants of God despised death to the degree that Jesus did. And no one was as anxious about it as he was. In the garden he actually says, "O God if you will let this cup pass from anyone of your creatures, let it pass from me." His skin from the agony flows with blood. He enters the place where his assailants have already agreed together to gather in upon him in order to kill him and his companions—the number of them being thirteen, including Jesus. The report goes on to mention the names of the Apostles of Jesus and concerns itself with whether there were thirteen, including Jesus, or fourteen, including Jesus. The report appears to resolve this by indicating that a man named Sergius was among the Apostles, making their number thirteen without Jesus. It also notes that the Christians deny the presence of Sergius because he was the one made to look like Jesus.

Ibn Isḥāq reports further that when the word from Allah comes to Jesus that God would raise him to himself, Jesus says, "O company of Apostles, which of you would like to be my companion in Paradise by being made to look like me to the people (*yushabbaha li-l-qawmi fī ṣūratī*) and by being killed in my place?" Sergius says, "I, O Spirit of Allah." Jesus then invites him to sit in his council, which he does. God then raises Jesus. Jesus' assailants enter in upon Sergius, take him, and crucify him.

Because the assailants do not know Jesus, they have to give Judas[31] thirty dirhams for the purpose of guiding them to him and identifying him for them. Accordingly, Judas says to them, "When you enter in upon him, I will kiss him, and he whom I kiss you take." When they come to the company of Jesus' companions, Jesus having been taken up, Judas sees Sergius in the form of Jesus, and having no doubt that it is Jesus, prostrates himself before him and kisses him. The assailants then seize Sergius and crucify him. Judas, regretting what he has done, hangs himself.

Ibn Isḥāq also reports that some Christians claim Judas was the one made to appear to them like Jesus, causing the Jews to crucify Judas. This report has Judas saying persistently, "I am definitely not your man; I am the one who guided you to him." Ṭabarī himself concludes, "God knows which of those it was."[32]

Ṭabarī next evaluates these reports and gives his reasoned judgment as to what the probable historical reality might be. Either one of the two reports traced back to Wahb ibn Munabbih wins his approval.[33] The first, transmitted by Hārūn ibn ʿAntarah, I call the *collective-casting narrative*. It recounts a substitutionist

30. Ibid., 9:371 (#10783).

31. Judas is surnamed here Zakarīyāyūṭī. Another source calls him al-Iskhāriyūṭī (Charfi, "Christianity in Ṭabarī," 123).

32. Ṭabarī, *Tafsīr*, 9:371-73 (#10785).

33. Ibid., 9:368-70 (#10779 and #10780).

solution to the *shubbiha la-hum* puzzle. In this scenario, God casts a likeness on all those who were in the house with Jesus at the time the Jews surrounded it. The Jews complain that they have been bewitched. Jesus asks for a volunteer, promising a place in paradise. The volunteer announces that he is Jesus; the Jews then crucify him, both they and the Christians thinking it was Jesus. According to this report, God merely "shamed the Jews" by this means and "rescued his Prophet from the hateful murder they wanted to commit against him."[34]

Ṭabarī's thinking proceeds as follows. If God had cast a likeness of Jesus on the one Apostle who volunteered in the presence of the others and had taken Jesus up also in the sight of the Apostles, they would have known for sure both that Jesus had been taken up and on whom his likeness had been cast. The matter would certainly not have been doubtful for them. Ṭabarī asks:

> How could that have been doubtful for them [the Apostles] if they had heard from Jesus his statement, "On whom shall my likeness be cast and become my companion in Paradise?"—if he did say that to them—and had heard the answer of the one among them who replied, "I," and had seen the transformation into the form of Jesus of the one who answered immediately . . . ?[35]

"In contrast," reasons Ṭabarī in support of the collective-casting narrative, "if, Lord willing, events worked out something like Wahb ibn Muhabbih's description of them, the Apostles, like the Jews, would not have been able to distinguish Jesus from any of themselves because of the similarity of all their appearances. For this reason, all of them, Jews and Christians, would have thought Jesus had been killed."

Ṭabarī insists elaborately that the Christians must have experienced the kind of doubt and confusion the Jews experienced. His argument implies that the Apostles of Jesus could not have led a flourishing Christianity in the wake of the crucifixion had they known their gospel was based on a gross misconception. In fact, later in his argument Ṭabarī states, "Those Apostles who narrated . . . [their understanding of the events] do not deserve to be called liars. Rather, they narrated what was true for them in appearance even if the matter for God in fact was different from what they narrated."[36] He needs less elaboration when he suggests the account of Wahb ibn Munabbih as transmitted by ʿAbd al-Ṣamad ibn Maʿqil (d. 799) would be a viable alternative to the one transmitted by Hārūn ibn ʿAnṭarah, the "collective-casting" report. According to Ibn Maʿqil's account,

> The company with Jesus in the house left him before the Jews would enter in upon him while Jesus remained. His likeness was cast on one of

34. Ibid., 9:374. The report mentioned in this paragraph from Wahb is Ṭabarī's report #10779.
35. Ṭabarī, *Tafsīr*, 9:374-75.
36. Ibid., 9:375-76.

> his companions who had been with him in the house after the company of them had left—except for Jesus and the one on whom his likeness had been cast. Jesus was taken up and then the one of his companions who had been changed into the form of Jesus was killed. Thus his companions and the Jews thought the one killed and crucified was Jesus when they saw the one who had been made to look like him—what happened to Jesus having been hidden from them—because his rapture and the transformation of the victim into his form took place after his companions had left him. In addition, they had heard Jesus in the night announcing his death and grieving when he had come to believe that he would be entering into death.[37]

Although Ṭabarī's choice represents the conclusion of a majority of the early commentators, some have been less sure. Another classical commentator, Ibn Kathīr (d. 1373), offers an additional substitution scenario, which emphasizes voluntary sacrifice for Jesus' sake. It has clear connections with narratives we have already seen.

> When God sent Jesus, the Jews were jealous of him because of all God had given him by way of prophethood and miracles. They called him a liar and rejected him, seeking to harm him as much as they could, so that Jesus could not settle down where they were. Thus, he and his mother had to travel a lot. This, however, did not satisfy them so they went to the king of Damascus of that time, a pagan Seleucid star worshipper. They warned him about a man in the Temple causing trouble for the people, leading them astray, and corrupting the king's subjects against him. This angered the king who wrote to his representative in Jerusalem to round this man up, put thorns on his head, and crucify him in order to prevent his harming the people. When the message reached the one responsible for the Temple, he complied with it, going with a group of Jews to the place where Jesus resided. He was among a group of his companions—twelve or thirteen—it is even claimed seventeen persons were in the company. This happened in the evening of Friday on the Sabbath. When Jesus sensed their having come, he asked his disciples, "Which one of you is willing for a likeness of me to be cast upon you? You will be my companion in Paradise." A young man among them accepted the challenge. Then Jesus appeared to be making little of this, repeating it a second and third time. Yet no one responded except that young man. So Jesus said, "You are the one." And God cast the likeness of Jesus upon him so that he looked like Jesus. A window opened in the roof and, sleep having overtaken him, Jesus was raised to heaven in accordance with God's statement, "O Jesus! I will take thee and

37. Ibid., 9:375.

> raise thee to Myself and clear thee (of the falsehoods) of those who blaspheme." (*Family of Imran* [3]:55)[38]

The criticisms of Ṭabarī identified above apply also to this narrative. Could the disciples reasonably have carried out the mission they accomplished after the end of Jesus' mission if they had known this transaction had taken place and, thus, that Jesus himself had not been crucified but taken up? Even Fakhr al-Dīn al-Rāzī, who accepts the substitutionist interpretation of the denial verse, gives some strong arguments against the dominant substitutionist position.

Al-Rāzī's Objections to the Substitutionist Interpretation of the Denial Verse

Rāzī finds six problems with the substitutionist interpretation of "they killed him not, nor crucified him, but *so it was made to appear to them*" (*Women* [4]:157). Although Rāzī responds to each objection on behalf of the substitutionist solution, in Mahmoud Ayoub's judgment his rejoinders seem "far less convincing than the objections themselves."[39] Chawkat Moucarry, an Arab Christian from Syria, also treats these objections in detail, finding them more convincing than Rāzī's refutation of them.[40]

1. Rāzī begins with the proposition that casting a likeness leads to confusion and supports his claim with an example. When parents see their children, they are confident that the children are theirs. But if we allow that people can be made to look alike, how then can parents be confident when they see their children that they are theirs and not someone else's on whom a likeness has been cast? How did Muḥammad's companions know that it was he and not someone made to look like him who was promulgating the guidelines for the community of faith?

For transmitted reports to be reliable, the first person reporting an event must see it clearly and experience it objectively. How can any reported information be certain, then, if the person who initiated it could not be sure what he saw was what he saw or something made to look like it? According to Mahmoud Ayoub, as mentioned at the outset of this chapter, substitution involves negating the divine covenant with humans (*Cow* [2]:38). Rāzī's refutation of this objection is simply the obvious truth that God is capable of casting the likeness of one person on another. In other words it does not make sense, but it is not impossible.

2. Rāzī next questions the whole substitution project by asking, "Why

38. Ibn Kathīr, *Tafsīr*, 2:426-27. The tradition I have paraphrased above is available in English in Ismāʿīl ibn ʿUmar Ibn Kathīr, *Tafsīr al-Qurʾān al-ʿaẓīm* [*Tafsīr Ibn Kathīr*], abridged by a group of scholars under the supervision of Safi-ur-Rahman al-Mubarakpuri, 10 vols. (Riyadh: Darussalam, 2000), 3:26.

39. Ayoub, *The Qurʾān and Its Interpreters: The House of ʿImrān*, 178.

40. Chawkat Moucarry, *The Prophet and the Messiah: An Arab Christian's Perspective on Islam and Christianity* (Downers Grove, IL: InterVarsity, 2001), 134-37.

couldn't the angel Gabriel have been adequate to protect Jesus from the Jews? God said he would strengthen him with the Holy Spirit" (*Table* [5]:110). Muslims generally believe that when the Qurʾān refers to the Holy Spirit it means the angel Gabriel. Rāzī adds another alternative to the substitution of a likeness of Jesus. "Since Jesus was able to heal, cast out spirits, and raise the dead," he asks, "could he not have caused a disease to descend on the Jews? Why was it necessary to sacrifice someone else for Jesus?"

3. He asks a third hard question before refuting his second objection, "If God is capable of taking Jesus up to himself, what purpose could possibly be served by casting his likeness on another person? Why condemn an innocent man to death?" Here is his response to this and the previous objection, "If God had simply taken Jesus up, it would have been such a great miracle that Christians would have been subject to even greater errors about his identity than they now are subject to." That is, they would have even greater reason to think he was superhuman.

4. The fourth objection resembles the first closely. Rāzī again expresses it in the form of a question. "If the people would have believed that the substitute look-alike was in fact Jesus, they would have been thrown into confusion. Is this congruent with God's providential wisdom?"

5. This is paired with another objection. "If we were to cast doubt on the basic conviction of Christians, so many of whom reported having seen Jesus being crucified and killed, do we not cast doubt on other historical reports, such as those about Muḥammad and, thus, about the existence of all the prophets?" Rāzī follows this up with another and final question based on common experience.

6. "Since the crucified person remained alive a long time, if this man had not been Jesus would he not have broken down and protested that he was not Jesus, that they had the wrong man?" Further, "If this had happened and been observed, would it not have been circulated?"

Rāzī responds on behalf of the dominant classical commentary position to objections 4, 5, and 6 together. "It may be that the people who actually observed the crucifixion were too few to count as a source of incontrovertible evidence." The man who assumed Jesus' identity may have chosen not to reveal it to anyone. Furthermore, these are only probabilities that cannot be verified with certainty. Rāzī finally rests his agreement with the substitutionist position on the "incontrovertible truth of the [sacred] text" and the trustworthiness of the Prophet.[41]

In this chapter, I have dealt with alternative ways of interpreting the sacred text, suggesting that the substitutionist interpretation does not exhaust the possible meanings of the verses under discussion. But this dominant interpretation does rest on Prophetic Tradition. In the next chapter I will discuss the authority of Islamic Prophetic Tradition (*ḥadīth*). But, first, let us turn briefly to the Shīʿī interpretation of end of Jesus' mission.

41. Rāzī, *Tafsīr*, 8:74-76 as presented in English by Ayoub, *The Qurʾān and Its Interpreters: House of ʿImrān*, 178-79.

Shīʿīte Commentators Opt for the Substitutionist Interpretation

Classical Shīʿī commentators such as al-Ṭūsī (d. 1067) hold that the Jews crucified someone else and that Jesus went into hermit-like seclusion.[42] They, however, venerate the person who volunteered to take Jesus' place.[43] According to the modern Shīʿī commentator al-Ṭabāṭabāʾī (d. 1982), "I will raise you to myself" refers to a spiritual ascension because God has no place for physical bodies. In this, he reflects a philosophical position called Muʿtazilī (Mutazilite) that denies anthropomorphic attributes of God.[44]

The classical commentators, following Ṭabarī, have resolved the apparent tension between the affirmation and denial verses on the basis of Prophetic Tradition (*ḥadīth*), a source of very high value for most Muslims. The next chapter looks at the authority of Prophetic Tradition.

---

42. Ayoub, "Towards an Islamic Christology," 110, and n. 74; also idem, *A Muslim View*, 171, 182 n. 53.

43. Mahmoud M. Ayoub, *Redemptive Suffering in Islam: A Study of the Devotional Aspects of ʿĀshūrāʾ in Twelver Shiʿism*, Religion and Society 10 (The Hague: Mouton, 1978), 116.

44. Muḥammad Ḥusayn Ṭabāṭabāʾī, *Al-mīzān fī tafsīr al-Qurʾān*, 20 vols. (Beirut: Muʾassasah al-Aʿlamī, 1971), 3:208; cited in Ayoub, "Towards an Islamic Christology," 110; idem, *A Muslim View*, 171. See also Muḥammad ibn al-Ḥasan al-Ṭūsī (d. 1067), *Tafsīr*, ed. Aḥmad Shawqī al-Amīn and Aḥmad Ḥabīb Quṣayr, 10 vols. (Najaf, Iraq: Maktabat al-Amīn, 1957), 2:478; 5:132.; cited in Ayoub, "Towards an Islamic Christology,"110; idem, *Muslim View*, 171.

4

"Before the Hour, Jesus Will Descend"

The Final Days of Jesus in the Prophet's *Sunnah*

The interpretation of the "affirmation verse" (*Family of Imran* [3]:55) and the "denial verse" (*Women* [4]:157) has been finally determined for most Muslim readers of the Qur'ān by a statement of the Prophet Muḥammad to the effect that Jesus will return before the final judgment, combat opposition, spread Islam, live for forty years, and then die and be raised in the general resurrection before the final judgment.

In this chapter we look at traditions of the Prophet Muḥammad in general, the tradition decisive for al-Ṭabarī's interpretation of the end of Jesus' mission, and those like it in particular. Each such report about what Muḥammad said and did has been handed on with a list or chain of people who transmitted the report. These "chains of authority" (*isnād*, pl. *asānīd*) have been thoroughly analyzed and validated by Muslim scholars. They represent for most Muslims an authoritative source of knowledge. Thus, as mentioned in chapter 1, the Muslims also have an authoritative source that is, like the Gospels, raised up.

The Sciences of Tradition

The classical Qur'ān commentators generally follow Ṭabarī in citing Prophetic Tradition to resolve the tension between the affirmation verse in the *sūrah* of the *Family of Imran*, which suggests that God caused Jesus to die, and the denial verse in the *sūrah* of *Women*, which indicates that the Jews neither killed nor crucified him.

The word translated "Prophetic Tradition" (*ḥadīth*) basically means "a report of something that happened." The basic verb, *ḥadatha*, means "to happen"; its intensive form, *ḥaddatha*, means "to talk about what happens." Early Muslims referred to stories about what the Prophet said and did as "the best *ḥadīth*." Eventually the word *ḥadīth* became fixed as the term for a tradition about what the Prophet said and did.[1] Thus, in English discourse about these reports, *ḥadīth* has come to be called simply "Tradition" or "Prophetic Tradition"—a singular and collective term. I refer to *ḥadīth* as "Tradition" when it means the Prophetic Tradition *collectively*. I use "a tradition" or "traditions" to refer to an individual *ḥadīth* or a group of them (*aḥādīth*).

The "Way" or *Sunnah* of the Prophet is, next to the Qurʾān, the most important source for determining the Islamic way of life and faith. *Sunnah* literally means "path," a path formed by usage, as opposed to one laid out by design (*sharīʿah*). Thus, the *Sunnah* represents the path laid out by Muḥammad's exemplary way of life and consists of the deposit of what he was believed to have said and done according to the Tradition. The Tradition provides the content of the *Sunnah*.[2]

Since the Qurʾān represents the will of God and the *Sunnah* the way of Muḥammad, these two major sources of the Islamic way of life cohere with the Word of Witness (*shahādah*) and first pillar of Islam, "I bear witness that there is no god but God and that Muḥammad is the Messenger of God." The Qurʾān itself in twenty-eight places links obedience and disobedience to God with obedience and disobedience to his Messenger (e.g., *Table* [5]:92). Tradition may be less sacred than the Qurʾān, but for most Muslims it is no less authoritative.

The traditions cited by Ṭabarī[3] and others that resolve the ambiguity of what we have called the affirmation and denial verses are referred to as the "descent-of-Jesus (*nuzūl ʿĪsā*) traditions." In general, they have Jesus returning to earth from heaven in the future, living a family life, performing certain tasks, dying a natural death, and rising again for the last judgment.[4] This eschatological death of Jesus also resolves the tension between the interpretation of *Family of Imran* [3]:55 that Jesus was taken to heaven and thus rescued from death and Jesus' own testimony in *Mary* [19]:33 that he will die, "So peace be upon me the day I was born, the day that I die, and the Day that I shall be raised up to life." It also resolves the tension between *Family of Imran* [3]:46, "He shall speak to the people in the cradle, in maturity (*kahl*), and among the righteous,"[5] since most interpreters hold that Jesus, having been taken up to heaven, did not reach maturity. In other words, he had to come back to earth in the future to speak as a mature man (*Family of Imran* [3]:46) and to die (*Mary* [19]:33). An example of the tradition Ṭabarī favors to interpret the end of Jesus' mission from the *Ṣaḥīḥ*, or collection of *sound* traditions, compiled by Muslim ibn al-Ḥajjāj al-Qushayrī al-Nisābūrī (d. 875) will follow. But first, a brief introduction to Muslim's work.

---

1. Muhammad Zubayr Siddiqi, *Ḥadīth Literature: Its Origin, Development, and Special Features*, ed. and rev. Abdal Hakim Murad (Cambridge: Islamic Texts Society 1993), 1.

2. Qurʾān and *Sunnah,* along with Analogy and Consensus, are referred to as the roots or sources of Islamic jurisprudence (*uṣūl al-fiqh*).

3. I identified these in chapter 3 above.

4. Here are the places where the traditions occur in Bukhārī (see n. 8 below): *maẓālim* 31; *buyūʿ* 103, 104; *anbiyāʾ* 49; in Muslim (see n. 6 below): *imān* 242, 343; and in Aḥmad ibn Ḥanbal (see n. 22 below): 7890.

5. My translation.

The work is known simply as *Ṣaḥīḥ* Muslim.[6] It is one of the two most authoritative collections of traditions. The title, *Ṣaḥīḥ*, means "sound" and indicates that the work is a collection of traditions the compiler considers completely reliable. Muslim examined a third of a million traditions attributed to the Prophet from which he selected about four thousand as sound.[7] The other work held in such high regard came from the hand of Abū ʿAbd Allāh Muḥammad ibn Ismāʿīl al-Bukhārī. It is also a *Ṣaḥīḥ*.[8] Historians have reported that Bukhārī was aware of some 600,000 traditions (although some reports indicate half that number), that he had memorized 200,000 of them (others say 100,000), and that his *Ṣaḥīḥ* preserves the 2,762 of the ones he considered genuine.[9]

For the record, the most important collections of *ḥadīth* according to mature Muslim assessment include in first rank the *Ṣaḥīḥ* of Bukhārī; the *Ṣaḥīḥ* of Muslim (d. 875); followed by the four *Sunans* that, along with the two *Ṣaḥīḥs* just mentioned, make up the "Six Books": the *Sunan* of Abū Dāʾūd (d. 888); the *Jāmiʿ* of al-Tirmidhī (d. 892); the *Sunan* of al-Nasāʾī (d. 915); and the *Sunan* of Ibn Mājah (d. 886). While a number of other works are surely important, one more should be mentioned, the *Musnad* of Aḥmad ibn Ḥanbal (d. 855).[10]

The Descent of ʿĪsā Tradition in *Ṣaḥīḥ* Muslim

We look now in the *Ṣaḥīḥ* of Muslim at the tradition Ṭabarī favors for deciding that Jesus did not die on the cross but was taken up to heaven to return to earth and die in the future after bringing victory to Islam.

> Qutaybah ibn Saʿīd *narrated to us*, "Layth related to us"; and Muḥammad ibn Rumḥ related to us, "al-Layth *informed us* from Ibn Shihāb, *from* Ibn al-Musayyab that he heard Abū Hurayrah say, 'The Prophet of God (PBUH) said, "*By the One who holds my soul in His hand, the son of Mary* (PBUH) *will soon come down* (yushikanna an yanzil) *among you*

6. Muslim ibn al-Ḥajjāj al-Qushayrī, *Ṣaḥīḥ Muslim*: *Being Traditions of the Sayings and Doings of the Prophet Muḥammad as Narrated by His Companions*, trans. A. M. Siddiqi, 4 vols. (New Delhi: Kitab Bhavan, 1982 [English only]), 1.92 #287-#293; *Ṣaḥīḥ Muslim,* 8 vols., trans. Mahmoud Matraji (Beirut: Dar al-Fikr, 1993) [English/Arabic]; *Ṣaḥīḥ Muslim bi-sharḥ al-Nawawī* (d. 1277), 18 vols. in 9 (Cairo: al-Maṭbaʿah al-Miṣrīyah bi-al-Azhār, 1929-30).

7. Siddiqi, *Ḥadīth Literature*, 59.

8. Abū ʿAbd Allāh Muḥammad ibn Ismāʿīl al-Bukhārī, *Ṣaḥīḥ al-Boukhari*, trans. Mahmoud Matraji, 9 vols. (Beirut: Dar al-Fikr, 1993) [English/Arabic]; *Ṣaḥīḥ*, trans. and ed., M. M. Khan [English/Arabic]; *Kitab al-jāmiʿ al-ṣaḥīḥ*, ed. M. Rudolf Krehl, 4 vols. in 3 (Leiden: Brill, 1894); Aḥmad ibn ʿAlī Ibn Ḥajar al-ʿAsqalānī (d. 1449), *Fatḥ al-bārī bi-sharḥ al-Bukhārī*, 17 vols. (Cairo: Shirkat Maktabat wa-Maṭbaʿat Muṣṭafā al-Bābī al-Ḥalabī, 1959[-1963]).

9. According to Siddiqi, out of 600,000 traditions, Bukhārī picked 7,275. He says Bukhārī included 1,725 traditions with incomplete *isnād* and weak authorities to head some of his more than 3,000 divisions (*Ḥadīth Literature*, 56-57).

10. For Bukhārī's and Muslim's *Ṣaḥīḥs*, see nn. 8 and 6 above. For Aḥmad ibn Ḥanbal, *Musnad*, see n. 21 below. For the other works mentioned in this paragraph, see Siddiqi, *Ḥadīth Literature*, 7-8, 43-69.

as a just arbiter (ḥakam muqsiṭ) *then break the cross, kill the pigs, and put down the* jizyah. *And wealth will abound to the extent that no one will accept it.*"'"

▯ ʿAbd al-Aʿlā ibn Ḥammād, Abū Bakr ibn Abī Shaybah, and Zuhayr ibn Ḥarb [also] related it to us. They said, "Sufyān ibn ʿUyaynah related to us"; and Ḥarmalah ibn Yaḥyā related to me, "Ibn Wahb informed us. He said, 'Yūnus related it to me'"; and Ḥasan al-Ḥulwānī and ʿAbd al-Malik / ʿAbd al-Raḥmān ibn Ḥumayd related to us from Yaʿqūb ibn Ibrāhīm ibn Saʿd, "My father related to us from Ṣāliḥ"—all of them from al-Zuhrī with this [same] chain of support (*isnād*) [i.e., Ibn Shihāb (al-Zuhrī)—Ibn al-Musayyab—Abū Hurayrah]. In his report, Ibn ʿUyaynah has "*as a just leader and fair arbiter.*" In the report of Yūnus, he uses, "*as a fair arbiter.*" He does not mention "*as a just arbiter.*" In his report Ṣāliḥ has, "*as a just arbiter,*" also the rendering of al-Layth. In his report he adds, "*To the extent that one prostration will be better than the world and all that is in it.*"

Then Abū Hurayrah says, "*Read if you wish*, 'And there is none of the People of the Book but must believe in him before his death . . .'—*the whole verse.*" (*Women* [4]:159)

Prophetic traditions contain two main categories of discourse. The portion in italics in the first paragraph quoted just above consists of the statement of Muḥammad that Jesus will return as a just ruler, break the crosses, kill the pigs, abolish the tax paid by People of the Book who decide not to accept Islam, and establish so much prosperity that no one will receive any welfare payments. According to the commentary of Muḥammad Fuʾād ʿAbd al-Bāqī, by "put down the *jizyah,* the tax People of the Book paid to remain in their own religious traditions, the tradition means only Islam will be accepted from them."[11] This may be the force of the last paragraph quoting *Women* [4]:159. The second paragraph cites differences in some of the reports that have been transmitted (noting their transmitters) of the same saying. This tradition in its various versions goes back to the Companion[12] of the Prophet Abū Hurayrah, who heard the original statement by Muḥammad. Scholars of tradition refer to the text of the tradition as its *matn* or "substance."

The other half of the discourse identifies the people who have handed the report down. As stated above, scholars refer to such a chain of authorities as the tradition's *isnād* or "support"—what it rests on and, thus, its "chain of authority."

Four distinct versions of this tradition have come down to the compiler

11. Muḥammad Fuʾād ʿAbd al-Bāqī, *Al-luʾluʾ wa-al-marjān fī-mā ittafaqa ʿalay-hi al-shaykhān al-Bukhārī wa-Muslim*, 3 vols. in 1 (Beirut: Dār Iḥyāʾ al-Turāth al-ʿArabī, 1986), 1:31, n. to #95.

12. "Companion" is capitalized as a technical term for an individual such as Abū Hurayrah who was a contemporary of the Prophet and who could have interacted with him directly. The transmitters of the next generation, who could not have interacted with Muḥammad directly, are called Successors, and the next generation, Followers.

Muslim, transmitted to him by eight individuals. But all the reports go back to one person, namely al-Zuhrī (d. 742), who received this tradition from al-Musayyab, who received it from Abū Hurayrah. It should come as no surprise, then, that the collection and criticism of tradition gave rise to an extensive study of biographical and geographical literature. One had to know the reliability of these authorities and whether or not they could have been in the same place at the same time in order to transmit their traditions one to the other. The very bulk of this literary production lends authenticity to the results of the criticism of Tradition. In fact the bulk of the criticism that traditional Muslim scholars apply to these traditions focuses on their chains of authority.

Criticism of the substance or text (*matn*, pl. *mutūn*) of the traditions does, however, come into play. In fact, Muhammad Zubayr Siddiqi identifies eight general principles for criticism of traditions based on their texts, such as, they may not contradict the substance of traditions already accepted as reliable, and they should not be against the dictates of reason, the laws of nature, or common experience.[13]

Muslim critics of tradition have been able to discern several categories of traditions according to their reliability and the structure of their chains of authority. Three categories of traditions relate to the number of transmitters during the early generations of transmitters. A tradition is deemed *mutawātir* (recurrent) if transmitted by so many transmitters during the first three generations[14] of transmitters that the possibility of fabrication vanishes. The tradition cited in the paragraphs quoted above from Muslim's *Ṣaḥīḥ* obviously does not qualify by itself at this level of authenticity because the transmitters in the first three generations are identical: Ibn Shihāb al-Zuhrī—Ibn al-Musayyab—Abū Hurayrah. In other words, any of the three could have conceivably invented the tradition.[15] Other descent-of-Jesus traditions, however, can be found in the major collections of Tradition, perhaps serving to qualify them as *mutawātir*.

Scholars refer to a tradition as *mashhūr* (well known) if transmitted by few in the first generation and transmitted by many in subsequent generations. The third category, *aḥādī* (based-on-one) traditions, includes traditions transmitted during the first three generations by one to four narrators only.[16]

Another way of assessing the authenticity of traditions relates to the collections they occur in. The highest grade of reliability accrues to those traditions included by both Bukhārī and Muslim; the next highest to those given by Bukhārī alone; and just below those, the traditions given by Muslim alone. Scholars have defined four categories below these three. Even though an *aḥādī* tradition, this eschatological tradition about Jesus' return occurs in both Bukhārī and Muslim, establishing its high level of reliability.

13. Siddiqi, *Ḥadīth Literature*, 114.

14. The first three generations (*ṭabaqāt*) include Companions, Successors, and Followers.

15. Muslim scholars have tended to exempt Companions of the Prophet from criticism, assuming that their high spiritual status would preclude forging a tradition.

16. Siddiqi, *Ḥadīth Literature*, 110.

Ṭabarī's Argument Revisited

Some traditions of Ibn ʿAbbās and Wahb ibn Munabbih, two early authorities on Qurʾān interpretation, reported that *mutawaffī-ka* in *Family of Imran* [3]:55 means "I shall cause thee to die."[17] They, it must be realized, were not reports from two transmitters telling how the Prophet interpreted the verse, but rather reports of how Ibn ʿAbbās and Wahb ibn Munabbih interpreted the verse. Based on what we have learned above about the authority of the Prophet's *Sunnah*, we can understand that the views of Ibn ʿAbbās and Wahb merit considerably less credence than traditions in Bukhārī and Muslim, which can be traced back to the Prophet himself. We also encountered Ṭabarī's own opinion on the whole matter, that God cast "a resemblance of Jesus on one of his followers so that they killed him instead of Jesus, God having raised Jesus beforehand."[18]

Ṭabarī bases his conclusion on what he terms "the recurrent (*mutawātir*) nature of the historical reports going back to the Messenger of God (PBUH) that he said, 'Jesus son of Mary will descend and kill the Antichrist. Then he will dwell on the earth for a mentioned period—the narratives differ as to its length. Then he will die and the Muslims will pray over him and bury him.'"[19]

> Ibn Ḥumayd told us, he said, "Salāmah told us from Ibn Isḥāq, from Muḥammad ibn Muslim [ibn Shihāb] al-Zuhrī, from Ḥanẓalah ibn ʿAlī al-Aslamī from Abū Hurayrah. He said, 'I heard the Messenger of God (PBUH) say, "*God will cause Jesus son of Mary to descend* (la-yuhbiṭanna) *as a just judge* (ḥakam ʿadl) *and a fair leader* (imām muqsiṭ). *He will break the cross, kill the pigs, remit the tax levied on non-Muslims* (jizyah), *cause property to abound until he cannot find anyone to accept it. And He will walk along the Rawḥāʾ doing the Ḥajj or the ʿUmrah or both of them.*" ' "[20]

The report is related by Aḥmad ibn Ḥanbal in his *Musnad*, #7890,[21] with one like it, but longer, from Yazīd ibn Hārūn (d. 821), from Sufyān ibn Ḥusayn (d. ca. 780),[22] from al-Zuhrī, from Ḥanẓalah (d. after 768). Aḥmad also transmits a

---

17. Muḥammad ibn Jarīr al-Ṭabarī, *Jāmiʿ al-bayān ʿan taʾwīl āyāt al-Qurʾān*, ed. Muḥammad Shākir and Aḥmad Muḥammad Shākir, 16 vols., Turāth al-Islām (Cairo: Dār al-Maʿārif, 1971), 6:457.

18. Ibid., 6:456.

19. Ibid., 6:458 (#7144).

20. Ibid. I have put the Arabic terms in parentheses because the many similar versions of this tradition itemized below vary at these points.

21. Aḥmad ibn Muḥammad Ibn Ḥanbal, *Musnad,* 6 vols. (no place: no pub., n.d.). The references in Wensinck's *Concordance* (Arent Jan Wensinck et al., *Concordance et Indices de la Tradition Musulmane: Les six livres, le Musnad d'al-Dārimī, le Muwatta' de Mālik, le Musnad de Aḥmad ibn Ḥanbal*, 8 vols. (Leiden: Brill, 1936-1988) are to the volumes and pages in this edition. A more recent edition is easier to use: *Musnad al-Imām Aḥmad ibn Ḥanbal,* ed. Shuʿayb al-Amaʾūt and ʿĀdil Murshid, 50 vols. (Beirut: Muʾassat al-Risālah, 1995-2001).

22. According to Shihāb al-Dīn Abī al-Faḍl Aḥmad ibn ʿAlī Ibn Ḥajar al-ʿAsqalānī (*Kitāb*

condensed version of the tradition (#7271) from Sufyān ibn ʿUyaynah (d. 814) and another version (#7667) from ʿAbd al-Razzāq (d. 826-827),[23] transmitted from Maʿmar ibn Rāshid (d. 770). Both of these reports are from al-Zuhrī, from Ḥanzalah. Again, in summary form, Aḥmad ibn Ḥanbal transmits it as report #10671 from the path of Ibn Abī Ḥafṣah (d. 749) and as report #10987 from the path of al-Awzāʿī (d. 774), both of them from al-Zuhrī, from Ḥanẓalah. Ibn Kathīr mentions many of its paths and narratives in his *Commentary* (*tafsīr*)[24] and his *History* (*taʾrīkh-hu*).[25]

The following tradition helps Ṭabarī explain the meaning of *Women* [4]:157. The "I" in the passage refers to the Prophet Muḥammad.

> The Prophets are brothers of one father, their mothers are each different but their religion is one. Of all men, I have the most rightful claim to Jesus son of Mary because there was no prophet between him and me. He will be my successor (*khalīfatī*) over my community. He will surely descend (*nāzil*). When you see him, you will recognize him. He shall be a man of medium height, with hues of red and white color, and of straight hair. His hair will appear as though dripping, although no water had touched it. He will be clad with two yellow garments. He shall break the cross and kill the swine, dispense abundant wealth, and wage war on behalf of Islam against men until God causes all other religions to perish in his time. At his hand, God will also destroy the Messiah of error, the deceiver, al-Dajjāl. Security will then cover the earth, so that lions will graze with camels, tigers with cattle, and wolves with sheep. Youths will play with snakes, but they will not harm them. He shall dwell in the earth for forty years. Then he will die, and Muslims will pray over him.[26]

The tradition from Muslim ibn al-Ḥajjāj quoted first in this chapter, the one quoted next above from Ṭabarī, and this one also from Ṭabarī represent three versions of this tradition. All three go back to the Companion Abū Hurayrah. Ibn Shihāb al-Zuhrī has transmitted two of them, one through Saʿīd ibn al-Musayyab and the other through Ḥanẓalah. Qatādah transmitted the longer one quoted just

---

tahdhīb al-Tahdhīb, 12 vols. in 6 [Haydarabad al-Dakkan: Maṭbaʿat Majlis Dāʾirat al-Maʿārif al-Niẓāmīyah, 1907-1909], 4:108), traditions related by Sufyān ibn Ḥusayn from al-Zuhrī were disputed.

23. This is ʿAbd al-Razzāq al-Ṣanʿānī (d. 826); see Herbert Berg, *The Development of Exegesis in Early Islam: The Authenticity of Muslim Literature from the Formative Period*, Curzon Studies in the Qurʾān (Richmond, Surrey, UK: Curzon, 2001), 36.

24. Ismāʿīl ibn Kathīr, *Tafsīr*, 7 vols. (Beirut: Dār al-Andalus, 1966), 2:44.

25. Idem, *Al-bidāyah wa-al-nihāyah*, 7 vols., 2nd ed. (Beirut: Maktabat al-Maʿārif, 1977), 1:2.91ff.

26. Ṭabarī, *Tafsīr*, 6:459 (#7145), as quoted by Mahmoud M. Ayoub, *The Qurʾān and Its Interpreters: The House of ʿImrān*, 2 vols. (Albany: State University of New York Press, 1984-1992), 2:171.

above via ʿAbd al-Raḥmān ibn Ādam. We followed the five paths of similar versions of Muslim's *Ṣaḥīḥ* and found that al-Zuhrī transmitted all of them from Abū Hurayrah via Saʿīd ibn al-Musayyab. The story of the descent of Jesus traditions does not end here, however.

The Descent of Jesus Traditions in Major Ḥadīth Collections

I examined descent-of-Jesus traditions mentioning Jesus' breaking or crushing the cross in Ṭabarī's commentary; the six principal books of Tradition; the *Musnad* of al-Dārimī (d. 868); the *Muwaṭṭāʾ* of Mālik ibn Anas; and the *Musnad* of Aḥmad ibn Ḥanbal.[27] In these ten sources I found thirty different paths or sets of *isnād*. Some of these represent different chains of attestation to the same or very similar traditions. Similar traditions about the return of Jesus that do not contain what he will do with the cross were not considered, though they may have contributed to Ṭabarī's *mutawātir* designation for the ones he cites. Only one of the thirty rested on some authority other than Abū Hurayrah. This one tradition forms part of a long narrative connected with the descent of Jesus in the last days. It turned up in the *Sunan* of Ibn Mājah traced back to Abū Umāmah al-Bāhilī (d. 700).

Generally speaking, these traditions have a discernible structure: a preamble, providing frame, setting, and/or emphasis; a declaration of the descent of Jesus; an indication of his role or identity; what actions he will perform or accomplish upon his descent; and the peace and prosperity that will result from his mission.

The following summary, organized according to the above structure, will give an idea of the number of variants in the descent-of-Jesus traditions available in the major *ḥadīth* collections. The meaning of the abbreviations is as follows: m=Muslim, b=Bukhārī, t=Tirmidhī, im=Ibn Mājah, T=Ṭabarī, ad=Abū Dāʾūd, ik=Ibn Kathīr, a=Aḥmad ibn Ḥanbal.

The Structure and Variants of the Descent-of-Jesus Traditions

Preamble: "By the One who holds my soul in His hand." (m, b, t, a)

"By God!" Other forms of intensification such as *inna-hu la-yanzilanna*, "Indeed he will come down." (T, m, a)

"The Hour will not arise until" (im, b)

"There is no prophet between him (that is, Jesus) and me." (ad)

"The Prophets are brothers of one father and many mothers and their religion (*dīn*) is one. Of all men, I have the most rightful claim to Jesus son of Mary because there was no prophet between him and me. He shall be my successor (*khalīfatī*) over my community." (T, a [details differ])

27. All sources but Ṭabarī are indexed in Wensinck's *Concordance* (see n. 21 above).

No preamble. (T, a [several, one with intensification])

Descent: "Jesus son of Mary will descend (*yanzil*) among you." (m, b, t, a)

"Jesus son of Mary will descend." (im, a)

"Jesus son of Mary will soon (*yushik an*) descend among you." (m, a)

"He will descend (*nāzil*)." (ad, T, a)

"God will bring down (*yuhbiṭ*) Jesus son of Mary." (T)

"He who lives among you will soon meet Jesus son of Mary." (a)

Role and Identity: "as a just arbiter (*ḥakam muqsiṭ*)." (m, b, t, a)

"as a fair (*ʿādil*) arbiter." (m, a)

"as a just (*qāsiṭ*) arbiter and a fair leader (*imām ʿadl*)." (a)

"as a just leader and a fair (*ʿadl*) arbiter." (m)

"as a fair (*ʿādil*) leader and a just arbiter." (a)

"as a fair (*ʿadl*) arbiter and a just leader." (im, T)

"as a rightly-guided (*mahdī*) leader and a fair arbiter." (a)

"when you see him, recognize him" (description follows). (ad, T, a)

Actions: "He will break (*yaksir*) the cross, kill (*yaqtil*) the pig and abolish (*yaḍaʿ*) the *jizyah*." (m, T, b, t, a)

"He will break the cross, kill the pig and abolish the *jizyah* (a [with intensive verbs])."

"He will crush (*yaduqq*) the cross, kill the pig, abolish the *jizyah*." (ad, T)

"He will crush the cross, slaughter (*yadhbaḥ*) the pig, abolish the *jizyah*." (im, a)

"He will break the cross, kill the pig." (a)

"kill the pig and break the cross." (a)

"He will kill the pig, wipe out (*yamḥū*) the cross." (a)

"He will abolish the *kharāj*" (addition). (a)

"He will fight the people over Islam" (addition). (ad)

"abandon almsgiving" (addition). (im, a)

"call the people to Islam" (addition). (a)

"descend the Rawḥāʾ then perform the Ḥajj or the ʿUmrah or both of them from it" (addition). (a)

"the prayer will be gathered for him." (a)

Results: Peace and Prosperity: "Wealth will abound so that no one will accept it (as welfare)." (m1, T2, b1, 2, 3, t1) "when he summons people to accept wealth, not even one will do so." (m, a)

"no one would try (to collect tax on) a sheep or a camel. Spite and mutual hatred will go away (*yurfa*ʿ), etc." (im)

"one could leave a young she-camel and no one would try (to collect *zakāt* on it) [another sign of prosperity]. Spite, mutual hatred, and jealousy against one another will certainly disappear." (m, im, a)

"and the summons [to Islam] will be one [i.e., no competing summons]." (a)

"and security will occur on the earth to the extent that the lions will graze with the camel, the leopards with the cows, the wolves with the sheep, and children will play with snakes, neither hurting the other." (T, im, a)

"Peace shall return. Swords will be taken as scythes and all [plants] that have thorns will lose them. And war will cease (*taḍa*ʿ*u l-ḥarbu awzāra-ha*)." (a)

"The sky will send down its daily bread and the earth will bring forth its bounty to the extent that the baby will play with the snake and it will not hurt him and the wolf will herd the sheep and not harm them. The lion will herd cows and not harm them." (a)

"to the extent that one prostration is better than the world and all it contains (addition)." (m, b)

"he will destroy (*yu*ʿ*aṭṭal*) the religious sects until God wipes out (*yahlak*) in his time all the sects other than Islam. God will wipe out in his time the lying false Messiah and security will come to the earth [plus other images of an ideal world]. Then he will dwell on earth 40 years; then he will be taken in death and the Muslims will pray over him (addition)." (a)

"and bury him (addition)." (T, a)

The plethora of variants exhibited in the preceding analysis does not by itself offer evidence that the Prophet never said anything like the saying Ṭabarī thinks is convincingly reliable, "God will cause Jesus son of Mary to descend as a just judge and a fair leader. He will break the cross, kill the pigs, remit the tax levied on non-Muslims (*jizyah*), and cause property/wealth to abound until he cannot find anyone to accept it." After all, as our discussions in chapters 9 and 10 will show, the passages in the Gospels supporting Jesus' predictions of the end of his mission also exhibit variation. We must keep in mind the urging of Hugh Goddard to avoid double standards (see chapter 1)! As a matter of fact, the wide variation in presentation of the return-of-Jesus traditions, along with the fact that several of them turn up in the two most important sources of the *ḥadīth* suggest that, for Muslims, variants do not detract from authenticity.

It should be clear by now that both the interpretation of the Qurʾānic passages related to the end of Jesus' mission and the majority Muslim view that has developed—with its several variants—rest on the conviction that the descent-of-Jesus eschatological traditions are authentic statements going back to Muḥammad.

Questions about the Authenticity of Ṭabarī's Eschatological Tradition

Keeping in mind that such traditions as the decisive one for Ṭabarī's conclusions about the end of Jesus' mission have very high value as truth for many Muslim readers, I want to raise some sincere questions in a spirit of enquiry.

Why Does the Qurʾān Itself Not Treat This Subject?

A question can be asked as to why in the Qurʾān and the earliest biography of the Prophet we do not find mention of, or allusion to, the descent of Jesus. The Qurʾān contains an eschatological scene narrating an interaction between God and Jesus at a future time when the messengers (*rusul*) will be gathered and asked about the response to their messages. God will ask Jesus to recall the grace of God to him and his mother, which suggests a number of blessings such as strengthening him with the Holy Spirit; teaching him the Torah and the Gospel; enabling miracles at his hand; defending him against detractors; and inspiring faith in his followers (*Table* [5]:109-11). After a brief digression related to God's inspiration of Jesus' Apostles (*ḥawāriyūn*) to follow him (verses 112-15), the heart of God's enquiry is given along with Jesus' reply:

> And behold! Allah will say: "O Jesus the son of Mary! didst thou say unto men, 'Worship me and my mother as gods in derogation of Allah'?" He will say: "Glory to Thee! never could I say what I had no right (to say). Had I said such a thing, Thou wouldst indeed have known it. Thou knowest what is in my heart, though I know not what is in Thine. For Thou knowest in full all that is hidden." (*Table* [5]:116)

The ethos or spirit of the passage has no resemblance to that of Ṭabarī's eschatological traditions.

Even though a cataclysmic end to the world order is vividly explicit in the Qurʾān and events related to the apocalypse are specified such as Gog and Magog (*Cave* [18]:94), a beast who will speak (*Ants* [27]:82), and the blowing of the trumpet or horn (*Ants* [27]:87; *Yāʾ Sīn* [36]:51; *Enfolded* [74]:8), the Qurʾānic grounding for the subject matter of the tradition Ṭabarī favors, namely, the advent of Jesus, consists of just a portion of one verse, *Gold* [43]:61, "And he will be a knowledge (*ʿilm*) for the Hour," interpreted as "his appearance will be a knowledge by which the coming of the Hour can be known." The "he" is naturally taken to refer to Jesus, since he is the subject of verses 57-59 and 63.

Furthermore, verses 65-78 mostly concern eschatology.[28] Some early exegetes, such as Qatādah, have concluded that the pronoun in question refers to the Qurʾān. Read accordingly, it appears less awkward, "It [the Qurʾān] is truly a knowledge (*ʿilm*) of the Hour."[29] Three other exegetes, Ibn ʿAbbās (d. 687/688), Abū Hurayrah, and al-Ḍaḥḥāk (d. 723), along with Qatādah, also read, "And he is truly the sign (*ʿalam*) for the Hour."[30] This reading resolves the awkwardness of the verse in the direction of Jesus as its subject. Whatever the exact rendering of *Gold* [43]:61, and even if it refers to Jesus' return, does it really require that he was not crucified?[31]

Otherwise, in spite of the fact that the Qurʾān contains a surprising amount of material about Jesus, it does not discuss anything similar to the content of Abū Hurayrah's descent-of-Jesus traditions—traditions decisive for Ṭabarī in interpreting verses about the end of Jesus' mission.

Why the Absence of This Subject in the Earliest Biographies of Muḥammad?

The earliest biographical literature dealing with the life of the Prophet Muḥammad contains no reference to this or any tradition dealing with Jesus' return. The earliest account of Muḥammad's life that has come down to us today is a version of the *Sīrah* of Ibn Isḥāq, edited by Ibn Hishām (d. 833). Since the biography of Muḥammad developed partly through explanation of the Qurʾān, it would seem strange that a story such as Jesus' return to break the crosses and slay the Antichrist did not turn up in it, if it were in fact something Muḥammad had stressed.

In a fragment of the lost book of Mūsā ibn ʿUqbah (d. 757), a dream of Muḥammad is recorded in which, while going round the Kaʿbah he sees Jesus and describes him as "a man with lank hair between two men, his head dripping with water." Turning away from the three, he sees "a red man, heavy, with curly hair, one eyed." When he asks who this was, they say, "The Antichrist." Some eschatological traditions depict Jesus' hair as looking as though it is dripping with water, but this is a dream and not a descent-of-Jesus tradition. Of interest to us, however, is Alfred Guillaume's comment, "The reference here to the 'two men' presumably refers to the two thieves on the cross."[32] This tradition also rests on the report of Ibn Shihāb al-Zuhrī from Sālim ibn ʿAbd Allāh on the authority of ʿAbd Allāh ibn ʿUmar (d. 693).

This reference to Jesus' dripping wet hair also occurs in Ibn Isḥāq's account

---

28. Neal Robinson, "Jesus," in *The Encyclopaedia of the Qurʾān*, ed. Jane Dammen McAuliffe, 6 vols. (Leiden: Brill, 2006), 3:17.

29. Abū ʿAbdallah Muḥammad ibn Aḥmad al-Anṣārī al-Qurṭubī, *Al-jāmiʿ li-aḥkām al-Qurʾān*, 20 vols. (Cairo: Dār al-kitāb al-ʿArabī, 1967), on *Gold* [43]:61.

30. Ibid.

31. Robinson, "Jesus," 3:17-18.

32. Alfred Guillaume, ed. and trans., *The Life of Muḥammad: A Translation of Ibn Isḥāq's* Sīrat Rasūl Allāh, *with Introduction and Notes* (London/New York/Toronto: Oxford University Press, 1955), xliii.

of the *isrāʾ*, or Night Journey, of Muḥammad, where Muḥammad describes the prophets he met on his ascent to the heavens.[33] A brief eschatological tradition going back to Abū Hurayrah occurs in Ibn Isḥāq, "The hour will not come until thirty antichrists come forth, each of them claiming to be a prophet."[34] The Antichrist does occur in some of the *ḥadīth*s we have looked at that have parallels with the substance of Ṭabarī's choice *ḥadīth*. But still there is no mention in the early biographical literature of Jesus' return to do away with the crosses.

Must We Interpret the Qurʾān by Means of This Tradition?

Ibn ʿĀshūr (d. 1867) argues that the use of transmitted traditions in Qurʾānic exegesis is not required.[35] His evidence for this comes from the fact that the Muslims, both the Companions and those who came after them, used their own original thinking in interpreting the Qurʾān. Ibn ʿĀshūr notes that the Prophet actually interpreted few verses himself and that the many traditions going back to the Companions exhibit a degree of diversity that defies harmonization. This flood of contradictory *tafsīr* traditions indicates convincingly that the Companions used their own original thinking in Qurʾānic exegesis. That is, if some of the traditions had really been heard from the Prophet, would these not have been used to correct the ones that contradicted them?[36]

Furthermore, given the fact that this particular descent-of-Jesus tradition with its mention of the breaking or crushing of the cross is an *aḥādī* tradition, that is, one dependent on only two transmitters at the earliest stage of its *isnād*, it might be more open to question, even though it does turn up in the main collections and even though Ṭabarī refers to it as *mutawātir*. And as Suleiman Darrat, of the University of Kentucky's Islamic Studies program, maintains, while its *aḥādī* status does not indicate that Abū Hurayrah's *ḥadīth* is fabricated, it does not bring the subject of either the return of Jesus or his death on a cross to the level of an Islamic creedal statement (*ʿaqīdah*).[37]

I am not here promoting an airtight argument in support of a revision in the value of Tradition as a source of interpreting the Qurʾān. But if my Muslim readers prove willing to consider at least the value of the interpretation of the

---

33. Ibid., 184.

34. Ibid., 648.

35. Other modern Qurʾān commentators raise significant questions about appealing to Tradition: ʿAbd al-Aʿlā al-Mūsawī Sabzawārī, *Mawāhib al-Raḥmān fī tafsīr al-Qurʾān*, 25 vols., 3rd ed. (Daftār Samāhat Āyat Allāh al-ʿUzmā al-Sabzawārī, 1993/1994), 10:148; Muḥammad ʿAbduh (d. 1905), quoted in Muḥammad Rashīd Riḍā, *Tafsīr al-Qurʾān al-ḥakīm al-shahīr bi-Tafsīr al-manār*, 12 vols. (Beirut: Dār al-Maʿārif, 1970), 3:317; and Sayyid Quṭb, *Fī ẓilāl al-Qurʾān*, 6 vols. (Beirut: Dār al-Shurūq, 1973), 2:802; translation: Sayyid Quṭb, *In the Shade of the Qurʾān: Fī Zilāl al-Qurʾān,* trans. and ed. Adil Salahi and Ashur Shamis, 30 vols. (Leicester: Islamic Foundation, 2001), 3:379.

36. Muḥammad al-Ṭāhir Ibn ʿĀshūr, *Tafsīr al-taḥrīr wa-al-tanwīr*, 13 vols. (Tunis: al-Dār al-Tunisīyah lil-Nashr, 1960-), 1:28-29.

37. Personal communication, January 2007.

affirming and denial verses proposed in chapter 2 above, they might be willing to consider the question, Is it possible that what is going on in the enterprise of *ḥadīth* studies as well as Qurʾān commentary is the solidification of a position derived from interaction with Christians after the time of the Prophet rather than a rediscovery of things that Muḥammad did in fact say?

5

"Would God Have Let His Messenger Be Killed?"

The Final Days of Jesus' Mission in Modern Qurʾān Commentary

The modern period in Qurʾān commentary began in the late nineteenth century with such modernist reformers as Muḥammad ʿAbduh (d. 1905).[1] Christine Schirrmacher maintains that nineteenth-century Muslim apologists claimed that People of the Book falsified the texts of the Old and New Testaments. In contrast to older apologists, these interpreters enlisted insights from European historical-critical study of the Bible.[2] Twentieth-century Muslim apologists, bolstered by the publication of the Gospel of Barnabas in 1907, have shifted their focus from the corruption of scripture to the person of Christ. Qurʾān commentary in its turn came to emphasize that the content of the Gospels, although not trustworthy as scripture, can be shown to support the Muslim interpretation of the end of Jesus' mission.

Mahmoud Ayoub asserts—relevant to our topic—that contemporary Sunnī thinkers have shifted their arguments to a discussion of the meaning of the cross in the Christian faith and to the question of the authenticity of the Gospel accounts of the death of Christ.[3] Muḥammad Rashīd Riḍā's (d. 1935) long discussion of issues

---

1. Oddbjørn Leirvik, *Images of Jesus Christ in Islam: Introduction, Survey of Research, Issues of Dialogue*, Studia Missionalia Upsaliensia 76 (Uppsala: Swedish Institute of Missionary Research, 1999), 71.

2. Christine Schirrmacher, *Mit den Waffen des Gegners: Christlich-muslimische Kontroversen im 19. und 20. Jahrhundert dargestellt am Beispiel der Auseinandersetzung um Karl Gottlieb Pfanders "Mizân al-haqq" und Rahmatullâh ibn Halîl al-'Uthmânî al-Kairâwânî's "Izhâr al-haqq" und der Diskussion über das Barnabasevangelium* (Berlin: Klaus Schwarz, 1992), 52; cited in Leirvik, *Images of Jesus*, 124.

3. Mahmoud M. Ayoub, "Towards an Islamic Christology, II: The Death of Jesus: Reality or Delusion?," *The Muslim World* 70, no. 2 (1980): 111; reprinted in Irfan A. Omar, ed., *A Muslim View of Christianity: Essays on Dialogue by Mahmoud Ayoub*, Faith Meets Faith (Maryknoll, NY: Orbis Books, 2007), 172. As early as the second and third Islamic centuries, Muslims had begun to demand a fuller treatment of the events of history from an Islamic perspective. For example, Ibn Isḥāq provided details of the life of Jesus that the Qurʾān omitted, such as Jesus' being born in Bethlehem, in a

connected with the crucifixion in his *Manār Commentary* includes a twenty-page section examining the issue of the cross. It includes subsections such as "The Christian Belief Concerning the Messiah and the Crucifixion," a refutation of the belief in the crucifixion, "Recompense and Salvation according to Islam," "The Belief in Crucifixion and Redemption Is Pagan," "Christian False Refutations against the Denial of the Crucifixion," "Proofs of the Untrustworthiness of the Gospels," and "The Claim of Some Christians That Christ Did Not Die by Crucifixion."[4] Sayyid Quṭb in his widely read commentary accepts only what the sacred text states concerning the death and ascension of Jesus. "As for the manner of his death and assumption," he writes, "these matters belong to the unseen (*ghaybīyah*), and they fall into the category of obscure verses (*mutashābihāt*), whose exegetical meaning (*taʾwīl*) is known to God alone."[5] Nevertheless he includes a lengthy discussion of the foolishness of the Christian conviction on these matters.

Abū al-Aʿlā Mawdūdī (d. 1979) in his widely read commentary, *Towards Understanding the Qurʾān*, takes a position similar to that of Quṭb. In his comment on *Women* [4]:157-58 he says,

> What is categorically asserted here is merely that the Jews did not succeed in killing the Messiah, but that God raised him unto Himself. The Qurʾān furnishes no detailed information about the actual form of this "raising." It neither states categorically that God raised him from the earthly sphere to some place in heaven in both body and soul, nor that his body died on earth and his soul alone was raised to heaven. Hence neither of the two alternatives can be definitely affirmed or denied on the basis of the Qurʾān.[6]

The one thing he concludes from reflection on the Qurʾān is that however Jesus ascended, it was an extraordinary event. The fact that Christians believed in the ascension of Christ indicates this. If some sort of exaltation of status were indicated, the wording of the Qurʾān would have been different. Furthermore, if this "raising" had been an ordinary kind, the refrain mentioning the divine name would not have been "Allah is exalted in Power, Wise."[7]

---

manger beside the palm tree; he also mentions a man called Sergius who had taken Jesus' place on the cross; and in al-Yaʿqūbī (d. after 891) "reveals an extensive knowledge of New Testament material" (Leirvik, *Images of Jesus*, 66-67).

4. Muḥammad Rashīd Riḍā, *Tafsīr al-Qurʾān al-ḥakīm al-shahīr bi-Tafsīr al-manār*, 12 vols. (Beirut: Dār al-Maʿārif, 1970), 6:23-42.

5. Sayyid Quṭb, *Fī ẓalāl al-Qurʾān*, 6 vols., 9th ed. (Beirut/Cairo: Dār al-Shurūq, 1980), 1:403. Ayoub cites another edition in "Towards an Islamic Christology, II," 111-12; idem, *Muslim View*, 182 n. 58.

6. Abū al-Aʿlā al-Mawdūdī, *Towards Understanding the Qurʾān*, trans. Zafar Ishaq Ansari, 7 vols. (London: Islamic Foundation, 1989), 2:108.

7. Ibid. The rhyme phrase at the end of many Qurʾānic verses corresponds to themes in the verses it climaxes (Neal Robinson, *Discovering the Qurʾān: A Contemporary Approach to a Veiled Text* [London: SCM Press, 1996], 200).

Nevertheless, as one would expect, some modern commentators take a rationalist position on both the mistaken identity of the one crucified and the nature of Jesus' exaltation. Al-Marāghī (d. 1945) interprets *rāfiʿu-ka*, "I will raise thee," as the raising of spiritual status, as in the case of Idrīs (Enoch).[8] Sayyid Ahmad Khan (d. 1898) in his *Tafsīr al-Qurʾān* (published 1903) takes a rationalist position that is generally positive toward the Christian scriptures. But his view of the crucifixion is that Jesus was taken down from the cross and resuscitated by his disciples.[9] The contemporary Muslim polemicist Ahmad Deedat, relying on the position of the earlier liberal Muslim, Sayyid Ahmad Khan, also holds that Jesus was resuscitated,[10] a position shared with the Ahmadiyyah movement.[11] The Muslim apologist Ruqaiyyah Waris Maqsood argues for the possibility that Jesus did not really die on the cross but revived in the grave.[12]

According to Ayoub, several commentators accept the Gospel of Barnabas.[13] Sayyid Quṭb says the Gospel of Barnabas was written during the period when many Gospels were written. But he points out that no valid tradition has been transmitted about this.[14] Others who accept the Gospel of Barnabas include Jammāl and Riḍā.[15] Maqsood, noting that some concepts occur in Barnabas that parallel concepts found among the Dead Sea scrolls, wants to accept Barnabas but does not finally do so, although she brings out all the evidence she can muster for the authenticity of that Gospel.[16]

Ibn ʿAshūr sees another possibility for the meaning of *shubbiha la-hum* ("so it was made to appear to them") in the denial verse. It could mean someone was made to look like Jesus and crucified in his place, but it could also mean the Jews received a false report that Jesus was crucified. The testimony of the Gospel of Barnabas that Judas was crucified in Jesus' place fits the first option.

---

8. Aḥmad Musṭafā al-Marāghī, *Tafsīr al-Marāghī*, 10 vols., 2nd ed. (Cairo: Musṭafā al-Bābī al-Ḥalabī, 1953), 6:12-13; cited in Ayoub, "Towards an Islamic Christology, II," 112; idem, *Muslim View*, 172. He also treats eschatological themes symbolically because of his rationalist approach. Muḥammad ʿAlī al-Munʿim al-Jammāl (*Al-tafsīr al-farīd li-al-Qurʾān al-majīd*, 4 vols. [Cairo: Dār al-Kitāb al-Jadīd, 1973], 353) mixes this view with other views. The Qurʾān permits two views, this one and the way of the eschatological *ḥadith;* see Riḍā, *Tafsīr*, 3:313.

9. Cited in Leirvik, *Images of Jesus*, 124-25. Leirvik deals briefly with the Ahmadiyyah movement (125-27), as does Riḍā at much greater length (*Tafsīr*, 6:43-59).

10. Ahmad Deedat, *What Was the Sign of Jonah?* (Birmingham, UK: Islamic Propagation Centre International, 1976); idem, *Who Moved the Stone?* (Birmingham, UK: Islamic Propagation Centre, 1977); and idem, *Resurrection or Resuscitation?* (Birmingham, UK: Islamic Propagation Centre, 1987).

11. See Malik Ghulam Farid's note 699 to *Women* [4]:157 (158 in the recension [*qirāʾah*] that the Ahmadiyyah use) in *The Holy Qurʾān: Arabic Text with English Translation and Short Commentary*, ed. Malik Ghulam Farid (Islamabad, Pakistan/Tilford, Surrey, UK: Islam International Publications, 1994), 232-33. Both Sunnī and Shīʿī Muslims consider the Ahmadiyyah movement heretical.

12. Ruqaiyyah Waris Maqsood, *The Mysteries of Jesus: A Muslim Study of the Origins and Doctrines of the Christian Church* (Oxford: Sakina Books, 2000), 171-91.

13. Ayoub, "Towards an Islamic Christology, II," 113; idem, *Muslim View*, 173.

14. Ayoub, "Towards an Islamic Christology, II," 113; idem, *Muslim View*, 173.

15. See nn. 4 and 8 above.

16. Maqsood, *Mysteries*, 229.

The report that Pilate in Rome denied having any knowledge of the crucifixion of Jesus coheres with the second option. What is required of the believer, however, according to Ibn ʿĀshūr, based on what the Qurʾān clearly teaches, is that Jesus was not killed and not crucified but that God raised him, rescuing him from those who were pursuing him.[17]

Finally, a rather startling proposal comes from a very recent discussion of this issue by Maqsood. She accepts the proposal of a writer from the Arab Christian community, Kamal Salibi, that the Qurʾānic Jesus, that is, ʿĪsā, was not the Jesus (Greek: *Iēsous*; Arabic: *Yasūʿ*) of the New Testament but a prophet revered in Arabia who lived some centuries before the Jesus of the Gospels.[18] The Jesus (Jeshu bar Nagara) of the Gospels, suitably modified into Salibi's idea of the historical Jesus, escaped and was only thought to have been crucified. He speculates that Judas Iscariot, Simon of Cyrene, or someone else was his substitute.[19]

Maqsood, in supporting Salibi's thesis, stresses the differences in what is said about ʿĪsā in the Qurʾān and what is said about Jesus in the Gospels.[20] Even granted the many differences in the depiction of Jesus in Christian and Muslim scriptures, it stretches credulity to the limit that there have to be two Marys who were believed to have been virgins, two Zechariahs, and two Johns. Maqsood tries to show how this is possible. But just because it is possible does not mean it is likely. Furthermore, both Salibi and Maqsood have to discount the earliest Muslim sources outside the Qurʾān that have uniformly equated the Jesus of Christianity with the ʿĪsā of the Qurʾān. This may not be a problem for Salibi because he is presumably not a Muslim; but Maqsood as a Muslim might have said more about why she ignores these sources.

Salibi also maintains that this Jeshu bar Nagara and ʿĪsā of the primordial Christianity of the Arabian peninsula, referred to in the Qurʾān, combined with a deity by the name of al-ʿĪsā, also called Dhu Khulasa, account for the New Testament Jesus of Nazareth, Son of God. The cult of Dhu Khulasa involved belief in a virgin birth, a dying and rising son, and a spiritual *gnosis* that results in salvation.[21]

It should not be assumed, however, that modern Muslims read mostly modern commentators. A popular Qurʾānic software program, *al-Qurʾān al-Karīm*, produced by the Global Islamic Software Company, features four commentaries by the following authors: al-Ṭabarī, Ibn Kathīr, al-Qurṭubī, and a commentary of the two Jalāls, Jalāl al-Dīn al-Suyūṭī (d. 1505) and Jalāl al-Dīn

17. Muḥammad al-Ṭāhir Ibn ʿĀshūr, *Tafsīr al-taḥrīr wa-al-tanwīr*, 13 vols. (Tunis: al-Dār al-Tunisīyah li-al-Nashr, 1960-), 6:21-22. Although Ibn ʿĀshūr died before the turn of the century, in 1867, his reference to the Gospel of Barnabas puts him among the modern commentators for our purposes.

18. Maqsood, *Mysteries,* 149. Kamal S. Salibi's works include *The Bible Came from Arabia* (London: Jonathan Cape, 1985); *The Secrets of the Bible People* (London: Saqi Books, 1988); *Conspiracy in Jerusalem* (London: Tauris, 1988).

19. Reported by Maqsood, *Mysteries*, 142.

20. Ibid., 146-50.

21. Ibid., 141.

al-Maḥallī (d. 1459), called *Jalālayn*.[22] The commentary of Muḥammad ʿAlī al-Ṣābūnī, a compilation of the essential features of six classical commentaries, also enjoys widespread circulation among contemporary Muslims.[23] The *Jalālayn Commentary,* in commenting on *Family of Imran* [3]:55, states simply that Jesus was taken and raised up without dying. Ṣābūnī opts for the view that Judas was substituted for Jesus and crucified in his place.

When we examine Qāsimī's commentary below in some detail, it will be clear that the most common conclusions of the classical commentators we encountered in chapter 3 are by no means neglected. Yet, like others of the modern commentators, he focuses significantly on the Gospels of the New Testament.

The Commentary of Qāsimī

One of the most complete discussions among the post-Barnabas commentators is that of Muḥammad Jamāl al-Dīn al-Qāsimī. Born in Damascus into a family well known for its juridical knowledge, Qāsimī became a Sunnī scholar. The edition of his commentary that I used was published in Cairo in 1957.[24] It shows clear influence from Muḥammad ʿAbduh as well as from the classical commentators. Qāsimī's commentary is distinguished by an extended treatment of the end of Jesus' mission.[25] Among other arguments, he argues from what the Gospels themselves say about the passion of Jesus.

In this chapter, I will use Qāsimī's commentary as a base and refer to other works as they relate to a particular passage or issue. Qāsimī starts right off with a basic interpretation of a key part of the denial verse.

> "They did not kill him and they did not crucify him; it only appeared that way to them." That is, their pride in having killed him is not legitimate because they did not kill him. And they have no substantiality in their claim to having crucified him because they did not crucify him. Rather they killed and crucified someone upon whom his likeness was cast.[26]

He follows this up with a long quotation of most of the material in Luke's Gospel related to the last days of Jesus' mission (Luke 22-24),[27] launching immediately

---

22. Jalāl al-Dīn Muḥammad ibn Aḥmad al-Maḥallī and Jalāl al-Dīn al-Suyūṭī, *Tafsīr al-Jalālayn* (Damascus: Dār al-Fikr li-al-Jamīʿ, 1965).

23. Muḥammad 'Alī al-Ṣābūnī, *Ṣafwat al-tafāsīr*, 3 vols. (Beirut: Dār al-Qurʾān al-Karīm, 1980-1981).

24. Muḥammad Jamāl al-Dīn al-Qāsimī, *Tafsīr al-Qāsimī: al-musammā bi-maḥāsin al-taʾwīl*, ed. Muḥammad Fuʾād ʿAbd al-Bāqī, 17 vols. (Cairo: Dār iḥyāʾ al-kutub al-ʿarabīyah/ʿĪsā al-Bābī al-Ḥalabī wa-shurakāʾ-hu, 1957), 5:1637-1700.

25. Hamidah al Nayfar, *Les Commentaires coraniques contemporains: Analyse de leur méthodologie*, Etudes Arabes 93. Collection "Studi arabo-islamici del PISAI" 10 (Rome: Pontifical Institute for the Study of Arabica and Islamica, 1998), 39. Qāsimī was born in Damascus in 1866 and died there in 1914. His commentary is one of around seventy works he left behind.

26. Qāsimī, *Tafsīr*, 5:1637.

27. Ibid., 5:1639-60.

into a critique of it entitled "Concerning the Futility of What They Relate and Its Incoherence, with Intellectual Proofs."[28]

The Gospels Reveal Confusion about the Last Days of Jesus

Qāsimī first delves into the Qurʾān commentary of Burhān al-Dīn al-Biqāʿī,[29] who claims all the Christian Gospels agree that knowledge on the matter of whether it was Jesus who was crucified goes back to just one person, Judas Iscariot. Other enemies did not recognize Jesus. Judas only laid his hand on Jesus and never really said that it was he. Furthermore, the time was night. Jesus himself had said to his companions, "All of you will have misgivings about me this night." His disciples subsequently fled and thus had no knowledge after that about what had happened to Jesus. Peter followed him from afar. Judas hanged himself. Only women at the tomb—but at a great distance—conveyed the angel's message that Jesus had returned to life. Such circumstances contribute only to speculation. The verses that resulted, assuming their soundness, do not compel us to recognize their veracity. The testimony of the Gospels, Biqāʿī says, serves only to confirm that those who would have arrested Jesus were in doubt about him. The one crucified, if it is true that they crucified him, was the one who guided them to Jesus.[30]

Qāsimī leans toward the same conclusion, namely, that the Gospel claim that Judas hanged himself possibly resulted from the surmise of Jesus' followers, based on their failure to see him any more after the crucifixion.[31]

The Gospel Narratives Support the Qurʾānic Interpretation

Referring to a work by al-Ālūsī (d. 1899), *Al-jawāb al-faṣiḥ* (*The Full Answer*),[32] Qāsimī reveals the way Muslims interpret events recorded in the Christian Gospels as supporting the following three convictions derived from the Qurʾān: (1) the one who was killed was the one made to look like Jesus; (2) the condition of those who crucified him was confusion; and (3) God esteemed Jesus highly and for this reason raised the Messiah up.

---

28. Ibid., 5:1660-68.

29. Burhān al-Dīn Ibrāhīm ibn ʿUmar al-Biqāʿī, *Maqāṣid al-naẓar li-al-ʿishrāf ʿalā maqāṣid al-suwar*, ed. ʿAbd al-Sāmiʿ Muḥammad Aḥmad Ḥasanayn, 3 vols. (al-Riyāḍ: Maktabat al-Maʿārif, 1987).

30. Cited in Qāsimī, *Tafsīr*, 5:1660. Qāsimī does not give the page numbers.

31. Ibid., 5:1660-61.

32. Nuʿmān ibn Maḥmūd Khayr al-Dīn al-Ālūsī, *Al-jawāb al-faṣīḥ li-mā laffaqa-hu ʿAbd al-Masīḥ* [Ibn Isḥāq al-Kindī], ed. Aḥmad Ḥijāzī al-Saqqā, 2 vols. (Cairo: Dār al-Bayān al-ʿArabī, 1987).

The Trial of Jesus

For one thing, the Gospel says that when the chief priest charges the one apprehended to swear by God, "Are you the Messiah Son of God?" the one apprehended replies, "You have said" (Luke 22:70). He does not answer him that he is the Messiah. If the one made to swear whether or not he was the Messiah had been the Messiah, he would have said, "Yes." Ālūsī is convinced that had Jesus been asked to swear in the name of God, he would not have been secretive nor would he have hesitated. This would have been true especially, he thinks, if Jesus were God, as Christians believe, the one who came down to save his devotees by sacrificing himself.

The Transfiguration

Ālūsī then turns to the Transfiguration (Luke 9:28-36). He says the appearance of Moses and Elijah and the overcoming of his companions by sleep can only mean that the Transfiguration was the time God raised Jesus. Clearly the Jews had heard Jesus say Elijah would come. This is why, when they raised him up on the cross,[33] according to the Gospels, they said, "Call on him so that we can see if Elijah will come and rescue him." In other words, while the Apostles slept, Moses and Elijah came and took Jesus to God. The one the Apostles saw after they awoke could have been one of the manifestations of his spirit, since Jesus surely had the power to change states. After all, he raised the dead, multiplied the loaves and fish, and healed the blind and lepers.[34]

The Arrest

Next Ālūsī deals with the scene where the Jews come to arrest Jesus (John 19:1-8). Using portions of verses 1 and 4, he says, "Jesus was with his disciples in the Garden when the Jews came in search of him. Jesus went out to them and said to them, 'Whom do you want?' They said, 'Jesus (his identity having been hidden from them). He says, 'I am Jesus.' He does this twice, since they were ignorant of his form." Ālūsī claims that Jesus acknowledges his identity under these circumstances because he knows God has taken responsibility for his protection from them and that they cannot take him for evil ends. He contrasts this with Jesus' response when the high priest asks about his identity. The clear answer in the Garden and the silence before the priest represent in his mind a decisive proof of what God in the Qurʾān says.[35]

---

33. Qāsimī almost never uses the word "cross." I have supplied the word here. Qāsimī actually says, "If Elijah came and they did not raise him [meaning "on the cross"] then he is the Messiah" (*Tafsīr*, 5:1662).

34. Ibid., 5:1662.

35. Ibid., 5:1662-63.

The Trial and Crucifixion

Ālūsī then turns to the events connected with the supposed killing of Jesus. He maintains that structural and semantic differences in the Gospel narratives of these events, the differences in their purposes, and their discrepancies represent proofs that Jesus was not killed. Ālūsī identifies a few statements of Jesus that contradict Christian claims or support the position of the Qurʾān. Some of these relate to the trial and the crucifixion, but not all. Statements contradicting Jesus' deity include his statement at the crucifixion, "My God, my God, why have you forsaken me?"; his statement in the Garden, "Oh Father, if it is not possible for you to let this cup (that is, death) pass from me, but necessary for me to drink it, then your will be done"; and his statement to the chief priest, "Indeed from now on you will not see the Son of Man until you see him seated on the right hand of power and coming on the clouds of heaven."[36]

The final statement he adduces supports the Muslim claim that Jesus was taken up. When the Pharisees and chief priests sent a guard to arrest Jesus, he said, "I will dwell among you for a while, then I will go to the one who sent me. Thus you will seek me and will not find me. You will not be able to find a way to where I will be." He notes that the commentators say this refers to Jesus' ascension to heaven. If Ālūsī is correct about the time when Jesus was taken up to heaven, he could not have been the one who said, "My God, my God, why have you forsaken me?" on the cross. That one, as Mawdūdī has pointed out, would have to have been someone else.[37] As someone else, it says nothing about Jesus' deity.[38]

The Gospels Support Substitution

Ālūsī concludes by asking his readers to stay with the Gospel narratives—in spite of the contradictions and incoherence they find in them—long enough to see how they demonstrate that the casting of Christ's likeness and his rescue took place just as God said, "but so it was made to appear to them" (*Women* [4]:157). He identifies nine features of the Gospel narratives supporting the Qurʾān's picture of the end of Jesus' mission.

1. The Gospels relate that Jesus was crucified before sundown on Friday and buried that evening. They also have the women coming to the tomb and finding it empty early Sunday morning. This contradicts what the Gospels say elsewhere that he remained in the tomb three days, just as Jonah remained in the fish three days and three nights.

2. As mentioned above, Jesus asked the Jews twice, "Whom do you seek?" And they answered twice, "Jesus of Nazareth." But they did not know him, even though he answered them, "I."

---

36. Qāsimī adds, "He meant by 'power' the Creator" (ibid., 5:1663).
37. Mawdūdī, *Towards Understanding*, 1:259.
38. Qāsimī, *Tafsīr*, 5:1663-64.

3. Judas was bribed to lead them to him, making kissing his hand the sign of identification. If they had known Jesus, they would have recognized him without any guidance and without any question, given the fact that he had been among them for the majority of the time in their Temple.

4. When the chief priest made Jesus swear that he was the Messiah, he did not say, "I am the Messiah," but said to him, "You have said."

5. Peter denied him. Since Peter was among the greatest of his messengers (*rusūli-hi*), and denial of Jesus would have amounted to unbelief (*kufr*), Peter could not possibly have denied Jesus.

6. When the governor said to him, "Are you he?" he returned no answer. If he had truly been Jesus, he would have acknowledged it and confessed it.

7. They arrested him at night, and his form had been altered and his visage disfigured by beating and punishment. Under such circumstances, something could easily be confused with something very different from it—how much more between something and its likeness? So, concludes Ālūsī, where would the certainty that it was Jesus have come from? Referring possibly to the Mount of Transfiguration, he adds, "especially since the Christians had decided the Messiah (peace be upon him) had been given power to change from form to form."[39]

8. The guards could have been bribed to let Jesus go just as Judas was bribed to lead the guards to him. They could then have taken someone else from among those who wanted to sacrifice themselves for Christ. The fact that he never acknowledged that he was the Christ supports this possibility.

9. Jesus said, "I will dwell with you for a time and then I am going to the one who sent me. So you will seek me but will not be able to find me. And you will not be able to find a way to where I am." He thus made it obvious that they will look for him and not find him and they will not harm him in any way, since he will ascend to heaven. A similar statement occurs in chapter 12 of the Gospel of John:

> The group said to him, "We have heard from the Law that the Messiah will remain forever, so how can you say that the Son of Man will be raised up? Who is this Son of Man?" Jesus said to them, "The light is with you a little while longer. Walk in the light while you have the light, lest the darkness overtake you and you be unable to see where you are going. Believe in the light while you have the light." Jesus said this and went away, hidden from their sight.[40]

Qāsimī then follows up with some observations of his own as evidence supporting the Qur'ānic statement, "Rather he raised him to himself" (*Women* [4]:158).

1. The Jews said to Jesus, "The Messiah mentioned in the Old Covenant/Testament will remain forever." They meant that the Messiah would not die in

39. Qāsimī, *Tafsīr*, 5:1665.

40. Ibid. (John 12:34-36).

this period, but would remain until the Final Hour. He did not deny their claim, a claim congruent with the Muslims' claim that he was raised alive to heaven, that he is now living there, and will come down at the end of time when the Hour draws near. Then he will kill the Antichrist and make judgments for the people according to the law (*sharīʿah*) of Muḥammad. He will die and be buried near the Prophet. The signs of the Great Hour include his return and his death.

Qāsimī and Ālūsī both work from the substitution position, supported by the eschatological, descent-of-Jesus tradition. Such modern commentators as Quṭb and Riḍā do not rely on this eschatological tradition. Mawdūdī, in contrast, accepts a form of it,[41] as does the Shīʿī Ayatollah Sabzawārī (d. 1993/94).[42] Qāsimī continues.

2. If he were a god, he would not have concealed himself from them for fear they would kill him, since God as their creator and the creator of their actions would know the temporal extent of their power over him.[43]

Before he turns to another source and line of argument, Qāsimī suggests an additional possible interpretation of the denial verses. God, he surmises, might have cast his likeness on Satan or on one of the rebellious jinn. He thinks this interpretation would seem possible to the Christians because they claim him to be god of the world and the creator of humans, jinn, and the children of Adam. He then asks, given the Gospel's contradictions, what could possibly require the despicable shame and intense torment Christians claim happened to the Lord of Lords? Here we find one of the strongest Muslim objections to the crucifixion.

God Did Not Foretell the Crucifixion of Jesus

Next, Qāsimī appeals to ʿIzz al-Dīn al-Muḥammadī's *Al-fāṣil bayn al-ḥaqq wa-al-bāṭil* (*The Distinguisher between Truth and Falsehood*) to refute a claim of Christians that by the prophet Amos, God foretold the crucifixion of Jesus. Rather, according to ʿIzz al-Dīn, the statement "Three transgressions I will receive from the Children of Israel, but the fourth I will not accept: their selling a righteous man" represents a proof against them, because God did not say "*their* selling me" or "their selling a god equal to me."[44] In fact, the passage puts Christians on the horns of a dilemma. If the passage does foretell the betrayal of Jesus, it requires Christians to say that Jesus is "the righteous man" and not a god to be worshipped. If "the righteous man" refers to someone else, then the passage allows for someone to be made to look like Jesus to those who bought him and crucified him.[45]

---

41. Mawdūdī, *Towards Understanding*, 2:109. See also his appendix to *sūrah* 33, *Confederates*.

42. ʿAbd al-Aʿlā al-Mūsawī Sabzawārī, *Mawāhib al-Raḥmān fī tafsīr al-Qurʾān*, 25 vols., 3rd ed. (Daftār Samāhat Āyat Allāh al-ʿUzmā al-Sabzawārī, 1993/94), 10:138-42.

43. Qāsimī, *Tafsīr*, 5:1666.

44. Amos 2:6. I do not know where this occurs in *Al-fāṣil*. (ʿIzz al-Dīn al-Muḥammadī, *Al-fāṣil bayn al-ḥaqq wa-al-bāṭil* [1889 or 1900]; cited in al-Qāsimī, *Tafsīr*, 5:1666 and 1667).

45. Qāsimī, *Tafsīr*, 5:1667.

Jesus Would Not Have Thirsted on the Cross

ʿIzz al-Dīn follows this up with three passages designed to show that Jesus was not crucified. First, he cites the event on the Mount of Transfiguration, which Qāsimī has already introduced from Ālūsī. Second, since Jesus went without food and drink for forty days and forty nights in the desert, he could not have been the crucified one who asked the Jews for a drink. In addition, Jesus said to his disciples, "I have food you know not of." Muḥammadī finds it incredible that someone who endured thirst and hunger for forty days and nights would show weakness before his enemies because of the thirst of one day—especially the elite of the prophets. If, as the Christians claim, he was the Lord, then it is even more absurd. The thirsty one had to have been the one made to look like Jesus.

Jesus Would Not Have Questioned His Destiny

Third, in the statement "My God, my God, why have you forsaken me?" the crucified one evidences dissatisfaction with his destiny as well as a lack of submission to God's command. Since Jesus could hardly have been guilty of dissatisfaction and lack of submission, the crucified one must have been someone else.[46]

While at this point in his commentary Qāsimī reiterates the arguments familiar to us from the classical commentaries,[47] other modern commentators do not rely on the traditions that Ṭabarī and others rely on. Muḥammad ʿIzzat Darwazah (d. 1984)[48] agrees with Riḍā that, since the traditions narrating that God took Jesus up to heaven rescuing him from death are *aḥādī* (based-on-one/nonrecurrent) traditions, they are not binding on believers. Darwazah concludes that the expression *mutawaffī-ka* (*Family of Imran* [3]:55) lends itself to both the position of Riḍā and that of the classical commentators with their traditions. Therefore *Family of Imran* [3]:55 could be interpreted literally that Jesus did die and then was raised to heaven. What Muslims clearly must believe, however, is that Jesus was neither killed nor crucified, since *Women* [4]:157 flatly denies these Christian claims.

Claims and Counterclaims of Christians

Since we dealt with the approach of the classical commentators, especially Ṭabarī in chapter 3, we may skip Qāsimī's reiteration of their arguments and proceed now to his responses to certain claims and counterclaims made by Christians.

46. Ibid., 5:1667-68.

47. Ibid., 5:1668-72.

48. Muḥammad ʿIzzat Darwazah, *Al-tafsīr al-ḥadīth: tartīb al-suwar ḥasab al-nuzūl*, 10 vols., 2nd ed. (Beirut: Dār al-Gharb al-Islāmī, 2001), 7:156-57. This edition is not identical with the 1962 edition, *Al-tafsīr al-ḥadīth* (Cairo: ʿĪsā al-Bābī al-Ḥalabī, 1962).

The Sophistry Argument

The first claim has already been mentioned by Rāzī as the first objection to the substitution interpretation of the phrase "it was made to appear that way to them" in *Women* [4]:157. Qāsimī adds that Christians also make this claim. According to Ālūsī, they say, if such a thing be possible, when a man sees his son or his wife, he will not be sure that it is his son or his wife. We know that necessarily a person knows his son is his son without uncertainty. The casting-a-likeness claim disallows certainty. Ālūsī responds with six rejoinders, summarized below.

1. Convincing proofs and clear arguments rest on the fact that God created humankind and all the constituents of the world. The state of being (*ḥukm*) of a thing is the state of being of what is like it. Nothing lies outside God's power to create its likeness. If God can create a likeness to everything in the world, then all the features of the body of Jesus have counterparts in the realm of possibility—in non-being—that God can create somewhere other than in the body of the Messiah. Thus, the claim of a likeness of Jesus cast on someone else represents a conviction about a possible reality and not about something contrary to necessary truth. As the Torah makes clear, God created all that belongs to a snake in the staff of Moses. Since making an animal resemble an animal or a human being resemble a human being is easier than making a plant like an animal, the transformation of Moses' staff was even more difficult than casting a likeness of Jesus on another. If Jews and Christians consider such a thing as the transformation of Moses' staff permissible, then they should not consider casting a likeness impossible. God had already contradicted his usual way of doing things in creating Jesus from one parent. Having his likeness placed on someone else is no more unusual than Jesus' creation from one parent. Furthermore, if it is true for the Christians that in the Mystic Supper the bread changes into the body of Jesus and the wine into his blood, why can his likeness not be cast on someone else?[49]

2. The Gospel gives ample evidence that Jesus was well known in his context. He grew up among the Jews, attending their ceremonies, festivals, and places of worship, preaching to them, teaching them, and dialoguing with them. They were amazed at his native capacities and acquired knowledge and abilities to the extent that they wondered about the sources of all this wisdom. Why, then, did they have to pay one of his disciples thirty dirhams to lead them to him if not that his likeness had been cast on someone else?[50]

3. Jesus was arrested, according to the Gospels, on a dark night among dark nights in a situation where his form would be distorted and his handsome features and bodily frame changed by beating, dragging, and other physical abuses. Such punishment would necessitate confusion between one thing and another—especially between a thing and something resembling it. The chief

49. This refutation implies a dimension of the argument different from the import of Rāzī's use of it. See above, chapter 3.

50. Qāsimī, *Tafsīr*, 5:1673-74.

priest when he summoned the person thought to be Jesus even made him swear whether he was Jesus the Messiah and Son of God. But he received no answer. Under these circumstances, how could the Christians and the Jews know for sure that the crucified one was really Jesus? Only supposition and speculation would have been possible for them—just as God said in the Qurʾān, "for of a surety they killed him not—nay Allah raised him up unto Himself" (*Women* [4]:157-58).[51]

4. Furthermore, as the Gospels present, when the Jews came to arrest Jesus, he went out to them and said, "Whom do you want?" They said, "Jesus." Evidently he had kept his identity hidden from them. He asked them twice and yet they did not recognize his form—another indication of the casting of a likeness and the taking up of Jesus.[52]

5. Again, according to the Gospel, Jesus said, "All of you will have doubts about me this night because it is written that I will strike the shepherd and the sheep will be scattered. However, after my resurrection I will precede you to Galilee" (Matthew 26:31-32).[53] This represents a testimony his Apostles would doubt—even Peter, the best of them, doubted. What God said turns out to be correct, "and those who differ therein are full of doubts with no certain knowledge, but only conjecture to follow" (*Women* [4]:157).[54]

6. Finally, in Matthew's Gospel, Judas, seeing that he had been condemned, regretted his betrayal, returned the thirty pieces of silver, and said, "I have sinned since I surrendered innocent blood." After throwing the silver into the Temple, he went off and hanged himself (27:3-5). Clearly, the Gospels are not decisive that it was Jesus who was crucified. Possibilities abound. Judas could have lied to the Jews in stating, "He is the one." One of the followers of Christ could have ensured his salvation with God by voluntarily claiming that he was Jesus, something that frequently happens among the followers of prophets. The guards may have taken a bribe from him, let him go, and arrested someone else. God may have sent a demon in Jesus' image to be crucified. The angel that descended to strengthen Jesus may even have taken his place as a ransom for him.[55]

Why Were the Apostles of Jesus Never Told of His Assumption before the Crucifixion?

After once again bringing up the Transfiguration (Luke 9) as evidence for the ascension of Jesus, Qāsimī responds to a question posed by Christians, "If Jesus were not really crucified but rather raised to heaven, why were the Apostles never told about it?" The answer is that Jesus did not announce this because he knew some people would lie about him and claim that he was divine. Furthermore, believing in the crucifixion of Jesus before the coming of Muḥammad was

---

51. Ibid., 5:1674-75.
52. Ibid., 5:1675.
53. Ālūsī erroneously cites Matthew 27 (ibid.).
54. Ibid.. 5:1675.
55. Ibid., 5:1675-76.

no big issue. But when the Prophet came, he cleared up two Christian errors: the belief that Jesus is a god and the belief that he was killed and crucified.[56]

Why Was it Necessary for Someone to Die in Jesus' Place?

The modern Shīʿī commentator ʿAbd al-Āʿlā al-Sabzawārī (d. 1993/1994) responds to a question Qāsimī, in spite of his detailed discussion, does not take up, "Why was it necessary for someone to die at all?" That is, "Why did God not simply raise Jesus up either secretly or openly, rescuing him from those who sought his life?" His response reminds us of Rāzī's. If Jesus had simply been raised to heaven for all to see, the perception of his likeness to deity would have become deeply rooted among those who believed in him. If he had been raised to God secretly without his form having been cast on someone else, his family and those who believed in him would have been accused of hiding him. As a result, trouble would have spread among them; fighting, mistreatment, and humiliation of women might have multiplied among them in the struggle to discover where he was being hidden. The divine wisdom of this means of avoiding these pitfalls may lie behind the choice of the rhyme phrase closing out the denial verses, "Allah is Exalted in Power, Wise" (*Women* [4]:158).[57] It reminds the reader of the verse in the *sūrah Family of Imran*, "And (the unbelievers) plotted and planned, and God too planned, and the best of planners is Allah" (*Family of Imran* [3]:54). God carried out his plotting and hidden ordering of affairs in wisdom. The power of God's plotting makes it invincible.[58]

Further Gospel Contradictions and Irrational Claims

According to Qāsimī, one argument from reason runs as follows. Every sound mind resonates with God's statement, "But they killed him not, nor crucified him, but so it was made to appear to them." It clearly contrasts with the irrationality of this statement from Matthew,

> So Jesus cried with a great cry and surrendered his spirit, and behold the veil of the temple was torn in two from top to bottom, and the earth shook, stones were split, the graves opened, and many bodies of the dead saints rose up and left the tombs after his resurrection. And they entered the holy city and appeared to many. (Matthew 27:50-53)

This contradicts the statement that the Jews bribed the guards to cover up the angel's descending from heaven upon the grave of Jesus. How could that ef-

---

56. Ibid., 5:1677. He attributes this argument to a book for which he designates no author, *Munyat al-adhikāʾ fī qiṣaṣ al-anbiyāʾ* (*Desire of the Wise about the Stories of the Prophets*).

57. See n. 7 above.

58. Sabzawārī, *Mawāhib*, 10:133.

fort have been successful at all if the miracles mentioned in the verses above had happened? Who would have failed to believe in the face of these miracles? What could the raising of the saints from their graves possibly have meant? God brought these corpses to life, but they could not help him before he was convicted and died.[59]

Next, Qāsimī mounts an attack on the transmission of reports found in the Gospels. Since we will deal with this argument in chapter 10 below, we turn here to Qāsimī's discussion of a Christian proposal resembling one I brought out in chapter 2 above. Qāsimī calls it a "wavering Christian's case."

A Wavering Christian's Case

One contemporary Christian who has begun to waver in his beliefs sets out to refute the Christians' trinitarian claims, showing them to be opposed to the texts of revelation. He accepts both the truthfulness of the Qurʾān and the idea that the currently extant Bible is not corrupt in any essential way. He also believes in the crucifixion of Jesus with certitude. In disputing with Qurʾān commentators over their interpretation of the crucifixion verses, he claims that the denial of the killing and the crucifixion of Jesus in the denial verse represents an upbraiding of the mockery and ridicule of the Jews and is not a denial that Jesus was crucified. He believes God, not the Jews, caused Jesus to be crucified. Qāsimī brings out some of the contentions of this essay, following them up with refutations.

This believer in the crucifixion holds that the ambiguity in what we are calling the denial verse lies mainly in the subject of the passive verb (*shubbiha*), the "it" in "so it was made to appear to them" (*Women* [4]:157). He wants to construe the "it" to be the verbal noun of the preceding verb "killed" or "crucified." So then his interpretation would be, "It looked as though they killed him and crucified him," or "their killing him and crucifying him was confused for them." A more expanded meaning would be, "It seemed as though, or came to their imagination as though, it had been they who were the killers and crucifiers." The Lord Christ was not killed, not forced into crucifixion, did not die by overwhelming power nor by necessity. Rather, he presented himself for crucifixion on the basis of his own desire, choice, and pleasure. So it is as though the Jews did nothing by their own power or choice alone that would enable them to be justly proud of their having killed him. Making Christ the passive subject for *shubbiha* complicates the issue and the flow of the language is lost, since the verse mentions no one literally or metaphorically who could be construed as the person Jesus was confused with.[60]

He also mentions that the Holy Qurʾān never reprimands Christians for erring in their belief about the crucifixion of Christ, his resurrection, nor for any

---

59. Qāsimī, *Tafsīr*, 5:1683.

60. Ibid., 5:1689. His book, *The Sound Affirmation Concerning the Crucifixion of the Messiah* (*Al-muʿtaqid al-ṣaḥīḥ fī ṣalb al-masīḥ*) expands on his thesis.

lying of the Gospel or the Apostles. It does not blame those who believe in the crucifixion of Jesus, in spite of referring time and again to other errors of theirs.[61] Furthermore, no sound traditions from the Messenger are adduced that deny the crucifixion of Jesus.

The wavering Christian adduces verses featuring actions attributed to God but performed by some agent other than God. They are similar to the verse denying that the Jews crucified Jesus, but meaning that while they had a hand in it, God brought it about. The Qurʾān states, "It was not ye who slew them; it was Allah: When thou threwest, it was not thy act, but Allah's" (*Spoils* [8]:17). Again it states, "Verily those who plight their fealty to thee do no less than plight their fealty to Allah: the hand of Allah is over their hands" (*Victory* [48]:10). Here the literal agent both in perception and in fact is clearly the Messenger Muḥammad. But the true agent is clearly God, the agent of everything that is.

Anticipating an objection that God in these verses is mentioned specifically as doing the throwing and the pledging, this Christian interpreter answers that in the same way the verses of crucifixion and its reports make clear many times in the Gospel that the agent and judge in the matter of the crucifixion was precisely God.[62]

He says that this Qurʾānic crucifixion verse is completely correct in itself and fully congruent with all the Qurʾān presents regarding this issue. An interpretation of the crucifixion verse as denying the crucifixion in an unrestricted way flies in the face of the meaning of all the books of both Testaments and continues to be counter to the truth and to linguistic taste. It contradicts what relates to it in other verses of the Qurʾān—and in texts of other revealed books, especially the Gospel. This Christian concludes that the Qurʾān teaches that Jesus was crucified, died, rose, and ascended to heaven and that he sent the Paraclete, Muḥammad, conveyor of the Holy Qurʾān, who brings together the spirit of trustworthiness and truth.[63]

Qāsimī says a profuse number of Muslim worthies have responded to this Christian, among them the author of *The Sharp Swords* (*Al-suyūf al-battārah*), whose author relies on trustworthy European historians.[64] He stresses that the Christians of Egypt and Syria, who ought to have known more about the end of Jesus' mission than the Greek-speaking Christians of the West, did not believe that Jesus was crucified. He cites some names of groups that he claims denied the crucifixion but got replaced by the churches that made the crucifixion of Jesus central.

Qāsimī concludes that Jesus was not crucified at all and never uttered the expressions of grief and sorrow the later Christian books attributed to him. In

61. Ibid., 5:1689-90.

62. Ibid., 5:1690.

63. Ibid., 5:1690-91.

64. I have not yet been able to identify the author of *Al-suyūf al-battārah* or of any of the European sources cited there except Éduard Sayous, *Jésus Christ d'après Mahomet*: *Notions et les doctrines musulmane sur le Christianisme* (Paris: Leroux; Leipzig: Schulze, 1880), 49; cited in Qāsimī, *Tafsīr*, 5:1692. .

summary, the crucified person was not Jesus. His persecutors did not have control over him. Rather, he was raised to heaven. On the premise of prophethood alone, it is not possible rationally to imagine his crucifixion.

This last proposition by Qāsimī may be an argument something like that of Abū al-Aʿlā al-Mawdūdī, "It seems perfectly reasonable that God would not have allowed such an extraordinary person to be crucified by unbelievers and should have raised him up to Himself."[65] Mawdūdī admits, however, that prophets and messengers have been killed. The Qurʾān says, "Why have you slain the prophets of God in times gone by?" (*Cow* [2]:91)[66] and, "Every time there came to them a messenger with what they themselves desired not—some they called imposters and some they slay [*sic*]" (*Table* 5:70).[67] Mawdūdī reports that John the Baptist was beheaded at the request of a dancing girl.[68] According to Muḥammad al-Jammāl, however, Jesus was one of a special class of messengers called *Ulū al-ʿAzm*, "those 'of inflexible purpose'" (*Dunes* [46]:35), and for this reason God did not allow the Jews to crucify him. These "Tenacious Messengers" include Noah, whom God rescued from drowning, Abraham, whom God rescued from the fire, Moses, whom God rescued from Pharaoh, Jesus, whom God rescued from the Jews, and Muḥammad, whom God rescued from the polytheists.[69]

As mentioned above, Qāsimī does not refute his wavering Christian by responding to the verses the latter uses to show that *Women* [4]:157 does not deny Jesus was actually crucified. The Shīʿī exegete Sabzawārī, however, does argue against claims like those the wavering Christian makes about the denial verse,[70] concluding that these verses deny Jesus died through assassination, execution, or even naturally. The words "they killed him not nor crucified him" deny his death by assassination by any means, a claim of one group of the People of the Book. They deny his death by the execution of crucifixion, a claim of another group of the People of the Book. They also deny that he died a natural death, since both groups hold he did not die a natural death.

He simply states that the words "but so it was made to appear to them" indicate that someone else on whom God had placed the likeness of Jesus was killed and crucified in Jesus' stead. "Nay, God raised him up unto Himself" indicates that the ascension was bodily, as does the denial of the claim that Jesus was killed or crucified itself. Such a raising up in place of death has to be both in body and soul. And the subsequent statement, "And there is none of the

65. Mawdūdī, *Towards Understanding*, 1:260.

66. See also *Family of Imran* [3]:21, 181; and *Women* [4]:155.

67. The present tense, *yaqtulūn* ("slay"), appears to be for the sake of the rhyme. Irving translates it as "would [like to] kill" in both *Table* [5]:70 and *Cow* [2]:87 (T. B. Irving, trans., *The Noble Qur'an: The First American Translation and Commentary* [Brattleboro, VT: Amana Books, 1992]).

68. Mawdūdī, *Towards Understanding*, 1:259.

69. al-Jammāl, *Al-tafsīr*, 1:647.

70. Mawdūdī takes on the position Qāsimī ascribes to a wavering Christian by simply saying, "As for those who try to interpret these Qurʾānic verses as indicating the death of Jesus, they actually prove only that God is incapable of expressing His ideas in clear, lucid terms" (*Towards Understanding*, 1:259).

People of the Book but must believe in him before his death," indicates that Jesus remained alive and did not die even after his ascension. Such an unusual life and future death for Jesus after his return are congruent with his lifetime of miracles, beginning with his miraculous birth.[71]

Muḥammad ʿIzzat Darwazah cites "a Christian evangelist" who calls himself al-Ustādh al-Ḥaddād ("Professor Smith").[72] Taking a position similar to that of Qāsimī's wavering Christian in *The Qurʾān and the Bible*,[73] Ustādh Ḥaddād interprets "they killed him not nor crucified him" in a way compatible with Christian belief. According to him, the verse denies that the Jews killed Jesus in the sense that they ended his existence with finality. That they had done so "was made to appear to them," when in fact they had not done so. Darwazah calls this position a contrivance, lacking in careful consideration. He does not, however, undertake his own detailed response, relying instead on Qurʾān commentators' work on the passage.[74]

The Gospels and the Crucifixion

The author of *The Sharp Swords*, mentioned above, wrote a second treatise called *Concerning the Discourse about the Gospel* (*Fī al-kalām ʿalā al-injīl*) in response to the wavering Christian's refutation of the historical claims of his earlier treatise, *The Sharp Swords*. That Christian, he contends, employs weak arguments, resorting to attacking as heretics and infidels the historians from Europe who agree with the Muslims that the crucifixion did not happen. The wavering Christian asserts further that the four canonical Gospels could not be charged with falsification since they bear witness from beginning to end to the event of the cross. He also reiterated his claim that the Qurʾān can be interpreted so as to agree with the Gospels.

71. Sabzawārī, *Mawāhib*, 10:146-47. The "his" in "before his death" can just as easily refer to the person believing as to the person believed in, namely, Jesus. Most commentaries discuss this issue at some length.

72. Al-Ustādh al-Ḥaddād is the pen name for a Lebanese Catholic clergyman whose name is given by the Library of Congress as Yūsuf Durrah al-Ḥaddād (b. 1915) (Kenneth E. Nolin, "Al-Ustādh al-Ḥaddād: A Review Article," *The Muslim World* 50, no. 2 [1970]: 170 n. 2).

73. This is volume 2 of Al-Ustādh al-Ḥaddād's work, *Durūs Qurʾānīyah*: vol. 1, *al-Injīl fī al-Qurʾān* (422 pp.); vol, 2, *Al-Qurʾān wa-al-Kitāb;* book 1, *Bīʾat al-Qurʾān al-kitābīyah* (280 pp.); book 2, *Atwār al-daʿwah al-Qurʾānīyah* (pp. 281-1074); book 3, *Al-ʿaqīdah wa-al-sharīʿah wa-al-ṣūfīyah fī al-Qurʾān;* vol, 3, *Mā bayn al-Injīl wa-al-Qurʾān;* vol. 4, *Naẓm al-Qurʾān wa-al-Kitāb;* book 1, *Iʿjāz al-Qurʾān* (202 pp.); and book 2, *Muʿjizat al-Qurʾān* (see Nolin, "Al-Ustādh al-Ḥaddād," 170).

74. Darwazah, *Tafsīr*, 8:278. (summary) The Christian opponents have contrived a saying that the Jews were not the ones who crucified and killed the Messiah so the denial of the Qurʾān is directed only at the Jews. The ones who did the crucifixion were Romans, and the denial does not include them. We answer this contrivance by saying that the spirit of the Qurʾānic expression intended to convey the denial of the killing and the crucifixion entirely. It was connected to the Jews only because—according to our belief—the Jews were claiming that they had crucified him. This section is missing in the 1962 edition of Darwazah's commentary.

Concerning the Discourse about the Gospel deals with European scholarly testimony to the preservation of the Qurʾān and the corruption of the Gospels, showing them to be further from the truth than the Torah. Its author points to the absence of any understanding of how the original Gospel separated into the four dissimilar accounts in the New Testament. He also finds no Christian answering adequately the question, "On the basis of what criteria do contemporary Christians consider legitimate these four contradictory Gospels?"

The Development of the Gospels

According to Qāsimī, *Concerning the Discourse about the Gospel* explains the development of the Gospels in the following way. Originally Christ uttered the one original Gospel orally. The Apostles transmitted it from him to the people orally also. So the populace memorized some of the sayings from it and added what they thought appropriate from biographies and stories, removing from them what clashed with their taste. These oral versions were passed on over time from person to person until they became widespread. Finally, different Gospels were written down based on these oral traditions. The churches then selected four of them as canonical. No one knows why Christians reject the Gospel of Barnabas, said to be revealed before the Qurʾān yet agreeing with it. It mentions Muḥammad by name and teaches that Christ, a prophet, a servant, and a created being, but not a god, was not crucified.[75]

Christians Exhibit No Consensus on the Crucifixion

According to Qāsimī, no consensus exists among Christians as to whether or not the crucifixion happened. Every school delves into it, their views differing in every way. They do not agree on how the crucifixion took place, what it means, or what it achieved. Their convictions rest on submission to blind tradition. Their leaders offer no proof greater than that religion requires a suspension of understanding in the face of mysteries not subject to conceptions of the mind. Furthermore, according to Christians, the crucifixion lies at the heart of their religion. It is as foundational to their creed as the concept of the unity and oneness of God (*tawḥīd*) is foundational to the creed of Muslims. Among Muslims, in contrast, the issue of the crucifixion has no more importance than other stories of luminaries, such as Noah, Abraham, and Moses, used to illustrate a sermon or a lesson. Because of the exactness and the preservation of the Qurʾān, the crucifixion and killing of Jesus has not occurred to the mind of any Muslim from the beginning of Islam to the present day. Not one of them has broken the Muslim consensus on that in any time or place.[76]

---

75. Qāsimī, *Tafsīr*, 5:1698.
76. Ibid., 5:1699-1700.

For the Apostle Paul, Crucifixion Is Metaphorical

Qāsimī ends his discussion of the crucifixion with the allegation that all European critics of history—as well as other historians—trace the forging of the issues of the crucifixion, the atonement, the divinity of Jesus, and other Christian doctrines back to the Apostle Paul. Paul says in his Letter to the Galatians, "It was before your eyes that Jesus Christ was publicly exhibited as crucified" (Galatians 3:1). In his Letter to the Romans he writes, "For if we have been united with him in a death like his, we will certainly be united with him in a resurrection like his. We know that our old self was crucified with him" (Romans 6:5-6a). These passages indicate that, according to Paul, Christ was not killed or crucified in reality. Rather, crucifixion serves him merely as a metaphor for the death of Christians to self.[77]

As we have seen in this chapter, Qāsimī and other modern interpreters turn to the canonical Christian Gospels to support the substitutionist interpretation of the Qurʾān's denial verses. They also criticize the reliability of these Gospels and, generally speaking, appeal to the Gospel of Barnabas as the most reliable of the Gospels. The next chapter therefore discusses the origin, nature, content, and authenticity of the Gospel of Barnabas.

77. Ibid., 5:1700. Qāsimī ends his discussion of the crucifixion of Jesus at this point. He does not deal with the Christian doctrine of the cross, the doctrines of original sin, atonement, and salvation in general. I deal with such objections in chapter 14 below.

6

Judas Crucified in Jesus' Place

The Final Days of Jesus' Mission in the Gospel of Barnabas

In February of 1976, the president of Libya, Muʿammar al-Qadhdhāfī, hosted a Christian-Muslim dialogue in Tripoli. The organizers of the event issued each of the seven hundred participants a copy of the Qurʾān and a copy of the Gospel of Barnabas (hereafter Barnabas). No Bibles were issued and no canonical Gospels were distributed. As a result of protest from the Vatican delegation, Barnabas was removed, but no documents were issued in its place. According to David Sox, an American journalist living in Britain, "One of the Catholic participants said later that Qadhdhāfī had asked him when the pope in Rome would at last produce the true Gospel, *Barnabas*, which he had been trying to hide for centuries."[1]

Two centuries earlier, George Sale (d. 1736) presented information about the Spanish text of Barnabas in the "preliminary discourse" to his translation of the Qurʾān. He says of the Spanish text, now lost except for fragments,

> The book . . . contains two hundred and twenty-two chapters of unequal length, and four hundred and twenty pages; and is said, in the front, to be translated from the Italian, by an Arragonian Moslem, named Mostafa de Aranda. There is a preface prefixed to it, wherein the discoverer of the original MS., who was a Christian monk, called Fra Marino, tells us, that having accidentally met with a writing of Irenaeus (among others), wherein he speaks against St. Paul, alleging, for his authority, the Gospel of St. Barnabas, he became exceeding desirous to find this gospel; and that God, of His mercy, having made him very intimate with Pope Sixtus V., one day, as they were together in that Pope's library, his Holiness fell asleep, and he, to employ himself, reaching down for a book to read, the first he laid his hand on proved to be the very gospel he wanted: overjoyed at the discovery, he scrupled not to hide his prize in his sleeve, and on the Pope's awaking, took leave of him, carrying with him that celestial treasure, by reading of which he became a convert to Mohammedanism.[2]

1. David Sox, *The Gospel of Barnabas* (London: George Allen & Unwin, 1984), 11.
2. George Sale, "To the Reader," in *The Koran: Commonly Called the Alkoran of Moham-*

A Dr. Holme, Rector of Hedley in Hampshire, had lent Sale the Spanish version of the Gospel. Joseph White refers to this Spanish translation of the Gospel of Barnabas in his eighth Bampton Lecture for 1784.[3] Only the fragments preserved in Sale's preface and in White's lecture—translated into English—are known to us now.[4]

In 1709, J. F. Cramer acquired an Italian manuscript of Barnabas in Amsterdam and lent it to John Toland, whom Sale mentions in his "To the Reader." Cramer later presented it to the bibliophile Count Eugène of Savoy. In 1738, it found its way with the count's books into the library of the royal court in Vienna, where it currently resides.[5]

In 1907 Canon Lonsdale Ragg and his wife, Laura Ragg, published an English translation, with introduction and notes, of Barnabas from this Vienna codex in which it was labeled "The True Gospel of Jesus according to the description of Barnabas his apostle."[6] In 1908, Khalīl Saʿādah's Arabic translation was published in Cairo. By the time Qāsimī was writing his commentary, Barnabas was being read in the Arab world.[7] By 1940 Professor Abū Zahra was using Barnabas in his religion classes at al-Azhār University in Cairo,[8] arguably the most prestigious of Islamic educational institutions.

Urdu editions, translated from Saʿādah's Arabic, were issued as early as 1916. Persian, Indonesian, and some subsequent Arabic translations have appeared. In 1973 a publishing company in Karachi brought out an edition of the Raggs' English translation, without their critical introduction. Popularized by Pakistani newspapers, this edition was widely distributed and stimulated a new edition in Urdu. Sayyid Abū al-Aʿlā Mawdūdī, a highly respected cleric and prolific writer, provided an introduction.

The Unity Publishing Company of Cedar Rapids, Iowa, published a fresh

---

med Translated into English from the Original Arabic with Explanatory Notes Taken from the Most Approved Commentators to Which Is Prefaced a Preliminary Discourse, ed. and trans. George Sale, Chandos Classics (London: Rederick Warne, n.d.), ix-x. Cited also by Lonsdale and Laura Ragg, "Introduction," in Lonsdale Ragg and Laura Ragg, eds. and trans., *The Gospel of Barnabas* (Oxford: Clarendon Press, 1907), xi-xii.

3. The Raggs say White used the Spanish text, although he provides no information about his source in the Bampton Lectures. See Joseph White, *A Comparison of Mahometism and Christianity in Their History, Their Evidence, and Their Effects in Nine Sermons*, Bampton Lectures (1784) (Oxford: D. Prince and J. Cooke/London: J. F. and C. Rivington, and T. Cadell, 1784), 328.

4. Luigi Cirillo and Michel Frémaux analyze all these fragments in detail in *Évangile de Barnabé: Recherches sur la composition et l'origine* (Paris: Beauchesne, 1977), 51-75.

5. Ragg and Ragg, "Introduction," xi.

6. Sox, *Gospel of Barnabas*, 10.

7. Iliyās Zahlāwī, *Ḥawl al-Injīl wa Injīl Barnaba* (Junayah, Lebanon: al-Maṭbaʿah al-Būlsīyah, n.d.), 62 and 105. Both La Monnoye in 1716 and Toland in 1718 held that behind the translations in romance languages lay an Arabic original. Sales (1734) mentions an Arabic original in his "Preliminary Discourse" (58), based solely on the reports of La Monnoye and Toland, neither of whom had seen any Arabic manuscripts. See also Ragg and Ragg, "Introduction," xvi. The Vienna manuscript contains Arabic glosses (included by the Raggs in their notes with translation) that an expert consulted by the Raggs considers written by a European ("Introduction," xvi n. 4).

8. Sox, *Gospel of Barnabas*, 10-11.

fifth edition of the Raggs' English translation of the Gospel in 1980. Altogether twenty-eight thousand copies were printed. It too omitted the Raggs' introduction. In its place this edition offered several essays: one offering Christian affirmation of the value of Islam, another two essays based on the Acts of the Apostles supporting the life and message of Barnabas as presented in his Gospel, another treating the survival of Barnabas, and, finally, an essay finding in the Bible the Islamic understanding of monotheism, Muḥammad, and Jesus.[9]

The omission of the Raggs' introduction in Muslim editions is not surprising, since in it they offered this evaluation of Barnabas:

> The internal evidence of the subject matter would point . . . to an Italian original of 1300-50 A.D. . . . [And] some one about 1575 . . . either copied out or invented this "Gospel of Barnabas." This much we may say with confidence. The Italian *Barnabas* is, to all intents and purposes, an original work . . . of one who, whether priest or layman, monk or secular, has a remarkable knowledge of the Latin Bible—as remarkable, perhaps as Dante's[10]—and like Dante, a special familiarity with the Psalter. It is the work of one whose knowledge of the Christian Scriptures is considerably in advance of his familiarity with the Scriptures of Islam: presumably, therefore, of a renegade from Christianity.[11]

A couple of non-Muslim analyses of Barnabas have lent some measure of prestige to the Gospel. In 1966, Shlomo Pines of the Hebrew University in Jerusalem suggested a "tenable hypothesis" that some of its ideas may have been connected with the Ebionites, a sect of Jewish Christians of the early centuries of Christianity.[12] And in 1977, Luigi Cirillo and Michel Frémaux published a French translation of Barnabas, featuring hundreds of pages of research and analysis. They theorized that a medieval writer produced Barnabas by elaborating on an apocryphal oriental core or base document.[13]

Both of these proposals appear congruent with the fact that the Gelasian Decrees, inaccurately attributed to Pope Gelasius (reigned 492-495) but probably compiled by a cleric at the outset of the sixth century,[14] mention a Gospel of Barnabas. Especially since this represents the unique reference to this Gospel—it

---

9. Lonsdale Ragg and Laura Ragg, trans., *The Gospel of Barnabas*, ed. and trans. from the Italian MS. in the Imperial Library at Vienna by Lonsdale and Laura Ragg with a facsimile [of page 132 of the original] (Cedar Rapids, IA: Unity Publishing, 1980). Hereafter cited in the notes as GB.

10. Dante Alighieri, "the greatest of Italian poets," lived from 1265 to 1321.

11. Ragg and Ragg, "Introduction," xlii-xliv.

12. Shlomo Pines, *The Jewish Christians according to a New Source* (Jerusalem: Hebrew Academy of Sciences and Humanitites, 1966), 70-73; cited in Sox, *Gospel of Barnabas*, 11.

13. *Évangile de Barnabé*, 96, 247 and passim. Jan Slomp has reviewed this massive work in detail ("The Gospel in Dispute: A Critical Evaluation of the First French Translation with the Italian Text and Introduction of the So-called Gospel of Barnabas," *Islamochristiana* 4 [1978]: 67-111).

14. Jan Slomp, "Preface," in Selim ʿAbdul-Ahad and W. H. T. Gairdner, *The Gospel of Barnabas: An Essay and Inquiry* (Hyderabad, India: Henry Martyn Institute of Islamic Studies, 1975), v-vi.

having been cited by no church father or in any other record at all—before the eighteenth century, the reference could very well be mistaking Barnabas for the Gospel of Matthew. The *Acts of Barnabas*, written before Cypriots allegedly found the remains of Barnabas in 478, mentions the first Gospel in connection with the Apostle Barnabas: "Barnabas, having unrolled the Gospel, which he had received from Matthew his fellow-labourer, began to teach the Jews."[15] It is also possible that a forger of Barnabas could have chosen that Apostle to present as the author of his forgery because of the otherwise unattested reference to his Gospel in the Pseudo-Gelasian Decrees.[16] At any rate, evidence presented below will demonstrate that even if there were a Gospel of Barnabas, it could hardly have been the 222-chapter Italian manuscript that is the only Gospel of Barnabas in existence today.

In spite of the fact that Cyril Glassé, a Muslim, can say of Barnabas, "there is no question that it is a medieval forgery,"[17] many in the Muslim world still seem certain that in it we have the authentic story of the end of Jesus' mission.

Qāsimī and the Gospel of Barnabas

In chapter 5, I mentioned that Muḥammad Jamāl al-Dīn al-Qāsimī, in his commentary published around the time Barnabas first appeared in English and Arabic, wondered why Christians rejected it.[18]

Here is a sample passage from the Gospel that Qāsimī refers to in his commentary. It is a statement made by Jesus and will introduce the flavor of this witness to the last days of Jesus' mission.

> And though I have been innocent in the world, since men have called me "God," and "Son of God," God, in order that I be not mocked of the demons on the day of judgement, has willed that I be mocked of men in this world by the death of Judas, making all men to believe that I died upon the cross. And this mocking shall continue until the advent of Mohammed, the Messenger of God, who, when he shall come, shall reveal this deception to those who believe in God's law.[19]

---

15. Quoted in Slomp, "Preface," vii.

16. Jan Slomp, "The Gospel in Dispute," 74.

17. Cyril Glassé, "Barnabas, Gospel of," *The New Encyclopedia of Islam*, rev. ed. of *Concise Encyclopedia of Islam* (Walnut Creek, CA/Lanham, MD/and New York: Altamira, 2001), 78.

18. *Tafsīr al-Qāsimī: Al-musammā bi-maḥāsin al-taʾwīl*, ed. Muḥammad Fuʾād ʿAbd al-Bāqī, 17 vols. (Cairo: Dār ihyāʾ al-kutub al-ʿarabīyah/ʿĪsā al-Bābī al-Ḥalabī wa-shurakāʾ-hu, 1957), 5:1698.

19. GB, 220/230a. The first number indicates the chapter number and the second, the page number in the manuscript the Raggs used. The Cedar Rapids, Iowa edition mentioned above (see n. 9), without the Raggs' introduction, indicates only the chapter divisions (1-222) of Barnabas. The Arabic translation Qāsimī worked from differs slightly, not tendentiously in this passage. In some places, however, its changes from the original Gospel of Barnabas are tendentious (e.g., it does not

What Qāsimī says about this passage represents well the conviction of some Muslims today about the value of this source.

> The English scholar Sale, famous in Europe for his translation of the . . . [Qur'ān], has called this gospel verse to witness in explicating the statement of God (Exalted be He) in the Sūrah of Āl ʿImrān, "And they plotted and God plotted and God is the best of the plotters." Scholars before Islam by nearly 300 years confirmed the Gospel of Barnabas so that the English scholar Toland could say, "And peace be upon Christianity," by virtue only of his seeing this Gospel.[20]

The Gospel of Barnabas on the Last Days of Jesus' Mission

Barnabas has no less than 222 chapters covering in the Raggs' translation 243 pages of 36 lines each. Page 11, for example, has an average of 11 words per line. Some of the passages will be quoted in accordance with the evaluation below. But we will have to be satisfied here with a broad outline of its contents followed by a summary in more detail of the entire section treating the end of Jesus' mission referred to by Christians as his passion and resurrection. Father Iliyās Zaḥlāwī summarizes Barnabas in five points: (1) The claim that Jesus of Nazareth is the Son of God is unbelief; (2) the claim that Jesus of Nazareth is the Messiah is unbelief; (3) Jesus is merely a prophet; (4) he was sent to prepare the way for the appearance of the true Messiah; and (5) the true Messiah is Muḥammad.[21] Organizing Barnabas according to its portrayal of the life of Jesus from his birth to his ascension, Zaḥlāwī divides it into two main sections with six divisions in the second section. The first section is made up of ten chapters narrating in detail the birth and childhood of Jesus. The second of the two main divisions deals with the whole of Jesus' public life from the time he begins preaching until the day when he is raised to heaven. It comprises the following six divisions.

1. Jesus begins his preaching and performs miracles (chapters 10-46).
2. Roman soldiers worship Jesus as a god, causing him a severe personal crisis. He gets free in the aftermath of it from the people calling him

---

render the Italian for Messiah as *al-masīḥ* when referring to Muḥammad but with *Masiyya*, obscurimg Barnabas's contradiction of the Qur'ān on this point; Slomp, "The Gospel in Dispute," 76).

20. Qāsimī, *Tafsīr*, 5:1698. I have not found this in Sale's "preface" to the Qur'ān. In my edition, what must be the "preface" is called "To the Reader."

21. Zaḥlāwī, *Ḥawl al-Injīl*, 63-64. According to Gerard A. Wiegers, the idea that Muḥammad is the Messiah represents a new concept characteristic of the polemical writings of the Moriscos in North Africa (Wiegers, "Muhammad as the Messiah: A Comparison of the Polemical Works of Juan Alfonso with the Gospel of Barnabas," *Biblioteca Orientalis* 52, nos. 3-4 (1995): 245.

first a God and second a Messiah. He prophesies of the coming of the expected Messiah, Muḥammad (chapters 47-98).

3. Jesus returns to spreading the good news. Then the people feel passionately about him and insist on making him a king. So Jesus escapes to Damascus and from there goes on to Tyre (chapters 99-126).
4. Jesus stays persistently with the education of his disciples, teaching them all about repentance, fasting, prayer, and virtues, charging them with carrying his message to the people (chapters 127-53).
5. Jesus meets Roman soldiers in the Temple and teaches (among other things) about sin, freedom, evil, predestination, and pollution (chapters 153-91).
6. Barnabas tells of the last days of Jesus on the earth, his supposed death, and ascension to heaven (chapters 192-222).[22]

Here are some excerpts from these last thirty chapters to provide a flavor of what Barnabas conveys to its readers.

> 210. . . . The high priest went in person to Herod and to the Roman governor, accusing Jesus that he desired to make himself king of Israel, and of this they had false witnesses. . . .
>
> 213. The day having come for eating the lamb, Nicodemus sent the lamb secretly to the garden for Jesus and his disciples, announcing all that had been decreed by Herod with the governor and the high priest. . . .
>
> When the lamb was eaten, the devil came upon the back of Judas, and he went forth from the house, Jesus saying to him again: "Do quickly that which thou must do."
>
> 214. Having gone forth from the house, Jesus retired into the garden to pray. . . .
>
> 215. When the soldiers with Judas drew near to the place where Jesus was, Jesus heard the approach of many people, wherefore in fear he withdrew into the house. And the eleven were sleeping.
>
> Then God, seeing the danger of his servant, commanded Gabriel, Michael, Rafael, and Uriel, his ministers, to take Jesus out of the world.
>
> The holy angels came and took Jesus out by the window that looketh toward the South. They bare him and placed him in the third heaven in the company of angels blessing God forevermore.
>
> 216. Judas entered impetuously before all into the chamber whence Jesus had been taken up. And the disciples were sleeping. Whereupon the wonderful God acted wonderfully, insomuch that Judas was so changed in speech and in face to be like Jesus that we believed him to be Jesus. And he, having awakened us, was seeking where the Master was. Whereupon we marveled, and answered: "Thou, Lord, art our master; hast thou now forgotten us?"

---

22. Zaḥlāwī, *Ḥawl al-Injīl*, 66.

And he, smiling, said: "Now are ye foolish, that know not me to be Judas Iscariot!"

And as he was saying this the soldiery entered, and laid their hands upon Judas, because he was in every way like to Jesus.

217. . . . [So they took Judas and he was condemned and crucified in the place of Jesus.] But they that stood firm in the doctrine of Jesus were so encompassed with sorrow, seeing him die who was entirely like to Jesus, that they remembered not what Jesus had said.

218. . . . Those disciples who did not fear God went by night [and] stole the body of Judas and hid it, spreading a report that Jesus was risen again; whence great confusion arose.[23]

The news reached Nazareth how that Jesus, their fellow-citizen, having died on the cross was risen again. Whereupon, he that writeth prayed the mother of Jesus that she would be pleased to leave off weeping, because her son was risen again. Hearing this, the Virgin Mary, weeping, said: "Let us go to Jerusalem to find my son. I shall die content when I have seen him."

219. . . . So the angels that were guardians of Mary ascended to the third heaven, where Jesus was in the company of angels, and recounted all to him.

Wherefore Jesus prayed God that he would give him power to see his mother and his disciples. Then the merciful God commanded his four favourite angels, who are Gabriel, Michael, Rafael, and Uriel, to bear Jesus into his mother's house, and there keep watch over him for three days continually, suffering him only to be seen by them that believed in his doctrine.

Jesus came, surrounded with splendour, to the room where abode Mary the Virgin with her two sisters, and Martha and Mary Magdalene, and Lazarus, and him who writeth, and John, James and Peter. Whereupon, through fear, they fell as dead. And Jesus lifted up his mother and the others from the ground, saying: "Fear not, for I am Jesus; and weep not, for I am alive and not dead."

221. And Jesus turned himself to him who writeth, and said: "See Barnabas, that by all means thou write my gospel concerning all that hath happened through my dwelling in the world. And write in like manner that which hath befallen Judas, in order that the faithful may be undeceived, and every one may believe the truth."[24]

It hardly needs saying that this narrative departs significantly from the accounts in the canonical Gospels of Matthew, Mark, Luke, and John. How shall we evaluate this unusual Gospel?

---

23. Cf. Matthew 28:13.
24. GB, 210/217a-221/223a.

Evaluation of the Gospel of Barnabas

Several features of the Gospel indicate that Barnabas is a medieval forgery: its geographical errors; its historical anachronisms; the absence in the Islamic tradition of any mention of it; its contradictions of the Qurʾān; and its comprehensive knowledge of the Bible.

Geographical Anomalies

In chapter 20, entitled "Miracles on the Sea Wrought by Jesus," Barnabas does not appear to be aware that he reports an additional miracle on land. "Jesus went to the Sea of Galilee," he writes, "and having embarked in a ship sailed to his city of Nazareth."[25] The writer apparently did not know that travel by water to Nazareth on the Sea of Galilee is not possible. One has to go by land. The author also possibly thinks that Jesus and his disciples went by boat to Jerusalem—at least so the Raggs conclude, based on Barnabas's chapters 151 and 152.[26]

Barnabas has Jesus and his disciples repairing to Damascus (chapters 139 and 143) and fasting for forty days on Mount Sinai (chapter 92). It seems strange that such trivial geographical references should contradict the whole of the geographical extent of Jesus ministry as portrayed in all four canonical Gospels. With the clear confusion about traveling from Galilee to Nazareth and possibly even to Jerusalem by boat, placing Jesus with thirty-six disciples in Damascus and having him fast for forty days on Mount Sinai contribute to the Raggs' judgment that Barnabas "possesses no first-hand knowledge of Palestine, still less of Palestine in the first century of our era."[27]

Historical Anachronisms

The context of the writer of Barnabas is medieval and not the environment of Palestine in late antiquity. This shows up in Barnabas's embellishments of the material we find in the canonical Gospels. Herod, Pilate, and Caiaphas frequently consult together.

> Then answered the priest, with the governor and the king, saying: "Distress not thyself, O Jesus, holy one of God, because in our time shall not this sedition be any more, seeing that we will write to the sacred Roman senate in such wise that by imperial decree none shall any more call thee God or son of God."[28]

25. GB, 20/19b.
26. Ibid., 152/166b.
27. Ragg and Ragg, "Introduction," xxi.
28. GB, 97/102b.

The authorities post this decree engraved in copper in the Temple.[29] Later the triumvirate has to reverse its position.

> The high priest therefore spake that under pain of anathema none should speak a word in defense of Jesus; and he spake to Herod, and to the governor, saying: "In any case we have an ill venture in our hands, for if we slay this sinner we have acted contrary to the decree of Caesar, and, if we suffer him to live and he make himself king, how will the matter go?"[30]

Again, according to the Raggs, Barnabas pictures Mary, Martha, and Lazarus as "proprietors of whole villages, like mediaeval 'signori.'"[31] The translators evidence astonishment that "the style of the book and the atmosphere which it breathes should have in them so much of the Occident, and of Italy." In fact, "the style bespeaks—if not a purely Italian and mediaeval or renaissance origin for Barnabas—at least a rare originality and individuality in him who first put its contents into their present form."[32] Their evidence for this follows, taking up no less than forty lines and ending with a reference to the villages of Magdala and Bethany being owned by private persons such as Mary, Martha, and Lazarus. They call this "more medieval than levitical, more natural in fourteenth- or fifteenth-century Italy than in first-century Palestine."[33]

David Sox[34] joins the Raggs[35] in pointing to another anachronism that sets Barnabas in medieval Italy rather than in first-century Palestine—the one-hundred-year Jubilee. In the course of Jesus' dialogue with the Samaritan woman, she asks him if he is the Messiah. Jesus replies,

> I am indeed sent to the house of Israel as a prophet of salvation; but after me shall come the Messiah, sent of God to all the world; for whom God hath made the world. And then through the entire world will God be worshipped, and mercy received, insomuch that the year of jubilee, which now cometh every hundred years, shall by the Messiah be reduced to every year in every place.[36]

Sox says this "tell-tale error" places Barnabas in the fourteenth century, if the Raggs are correct, or the sixteenth, if Jan Slomp[37] is correct—but certainly not

29. GB, 98/104a.
30. Ibid., 210/217b-218a.
31. Ragg and Ragg, "Introduction," xxi.
32. Ibid., xxxvi-xxxviii.
33. Ibid., xxxix.
34. Sox, *Gospel of Barnabas*, 29.
35. Ragg and Ragg, "Introduction," xli-xlii.
36. GB, 82/87b.
37. Slomp, "The Gospel in Dispute," 111.

in the first century.[38] In biblical times, the Jewish Year of Jubilee came every fifty years. It was a year when slaves were set free and land returned to owners who had previously been forced to sell it to live (Leviticus 25). Barnabas's one-hundred-year Jubilee dates it, according to the Raggs, between 1300 and 1350. In 1300 Pope Boniface proclaimed for Christians a Jubilee that he intended to occur again every century. The measure so successfully brought pilgrims to Rome—and with them financial success—that Pope Clement VI shortened the interval and celebrated the next Jubilee in 1350.[39]

Slomp finds a later date more probable based on Barnabas's centennial Jubilee. He focuses on Jesus' prediction that, when Muḥammad comes, the interval between Jubilees will "be *reduced* to every year in every place."[40] The reduction of the period of Jubilee years did not end with the fifty-year interval of Pope Clement VI. In 1470 the period was reduced to twenty-five years, and in 1585 Pope Sixtus V started his reign with a Jubilee year. This might lead to the surmise that just about any year could be designated a Jubilee. Slomp then hypothesizes that 1585 is the exact date of the Jubilee passage in Barnabas.[41] Sixtus V is the pope who was said to have gone to sleep on Fra Marino, the monk who, according to the "preliminary discourse" of George Sale's English translation of the Qur'ān, stole Barnabas out from under the pope's nose.

Another interesting detail in Barnabas is the mention of a *Quadragesima*, the Latin term for the forty days of Lent.

> The Roman soldiery, through the operation of Satan, stirred up the Hebrews, saying that Jesus was God come to visit them. Whereupon so great sedition arose, that nigh upon the Forty Days (*quadragessima*) all Judea was in arms. . . .[42]

This term *quadragessima* (although usually spelled *Quadragesima*) means Lent, the period of fasting before Easter, and the first Sunday of Lent. The name for Lent occurs among the pronouncements of the Council of Nicaea (325), and the practice of fasting before Easter is very early. But the practice of fasting for *a forty-day period*, probably modeled after Jesus' own fast as recorded in the Synoptic Gospels, started in the seventh century.[43] Barnabas contains a lot of material on fasting; but why would Barnabas want to suggest the Lenten fast, an event marking the significance of the passion and resurrection of Jesus, while attempting to deny the occurrence of both? It makes most sense to add this to Barnabas's anachronisms.

---

38. Sox, *Gospel of Barnabas*, 28-29.
39. Ragg and Ragg, "Introduction," xli-xlii.
40. GB, 82/85b. Slomp provides the emphasis ("Gospel in Dispute," 84).
41. Ibid.
42. Ibid., 96/96a.
43. Howard Sainsbury, "Lent," in J. D. Douglas, Earle E. Cairns, and James E. Ruark, eds., *The New International Dictionary of the Christian Church*, Regency Reference Library (Grand Rapids: Zondervan, 1978), 590.

Unusual Knowledge of the Whole Canon of Christian Scripture

Like the great Italian poet Dante, the author of Barnabas exhibits a comprehensive knowledge of Christian scripture. Barnabas features quotes or references to twenty-two of the thirty-nine books of the Hebrew Bible. It generally evidences full and accurate knowledge of these books, showing preference for the Psalms and Isaiah. After them it refers most frequently to the Pentateuch and the Former Prophets. Barnabas cites the Latter Prophets only once and has Daniel writing the books of Kings. As far as the New Testament is concerned, reference is made in some way to nineteen of the twenty-seven canonical books. The Barnabas material from the Epistles of the New Testament, Acts, and Revelation does not spring from some substratum of tradition common to the earliest followers of Jesus but evidences direct dependence on the New Testament books themselves.[44] Ironically, the books cited include the writings of Paul, even though Barnabas writes to counteract his influence (chapters 1 and 222).

Barnabas features quotes from all four canonical Gospels and structures the whole of its discourse according to a harmony of them.[45] The Raggs can say that the Gospels "form the fundamental substratum of the whole document."[46] If it were just a matter of noticing the heavy dependence of Barnabas on the Gospels of Matthew, Mark, Luke, and John, however, one might attribute this dependency to Barnabas's drawing on the same historical experiences and documents as the canonical evangelists. But, as in the case of the Epistles and other books of the New Testament, his copying of passages virtually verbatim from these sources raises considerable doubt that this is the case.

For example, in chapter 166, Barnabas depicts Andrew referring to the Torah of Moses while actually quoting the Apostle Paul. Andrew asks, "But how is that to be understood which God said to Moses, that he will have mercy on whom he willeth to have mercy and will harden whom he willeth to harden?"[47] Exodus 33:19 reads, "I will be gracious to whom I will be gracious, and will show mercy on whom I will show mercy." Exodus 4:21 reads, referring to Pharaoh, "I will harden his heart, so that he will not let the people go." Andrew, however, combines the quotations, reversing their order: "He will have mercy on whom he willeth to have mercy," he says, "and will harden whom he willeth to harden."

---

44. Ragg and Ragg, "Introduction," xviii.

45. Barnabas follows the basic structure of Gospel harmonies, sometimes agreeing with the eastern Syriac and Persian traditions and sometimes with the several medieval harmonies. Cirillo and Frémaux (*Évangile de Barnabé*, 203-4) have made the most elaborate case for this conclusion.

46. Ragg and Ragg, "Introduction," xviii.

47. Ibid. I have chosen the English translation of Ronald A. Knox for these quotations because of its connection with the Latin Vulgate, although the New Testament translation comes from the Greek (*The Old Testament Newly Translated from the Latin Vulgate*, trans. Ronald A. Knox, 2 vols. [London: Burns Oates & Washbourne, 1949]; and Ronald A. Knox, trans., *The New Testament of Our Lord and Saviour Jesus Christ: A New Translation* [New York: Sheed & Ward, 1948]).

Clearly, Barnabas has Andrew quoting Romans 9:18: "So then he has mercy on whomever he chooses, and he hardens the heart of whomever he chooses."[48]

Barnabas Contradicts the Qurʾān

Barnabas tries to convey at least four major ideas: that Jesus is not God; that he was not killed or crucified; that he was not the Messiah; and that Muḥammad, the true Messiah, would be coming. The first idea supports the contention of the Qurʾān; the second agrees with the standard interpretation of one of its verses (*Women* [4]:157); but the third and fourth stand in stark contrast to the Qurʾān.

Since Barnabas strips Jesus of the messianic identity the canonical Gospels give him, it must provide him with some other identity. Barnabas provides for Jesus the role that the canonical Gospels ascribe to John the Baptist. In fact, Barnabas evidences no trace of John the Baptist. This omission also contrasts with the Qurʾān. So in two instances Barnabas contradicts the Qurʾān. It denies Jesus' messiahship and attributes it to Muḥammad, and it presents Jesus as the one who prepares the way for Muḥammad, the expected Messiah. Barnabas has Jesus himself at numerous points making these convictions known, so that no doubt can possibly remain that Jesus is not the Messiah—but his forerunner.[49]

In chapters 92 through 97, Jesus leaves Mount Sinai where he has kept the Lenten fast with his disciples, attempts to enter Jerusalem, clarifies who he is, and foretells the coming of Muḥammad. Before he can enter the city, everyone pours out to greet him. When the crowd recognizes him, they shout,

> "Welcome to thee, O our God!" and they began to do him reverence, as unto God. Whereupon Jesus gave a great groan and said: "Get ye from before me, O madmen, for I fear lest the earth should open and devour me with you for your abominable words!" Whereupon the people were filled with terror and began to weep.[50]
>
> Then Jesus, having lifted his hand in token of silence, said: "Verily ye have erred greatly, O Israelites, in calling me, a man, your God. And I fear that God may for this give heavy plague upon the holy city, handing it over in servitude to strangers. O a thousand times accursed Satan, that hath moved you to this!"[51]

---

48. See also Ragg and Ragg, "Introduction," xviii. At issue in this part of Barnabas is predestination. Barnabas takes a strong stand in favor of human freedom. But, as the church historian Dirk Jellema says, "In the first centuries of the Christian Church, predestination was not an issue" ("Predestination," in J. D. Douglas, Earle E. Cairns, and James E. Ruark, eds., *New International Dictionary of the Christian Church,* 798). It is also not an issue in the Qurʾān, although it became an issue within a hundred years of Muḥammad's death. See on this subject Ragg and Ragg, "Introduction," xxxiii. This issue could also have been listed under anachronisms in Barnabas above.

49. See, for example, GB, chapters 70, 82, 96, 198.

50. GB, 92/97b.

51. Ibid., 93/97b.

> And having said this, Jesus smote his face with both his hands, whereupon arose such a noise of weeping that none could hear what Jesus was saying. Whereupon once more he lifted up his hand in token of silence, and the people being quieted from their weeping, he spake once more: "I confess before heaven, and I call to witness everything that dwelleth upon the earth, that I am a stranger to all that ye have said; seeing that I am man, born of mortal woman, subject to the judgement of God, suffering the miseries of eating and sleeping, of cold and heat, like other men. Wherefore when God shall come to judge, my words like a sword shall pierce each one [of them] that believe me to be more than man."[52]

At this point a great company of horsemen arrive with Pilate, Herod, and the high priest. Jesus repeats his confession before the high priest. He responds in repentance, and the two of them go before the masses to quiet them and to convince them that Jesus is not God. This results in mass repentance and tears of remorse from among the people who ask Jesus to pray for them, "everyone crying: 'So be it,' 'Amen.'"[53]

> When the prayer ended, the priest said with a loud voice: "Stay, Jesus, for we need to know who thou art, for the quieting of our nation."
>
> Jesus answered: "I am Jesus, son of Mary, of the seed of David, a man that is mortal and feareth God, and I seek that to God be given honour and glory."
>
> The priest answered: "In the book of Moses it is written that our God must send us the Messiah, who shall come to announce to us that which God willeth, and shall bring to the world the mercy of God. Therefore I pray thee tell us the truth, art thou the Messiah of God whom we expect?"
>
> Jesus answered: "It is true that God hath so promised, but indeed I am not he, for he is made before me, and shall come after me." [cf. John 1:30]
>
> The priest answered: "By thy words and signs at any rate we believe thee to be a prophet and an holy one of God, wherefore I pray thee in the name of all Judaea and Israel that thou for love of God shouldst tell us in what wise the Messiah will come."
>
> Jesus answered: "As God liveth, in whose presence my soul standeth, I am not the Messiah whom all the tribes of the earth expect, even as God promised to our father Abraham saying: 'In thy seed will I bless the tribes of the earth.' But when God shall take me away from the world, Satan will raise again this accursed sedition, by making the

52. Ibid., 93/98a.
53. Ibid., 93/98b-95/101b.

> impious believe that I am contaminated, insomuch that scarcely shall there remain thirty faithful ones: whereupon God will have mercy upon the world, and will send his messenger for whom he hath made all things; who shall come from the south with power, and shall destroy the idols with the idolaters; who shall take away the dominion from Satan which he hath over men. He shall bring with him the mercy of God for salvation of them that shall believe in him, and blessed is he who shall believe his words.[54]
>
> "Unworthy though I am to untie his hosen, I have received grace and mercy from God to see him."
>
> Then answered the priest, with the governor and the king, saying: ". . . We will write to the sacred Roman senate in such wise that by imperial decree none shall any more call thee God or son of God. . . ."
>
> Then said the priest: "How shall the Messiah be called, and what sign shall reveal his coming?"
>
> Jesus answered: "The name of the Messiah is admirable, for God himself gave him the name when he had created his soul, and placed it in a celestial splendour. God said: 'Wait Mohammed; for thy sake I will to create paradise, the world, and a great multitude of creatures, whereof I make thee a present, insomuch that whoso shall bless thee shall be blessed, and whoso shall curse thee shall be accursed. When I shall send thee into the world I shall send thee as my messenger of salvation, and thy word shall be true, insomuch that heaven and earth shall fail, but thy faith shall never fail.' Mohammad is his blessed name."
>
> Then the crowd lifted up their voices, saying: "O God, send us thy messenger: O Mohammed, come quickly for the salvation of the world!"[55]

These testimonies of Jesus in Barnabas contradict explicit statements of the Qur᾿ān about the identity of Jesus. According to the Qur᾿ān, the Messiah is ʿĪsā ibn Maryam.

> The angels said: "Mary, God gives you news of a Word from Him, whose name will be the Messiah (*al-masīḥ*), Jesus, son of Mary; who will be held in honor who will be one of those brought near to God." (*Family of Imran* [3]:45)[56]

Other passages where Jesus is named the Messiah include *Women* [4]:171; *Table* [5]:72; and [5]:75.

54. Ibid., 96/101b-102b.

55. Ibid., 97/102b-103b.

56. M. A. S. Abdel Haleem translation (*The Qur'an*, trans. M. A. S. Abdel Haleem, Oxford World's Classics [Oxford/New York: Oxford University Press, 2005]).

The second contradiction between Barnabas and the Qur'ān relates to the role of Jesus. Jesus prepares the way for the Messiah in Barnabas, whereas the Qur'ān ascribes that role to John the Baptist, Yaḥyā ibn Zakarīyā, who confirms Jesus among the people and announces his coming. In answer to Zechariah's request for an heir, God addresses him directly: "O Zakariya! We give thee good news of a son: His name shall be Yahya: On none by that name have We conferred distinction before" (*Maryam* [19]:7). Barnabas completely ignores John the Baptist.

The mission of John is clearer in a passage from a portion of the *sūrah Family of Imran* [3] that shows Zechariah again beseeching his Lord for an heir.

> There did Zakariya pray to his Lord, saying: "O my Lord! Grant unto me from Thee a progeny that is pure: For Thou art He that heareth prayer!" While he was standing in prayer in the chamber, the angels called unto him: "Allah doth give thee glad tidings of Yahya, witnessing [*muṣaddiqan*] the truth of a Word from Allah, and (be besides) noble, chaste, and a Prophet—of the (goodly) company of the righteous." (*Family of Imran* [3]:38-39)

The absence of any mention of John the Baptist in Barnabas could hardly be accidental, because his role as forerunner has been so clearly taken by Jesus: "[Jesus said:] 'Unworthy though I am to untie his hosen, I have received grace and mercy from God to see him.'"[57]

We turn now to our final evidence that Barnabas is not the work of the Apostle Barnabas of the New Testament.

Silence on Barnabas in the *Sunnah* of the Prophet

In spite of the many parallels with the Gospels and other Christian literature of the earliest period in the *Sunnah* of Muḥammad, we find no mention anywhere of a Gospel of Barnabas. In fact, no citations distinctly from Barnabas turn up in the sources of the Prophet's *Sunnah*. That the *Sunnah* affirms Jesus as only human and not divine needs no documentation here. That the Qur'ānic commentaries and the Prophetic Tradition deny that Jesus was killed and crucified is similarly quite obvious, although, as we have seen, some dissonance exists among the interpretive traditions adduced by Muḥammad ibn Jarīr al-Ṭabarī. But I know of nothing distinctive about Barnabas found among them.

The Jesus of Barnabas knows a startling amount of information about Muḥammad's identity and mission long before the Seal of the Prophets appeared on the scene. Yet the massive storehouse of Muḥammad's deeds and sayings

57. GB, 97/102b. See Mark 1:7; see also GB, 72/74a and GB, 82/85b.

evidences nothing about the very source that reports the amazing foreknowledge of the one who heralded his coming.

In other words, Glassé, whom we mention above, is correct in his conclusion that Barnabas comes not from the first century East but from the medieval West. We turn now to the prevalence of a belief in Jesus' death and resurrection in the earliest Christian communities of faith.

7

Did Early Christians in Egypt and Syria Deny the Crucifixion of Jesus?

Several Muslim commentators on the Qurʾān and other apologists have claimed that early Christians in Syria and Egypt believed that Jesus was not crucified; and, because these Syrians and Egyptians were closer to the events of Jesus' life and mission than the churches founded by the Apostle Paul in the West, they had a better understanding of what really happened at the end of Jesus' mission. In this chapter I respond to these claims by studying the lost Christianity that Qurʾān exegetes cite to support them. Then in the second half of the chapter, I look at the earliest churches the Apostle Paul did *not* found—at Jerusalem, Antioch, Rome, and Alexandria—to show that they did believe Jesus was crucified.

According to al-Qāsimī in the commentary we followed closely in chapter 5 above, history shows that the issue of the crucifixion emerges as among the most important questions giving birth to division and hostility among Christians in general and among the first generations of Christians in Egypt and Syria in particular. Christians denied solidly the occurrence of the crucifixion because some of them thought it disgraced Christ and compromised his honor. Others denied it based on historical evidence. Some of the many sects denying the crucifixion include the followers of Saturninus, the Marcionites, Docetists, followers of Bardesanes, Tatianites, followers of Carpocrates, followers of Mani, and the Valentinians. Along with many others, none of these sects could accept in any way that Christ was actually nailed to or died on the cross. Accordingly, they attached no importance to the cross and the crucifixion. Some esteemed historians say the differences occurring among the Christians in the beginning on the matter of the crucifixion resulted in the abandonment of most of these sects by the members, their scattering, and their being considered, in the opinion of others, apostates from the faith. Nevertheless, the ideas of these persecuted and oppressed sects were congruent with Christian sources both in content and in transmission.[1]

1. Muḥammad Jamāl al-Dīn al-Qāsimī, *Tafsīr al-Qāsimī: al-musammā bi-maḥāsin al-taʾwīl*, ed. Muḥammad Fuʾād ʿAbd al-Bāqī, 17 vols. (Cairo: Dār iḥyāʾ al-kutub al-ʿArabīyah/ʿĪsā al-Bābī al-Ḥalabī wa-shurakāʾ-hu, 1957), 5:1691-92. He also mentions the Bārskālyūniyūn and the Būlīsiyūn, whom I have been unable to identify.

Muḥammad ʿIzzat Darwazah also makes much of sects of Christians who have rejected the crucifixion. He believes that *Table* [5]:82-83 identifies these Christians:

> The nearest . . . [people] in love to the Believers wilt thou find those who say, "We are Christians": Because amongst these are men devoted to learning and men who have renounced the world, and they are not arrogant. And when they listen to the revelation received by the Apostle, thou wilt see their eyes overflowing with tears, for they recognize the truth: They pray: "Our Lord! We believe; write us down among the witnesses."

He cites Muḥammad Rashīd Riḍā who mentions, in addition to some groups Qāsimī mentions, a Photius, who reports reading in a book featuring the journeys of Peter, John, Andrew, Thomas, and Paul that someone else was crucified in the Messiah's place. He also cites a second-century Christian monk, Ībūn, who claimed, "The Messiah was born from Joseph and the Virgin and we do not know when and how his life was ended."[2]

Qāsimī references the European Éduard Sayous, a member of the French Institute in Paris, who affirms that some sects of Christianity, among them the followers of Basilides, held that, while going to the place of crucifixion, Jesus and Simon the Cyrene were made to look like each other. Jesus then hid himself to laugh in derision over his misguided persecutors. Among these Christian sects, the Cerinthians (al-Sīrintiyūn) held that one of the Apostles was crucified in the place of Jesus.[3]

Given the presence of these sects arguing against the crucifixion, Qāsimī concludes that to claim a Christian consensus for the crucifixion of Jesus turns out to be untenable.

A Look at the Christians Cited by Qāsimī and Riḍā

Several lines of dialogue might be followed in responding to this conclusion. After I respond to the specific claims that Qāsimī and Riḍā have laid out, I will show that witnesses to the crucifixion of Jesus originating in Palestine and Syria preceded any dispute about whether Jesus was the one who died on the cross. But first it may be helpful to distinguish between those, like the writer of the Gospel of Barnabas, who hold that someone other than Jesus was crucified in his place, and those who believed that Jesus or the Christ only *seemed* to be suffer-

2. Muḥammad ʿIzzat Darwazah, *Al-tafsīr al-ḥadīth: Tartīb al-suwar ḥasab al-nuzūl*, 10 vols., 2nd ed. (Beirūt: Dar al-Gharb al-Islāmī, 2001), 8:274-75.

3. Qāsimī, *Tafsīr*, 5:1692. The work cited by Qāsimī is Éduard Sayous, *Jésus-Christ d'après Mahomet: Notions et les doctrines musulmane sur le Christianisme* (Paris: Leroux; Leipzig: Schulze, 1880), 49.

ing and dying on the cross. The latter position can be called *gnostic* or *docetic*: Christ only *appeared* to be human; or he only *seemed* to be crucified; or Jesus was crucified, but only after the spirit of the Christ had departed from him.

Jewish and Aramaic Christianity

Cerinthus was an early-second-century Jewish Christian from Asia.[4] We know his influence only through Christian apologists such as Irenaeus (d. 202) and Hippolytus (d. 236). Cerinthus emphasizes the law strongly, and requires circumcision and Sabbath observance. According to him, Jesus was "a man upon whom the Christ descended at baptism and departed before the cross."[5] Since Cerinthus and his followers used the same Gospel that the Ebionites (see below) used, a "truncated version of Matthew,"[6] apparently containing the passion narrative, and since no one seems to have recorded that the Cerinthians rejected the death of Jesus, we should be justified in concluding that Cerinthus believed Jesus was crucified, *but not while he was still the Christ.*[7] Among the things modern historians can dig up, none suggests that the Cerinthians rejected the death of Jesus in favor of a substitute. According to Hippolytus, Cerinthus taught that Jesus will be resurrected on the day of resurrection.[8] If he did not die, how will he be resurrected in the last days?

Ebionites. The Christian monk whom Riḍā referred to as Ībūn probably refers to Ebion, the supposed founder of the Ebionites. The name "Ebion" comes from the Hebrew word for "the poor" and therefore does not refer to the person upon whose teachings the Ebionites relied. All our knowledge of the Ebionites comes from the pens of those who wrote against them, and what

---

4. Donald A. Hagner, "Jewish Christianity," in Ralph P. Martin and Peter H. Davids, eds., *Dictionary of the Later New Testament and Its Development* (Downers Grove, IL/Leicester: InterVarsity, 1997), 584.

5. Ibid.

6. Henri-Charles Puech and Beate Blatz, "Other Gnostic Gospels and Related Literature," in Wilhelm Schneemelcher, ed., *New Testament Apocrypha*, 2 vols.; vol. 1, *Gospels and Related Writings,* rev. ed., trans. R. McLane Wilson (Cambridge: James Clarke/Louisville, KY: Westminster John Knox, 1991), 1:397.

7. Jean Daniélou, *A History of Early Christian Doctrine*, 3 vols., vol. 1, *The Theology of Jewish Christianity,* 3 vols. (London: Darton, Longman, & Todd, 1964), 1:68-69.

8. Louis Duchesne, *Early History of the Christian Church from Its Foundation to the End of the Fifth Century*, 4th ed. (London: John Murray, 1957 [1905], 58 n. 1. This must be the "one report," mentioned by Robert M. Grant, that "Christ died at the crucifixion, but he has not yet risen" (Grant, *Gnosticism and Early Christianity* [New York: Columbia University Press, 1959], 98). Abbé Duchesne comments in this same note, "This improbable statement of his tenets is contradicted by Irenaeus." What Irenaeus contradicts, however, is the claim that Cerinthus rejected the resurrection: "But at last Christ departed from Jesus, and . . . then Jesus suffered and rose again, while Christ remained impassible, inasmuch as he was a spiritual being" (*Against Heresies* 26.1; Alexander Roberts and James Donaldson, eds., rev. and annotated by A. Cleveland Cox, *The Ante-Nicene Fathers: Translations of the Writings of the Fathers Down to A.D. 325* [American reprint of the Edinburgh edition], vol. 1, *The Apostolic Fathers—Justin Martyr—Irenaeus* [Edinburgh: T&T Clark/Grand Rapids: Eerdmans, 1989], 352).

the several pens wrote does not cohere completely.[9] Irenaeus first mentions this group among the Jewish Christians. They took strong opposition to the Apostle Paul's attitude toward the law and followed the law themselves. They believed in God's creation of the world and held the same opinions about Jesus as the Cerinthians. Tertullian (d. 225?) says Ebion was the successor to Cerinthus, who denied the virginal conception of Jesus and taught that he was a prophet, Son of God, and elected Messiah through the descent of the dove—but not God.

According to Riḍā, Ebion was uncertain about the death of Jesus. The fragments of the Gospel of the Ebionites (dated to the beginning of the second century) that Epiphanius (315-403) preserves contain a snippet from the preparation for the Last Supper. After pointing this out, Phillip Vielhauer and Georg Strecker speculate that the Gospel probably also contained "a history of the passion and Easter, about which, however, we know nothing in detail."[10]

If it were known that the Ebionites denied the passion of Jesus, could Vielhauer and Strecker possibly have speculated thus? The fact that Felix Scheidweiler can entertain the possibility that an Ebionite authored the Acts of Pilate suggests that Ebionites did not reject the crucifixion of Jesus, since the Acts of Pilate adheres closely to the resurrection and ascension as depicted in the Gospel of Matthew.[11] Bart Ehrman, in connection with stressing that Ebionites believed God adopted Jesus as son because he alone kept the Jewish law perfectly, states explicitly, "God . . . assigned to him a special mission, to sacrifice himself for the sake of others. Jesus then went to the cross, not as a punishment for his own sins but for the sins of the world. . . . As a sign of his acceptance of Jesus' sacrifice, God then raised Jesus from the dead and exalted him to heaven."[12]

Tatian (d. after 173) was born in Syriac-speaking territory. After extensive wanderings he encountered the scriptures and converted to Christianity in Rome. Justin Martyr (d. ca. 165) mentored him. He is well known for having created a harmony of the Gospels called the *Diatessaron* and an eloquent treatise, *Oration to the Greeks*. While his opposition to marriage and eschewing of meat reminds one of Gnosticism, and while one finds traces of Gnosticism in the *Oration*, the only traces of it in the *Diatessaron* are those already present in the canonical Gospels. Given the fact that the twelfth and last chapter of his harmony covers Gethsemane, the trials, the crucifixion, and the resurrection of Jesus, it seems unlikely that he proceeded according to the motivations Qāsimī attributes to him.

The fact that no doubt can legitimately be raised against the *Diatessaron*

---

9. Bart D. Ehrman, *Lost Christianities: The Battle for Scripture and the Faiths We Never Knew* (Oxford: Oxford University Press, 2003), 100.

10. Phillip Vielhauer and Georg Strecker, "Jewish-Christian Gospels," in Schneemelcher, ed., *New Testament Apocrypha*, 1:167.

11. Felix Scheidweiler, "The Gospel of Nicodemus, Acts of Pilate, and Christ's Descent into Hell," in Schneemelcher, ed., *New Testament Apocrypha*, 1:503.

12. Ehrman, *Lost Christianities*, 101. See also David F. Wright, "Ebionites," in Martin and Davids, eds., *Dictionary of the Later New Testament*, 313-17; Daniélou, *History of Early Christian Doctrine*, 55-64; and Schneemelcher, ed., *New Testament Apocrypha*, 1:135-41, 152, 166-71.

(which means a harmony of four) being a harmony of the four canonical Christian Gospels[13] suggests that Tatian cannot be cited as a person testifying to the view of the end of Jesus' mission espoused by the exegetes of the Qurʾān cited above. Tatian did separate himself from the orthodox church, inclining even more toward asceticism, and, according to Franco Bogiani, of the University of Turin, became virtually a Gnostic.[14] No one, however, says he rejected the crucifixion of Jesus, and even if he did, his position would not support the allegation that Christians with greater access to the events at the end of Jesus' mission rejected the crucifixion of Jesus.

Marcion (d. ca. 160), a native of Sinope, a port on the Black Sea, after a falling out with his father, a Christian bishop, went to Rome as a Christian in 139 or 140 where he met a Gnostic teacher whose ideas he ended up enhancing and promulgating. When he expounded his views to the leaders of the church in Rome, he was excommunicated. His views became very popular, but they did not stem from a historical conviction that the crucifixion did not take place, or because he thought the cross was shameful. His reasons were theological.

He distinguished between the inferior Creator of the Hebrew Bible and the Supreme God of the New Testament. Since the earthly body is evil and cannot be a fit dwelling place for the divine, Jesus could not have had a real human body. Marcion accepted, however, his version of the teachings of Paul and rejected all the New Testament books except an expurgated Gospel of Luke and ten expurgated letters of Paul.[15] He did not deny the death of Christ but taught that Christ's blood was the necessary purchase price for freeing humans from their allegiance to the Creator.[16] According to Marcion, Jesus—as Paul had written—came "in the likeness of sinful flesh" (Romans 8:3) and "paid the penalty for other people's sins by dying on the cross."[17] How Marcion could believe a person who is not really flesh and blood could die and shed redemptive blood remains a mystery. What we do know is that he cannot be counted among the Christians who did not believe in the crucifixion of Jesus.

Bardaisan, or Bardesanes (d. ca. 222), a philosopher and poet from Edessa, a city near the Euphrates River in what is now southeastern Turkey, was born and raised in the traditional religion of his area but converted to Christianity at a young age and even wrote in opposition to heretics.[18] A strophe of one of his hymns,

---

13. J. Hamlyn Hill, "Introduction," in J. Hamlyn Hill, ed., *The Earliest Life of Christ Ever Compiled from the Four Gospels: Being the Diatessaron of Tatian (circ. A.D. 160) Literally Translated from the Arabic Version and Containing the Four Gospels Woven into One Story* (Edinburgh: T&T Clark, 1894), 22.

14. Franco Bolgiani, "Tatian," in Angelo Di Berardino, ed., *Encyclopedia of the Early Church*, trans. Adrian Walford, with a foreword and bibliographic amendments by W. H. C. Frend, 2 vols. (Cambridge: James Clarke, 1992), 2:815.

15. Schneemelcher, ed., *New Testament Apocrypha*, 1:23.

16. E. C. Blackman, *Marcion and His Influence* (London: SPCK, 1948), 101-2.

17. Ehrman, *Lost Christianities*, 105.

18. René Lavenant, "Bardesanes," in Di Berardino, ed., *Encyclopedia of the Early Church*, 1:110.

preserved by Ephrem Syrus (d. 373), contains the triad Father, Mother, and Son, represented by the symbol of a fish, although the fish could also symbolize the fertility of the Mother.[19] He lauded the Father, Mother, and Son of Life in his poetry in which the sun symbolized the Father and the moon the Mother.[20] His commitment to the unrestricted positive value of the creation distinguished him from the Gnostics,[21] although his Christology was apparently docetic.[22] At the same time, his position that the death and resurrection of Christ are not really necessary for the justification of humans at the final judgment distinguished him from orthodoxy. Nevertheless, he considered himself a Christian.[23]

His doctrine of creation involves the cross. Christ is the pure thought or *Logos* that descends at the command of the All-highest when the pure elements of the cosmos complain about the negative effects of darkness mingling with them. The Christ then separates the darkness from the good elements, but with only partial success. From the remaining mixture—"after ordering the elements according to the mystery of the Cross"—he creates the world. The cross represents the principle of bringing order out of chaos, beginning with creation.[24] No evidence suggests he taught that Jesus did not die on a cross.

Mani (d. 277), the Apostle of Babylon, of Iranian ethnicity from Ctesiphon in Mesopotamia, grew up among a variety of religious traditions. He learned from a group of Jewish-Christian baptists, called al-Mughtasilūn by the Muslim scholar al-Nadīm (d. 988). This movement, founded by a Jewish Christian that Nadīm called al-Khasayh or Elkesai (fl. 100), has been identified as the Elkesaites mentioned by some of the apostolic fathers.[25] Elkesaism draws heavily from the Ebionites but is influenced by orthodox Christian teaching. Jean Daniélou says that Elkesaism's "heresy lies in the fact that it regarded Jesus as a mere prophet."[26] This heterodox sect of Jewish Christianity, however, did not reject the death of Jesus.

Mani's father had evidently been converted to Elkesaism about the time

---

19. H. J. W. Drijvers, *Bardaisan of Edessa*, Studia Semitica Nederlandica 6 (Assen: Van Gorcum, 1966), 140-41, 151; and idem, *Cults and Beliefs at Edessa*, Études préliminaires aux religions orientales dans l'Empire romain 82 (Leiden: Brill, 1980), 79.

20. Ibid., 157-58.

21. Drijvers identifies the elements in Bardaisan that distinguish him from the Gnostic paradigm (*Bardaisan*, 223-24).

22. Ibid., 183. "Docetic" (from the Greek: *dokeō*) means Jesus "seemed" or "appeared" to be fully human.

23. Albrecht Dihle, "Zur Schicksallehre des Bardesanes," in Adolf Martin Ritter, ed., *Kerygma und Logos, Beiträge zu den geistesgeschichtlichen Beziehungen zwischen Antike und Christentum: Festschrift für Carl Andresen zum 70. Geburtstag* (Göttingen: Vandenhoeck & Ruprecht, 1979), 124-25.

24. Dijvers, *Bardaisan*, 110, including n. 1. This represents, however, only one of several not-always-consistent traditions reporting the cosmology of Bardaisan, and it is the only reference to the cross in the whole of Drijvers's book.

25. Eusebius (*History*, 6:38) calls him Helkesai (Eusebius, bishop of Caesarea, *The Ecclesiastical History and the Martyrs of Palestine*, trans. Hugh Jackson Lawlor and John Ernest Leonard Oulton, 2 vols. [London: SPCK, 1954], 1:204).

26. Daniélou, *History of Early Christian Doctrine*, 1:67.

Mani was conceived. Iranian Gnosticism also had a profound effect on Mani, along with the teachings of two Syrian Gnostics, Marcion and Bardaisan of Edessa (d. 222). Mani, born in 216, began his public ministry as a prophet at the age of twenty-five. His teachings spread widely, aided by the journeys he made to disseminate them. He primarily covered the territory to the east of Mesopotamia, extending into India. The support of the Parthian ruler Shapur I contributed to his success. In fact, when this political protection dissolved, the Zoroastrian priests managed to get him killed.[27]

In brief, Mani taught a form of dualism: darkness, a spiritual kingdom, opposed light. God, who is over the realm of light, is radiant with love. Darkness, on the other hand, comprises an impersonal force or kingdom. Satan, an emanation from darkness, created humankind, packing them with rays of light. In this way he sought to control the light. Life then consists of a struggle between the influences of demons that try to bind humans to darkness through sensuality and false religion—the religion of Moses and the prophets being the worst. The spirits of light try to save humans by imparting an esoteric knowledge (*gnosis*) about nature and its forces and by drawing humans away from darkness and sensuality. God also sends prophets to proclaim this knowledge. Mani is the final and superior prophet.

Jesus—though not the historical Jesus—was accounted a prophet, but also a phantom incapable of suffering and death. Mani, then, is hardly an example of early Christians who did not believe it was Jesus who was crucified. He was, after all, a figure of the late-second and early-third century.

Leucius Charinus. As we saw above, Riḍā appeals to a report of Photius (patriarch of Constantinople 858-867 and 877-886), who read a book called *The Journeys of the Apostles*, which contained the Acts of five Apostles, one of whom taught that someone was crucified in Christ's place. As the book itself makes clear, Leucius Charinus (or Carinus), otherwise unknown, is its author.[28] Knut Schäferdiek, who identifies this book as Manichaean, quotes the long passage from Photius describing it. Among other things, Photius reports that the book claims "it was not Christ that was crucified, but another in his place, and that for this reason he derided those who crucified him."[29] Photius apparently refers to the Acts of John §97-§102, where Jesus appears to John in a cave on the Mount of Olives and explains to him,

> This Cross . . . is not that wooden Cross which you will see when you go down from here; nor am I the (man) who is on the Cross, (I) whom now you do not see but only hear (my) voice. I was taken to be what I

27. Gherardo Gnoli ("Mani," in Mircea Eliade et al., eds., *Encyclopedia of Religion*, 16 vols. [Chicago, IL: Macmillan, 1987], 9:160) and Duchesne (*The Early History*, 1:405) disagree over the manner of death.

28. Knut Schäferdiek, "The Manichaean Collection of Aprocryphal Acts Ascribed to Leucius Charinus," in Schneemelcher, ed., *New Testament Apocrypha*, 2:87.

29. Ibid.

> am not, I who am not what for the many I am; but what they will say of me is mean and unworthy of me. (§99)[30]

Schäferdiek's painstaking analysis of all the research connected with the *Journeys* and the five Acts they contain allows him to date the composition of the Acts of John in "the first half of the 3rd century . . . in the region of East Syria."[31]

Gnostics in Antioch and Egypt

Valentinus (fl. 120-160), a Greek and Christian Gnostic teacher born in the Nile Delta around the year 100 and schooled in Alexandria, moved to Rome and became a teacher of note (138-158).[32] He came close to being made a bishop there. His influence spread very widely, as illustrated by the influence of his school in the Gospel of Philip. Although the origin of this probably late-second-century composition cannot be discerned for certain, indications in it point to Syria.[33] He may have been the author of the Gospel of Truth found in the collection at Nag Hammadi in Egypt.[34]

In Rome he engaged in disputes with Justin Martyr, becoming known by even his detractors as brilliant and eloquent. His students came to represent the most prolific school of Gnostic teachers. Some of his followers wrote documents discovered in the now-famous Nag Hammadi collection, including possibly the Gospel of Philip.[35] Basilides was among Valentinus's most accomplished students. Through the teaching of these two men, Gnostic Christianity gained a strong influence in Egypt, especially in Alexandria.[36]

---

30. Knut Schäferdiek, "Acts of John," in Schneemelcher, ed., *New Testament Apocrypha*, 2:185. In this passage, John laughs at the crowd. *The Second Treatise* (Logos) *of the Great Seth* and the Nag Hammadi *Apocalypse of Peter* (NHC VII 3:81:3-82:32, in Birger A. Pearson, ed., *Nag Hammadi Codex VII*, Coptic Gnostic Library [Leiden/New York/Cologne: Brill, 1996], 241-45) feature Jesus laughing at his crucifiers because they were nailing another man to the cross (Schäferdiek, "Manichean Collection," 2:95).

31. Schäferdiek, "Acts of John," 2:167.

32. Hans Martin Schenke, "The Gospel of Philip," in Schneemelcher, ed., *New Testament Apocrypha*, 1:182.

33. Ibid., 1:183.

34. Nag Hammadi Codex I, 3, "The Gospel of Truth," ed. and trans. Harold W. Attridge and George W. MacRae, S.J., in Harold W. Attridge, ed., *Nag Hammadi Codex I (The Jung Codex): Introductions, Texts, Translations, Indices*, Coptic Gnostic Library, Nag Hammadi Studies 22 (Leiden: Brill, 1985), 55-122.

35. Pheme Perkins, "Gnosticism," in Everett Ferguson et al., *Encyclopedia of Early Christianity* (New York/London: Garland, 1990), 373. For example, the Gospel of Philip teaches that this Mary, a "virgin whom the powers did not defile," was childless. This is exactly parallel to Valentinus's statement that "Christ passed without contact through the virgin womb 'like water through a pipe'" (Wolfgang A. Biener, "The Relatives of Jesus," in Schneemelcher, ed., *New Testament Apocrypha*, 1:481).

36. James E. Goehring, "Egypt," in Ferguson et al., eds., *Encyclopedia of Early Christianity*, 292.

According to Valentinus, before the creation, the divine reality included a *pleroma* (Greek: *plērōma*, "fullness"), consisting of a male-female duality he called "Depth" and "Silence." The ultimate Father and unknown God consists of "the transcendental unity of Depth and Silence."[37] From these two emanates a second duality and from them a further quartet. An additional eleven pairs of male-female aeons (Greek sing.: *aiōn,* "power") emanate from the first Ogdoad or eightfold structure. The Ogdoad and the eleven pairs together make up the thirty aeons of the *pleroma*. Valentinus considered the aeons "thoughts, feelings and emotions of the divine." Ptolemy, his student, considered the aeons "personalized substances, characterized independently of God."[38] The last aeon of the *pleroma,* Sophia (Wisdom), revolts, being filled with desire. And from her error or fall, the whole of the creation, including the Demiurge, or Creator, the Elohim, and YHWH of Genesis in the Torah, comes into being.

Christ the male aeon counterpart of Sophia, left unpaired within the *pleroma* by her fall, comes to her rescue. Since the fall of Sophia has resulted in humans coming into being as a mixture of spirit (Greek: *pneuma*) and soul (Greek: *psychē*) trapped in flesh, this heavenly Christ comes as the savior Jesus to teach humans how to "ascend to their true home above."[39] Valentinus referred to the savior as the bridegroom of the lower Sophia and believed that Christ revealed the ultimate but unknown God.

Harold W. Attridge and George W. MacRae, S.J., in introducing the Gospel of Truth, mentioned above, conclude that the supposition that Valentinus composed the document is compatible with the evidence from the underlying theological system and from a comparison with the fragments of Valentinus's known writings.[40] If this is the case, it means that what we have outlined above pertains more to the school Valentinus gave birth to than to his own theological system. For one thing, his system is more monotheistic than the works of the later Valentinians.[41] The Christology of the Gospel of Truth—given the fact that it is a Gnostic writing—strikes one as surprisingly close to that of the canonical Gospels, especially when it comes to the end of Jesus' mission. While the relationship of the Son to Jesus Christ defies exact definition, Jesus' mission of saving revelation through teaching certainly participates in the divine plan (19:19-20:5). Although Jesus was persecuted by Error (18:22-23), was crucified

37. Gilles Quispel, "Gnosticism from Its Origins to the Middle Ages," in Eliade et al., eds., *Encyclopedia of Religion*, 5:571-72.

38. Jean Pepin, "Logos," trans. Denis O'Brien, in Eliade et al., eds., *Encyclopedia of Religion*, 9:10.

39. Karen L. King, "Valentinus," in Ferguson et al., eds., *Encyclopedia of Early Christianity*, 923.

40. Attridge and MacRae, "The Gospel of Truth: Introduction," 76.

41. Ibid., 79. Kendrick Grobel sees the differences as more dramatic and calls for a revision of our understanding of the teachings of Valentinus (*The Gospel of Truth: A Valentinian Meditation on the Gospel: Translation from the Coptic and Commentary* [London: Adam & Charles Black, 1960], 7-31).

(18:25; 20:25), and died (20:11), these events seem not to have involved the Son, whose mission is restricted to the transcendent realms.[42]

Although Valentinus and his successors clearly were Gnostics, or Gnostic Christians, none of them seems to have denied the cross. Not only do I not find such claims made by Christian apologists, but I find no reference to such a rejection, or a teaching such as that of Basilides, the *Treatise of the Great Seth*, and *The Journeys of the Apostles*. As in the Gospel of Truth, the Jesus who died there may not have been the *Logos* or Son at the point of his death; but a denial of the death of Jesus does not play a role in the Gospel of Truth: "Jesus . . . was nailed to a tree; he published the edict of the Father on the cross. O such great teaching! He draws himself down to death though life eternal clothes him."[43]

Saturninus, or Satornilus (fl. ca. 120 or 150), a contemporary of Basilides and native of Antioch, was a disciple of Menander of Samaria, who taught at Antioch. Saturninus held that the God of the Jews was evil; that angels created humankind—some good and some bad; and that God finished creating them. According to Saturninus, bad angels support the bad people and good angels, the good. Saturninus held that Jesus taught abstention from marriage and that bearing children comes from Satan, who is essentially the Creator God of the Jews. The Christians were wrong about Jesus' being "the word become flesh." Rather "the Savior was actually unbegotten, incorporeal, and formless."[44] The cross of Jesus has no place in his theological system, but he did not focus on denying the crucifixion.

Basilides, presumably from Syria, was active as a teacher and leader in Alexandria from ca. 117 to ca. 160. The Basilideans, according to Clement of Alexandria (d. 215), claimed that their teaching went back to the Apostle Matthias (Acts 1:15-26). A certain Glaucius, Peter's interpreter, taught Matthias. Understanding the full teaching of Basilides must be incomplete because the several Christian heresiographers on whom we must depend for our knowledge differ in their descriptions.[45] Typical docetic/Gnostic features turn up in Basilides' Christology, as summarized by Irenaeus.

The *Nous* (Greek: *nous*, "mind") of the unborn Father and the one called Christ appeared on earth in the person of Jesus to deliver those who believed in him. He did not suffer death, but rather authorities compelled Simon of Cyrene to carry his cross. Jesus grasped this opportunity to transform himself to look like Simon and Simon to look like him. The Romans then crucified Simon, people thinking he was Jesus. Jesus, on his part, stood by laughing.[46]

42. Attridge and MacRae, "Gospel of Truth," 75, 87-88.

43. *Gospel of Truth*, 20:20-30a.

44. Grant, *Gnosticism and Early Christianity*, 106.

45. Adele Monaci Castagno, "Basilides, Basilideans," in Di Berardino, ed., *Encyclopedia of the Early Church*, 1:113. The passage in Clement is *Miscellanies* 3.1. See also Roberts and Donaldson, eds., *Ante-Nicene Fathers*, vol. 2, *Fathers of the Second Century*, 381-82.

46. This view of the cross shows up also in the Nag Hammadi Gnostic text *The Second Treatise of the Great Seth*, 55:1-56:34; and in *The Apocalypse of Peter*, 81:3-82:32 (Pearson, ed., *Nag Hammadi Codex VII*, 137, 163-67). Gregory Riley dates *Treat. Seth* in the latter half of the second

The *Nous* was the firstborn of the unborn Father. From him came a series of emanations, which resulted in angels who occupy the lowest heaven. It was these angels who created the world; the chief of these angels is the one thought to be the God of the Jews. Those who know that the Christ was the *Nous* and that he was not crucified are "acquainted with the dispensation of the unborn Father."[47] The fact that Irenaeus here states explicitly that Basilides held a substitutionist view of the crucifixion supports the assumption that Irenaeus would have mentioned it if any of the others he discussed had believed someone was substituted for Jesus on the cross.

Carpocrates (fl. first half of the second century), a Platonic and Gnostic interpreter of Christianity from Alexandria, maintained the world was created by angels who were considerably inferior to the true God. Jesus, according to him, was born in a natural way the son of Joseph; but his soul was pure, and he was endowed from on high with the ability to recall his past lives. He was given the power to return to the true God. The soul of Jesus renounced the practices of Judaism in which he was raised. He was able to destroy in himself those typical human passions that are the result of sin.[48] His followers overcame these human passions by experiencing them.[49] They thus developed a reputation for loose morals. Jesus gave his true teachings to his disciples secretly, according to the Carpocratians. Irenaeus, who "provides the only account of Carpocratian theology which can pretend to reliability,"[50] has only this to say about Carpocratian teaching about the life of Jesus.

> Jesus was the son of Joseph, and was just like other men, with the exception that he differed from them in this respect, that inasmuch as his soul was steadfast and pure, he perfectly remembered those things which he had witnessed within the sphere of the unbegotten God.[51] On this account, a power descended upon him from the Father, that by means of it he might escape from the creators of the world;[52] and they say that it, after passing through them all, and remaining in all points

century, probably composed in Alexandria—definitely originally in Greek ("Second Treatise of the Great Seth: Introduction," in Pearson, ed., *Nag Hammadi Codex VII,* 142). The Apocalypse of Peter could have been written in Greek in any Christian community between 150 and 250 ("Apocalypse of Peter: Introduction," in Pearson, ed., *Nag Hammadi Codex VII,* 214).

47. Irenaeus, *Against Heresies* 1.24.4.

48. Ibid., 1.25. Norbert Brox in a recent critical edition of this text suggests there have been doubts about the historicity of Carpocrates that cannot be completely assuaged (Irenäus von Lyon, *Adversus Haereses=Gegen die Häresien 1*, Fontes Christiani 8.1 [Freiburg: Herder, 1993], 1.307). Readers who understand Latin can see also Clement of Alexandria, *Miscellanies* 3.2 (Roberts and Donaldson, *Ante-Nicene Fathers*, vol. 2, *Fathers of the Second Century*, 382-83).

49. Grant, *Gnosticism and Early Christianity*, 95-96.

50. Morton Smith, *Clement of Alexandria and a Secret Gospel of Mark* (Cambridge, MA: Harvard University Press, 1973), 270.

51. That is, before he took on flesh for this incarnation.

52. That is, the angels who created the world.

> free, ascended again to him, and the powers, which in the same way embraced like things to itself.[53]

This is as close as the Carpocratians come to the position espoused by Qāsimī. In responding to Carpocrates, Irenaeus reports nothing about a substitutionary view of the crucifixion.

In summary, few of the individuals and their followers cited by the Muslim commentators on the Qur'ān *who taught that someone was substituted for Jesus on the cross* lived and taught closer in time and place to the events at the end of Jesus' mission than the writers of the New Testament Gospels. Furthermore, as we will see in the remainder of this chapter, the teaching about Jesus' saving death and resurrection cannot be attributed to the creativity of the Apostle Paul alone as Qāsimī alleges.[54]

Believers in the Cross at Centers of Christianity before Paul

In the aftermath of the end of Jesus' mission, Christianity spread rapidly from Jerusalem throughout the Mediterranean world. Six cities can be identified as key centers of the early Christian movement: Jerusalem, Antioch in Syria, Ephesus in Asia Minor, Corinth in Greece, Alexandria in Egypt, and Rome.[55] The Apostle Paul founded only the churches in Ephesus and Corinth. The discussion below of the non-Pauline churches in the other four principal cities will show that as far as can be discerned by disciplined historical methods, the earliest churches in these widely diverse cities taught that Jesus died and rose again. The Christians whom Saul of Tarsus sought to defeat before he became a believer in Jesus as the Messiah already believed in Jesus' death and resurrection.

The Jerusalem Believers

On the day of Pentecost, the church was inaugurated. The people who were gathered there to witness the first pouring out of the Holy Spirit and to hear Peter's sermon included "Parthians, Medes, Elamites, and residents of Mesopotamia, Judea and Cappadocia, Pontus and Asia, Phrygia and Pamphylia, Egypt and the parts of Libya belonging to Cyrene, and visitors from Rome, both Jews and proselytes, Cretans and Arabs" (Acts 2:9-11).

While Acts provides evidence for discerning the differences of opinion in

---

53. Irenaeus, *Against Heresies* 25.1.

54. Qāsimī, *Tafsīr*, 5:1700.

55. Clinton E. Arnold, "Centers of Christianity," in Martin and Davids, eds., *Dictionary of the Later New Testament and Its Developments*, 141-52.

the early church (Acts 5:37; 23:2), it gives no evidence that the death of Jesus was at all a point of controversy.[56] The early chapters of Acts provide insights into the Jerusalem church. And the speeches of this section help us discern the content of the message disseminated from Jerusalem.

The value of the speeches in the Acts of the Apostles for insights into the convictions of early Palestinian Jewish Christianity[57] prior to the conversion of the Apostle Paul (Acts 9) has been disputed. But what can be discerned reliably from them is that, while they contain no developed theology of the cross, Jesus is clearly presented as unjustly put to death and vindicated by God's raising him from the dead (e.g., Acts 3:15). According to Christopher Rowland, professor of exegesis of holy scripture at Oxford University, in these speeches "Jesus is spoken of in ways which have few parallels elsewhere in the New Testament."[58] This factor militates against the supposition that the author of Acts forges his history to support the Pauline church. While he supports the Christianity of Paul and emphasizes the unity of the church's witness, he does not do so by obscuring the tensions existing between what he supports and the facts on the ground. The death and resurrection of Jesus are affirmed in the early speeches. Furthermore, the records of the speeches of Peter and Stephen in Acts provide no evidence of the justification theology of the cross familiar to readers of Paul's letters. These speeches announce the age of fulfillment's arrival (2:16-21), lay out the life, death, and resurrection of Jesus (2:22-24), bring in evidence from the Hebrew scriptures to show he is the Messiah (2:25-28), and call their audience to repentance (2:37-41). Paul, speaking in the synagogue at Antioch in Pisidia, however, in addition to the basic outline just mentioned, offers in Christ remission of sins and justification (Acts 13:38-41). Clearly a community existed in Jerusalem that proclaimed the death and resurrection of Jesus before the wide influence of Paul.

Despite its prominence as the epicenter for the spread of the gospel to the ends of the earth,[59] Jerusalem was the place of writing of only the book of James, and possibly the Letter of Jude. This may be because the Romans destroyed the city not more than forty years after the end of Jesus' mission, and the Christians scattered, along with most of the other Jews.[60] Antioch may have contributed more to Christian faith and the literature that supported it than did Jerusalem.

---

56. Christopher Rowland, *Christian Origins: An Account of the Setting and Character of the Most Important Messianic Sect of Judaism*, 2nd ed. (London: SPCK, 2002), 75.

57. By this I mean Christians who were of Jewish identity. For a more complete discussion of types of Jewish Christianity, see Glen A. Koch, "Jewish Christianity," in Ferguson et al., eds., *Encyclopedia of Early Christianity*, 489; and Oskar Skarsaune and Reidar Hvalvik, eds., *Jewish Believers in Jesus: The Early Centuries* (Peabody, MA: Hendrickson, 2007), 3-15.

58. Rowland, *Christian Origins*, 195-96.

59. This expansion is nicely summarized by Howard Clark Kee, *Who Are the People of God? Early Christian Models of Community* (New Haven/London: Yale University Press, 1995), 192-207.

60. Arnold, "Centers of Christianity," 145.

The Church in Antioch

The second great city in the story of the early Christian church is Antioch on the Orontes river in what was then the Roman province of Syria and in what is now the modern state of Turkey, near the border of Syria. It was the third or fourth largest city in the Roman Empire with nearly half a million people, about forty thousand of whom were Jews. Many of the Christians at Antioch were Jewish Christians who were forced to leave the environs of Jerusalem in connection with the persecution associated with Stephen's martyrdom (Acts 7). But a great number of Gentiles also became disciples of Jesus there so that the movement gained a name as a separate sect. Luke puts it simply, "it was in Antioch that the disciples were first called 'Christians'" (Acts 11:26). Some of the leaders of the Antioch church there were from outside the region (Acts 13:1).

Raymond E. Brown (d. 1998) and John P. Meier, two prominent contemporary authorities on the New Testament, after surveying the broad range of possible sites for the composition of Matthew, conclude that Matthew reflects the circumstances of the church in Antioch between its early days when Paul and Barnabas were engaged in their missionary journeys (40-70; Galatians 2; Acts 11-15) and the circumstances that prevailed there when Ignatius (d. 117) wrote his corpus of letters (108-117).[61] Meier, who wrote the sections on Antioch for their book *Antioch and Rome*: *New Testament Cradles of Catholic Christianity*, dates "with a high degree of probability" the writing of Matthew to sometime during the years 80 through 100.[62] The tradition that Matthew's Gospel embodies "was shaped in Jewish Christianity."[63]

With hesitation, Meier includes the *Didache*[64] in his discussion of the church at Antioch because he sees its connection with the city as less clearly established than that of the Gospel of Matthew and the letters of Ignatius. The *Didache*, or the *Teachings of the Twelve Apostles*, was an instruction manual to prepare Gentile Christian converts for baptism.[65] In a very recent detailed study, however, Michelle Slee demonstrates to a high degree of probability that the *Didache* originated in Antioch at a time just prior to the Jewish War of 66-70. While significant passages parallel to the Gospel of Matthew are found in the

---

61. Raymond E. Brown and John P. Meier, *Antioch and Rome*: *New Testament Cradles of Catholic Christianity* (London: Geoffrey Chapman, 1983), 27. The letters of Ignatius that Brown and Meier consider authentic include those to the Ephesians, Magnesians, Trallians, Romans, Philadelphians, Smyrneans, and Polycarp.

62. Ibid., 81.

63. Raymond E. Brown, *The Churches the Apostles Left Behind* (New York: Paulist, 1984), 129.

64. The *Didache* is a handbook for Christian formation, giving instruction in ethics and church order.

65. *The Didache; The Epistle of Barnabas; The Epistles and the Martyrdom of St. Polycarp; The Fragments of Papias; The Epistle to Diognetus*, Ancient Christian Writers—the Works of the Fathers in Translation, newly translated and annotated by James A. Kleist, undated reprint (New York: Newman, 1948), 3-25, including Kleist's introduction.

Didache, they represent traditions earlier than the final composition of all three Synoptic Gospels.[66]

Slee shows how the *Didache* turns out to be a response to the controversy represented in Galatians 2 and Acts 15 about inclusion of Gentiles in the church. The issue revolves around table fellowship between believers of Jewish background and converts directly from a Gentile ethnic identity. This manual for preparation of Gentile converts is designed to provide them with ethical and communal readiness to share with Jewish Christians. The Gentiles are expected, however, to learn and obey Torah if they are to go on to perfection and to stand fully confident at the final judgment. No record of any controversy over the death or crucifixion of Jesus surfaces in the *Didache*. The Gospel of Matthew that comes into circulation at Antioch after the destruction of Jerusalem (70), that is, a decade or two after the *Didache*, shares in the intense focus on the cross prevailing throughout the Synoptic Gospels.

When we come to the third period of Meier's study of Antioch, the period at least a decade after the composition of the Gospel of Matthew, we find Meier looking at Antioch's Christian community through the lens of the genuine letters of Ignatius. By this period, the issue of belief in the cross can no longer be merely stated, ignored, or assumed.[67] By the beginning of the second century, some Christians are challenging the reality of the death of Jesus by crucifixion. These people participate in a *docetic* movement.[68] As already mentioned, this tendency, later developing into Gnostic Christianity, de-emphasizes the full humanity of Jesus, proposing that he only *seemed* or *appeared* to be human.

The cross of Christ is central to the teachings of both Acts and Galatians. It is also central to the teaching of the Gospel of Matthew and pervades the message of the letters of Ignatius (e.g., see the letter of Ignatius to the Ephesians, chapter 18). But for the recipients of Ignatius's letters the passion and death of Jesus had become a matter of dispute—as a spin-off of the rejection of Jesus' humanity. In his Letter to the Magnesians (chapter 9), Ignatius mentions that some deny Jesus' death.

The traditions that Jesus was crucified, died, and was buried, passed on by the Christian community at Antioch in Syria, were earlier than the traditions that Jesus only seemed to have died. If Antioch can speak for the Palestinian and Syrian churches in general, docetic claims that Jesus did not die surfaced only at the very end of the first century at the earliest.

The Church in Rome

By the end of the first Christian century, Rome was a major center of Christianity. Like Jerusalem, Antioch, and Alexandria, Rome had Christian communi-

---

66. Michelle Slee, *The Church in Antioch in the First Century CE: Communion and Conflict*, Journal for the Study of the New Testament Supplement Series 244 (London: Sheffield Academic Press, 2003), 75.

67. John P. Meier, "Part One: Antioch," in Brown and Meier, *Antioch and Rome*, 79.

68. See n. 22 above.

ties before the missionary activity of the Apostle Paul. No one knows for sure how followers of Jesus as the Messiah first established communities of faith in Rome. Possibly some of those from Rome who heard the gospel first while attending the festival of Pentecost in Jerusalem brought the message back home with them. Even before Christian times, direct relationships prevailed between the Jews of Rome and Jerusalem. This direct contact continued to characterize the relationship between Christian Jews in Rome and those in Jerusalem.

Jews in Rome during the period when Christianity got its start there numbered between forty and fifty thousand. Thirteen synagogues flowered in Trastevere, Rome's Jewish quarter.[69] In 49, during the reign of Claudius (41-54), the Jews were expelled from their quarter. The Roman historian Suetonius (70-140) attributes this punishment to the fact that "they were always making disturbances because of the instigator Chrestus."[70] Scholars agree that Chrestus refers to Christ. In any case, this expulsion of Jews must have thrown the leadership of the Roman church into the hands of Gentiles.

According to Raymond E. Brown, "the dominant form of Christianity at Rome in the 40s and early 50s was probably one close to Jerusalem and Judaism."[71] Paul writes in his letter to the church at Rome about the year 58, "I desire, as I have for many years, to come to you when I go to Spain" (15:24). He has already made the claim that the faith of the Roman church "is proclaimed throughout the world" (1:8). According to Acts 18:2-3, when Paul came to Corinth (49-50), he stayed with Aquila and Priscilla, Christian Jews probably expelled from Rome in connection with the expulsion of 49.[72] In other words, by 49, Christians had a significant-enough presence in the Jewish community to be able to cause a disturbance that reached the attention of the emperor.

Another indication of the Jewish roots of Christianity in Rome at the time Paul wrote surfaces in the fact that, because the Roman church had close connections with Jerusalem, Paul could appeal to them for aid to help the poor Christians in Jerusalem. As Brown puts it, "*The dominant Christianity at Rome had been shaped by the Jerusalem Christianity shaped by James and Peter. . . .*"[73] It is also clear from the Letter to the Romans that Paul had to reason his way into having his understanding of the Christian gospel heard in Rome. This much can be gained just from reading the letter. But Brown holds that Paul, writing to a largely Gentile Christian church in Rome but one sympathetic with the viewpoint prevailing in Jerusalem, hopes that he will set their minds at ease about his mission. Among other reasons, he wants the Christians in Rome to

---

69. Graydon F. Snyder, "Rome, Christian Monuments at," in David Noel Freedman et al., eds., *The Anchor Bible Dictionary*, 6 vols. (New York: Doubleday, 1992), 5:834.

70. Gaius Suetonius Tranquillus, *Lives of the Caesars*, book 5, *The Deified Caesars*, 25.4; cited in Robert E. Van Voorst, *Jesus Outside the New Testament: An Introduction to the Ancient Evidence* (Grand Rapids: Eerdmans, 2000), 30.

71. Brown and Meier, *Antioch and Rome*, 90.

72. Brown gives the argument for their being Christians in *Antioch and Rome*, 100.

73. Ibid., 110. Italics supplied by Brown.

support his self-defense in Jerusalem before Jewish Christians there.[74] He is very complimentary (1:7-8; 6:3-4; 15:14; 16:17); he carefully states his credentials (1:1, 14-15 [cf. Galatians 1:1]; 15:15-16, 20); and he uses diplomatic rhetoric (Greek: *parakalō*, "I appeal") (12:1; 15:30). Brown says a scholarly consensus holds that Paul states his summary of the gospel to the Roman Christians in typical Jewish Christian terms.

> In 1:3-4 he summarizes "the gospel of God" (1:1) to preach which he has been especially chosen: It is the gospel concerning God's Son "who was born of the seed of David according to the flesh, designated Son of God in power according to a Spirit of Holiness as of resurrection from the dead." Critical scholarship recognizes that here Romans is offering a Jewish Christian formulation of the gospel that would be familiar to the readers.[75]

In his effort to be as persuasive as possible in representing himself and his message to the Roman Christians, *Paul never needs to defend the fact that Jesus died on the cross.* It must be the case that the Christianity planted in Rome from the beginning believed that *it was Jesus who died on the cross.* In his letter to Rome Paul argues *from* the death and resurrection of Jesus not for or toward them.[76]

In Romans 1-5 Paul argues for the fact that, while the Jews have special advantages as God's chosen people, both Jews and Gentiles are one in being sinners who need the salvation God offers in the death and resurrection of his Messiah. In Romans 6-8 he argues that the Law is good in that it makes people aware of their sin, but that God's grace through the gift of the Holy Spirit accomplishes the righteousness the Law failed to deliver for those who followed it. In Romans 9 through 11, Paul deals with the question of why the Jews failed to accept the gospel if it is so effective. In Romans 12-15 he gives guidance for living the Christian life.

These are the issues Paul addresses. He does not address any issue related to whether or not Jesus was crucified. Rather, he *assumes the death of Jesus in all his argumentation.* For example, in Romans 4 he shows that Abraham was saved by faith before he was circumcised and before the Law was given through Moses. As the father of both Jews and Gentiles, he, like all Christians—Jew and Gentile—was saved by faith "in him who raised Jesus from the dead" (4:25; see also 6:1-4, 11, and 13). Paul concludes Romans 8 by stressing the adequacy of God in spite of all possible obstacles. He appeals to the death of Jesus as evidence for the degree to which God will support those who trust in Him: "He who did not withhold his own Son, but gave him up for all of us, will he

74. Ibid., 111.

75. Ibid., 117-18.

76. In 1 Corinthians 15, Paul argues for the resurrection of Jesus. He does not argue for the crucifixion of Jesus.

not with him also give us everything else?" (8:32). In offering a concluding section of guidance for living (12:1-15:13), Paul appeals to Christ's death as an example. In a passage where he is encouraging believers to be tolerant of other believers whose scruples over food differ from their own, he stresses their interdependence. Notice the appeal to the death and resurrection of Christ.

> We do not live to ourselves, and we do not die to ourselves. If we live, we live to the Lord, and if we die, we die to the Lord; so then, whether we live or whether we die, we are the Lord's. For to this end Christ died and lived again, so that he might be Lord of both the dead and the living. (14:7-9)

Further along in the passage, he identifies the brother or sister who differs with the implied readers as one for whom Christ died: "If your brother or sister is being injured by what you eat, you are no longer walking in love. Do not let what you eat cause the ruin of one for whom Christ died" (14:15). This designation supports the value of the brother or sister who might be hurt by open defiance of dietary scruples. Would such an appeal be made if even some of the receptors of the letter believed Christ had not died?

The Church in Alexandria

Jews from Alexandria, the most important city in Egypt, with a population of around half a million, and the second largest city in the Roman world, were present on the day of Pentecost (Acts 2:10). Alexandria could boast "the largest and most powerful Jewish settlement in the entire Greek-speaking world."[77] The Coptic (i.e., Egyptian) church accepts the hearsay report recorded by Eusebius that the evangelist Mark brought the gospel to Egypt. Eusebius cites a tradition that Mark was succeeded in ministry to the church in Alexandria by Annianus "while Nero was in his eighth year" (62).[78] A better-attested tradition, also recorded by Eusebius, has Mark being in Rome with Peter "in the days of Claudius" (41-54) where he later wrote his Gospel.[79] According to a fragment of a letter from Clement of Alexandria (150?-215?), Mark arrived in Alexandria after Peter's death in Rome. Clement says nothing about Mark's founding the church there or serving as bishop.[80] Whatever the case may be with Mark, it is virtually certain that those who first brought the gospel to Alexandria were Jewish believers from Jerusalem and that the first converts there were from the Jewish community.

Among the Jews who disputed with Stephen were Alexandrians (Acts 6:9).

77. Birger A. Pearson, "Christians and Jews in First-Century Alexandria," *Harvard Theological Review* 79 (1986): 207.

78. Eusebius, *History*, 2.16.1; 2.24.1. Nero reigned from 54-68.

79. Ibid., 2.17.1; 3.39.15. The superiority of the Rome/Peter tradition over the Alexandrian one has been promoted by a number of scholars, e.g., Raymond E. Brown, in Brown and Meier, *Rome and Antioch*, 193-94; and Arnold, "Centers," 149.

80. Pearson, "Christians and Jews," 210.

Stephen himself, as one of the Hellenist leaders, may have been from Alexandria (6:5). Some of the Hellenist Jewish Christians expelled from Jerusalem (8:1) could have come to Alexandria—traffic between the two cities was extensive.[81] L. W. Barnard showed that Stephen's interpretation of the history of Israel (Acts 7:2-53) had a significant influence on the Epistle of Barnabas, which increases the sense of connection between the first martyr and Alexandrian Christianity.[82]

Apart from the Gospel of Mark, if Mark was in fact written in Alexandria, the oldest Christian document from that city would be the Epistle of Barnabas. Written after a massacre of Jews in 66, the destruction of the Temple in 70, and the destruction of Jewish life in Alexandria after the Jews rose up against the authorities in the time of Trajan (115-117), the Epistle of Barnabas combines a transparently Jewish method and approach with a caustic rejection of Judaism as completely replaced by Christianity's new covenant.

Written by an anonymous teacher, probably a rabbi converted to Christianity, the Epistle of Barnabas features typical Alexandrian Jewish interpretive methods such as allegorical/spiritual interpretation of scripture and a method called *pesher*, which is characterized by the application of texts of scripture to current situations and concerns.[83] It also features a version of a common Jewish form of ethical guidance called the "Two Ways"—one of light and one of darkness. The author presents this Two-Ways teaching as another type of *gnosis*. But this thoroughly Jewish idea of knowledge contrasts with that of Gnosticism, for which *gnosis* "refers to the comprehension of the soul's origin and nature by a mystical enlightenment."[84]

The Epistle of Barnabas, which is older than the works of Gnostics such as Basilides (fl. ca. 150) and Valentinus (fl. ca. 140), places the actual suffering, death, and resurrection of Jesus in high regard. The whole of chapters 5 through 8 deal with the suffering of Christ. The section begins, "For it was for this reason that the Lord endured the deliverance of his flesh to corruption, that we might be cleansed by the forgiveness of sins, that is, by his sprinkled blood" (5:1).[85] Barnabas follows this up with a quotation from Isaiah 53:5, 7. Barnabas 11 and 12 focus on baptism and the cross. In this section, Barnabas interprets Psalm 1:3-6 in the following way: "blessed are those who, having set their hope on the cross, descended into the water . . ." (11:8).[86]

Alexandria represents another somewhat independent stream of Christian

81. Ibid., 209-10.

82. L. W. Barnard, *Studies in the Apostolic Fathers and Their Background* (Oxford: Basil Blackwell, 1966), 62-72. The Epistle of Barnabas should not be confused with the Gospel of Barnabas. See chapter 6 above.

83. Illustrated by Barnard in *Studies*, 49.

84. Ibid., 50.

85. The translation is by J. B. Lightfoot, edited and revised by Michael W. Holmes, in *The Apostolic Fathers: Greek Texts and English Translations*, ed. and rev. Michael W. Holmes (Grand Rapids: Baker, 1992, 1999), 283. Holmes also does the article on Barnabas in *Dictionary of the Later New Testament*, 125-27, where he provides a helpful outline of the letter.

86. Holmes, *Apostolic Fathers*, 305.

teaching inspired by the more radical Hellenist approach featured in Stephen's speech of Acts 7 and carried through to the Epistle of Barnabas of the early second century. Like the earliest strands of Christian faith in Jerusalem, Antioch, and Rome, it features a central conviction about the death of Jesus and its meaning.

No evidence for a rejection of the crucifixion of Jesus can be adduced from Syria and Egypt until after the documents we have examined associated with these four cities, Jerusalem, Antioch, Rome, and Alexandria. To the contrary, the churches of all these cities clearly believed Jesus was crucified and raised from the dead. This conviction stemmed from the earliest Christianity we know of. It in no way contrasted with a Christian tradition that was closer in time and space to the events of the end of Jesus' mission. The movements and leaders cited by Qāsimī and others, although from Syria and Egypt, came on the scene later than the communities in the principal cities we looked at in the last part of this chapter. Though a few leaders did reject the crucifixion of Jesus, they were not closer in time and space than the vast majority of Christians who recognized the canonical Gospels as scripture and based their faith in part on the death and resurrection of Jesus the Messiah.

8

Sent Down or Raised Up?

A Comparison of Islamic and Christian Scriptures

Christianity and Islam are founded on written sacred sources. While the Gospels say nothing about Islamic scripture, the Qurʾān frequently mentions the Gospel (*injīl*). For Christians, the singular noun *gospel* means the "good news" about the action of God in Jesus the Messiah (Mark 10:29) that has liberating potential for all humanity (Romans 1:16). The plural noun *Gospels* refers to the four books in the New Testament that narrate that good news: the Gospel according to Matthew, the Gospel according to Mark, the Gospel according to Luke, and the Gospel according to John.

The Qurʾān, in contrast, speaks only of the Gospel *(injīl)* in the singular: "We gave him *(ataynā-hu)*[1] [Jesus] the Gospel (*al-injīl*): therein was guidance and light, and confirmation of the Torah that had come before him: a guidance and admonition to those who fear Allah" (*Table* [5]:46). Consequently, many Muslims suspect that Christians have corrupted the New Testament Gospels because they contain the words of Jesus embedded in the narratives of their authors. The Gospels rarely quote God directly, as they do, for example, in the event of the Transfiguration: "This is my Son, the Beloved; listen to him" (Mark 9:7). Thus, the Gospels do contain "sent down" revelation. But, while not every verse of the Qurʾān features first person discourse, "God is the implied speaker throughout."[2] And, as we mentioned earlier, the Tradition is "raised up."

The Qurʾān confirms the Gospel, leading some Muslim readers to look for passages in the Gospels that agree with the Qurʾān and to consider passages in them corrupt that contradict the Qurʾān. One Muslim stated to a group I was in, "If a source contains 10 percent error, it is not 90 percent accurate. It is 100 percent unreliable." According to him, any error or discrepancy makes the whole unreliable.

Consequently, before exploring Jesus' predictions of his death in the Gospels, I must interpret the Christian understanding of scripture[3] by describing

1. A. Yusuf Ali uses "sent" here even though the text says "gave." This shows the influence of the Islamic "sent-down" concept of scripture; see also *Mary* [19]:30.

2. Neal Robinson, *Discovering the Qur'an: A Contemporary Approach to a Veiled Text* (London: SCM, 1996), 234.

3. See Kenneth Cragg, *The Call of the Minaret*, 2nd ed. (Maryknoll, NY: Orbis Books/Ibadan,

the formation of the Gospels in the New Testament and the nature of their affirmation as authoritative scripture for the Christian community. But first a glance at the collection of the Qurʾān.

Recently I had the privilege of visiting the relics collection in Istanbul's Topkapi Palace where I saw a copy of the Qurʾān believed to have belonged to Caliph ʿUthmān (d. 656).[4] The Qurʾān as we know it today descends directly from this *muṣḥaf,* or codex, that ʿUthmān ordered prepared in 650 or 651. In Bukhārī's *Ṣaḥīḥ*,[5] the story of ʿUthmān's creation of a single authoritative text of the Qurʾān runs as follows.

> ʿUthmān asked Ḥafṣah, the daughter of the Second Caliph, ʿUmar ibn al-Khaṭṭāb, and widow of the Prophet, to send the sheets she had in her possession from an earlier effort to collect the Qurʾān under the First Caliph, Abū Bakr, so they could be copied into codices, and returned. Ḥafṣah sent the sheets. Next ʿUthmān enlisted Zayd ibn Thābit, ʿAbd Allāh ibn al-Zubayr, Saʿīd ibn al-ʿĀṣ, and ʿAbd al-Raḥmān ibn al-Ḥārith ibn Hishām to copy them into codices. ʿUthmān instructed the three of them who were from the tribe of Quraysh, ʿAbd Allāh, Saʿīd, and ʿAbd al-Raḥmān, "If you and Zayd ibn Thābit [Zayd was from Medinah and not of the Quraysh ethnic group] differ in anything from the Qurʾān, write it in the tongue of the Quraysh, since it was sent down in their tongue." They followed this procedure in copying the sheets into the codices. ʿUthmān returned the sheets to Ḥafṣah and sent one codex to each province of the Islamic Empire. He then ordered all other Qurʾānic material—sheet or codex—burned.[6]

The need ʿUthmān felt to establish an authoritative text of the Qurʾān and to dispose of all alternatives is congruent with the Muslim understanding of the nature of revelation. The Qurʾān in Islamic dogma amounts to the very words of God preserved on tablets in heaven (*Constellations* [85]:22) and dictated to Muḥammad. God sent it down to Muḥammad. As a single infallible authority, divinely sent down, the Qurʾān requires a single reliable original codex. The Gospels, in contrast, arise out of different communities of Christian faith with particular perspectives and their own memory of events. Therefore, any

---

Nigeria: Daystar, 1985), 247-58. *The Call of the Minaret* has also been republished by Oneworld Publications, Oxford.

4. Another copy is housed in Tashkent, according to Ahmad Von Denffer (*ʿUlūm al-Qurʾān: An Introduction to the Sciences of the Qurʾān*, rev. ed. [Leicester: Islamic Foundation, 1996], 60-66).

5. Muḥammad ibn Ismāʿīl al-Bukhārī, *Al-jāmiʿ al-ṣaḥīḥ* (Cairo, 1930), *Kitāb faḍāʾil al-Qurʾān*, *Bāb* 2 and *Bāb* 3. For an English translation, see *Ṣaḥīḥ al-Bukhāri: The Translation of the Meanings of Sahih al-Bukhari: Arabic-English*, trans. Muhammad Muhsin Khan, 9 vols., 6th ed. (Lahore, Pakistan: Kazi Publications, 1983), 6:475-80.

6. Ṣubḥī al-Ṣāliḥ's *Mabāḥith fī ʿulūm al-Qurʾān* (*Studies in the Qurʾānic Sciences*), 5th ed. (Beirut: Dār al-ʿIlm li-l-Malāyīn, 1968), 78. The Shīʿī branch of Islam contends that the caliphs Abū Bakr, ʿUmar, and ʿUthmān had the references to the designation of ʿAlī as Muḥammad's successor eliminated from the standard copies of the Qurʾān.

Christian understanding of scriptural inspiration and authority does not require a single authoritative rendering of every event and statement. In addition, Christians believe that the Holy Spirit aids the reader or hearer of the scripture in understanding and applying it.

Many Muslims, whose Qurʾān testifies to one reliable Christian Gospel, find our four Gospels puzzling. Nevertheless, the fact that more than one scriptural story of Jesus has been preserved in many ancient manuscripts is in its turn congruent with the nature of the revelation—as Christians understand it. Anglican bishop Kenneth Cragg, the dean of Christian interpreters of Islam, puts it succinctly, "The gospels bring a cumulative witness to a central figure without conspiring to eliminate secondary divergences."[7] This central figure, of course, is Jesus. The Scandinavian biblical scholar Harald Riesenfeld puts it in another way, "for our assurance of the historicity of Jesus and for our general knowledge of who and what he was, the fact that we have a plurality of four Gospels is a fundamental advantage."[8] In this sense, the Gospels parallel the Tradition of Muḥammad rather than the Qurʾān. This especially applies to a type of tradition known as Sacred Tradition (*ḥadīth qudsī*). A Sacred Tradition contains God's word but in human language—the language of the Prophet Muḥammad.[9]

The Canonization and Composition of the Gospels

The common focus of these two competent scholars on Jesus should come as no surprise. The central feature of divine disclosure, as Christians see it, is Jesus. The Gospel of John puts it clearly, "The Word became flesh and lived among us" (John 1:14). God sent Jesus down—not the Gospels (John 6:38). The normative scriptures of Christianity do not come down from God; they are not the very words of God; they are not preserved on a tablet in heaven. Christian scriptures arise out of their communities of faith. They represent the product of God's involvement in the communities of faith that arose in the aftermath of the end of Jesus' mission. Initially, the authoritative scriptures of Christianity consisted of the Hebrew and some Greek writings of Judaism. The most important of these Christians now call the Old, or Ancient, Testament. It corresponds in content to the Hebrew scriptures or Bible of Judaism.

Over time, the widely diverse Christian communities of faith recognized the books of the New Testament as authoritative and reliable guides for Christian faith and life. Letters were written to address problems faced by churches in places such as Galatia in what is now the Asian part of Turkey, Corinth in

7. Cragg, *Call of the Minaret*, 248.

8. Harald Riesenfeld, *The Gospel Tradition: Essays by Harald Riesenfeld* (Oxford: Basil Blackwell, 1970), 1.

9. William A. Graham, *Divine Word and Prophetic Word in Early Islam: A Reconstruction of the Sources, with Special Reference to the Divine Sayings or Ḥadīth Qudsī* (The Hague: Mouton, 1977).

Greece, and Rome. Christians believe God supported the wide circulation of these letters to assist many churches in understanding the gospel, or good news, of what God had done in Jesus the Messiah and was doing through the Spirit after Jesus' departure to heaven. They also aided in the practice of the faith so effectively and in so many Christian contexts that the churches came to realize that God had selected and used them for the edification and spiritual formation of believing individuals and communities.

At the same time, the churches began to recognize that clarifying the truth about the events and sayings of Jesus required written accounts. They needed to show how Jesus' life, death, and resurrection represented clear fulfillment of intimations in the scriptures of Judaism. Stimulating and nurturing faith in Jesus as the Messiah required the recording of Jesus' sayings and actions in writing. The resulting documents rested on the authority of the Apostles as eyewitnesses. They incorporated testimonies, stories, and recollections already circulating in the churches through the media of preaching, teaching, storytelling, and worship.

The most widely attested of these accounts, now referred to as "Gospels," were four. None of them contains any direct reference to the identity of its author. Church tradition, however, has referred to them as the "Gospel according to Matthew," the "Gospel according to Mark," the "Gospel according to Luke," and the "Gospel according to John." Matthew and John were among the original twelve Apostles. According to early church tradition, Mark's work reflects the eyewitness influence of Peter.

When they talk about their scripture, Christians naturally use phrases such as "emerged out of" and "arose from." God did not send down the Christian scriptures. Rather, God raised them up. In God's providence the scriptures emerged from the communities who believed in Jesus as God's Messiah. These scriptures were recognized as sharing in the divine inspiration that believers had discerned in the Hebrew scriptures. In other words, God sent down Jesus and raised up documents composed by humans—letters, Gospels, and other treatises—to bear witness to who Jesus was and what that means for all humankind. Each Gospel represents "the voices of Christians explaining what led to their existence," clarifying the stories of Jesus for themselves and proclaiming them to others.[10]

Most devout New Testament scholars have concluded that Mark's Gospel, written between 60 and 70,[11] was the earliest of the four Gospels in the New Testament. David Wenham and Steve Walton identify four reasons for the composition of these Gospels.

---

10. C. F. D. Moule, *Birth of the New Testament* (San Francisco: Harper & Row, 1981), 131.

11. David Wenham and Steve Walton (*Exploring the New Testament*, 2 vols.; vol. 1: *Introducing the Gospels and Acts* [London: SPCK, 2001], 1:206) place the date at 60, and Norman Perrin puts it shortly after 70 (*The New Testament: An Introduction* [New York: Harcourt Brace Jovanovich, 1974],163).

1. Historically, the eyewitnesses to the events of Jesus' life, death, and resurrection were dying. This becomes clear in the introduction to Luke's Gospel, where he clearly represents himself as a member of the second generation of believers who has received his information from eyewitnesses (1:2).
2. The Gospels were written for evangelistic reasons as well. John's Gospel addresses this purpose explicitly, "These are written so that you may come to believe that Jesus is the Messiah, the Son of God,[12] and that through believing you may have life in his name" (20:31).[13]
3. The Gospel writers wrote to instruct believers also. Matthew's Gospel reveals this purpose transparently through its five major discourses to disciples.[14] In Jesus' last challenge to his disciples, often called the Great Commission, Jesus specifies teaching as one of the two major tasks of making disciples (Matthew 28:19-20).
4. Finally, writing enabled a more widespread and rapid dissemination of the proclamation of Jesus as God's Messiah. The written Gospels' brevity made them easily copied and lightweight for transport by travelers.[15]

This analysis coheres with Kenneth Cragg's observation about the Gospels: "They arose in the heart of the church to perpetuate its saving memory of Christ when time was thinning the contemporary generation and the wider world beyond the Palestinian was entering the fellowship."[16]

From as early as the second century, the Christian churches recognized the four Gospels of the New Testament as documents authoritative for Christian believers. Tatian, a contemporary of Justin Martyr, produced a harmony or unification of the four Gospels into one Gospel, called the *Diatessaron*. This fact of history "supplies proof that by about 170 all four Gospels were regarded as authoritative, otherwise it is unlikely that Tatian would have dared to combine them into one gospel account."[17] Scholarship has focused a vast amount of attention on these four documents in an effort to discern their sources, composition, and relationship to one another.

---

12. Some Jewish texts from the time of Jesus refer to the Messiah as "Son of God," that is, as "Israel's representative" (N. T. Wright, *Jesus and the Victory of God*, Christian Origins and the Question of God 2 [Minneapolis: Fortress, 1996], 485-86).

13. All biblical quotations are from the New Revised Standard Version unless otherwise indicated.

14. David R. Bauer, *The Structure of Matthew's Gospel: A Study in Literary Design*, Journal for the Study of the New Testament Supplement Series 31; Bible and Literature Series 15 (Sheffield: Almond, 1988), 130-31.

15. Wenham and Walton, *Exploring the New Testament*, 1:53-54.

16. Cragg, *Call of the Minaret*, 248.

17. Bruce Metzger, *The Canon of the New Testament: Its Origin, Development, and Significance* (Oxford: Clarendon, 1987), 115.

Disciplines of Gospel Research

Among the most important disciplines scholars have used in Gospel research are *form criticism*, *source criticism*, and *redaction* or *composition criticism*. Criticism in this context means "making careful, thoughtful judgments about matters of history, literary presentation, text and language in the light of the evidence available."[18] Many scholars have undertaken this task from within a devout appreciation for the Gospels as scripture. Others have approached them strictly as documents of late antiquity. Both groups of scholars have given painstaking attention to the passages they study in order to be as accurate as possible in assessing the history and the composition of Gospel tradition. Believing scholars have undertaken their work with respect and reverence. They take seriously that the church identified early in its experience these testimonies to the story of Jesus as providentially ordered to edify and to equip believing Christian communities and individuals for engagement in the tasks of the kingdom.

I will offer here a brief overview of the scholarship I appeal to below in showing that Jesus explicitly predicted his death and resurrection. The overview also supports my contention that God raised Christian scripture up out of the communities of Christian faith.

Form Criticism

In the introduction to his Gospel, Luke tells Theophilus that the many written accounts of the events of Jesus' life were based on information "handed on to us by those who from the beginning were eyewitnesses and servants of the word" (1:2). The Gospels give evidence that their authors composed them using information from eyewitnesses. For example, in Mark 4:35-38 the marks of eyewitness reporting include the details "when evening had come" and "on the cushion" (emphasized in italics).

> On that day, *when evening had come*, he said to them, "Let us go across to the other side." And leaving the crowd behind, they took him with them in the boat, just as he was. Other boats were with him. A great windstorm arose, and the waves beat into the boat, so that the boat was already being swamped. But he was in the stern, asleep *on the cushion*. . . .

Form critics examine such reports, analyzing them to determine what their origins in the life of the earliest churches may have been. Scholars pursuing this kind of criticism call it *form* criticism because the reports used by the Gospel writers occur in consistent forms, such as tales, exhortations, legends, miracle stories, sayings, and parables. These forms blossomed as Christians shared their

18. Wenham and Walton, *Exploring the New Testament*, 1: 58.

faith in Jesus and their memories of his sayings, actions, and attitudes in various life contexts.

For example, one form is called a *pronouncement story*. Preachers proclaiming the gospel used these stories in their sermons. Pronouncement stories have a typical structure, although they do not always exhibit it exactly. The Gospel writers incorporated these stories into their own narratives. The first explicit prediction Jesus made of his coming death and resurrection (Mark 8:27-33) can be shown to have been earlier than the Gospel of Mark because it occurs in a *form* critics recognize as a *didactic discourse*. Such discourse typically features an "introductory dialogue" (verses 27-30), a "central instruction" (verse 31), and a "conclusion to the instruction" (verses 32-33).[19]

Form critics also focus on the history of the traditions preserved in the Gospels. In the earliest period, believers shared their recollections of the sayings and deeds of Jesus orally. This oral period lasted until the destruction of Jerusalem in the year 70. This period gave birth to the use of specific isolated units in preaching and teaching. For example, in Acts 20:35b we find, "remembering the words of the Lord Jesus, how he said, 'It is more blessed to give than to receive.'" A story of Jesus' suffering and death, used with the Lord's Supper, surfaced in this very early period, representing an exception to the practice of teaching and preaching based on specific isolated units of tradition (Paul refers to this in 1 Corinthians 11).[20]

Scholars have evaluated differently the authenticity of the oral traditions and their forms used by Gospel writers in composing their Gospels. Rudolf Bultmann (d. 1976), a pioneer in the area of form criticism, thought that scholars could not learn anything authentic about the life and personality of Jesus from the Gospels. He viewed New Testament writers as uninterested in either of these topics, concluding that they present us with largely fragmentary and legendary information about the life and person of Jesus. Therefore, according to him, what we know about Jesus comes from the preaching and teaching of the early church, not from the words and deeds of Jesus himself. Bultmann believed that, although a tradition going back to Jesus did exist, it had faded out by the time of the writing of the Gospels. The Christian community's transmission was *informal* in that, according to Bultmann, no person or institution supervised the process of handing it down.[21]

---

19. See Craig L. Blomberg, "Form Criticism," in Joel B. Green, Scot McKnight, and I. Howard Marshall, eds., *Dictionary of Jesus and the Gospels* (Downers Grove, IL: InterVarsity, 1992), 243-50.

20. For evidence of the early passion narrative, see Joel B. Green, *The Death of Jesus: Tradition and Interpretation in the Passion Narrative*, Wissenschaftliche Untersuchungen zum Neuen Testament 2, Reihe 33 (Tübingen: Mohr, 1988), 157-74; and Bruce Chilton, "Tradition-Historical Criticism and Study of Jesus," in Joel B. Green, ed., *Hearing the New Testament: Strategies for Interpretation* (Grand Rapids: Eerdmans/Carlisle, UK: Paternoster, 1995), 37-59.

21. Rudolf Bultmann, *Jesus and the Word*, trans. Louise Pettibone Smith and Erminie Huntress Lantero (London and Glasgow: Scribners/Collins/Fontana, 1958 [1934]), 14-17; summarized from a different Scribners edition of the same work, pp. 8-13, by Kenneth E. Bailey, "Informal Controlled

In contrast, a later Scandinavian School represented by Birger Gerhardsson and Harald Riesenfeld argued that the Gospel tradition stems from the person of Jesus. According to them, his followers memorized the words and deeds of Jesus as "holy words."[22] The materials the evangelists used to construct their Gospels were passed down in an institutional form very much like the rabbinic schools of the time. The institution controlled the transmission to insure its reliability.[23]

Kenneth E. Bailey, a New Testament scholar with more than thirty-years experience teaching New Testament in the Middle East, affirms a mediating but constructive position between the school of Bultmann and the Scandinavian school. He bases his presentation on a process of transmission less formal than the rabbinic system proposed by Riesenfeld and Gerhardsson and more reliable than that supposed by Bultmann and his followers. Bailey rejects the *informal uncontrolled* model of transmission proposed by Bultmann and the *formal controlled* model proposed by the Scandinavians in favor of an *informal controlled* model based on a practice still in place in contemporary Middle Eastern villages for transmitting oral information.

Bailey demonstrates that archaeology has unearthed evidence indicating a high degree of continuity between cultural patterns of the ancient Near East and those of its contemporary inhabitants, especially in rural villages. He therefore considers it useful to look to current Middle Eastern practices of oral transmission for help in assessing the probable quality of the oral transmission that Gospel writers and their predecessors drew upon.

He says the way rumors are spread in the modern Middle East corresponds to the informal and uncontrolled model proposed by Bultmann for the New Testament oral tradition. The contemporary Muslim system for memorization and recitation of the Qurʾān represents the modern Middle Eastern equivalent of the rabbinic *formal* and controlled system the Scandinavians hold to have been the model for the transmission of oral traditions about Jesus. A third model, however, also turns up in the modern Middle East. The people of traditional villages in the region transmit important proverbs, riddles, poetry, parables, stories, and "well-told accounts of the important figures in the history of the village or community" in a way that can be described as *informal* but *controlled*. That is, the accuracy of the transmitted material is controlled, not by any such

Oral Tradition," *Themelios* 20, no. 2 (January 1995), 4-11 (reprinted from *Asia Journal of Theology* 5 [1991], 34-54), 4.

22. Riesenfeld, *Gospel Tradition*, 11-29; summarized by Bailey in "Informal," 5.

23. Birger Gerhardsson, *Memory and Manuscript: Oral Tradition and Written Transmission in Rabbinic Judaism and Early Christianity*, Acta Seminarii Neotestamentici Upsaliensis 22 (Uppsala: Almqvist & Wiksell/Copenhagen: Ejnar Munksgaard, 1961), 335; and idem, *Tradition and Transmission in Early Christianity*, Coniectanea Neotestamentica 20 (Copenhagen: Ejnar Munksgaard, 1964), 40-47. Eerdmans has published these two works under one cover with the original pagination of both in *Memory and Manuscript: Oral Tradition and Written Transmission in Rabbinic Judaism and Early Christianity* with *Tradition and Transmission in Early Christianity* (Grand Rapids: Eerdmans, 1997). Bailey summarizes Gerhardsson's position in "Informal," 5.

formal institution as the rabbinic school or the institutions of Qurʾān recitation, but by the collective involvement of villagers. The control is communal rather than institutional. Material is transmitted orally with degrees of control that differ according to the form and content of the lore transmitted.

Villagers allow no flexibility in transmission of poems and proverbs. These forms have to be transmitted verbatim over the generations. For example, in the area of Syria and Lebanon, the Syriac hymns of Ephrem Syrus (d. 373) are so well known today that people dare not recite them unless they can do so verbatim from memory. In the case of parables and the recollections of historical people and events, villagers allow no flexibility in the important structure of events and crucial things said. They do allow flexibility, however, in details and in the way the parables or stories are told.

Bailey provides an example from a village in Egypt of a story he heard from at least half a dozen different individuals, told from their distinctive perspectives. These informants told of a groom who was accidentally shot during the traditional celebration of his wedding. The parts of the event that everyone got exactly right were the details establishing it as an act of God, "the gun went off" (the passive voice was used in Arabic), and the exact words of the people in reporting the death of the groom to the police, "A camel stepped on him." The communal lie occurred out of necessity because reporting the actual cause of death to authorities would have required the family of the groom to exact blood revenge from the one holding the gun when it went off.

Historical narratives of events and people important for the identity of the villagers or their community are informally controlled for this level of reliability. Bailey thinks oral transmitters of the deeds and words of Jesus had to conform to this level of transmission reliability, namely, flexibility of detail with rigidity of event structure and crucial statement.[24] His conclusions harmonize with the similarities and differences in stories about, and sayings of, Jesus as we find them in the Synoptic Gospels (Matthew, Mark, and Luke). See, for example, figure 8.1, p. 128 below.[25]

The kind of informal but controlled transmission Bailey ascribes to the early church is culturally consistent with contemporary methods among traditional communities in the same geographical region. Furthermore, the assumption of this continuity accounts for the fluidity prevailing in the transmission enshrined in the Gospels. It cannot be denied that the form criticism presented by Bultmann and modified by generations of scholars following him provides important insights into the history of the development of the four Gospels. At the same time, given the analysis of Bailey, serious students of the Gospels are warranted in considering reliable the orally transmitted words and deeds of Jesus now embedded in our Gospels.

---

24. Bailey, "Informal," 4-9.

25. These three Gospels are similar enough that they can be "seen together," and thus compared and contrasted.

As time went on, the isolated units of oral tradition took on stereotypical forms very similar to the types of orally transmitted material identified by Bailey: individual sayings, including (among other things) proverbs, pronouncement stories, parables, speeches, miracle stories, and historical narratives.[26] These were collected into documents, such as the apparent collection of sayings used by Matthew and Luke but not found in Mark, and connected narratives, such as the Gospel according to Mark. The authors of the four Gospels, then, used these sources in their compositions. The church came to realize that these Gospels belonged to a new set of writings that God had providentially ordered and inspired. As we have put it above, God raised the Gospels up out of the communities of people who followed Jesus. He did not send them down. They were constructed from oral traditions and from sources composed of oral tradition. Source criticism looks at the major sources that help form the four Gospels.

Source Criticism

Returning to Luke's introduction to his Gospel, we find this phrase, "Since *many* have undertaken to set down an orderly account of the events that have been fulfilled among us . . ." (1:1). Evidently, Luke had available for his use many orderly accounts—or attempts at orderly accounts. These accounts offered him sources of information about Jesus' sayings and deeds. Here he emphasizes the events fulfilling scripture, but he had sources for the sayings of Jesus as well. Source criticism accordingly looks at the similarities and differences in the various passages of the Gospels to discern the sources they depend on.

Most New Testament scholars subscribe to what they call the two-document hypothesis, namely, that Matthew and Luke utilize two basic documents, along with other material, in composing their Gospels: the Gospel of Mark and an independent and as yet undiscovered sayings source. Matthew and Luke share 235 verses that do not show up in Mark. Many of these verses are so nearly identical in Matthew and Luke that they must have been taken from a common source. Scholars call this source "Q" from *Quelle*, German for "source." Q may have been purely oral.[27]

Wenham and Walton offer an important caution about interpretation based on source criticism. Since stories about Jesus and his disciples in their oral form enjoyed wide circulation among the churches, it is likely that Matthew and Luke had knowledge of material in Mark's Gospel from oral sources as well. For this reason, we cannot assume that the way Mark presents a story necessarily adheres more closely to Jesus' actual actions and words than does the way one or both of the other two Synoptic evangelists present it.[28] For example, Matthew 20:20 and Mark 10:35 both transmit the story of the brash request of James and John,

26. Bailey, "Informal," 10.

27. Robert H. Stein, *Gospels and Tradition: Studies on Redaction Criticism of the Synoptic Gospels* (Grand Rapids: Baker, 1991), 47.

28. Wenham and Walton, *Exploring the New Testament*, 1:69.

the sons of Zebedee, for places of prominence in Jesus' kingdom. Matthew's account has the mother of the brothers making the request, while Mark omits the mother's mediation. Since it is more likely that a transmitter would omit the mother than that another transmitter would add her, and since traditional societies look on maligning someone's mother as a great error, Matthew's account probably adheres more closely to the details of the original event.[29]

Source criticism allows interpreters to judge the likelihood that traditions about sayings and deeds of Jesus genuinely go back to him. The criterion of *multiple attestation* can be stated as follows: if a saying or deed of Jesus shows up in more than one independent source, it is much more likely to have been something Jesus actually said or did than if it occurs in only one source. For example, the crucifixion of Jesus shows up in all strands of the tradition except Q; and even this source contains the challenge for all followers of Jesus to take up their *crosses* and follow him (Matthew 10:37-38; Luke 14:26-27).

The criterion of *dissimilarity* states that, if a Gospel tradition differs from topics and issues occurring in the writings of the early church, it probably goes back to Jesus rather than to someone later. The prayer of Jesus in the Garden of Gethsemane to be released from the suffering of death (Mark 14:36) meets this criterion because his agonizing over the approaching ordeal differs significantly from the more triumphant Christology of the early churches. If a tradition differs from both issues and topics prevalent in the Judaism of Jesus' time *and* those of the early church, then the criterion of *double dissimilarity* comes into play. This same apparent fear of martyrdom on Jesus' part contrasts also with the attitude of the Jewish Maccabbean martyrs of the second century BCE (2 Maccabees 7:1-42), thus fulfilling the criterion of double dissimilarity. Dissimilarity to Judaism alone, however, should not be used as a criterion because Christians could have invented traditions that differ from Jewish topics. Furthermore, the results of applying such a criterion would only serve to separate Jesus from Judaism.[30]

These criteria, however, should only be used *positively*, namely, to increase the probability that a tradition goes back to Jesus and not finally to discredit it. If we were to judge against a saying of Jesus simply because we find a counterpart in early Christianity or Second Temple Judaism, we would be making the absurd implication that Jesus said nothing that was said by his contemporaries and his followers. It is also impossible to argue that Jesus never said anything only once; or that nothing he said could be picked up by only one Gospel writer.[31]

The criterion of *coherence* suggests that, if a Gospel tradition proves congruent with traditions already validated, it too probably goes back to Jesus. Even though the Gospel of Thomas was produced in the second century after Christ, it contains some sayings so nearly identical to those already recognized as genuine in the earlier Gospels that these Thomas sayings too are considered

29. I am indebted to my colleague Dale Walker for this example.

30. Tom Holmén, *Jesus and Jewish Covenant Thinking*, Biblical Interpretation Series 55 (Leiden/Boston/Cologne: Brill, 2001), 28.

31. Ibid., 30-31.

genuine. Here is a bit of one of these sayings, "Whoever does not . . . carry the cross as I do, will not be worthy of me" (Gospel of Thomas 55).[32]

Two criteria can be used to decrease the probability that a tradition is genuinely from Jesus himself. The criterion of *implausibility* can be used to show that something could not have happened at the time of Jesus or in the place where he carried out his mission. We used this criterion in discussing the Gospel of Barnabas's *quadragesima,* or Lenten fast, in chapter 6 above. And the criterion of *incoherence* comes into play when a tradition appears incompatible with other established and validated Jesus traditions. This too can be exemplified from the Gospel of Barnabas in which Jesus applies to himself attributes applied to John the Baptist in the established Jesus traditions.[33]

Composition Criticism

Luke introduces his Gospel in these words, "I too decided, after investigating everything carefully from the very first, to write an *orderly* account for you, most excellent Theophilus" (1:3). He had already said, as noted above, that many others had "undertaken to set down an *orderly* account of the events" that had taken place among the believers (1:1). Clearly, Luke has taken pains to compose his Gospel in a meaningful and orderly way. Matthew, Mark, and John also show evidence of care in composition. Scholars have traditionally called this study of the contributions the author of a Gospel has made to its final form through the way he has composed it *redaction criticism*. Redaction means "editing," and the Gospel writers do much more than edit the sources they use. They have produced a meaningful composition of their own. I, therefore, prefer—along with Wenham and Walton—the term *composition criticism*.[34]

Luke identifies his reader—someone named Theophilus. Although Mark and Matthew do not identify their readers, they also write for an *implied readership*. In their case this has to be discerned from the unique contributions they each make to the final composition of their Gospels. This difference in purpose for writing helps to explain the clear differences in the Synoptic Gospels. The striking similarities in the three compositions help us appreciate their faithfulness to the oral and the written sources they use to portray what Jesus said and did, that is, as Luke puts it, "the events that have been fulfilled among us" (Luke 1:1).

At several points in our discussion of Jesus' predictions of his death and resurrection and of the events in his life appealed to by Muslim commentators,

---

32. The Gospel of Thomas is a collection of Jesus' sayings; it was mentioned by Hippolytus and Origen in the third century and discovered in 1945 at Nag Hammadi in Upper Egypt.

33. All the above criteria are discussed most helpfully in Holmén, *Jesus and Jewish Covenant Thinking*, 27-36.

34. Wenham and Walton, *Exploring the New Testament*, 1:75. Richard A. Burridge in *Four Gospels, One Jesus?* 2nd ed. (Grand Rapids/Cambridge: Eerdmans, 2005) offers an imaginative and sophisticated essay on the composition of each of the four Gospels.

we base our conviction about the authenticity of the material under discussion partly on the *criterion of divergent patterns from the composition*: when a particular evangelist includes something in his Gospel in spite of the fact that it does not contribute to his purpose or is not characteristic of his writing, he must have included it because he knew it happened or because it occurred in his source or sources. Such a criterion helps scholars discern, for example, that Mark 9:9b did not originate with Mark, "As they were coming down the mountain, [Jesus] ordered them to tell no one about what they had seen, until *after the Son of Man had risen from the dead*." Since Mark typically stresses the death of Jesus and not his resurrection, it is unlikely that he would have fabricated this verse, omitting the death of Jesus and mentioning only his resurrection. Jesus' response to Simon Peter's confession of Jesus' identity exemplifies this criterion as well. Jesus said that "flesh and blood" had not revealed to Peter the truth of what Peter confessed. The phrase "flesh and blood" is not characteristic of Matthew but is a phrase that may have originated when the church was still speaking Aramaic (Matthew 16:17).[35] While composition criticism includes both editorial and stylistic dimensions of the Gospel writer's impact on his composition, editorial features that help the evangelist achieve his theological purpose may prove more helpful in detecting his sources.

All these criticisms—form, source, and composition—are possible because the Gospels emerge from within communities of Christian faith. They result from the ministry of the Holy Spirit through the normal channels of God's mission through the church itself. That is, God raised them up rather than sent them down.

Another feature of the opening verses of the Gospel of Luke deserves to be noted. Luke says the events of the life of Jesus "were delivered (*paredosan*) to us by those who from the beginning were eyewitnesses and ministers (*hypēretai*) of the word" (1:2). In addition to the fact that *paredosan* is a technical term for passing on tradition, the Greek term *hypēretai* (sing. *hypēretēs*) is the equivalent of the Hebrew *ḥazzān* and probably refers to someone qualified to recite the tradition[36] (Arabic *muḥaddith*).

The Gospels Were Not Sent Down from Heaven

Source criticism, for example, makes clear that the writers of the Gospels do not always intend to provide us with the exact words of Jesus. In some instances they obviously paraphrase, modify, and explain the meaning of Jesus' words. These authors had the authority to interpret the words of Jesus in light of the needs of their context. While the exact words Jesus must have said do not always emerge clearly from the four Gospels, they can often, if not infallibly, be discerned, as we can see when we arrange texts from several Gospels side by side.

35. Ibid., 70. See Grant R. Osborne, "Redaction Criticism," in Green, McKnight, and Marshall, eds., *Dictionary of Jesus and the Gospels*, 662-69.

36. Bailey, "Informal," 10-11 n. 33.

Figure 8.1 Jesus Calms a Storm in the Synoptics
Common Witness and Distinct Features
(Boldface type indicates distinct features.)

Matthew 8:23-27	**Mark 4:35-41**	**Luke 8:22-25**
And when he got into the boat, **his disciples followed him**.	On that day, **when evening had come,** he said to them, "Let us go across to the other side." And leaving the crowd behind, they took him with them in the boat, just as he was. **Other boats were with him.**	One day he got into the boat with his disciples, and he said to them, "Let us go across to the other side **of the lake.**" **So they put out, and while they were sailing** he fell asleep. **[order]**
A windstorm (*seismos*) arose on the sea, so great that the boat was being swamped by the waves; but he was asleep.	A great windstorm (*lailaps*) arose, and the waves beat into the boat, so that the boat was already being swamped. But he was in the stern, asleep **on the cushion**;	A windstorm (*lailaps*) swept down the lake, and the boat was filled with water, and they were in danger.
And they went and woke him up, saying, "**Lord, save us!** We are perishing!" And he said to them, "Why are you afraid, you of **little** faith?" Then he got up and rebuked the winds and the sea; and there was a dead calm. They were amazed, saying, "What sort of man is this, that even the winds and the sea obey him?"	and they woke him up and said, "**Teacher, do you not care** that we are perishing?" He woke up and rebuked the wind, and said to the sea, "Peace! Be still!" Then the wind ceased, and there was a dead calm. He said to them, "Why are you afraid? Have you still **no** faith?" And they were filled with great awe and said to one another, "Who then is this, that even the wind and sea obey him?"	They went to him and woke him up, shouting, "**Master, Master**, we are perishing!" And he got up and rebuked the winds and the raging waves; they ceased, and there was a calm. He said to them, "Where is your faith?" They were afraid and amazed, and said to one another, "Who then is this, that he commands even the winds and the water, and they obey him?"

The arrangement of the three versions of Jesus calming a storm is taken from the three Synoptic Gospels, offering a sample of the divergences one encounters. I have highlighted these differences with boldface type. A few comments on the comparison between Matthew's and Mark's versions follow to illustrate how these "criticisms" work. Eyewitness touches show up in Mark. The time of day is specified: "When evening had come." Jesus went "just as he was." There were "other boats." The cushion in the stern may have been the boatman's cushioned seat. The disciples' reproach of Jesus, "Do you not care that we are perishing?" impresses us with its specificity. Jesus speaks directly to the wind and waves. Mark tells his readers that Jesus rebukes his disciples and why he does so. Matthew eliminates details he feels are not essential, including all the eyewitness touches. He emphasizes Jesus' authority. The disciples address Jesus as "Lord" (a favorite word of Matthew). He uses the word "save." Because of his emphasis on discipleship, Matthew adds the word "follow" as a link with other parts of his discourse. Matthew is less critical of the disciples. Composition criticism observes that Matthew adapts Mark's account to emphasize Jesus' authority and the importance of discipleship.[37]

If we had but one Gospel, we would be unaware of any divergence from the very words Jesus must have said. We would have to take what our one source gave us on faith—bolstered by the character of the document itself and its ability to convey a transforming message—that this Gospel was the inspired word of God. Similarly, Muslims take it on faith—bolstered by the character of the document itself and its ability to convey a transforming message—that the Qurʾān is the word of God. We mentioned Tatian's harmony of the Gospels above. Produced in the middle of the second century, it represented a response to criticism from outsiders of the failure of the four Gospels to agree on every detail of Jesus' sayings and deeds. It remained in use as the Gospel of choice for Syriac-speaking Christians until the fifth century.[38]

Nevertheless, the one-Gospel solution did not prevail universally in the Christian church. It is better that we have four. Since we have four Gospels, we have two valuable kinds of evidence. For one thing, because discrepancies exist in the four Gospels, we can be sure they are not the result of a conspiracy to press an ideology or religious tradition upon the world. Their divergence points to their authenticity. For another, the points where the several strands of tradition agree have greater significance because the various Gospels do not agree on everything. In other words, the divergence of the Gospels points to their independence and authenticity. Again, as Cragg says, "The gospels bring a cumulative witness to a central figure without conspiring to eliminate secondary divergences."[39]

This quote reminds us also that the central self-revelation of God is in Jesus the Messiah, not in a book or set of documents—indispensable though they are. Interestingly enough, as we noted in chapter 1 above, the Qurʾān the Muslims believe was sent down from heaven appears to support our conviction that the Jewish and Christian scriptures are reliable.

What is the theological significance of a scripture raised up? Very briefly, it is congruent with the Christian conviction that God is involved in the life of the Christian community. The authors of the Gospels, and the communities that received these documents and discerned the inspiration of God in them, obviously believed that Jesus had been crucified and that he had predicted both his death and his resurrection. Did Jesus himself—as best we can discern through historical investigation of these Gospels—envision his own death and resurrection as part of the divinely ordered end of his mission?

37. Wenham and Walton, *Exploring the New Testament*, 1:77.

38. David Bundy, "Tatian," in Scott W. Sunquist et al., eds., *A Dictionary of Asian Christianity* (Grand Rapids: Eerdmans, 2001), 822.

39. Cragg, *Call of the Minaret*, 248.

9

"The Days Will Come When the Bridegroom Is Taken Away"

Jesus' Final Days in the Context of His Life

When Scot McKnight, Karl A. Olsson Professor in Religious Studies at North Park University, published *Jesus and His Death* in 2005, it had been about "fifty years since anyone dedicated an entire volume to analyzing how Jesus understood his death."[1] His nearly four-hundred-page study calls attention to "the stubborn presence of numerous texts where Jesus anticipates his death."[2] He carries out this project by applying such tools of historical analysis as we summarized in chapter 8 to the whole of Jesus' life and teaching. In this chapter, with the help of McKnight and others, we will look at Jesus' anticipation of a premature death.

"When the Bridegroom Is Taken Away"

Early in his public ministry, in the region of Galilee, when asked why his disciples did not fast, Jesus hinted at his premature death.

> Jesus said to them, "The wedding guests cannot fast while the bridegroom is with them, can they? As long as they have the bridegroom with them, they cannot fast. The days will come when the bridegroom is taken away from them, and then they will fast on that day." (Mark 2:19-20)

Mark refers to the questioners as "they" (2:18), presumably a reference to people in general. Luke (5:33-35) follows Mark in this respect; but Matthew (9:14-15) has the disciples of John the Baptist asking the question.[3] The passage features

1. Scot McKnight, *Jesus and His Death: Historiography, the Historical Jesus and Atonement Theory* (Waco, TX: Baylor University Press, 2005), 336.

2. Ibid.

3. McKnight notes that since in Matthew reference is made to John's disciples asking the question about fasting, the interchange may have taken place at a time after John had been executed and not in Jesus' early Galilean ministry. But it should be noted that the events in Mark 2 show the controversy already arising as a result of Jesus' ministry: forgiveness of sins, eating with tax col-

other minor differences in the three Gospels; but Jesus' statement, "The days will come when the bridegroom is taken away from them, and then they will fast on that day," is only slightly edited by Matthew, who omits "on that day" (15), and by Luke, who ends the saying with "those days" (35)—both evangelists removing some of the rough edges of Mark's Greek.[4] This may be an example of the informal controlled method of transmission of reports identified by Kenneth E. Bailey and summarized in chapter 8 above. In this form of control for accuracy of transmission, details may differ from one telling to another, but specific sayings are treated with greater faithfulness to their original content.[5]

Taken alone, however, this passage cannot establish that Jesus anticipated his premature death because many scholars take Mark 2:20 to be an insertion into this set of verses—before Mark incorporated them into his Gospel but after Jesus had been crucified. Nevertheless, when viewed in the light of subsequent events and statements of Jesus, it seems certain that Jesus "thought he would die prematurely and that his death was willed by God as part of his eschatological plan to purge Israel at the end of times."[6] One poignant event surely offered Jesus a clue to his own fate, the execution of his kinsman and mentor, John the Baptist.

"When Jesus Heard This, He Withdrew to a Deserted Place"

The premature death of John the Baptist probably served as a clue to Jesus that he, as a prophet like John, could also be facing a premature death. Mark and (especially) Matthew detail the story of the beheading of John the Baptist at the request of Herod's wife, offered through the medium of her daughter, who had just pleased the ruler with an excellent dance (Matthew 14:3-12; Mark 6:17-29). Only Matthew indicates a brief time of mourning for John on Jesus' part before needy people require his attention:

> Now when Jesus heard this, he withdrew from there in a boat to a deserted place by himself. But when the crowds heard it, they followed him on foot from the towns. When he went ashore, he saw a great crowd; and he had compassion for them and cured their sick. (14:13-14)

lectors, and doing what was not lawful on the Sabbath. Jesus may have perceived early on that his faithfulness to his divine mission to implement God's priorities would get him into the kind of hot water (baptism!) that ended John's life.

4. Evidence for the dominant view among scholars that Matthew and Luke use Mark as a source is the tendency—evidenced here—for both of them to refine Mark's Greek (Richard A. Burridge, *Four Gospels, One Jesus?* [Grand Rapids: Eerdmans, 1994], 10).

5. Kenneth E. Bailey, "Informal Controlled Oral Tradition," *Themelios* 20, no. 2 (January 1995), 4-11; reprinted from *Asia Journal of Theology* 5 (1991): 34-54.

6. McKnight, *Jesus,* 138.

Luke includes only the following verses, but they capture the close connection between the two prophets:

> Now Herod the ruler heard about all that had taken place, and he was perplexed, because it was said by some that John had been raised from the dead, by some that Elijah had appeared, and by others that one of the ancient prophets had arisen. Herod said, "John I beheaded; but who is this about whom I hear such things?" And he tried to see him. (9:7-9)

Indeed, as McKnight remarks, the death of John the Baptist "was undoubtedly scorched on" the memory of Jesus.[7] According to the thorough analysis of N. T. Wright, John was "the role model" for Jesus' own vocation, at its beginning at least.[8]

"Are You Able to Be Baptized with My Baptism?"

Another passage corroborating the conclusion from Mark 2:19-20 that Jesus would die a premature death is Mark 10:35-40.

> James and John, the sons of Zebedee, came forward to him and said to him, "Teacher, we want you to do for us whatever we ask of you." And he said to them, "What is it you want me to do for you?" And they said to him, "Grant us to sit, one at your right hand and one at your left, in your glory." But Jesus said to them, "You do not know what you are asking. Are you able to drink the cup that I drink, or be baptized with the baptism that I am baptized with?" They replied, "We are able." Then Jesus said to them, "The cup that I drink you will drink; and with the baptism with which I am baptized, you will be baptized; but to sit at my right hand or at my left is not mine to grant, but it is for those for whom it has been prepared."

Because of the cup metaphor in this passage, some scholars have argued that it was constructed by the early church based on Jesus' agony in the Garden of Gethsemane (Mark 14:36) or his serving of the Last Supper (Mark 14:22-25). Some think the metaphor of baptism recalls Paul (Romans 6:3-4) and therefore does not represent something Jesus himself said.[9] But McKnight offers a number of telling indications that this intimation of Jesus' ultimate ordeal is authentically his.

---

7. Ibid., 132. This event attracted the attention of the Jewish historian Josephus (*Antiquities* 18.2).

8. N. T. Wright, *Jesus and the Victory of God*, Christian Origins and the Question of God 2 (Minneapolis: Fortress, 1996), 162.

9. For the bibliography, see McKnight, *Jesus*, 124-25.

The context of this verse shows that Jesus—in contrast to the view of him in the early church—is limited in power in that he is not able to assign places at the final banquet (40), which meets the criterion of *dissimilarity*. The baptism metaphor here meets the test of authentic Jesus material called *multiple attestation* because it turns up also in Luke's special tradition, a different tradition altogether from Mark, "I came to bring fire to the earth, and how I wish it were already kindled! I have a baptism with which to be baptized, and what stress I am under until it is completed!" (Luke 12:49-50).[10]

Furthermore, in the passage under discussion, Jesus suggests that James and John will also undergo a baptism like his. "The cup that I drink," he says, "you will drink; and with the baptism with which I am baptized, you will be baptized" (Mark 10:39). If this amounts to an after-the-event-of-Jesus'-death insertion into his discourse on the part of the early church, why would the inserter include with it a prediction of the martyrdom of John, who was never martyred? Would they have attributed to Jesus a prophecy that did not come true?

In addition, the parallel with Romans 6 is overdrawn because there Paul refers to the *literal* baptism of believers as a participation in the death of Jesus, while the metaphor here points to the parallel ordeals of Jesus and his disciples. Finally, in the body of tradition called Q, shared by Matthew and Luke but missing in Mark, John promises that Jesus will *baptize* with "the Holy Spirit and fire" and goes on to say, "His winnowing fork is in his hand, to clear his threshing floor and to gather the wheat into his granary; but the chaff he will burn with unquenchable fire" (Luke 3:16-17; Matthew 3:11-12). Baptism for John stands for the ordeal of judgment, similar to the way Jesus uses baptism in Mark 10:38, but *dissimilar* to Paul's reference to ritual participation in the death of Jesus. Together, the witness of Mark and Q to this metaphor in light of Paul's different use of baptism meets the criterion of *dissimilarity*.[11]

According to Hans F. Bayer, head of the department of New Testament at German Theological Seminar, Giessen, Germany, the metaphor of baptism as a divine imperative, requiring a divine humiliation of Jesus, occurs in the scriptures that Jesus knew. In the Hebrew scriptures, the word *ṭābal,* which corresponds to the Greek *baptō* (*baptizō*), refers to inundation and occurs frequently as a metaphor for divine judgment (e.g., Job 9:31). The Hebrew scriptures use the image of inundation to describe the force of powerful oppression. For example, David writes about God's deliverance: "For the waves (*mishberēy*) of death encompassed me. . . . He . . . drew me out of mighty waters" (2 Samuel 22:5 and 17). The prophets use this image when oppressors become agents of divine judgment (e.g., Isaiah 8:7 and 8). This second usage of the image corresponds most closely to the content of the passage under discussion here. In Jonah 2:3-4, the reluctant prophet says God threw him into the waters as judgment for his disobedience: "You cast me into the deep, into the heart of the seas, and the flood surrounded me; all your waves and your billows passed over me. . . ."

---

10. This is from the tradition peculiar to Luke.

11. McKnight, *Jesus,* 124-25.

This judgment does not, however, necessarily imply death. The external flood of baptism is more closely associated with suffering from persecutors, while the cup is more closely associated with the direct outpouring of divine wrath and judgment.[12] Or, as McKnight phrases it, "the baptism about which both John and Jesus spoke was an image of what will happen to those who experience the day of YHWH [the Lord][13] when he comes to purify his land and his people for his perfect rule."[14]

"Are You Able to Drink the Cup That I Drink?"

What can we make of the metaphor of the cup? The most frequent use of a word for cup in the Hebrew scriptures is metaphorical, usually represented by the word *kōs* (a word sometimes used for a literal cup), but once by the synonym *saf* (Zechariah 12:2). Usually different words signify a literal cup: *qāśah* (only in 1 Chronicles 28:17); *gābīa*ʿ (only in Genesis 44:2, 12, 16, 17); ʾ*aggān* (only in Isaiah 22:24). Some sample passages from the scriptures Jesus knew illustrate the metaphorical use of cup.

> Rouse yourself, rouse yourself!
> Stand up, O Jerusalem,
> you who have drunk at the hand of the Lord
> the cup of his wrath,
> who have drunk to the dregs
> the bowl of staggering. (Isaiah 51:17)
>
> Thus says your Sovereign, the Lord,
> your God who pleads the cause of his people:
> See, I have taken from your hand the cup of staggering;
> you shall drink no more
> from the bowl of my wrath. (Isaiah 51:22)
>
> For thus the Lord, the God of Israel, said to me:
> Take from my hand this cup of the wine of wrath, and make all the nations to whom I send you drink it. (Jeremiah 25:15)

---

12. Hans F. Bayer, *Jesus' Predictions of Vindication and Resurrection: The Provenance, Meaning, and Correlation of the Synoptic Predictions*, Wissenschaftliche Untersuchungen zum Neuen Testament, 2. Reihe, 20 (Tübingen: Mohr, 1986), 78-81; and idem, "Predictions of Jesus' Passion and Resurrection," in Joel B. Green, Scot McKnight, and I. Howard Marshall, eds. *Dictionary of Jesus and the Gospels* (Downers Grove, IL: InterVarsity, 1992), 631-32.

13. YHWH represents God's name in Hebrew. Since no one knows how to pronounce the word and it is too holy to be said, only its consonants are written. Jews pronounce "Adonai" when reading YHWH. English translations use "Lord" for YHWH because the Greek translation of the Hebrew Bible uses *kyrios*, "Lord," to translate YHWH.

14. McKnight, *Jesus*, 128.

You will be sated with contempt instead of glory.
Drink, you yourself, and stagger!
The cup in the Lord's right hand
will come around to you,
and shame will come upon your glory! (Habakkuk 2:16)

On the wicked he will rain coals of fire and sulfur;
a scorching wind shall be the portion of their cup. (Psalm 11:6)

As these passages indicate, the key to the image of cup is not the container itself but its contents. Although the cup can stand for the many blessings God provides, as in Psalm 23, "my cup overflows," more often the Hebrew scriptures use the cup image to symbolize God's judgment against sin, as in Isaiah 51:17 above.

Although drunkenness, as depicted in the Isaiah and Habakkuk passages above, seems to pale in comparison to such evils as war and disease, it represents a telling image for a painful experience people inflict on themselves. Drunkenness involves a progression that is humiliating. People begin drinking in confidence and possibly even arrogance and end up in staggering, vomiting, illness, and performing deeds they later regret. Passages such as Psalm 75:4-5; Jeremiah 49:12-16; and Revelation 18:6 reflect this progression.[15] As in the quotes above, sinners stagger and fall in the streets, suffer exposure, and are disgraced. In other passages they are scorned and humiliated by their enemies (Isaiah 51:23) and finally go insane (Jeremiah 51:7).[16]

Bayer summarizes the consistent features of the prophetic references to the cup, which, unlike references to the cup in the Psalms, are uniformly of judgment: God primarily administers it; the people of God receive it first; and while the cup will be fully emptied, the removal of the cup will follow a limited period of judgment.[17]

In the prayer Jesus taught his disciples—probably genuine Jesus material[18]—we find the following petition: "And do not bring us to the time of trial" (Matthew 6:13a; Luke 11:4).[19] "Trial" here does not refer to the little temptations and tests that spread themselves out on the path of daily living but to the "final persecution and testing of God's saints,"[20] which will accompany the in-breaking of God's kingdom and the pouring out of God's judgment. Scholars refer to this time of

15. In Revelation 18:4-10 the cup for Babylon contains plagues of death, mourning, and famine (verse 8).

16. Leland Ryken, James C. Wilhoit, and Tremper Longman III, "Cup," in *Dictionary of Biblical Imagery* (Downers Grove, IL: InterVarsity, 1998), 186.

17. Bayer, *Jesus' Predictions,* 71-72.

18. McKnight, *Jesus*, 107-9.

19. Scholars refer to this as Q 11:4 (see chapter 8 above). Matthew adds, "but rescuc us from the evil one" (6:13b).

20. Joachim Jeremias, *The Prayers of Jesus* (London: SCM, 1967), 105-6; cited in McKnight, *Jesus*, 111.

tribulation as the messianic woes or the final ordeal. Raymond E. Brown refers to this time of trial as the "titanic struggle between God and Satan which must introduce the last days."[21] Jesus describes it in Mark 13:5-36.

When Jesus agonizes over the end of his mission in the Garden of Gethsemane, he prays, "Abba [Aramaic for *Father*] . . . for you all things are possible; remove this cup from me; yet, not what I want, but what you want" (Mark 14:36). In both the Lord's Prayer and this agonizing petition in the Garden, Jesus asks God's deliverance from the cataclysmic events, "the time of trial," the cup of suffering that he sees on the horizon. Jesus assumes that the coming of the kingdom of God will be accompanied by great tribulation.

This fear of the final events Jesus would suffer as a result of his mission also fits the criterion of *double dissimilarity*. The view of Christ prevalent in the early church would not have drawn them to fabricating this desire to escape the final events of his mission. Nor were the stories of martyrdom in the Jewish writings of his time supportive of this agonizing reluctance to suffer. For example, the seven martyred brothers and their mother from the time of the Maccabees show no such reluctance in the face of crushing torture and death (2 Maccabees 7:1-42). Jesus wanted the kingdom of God to come; yet, it looked to him increasingly as if he would be inundated by the waves of death in the cataclysmic events of the coming of the kingdom.

This evidence puts us on solid ground for concluding that when Jesus used the metaphor of "*cup* his audience . . . understood the purification of the Final Ordeal"[22]—the time when God would come in judgment and pour out his fury on Israel for unfaithfulness as he prepared them for redemption.[23]

Given this analysis, we have in Mark 10:38 a prediction of suffering in the final ordeal. Although Jewish literature of Jesus' time differs on details, it clearly looked for a future time of tribulation characterized by apostasy, communal upheaval, disruptions of cosmic proportions, and great human suffering.[24] In Jesus' Garden ordeal, his cup surely includes a very personal engagement with that final time of intense suffering.

"She Has Anointed My Body Beforehand for Its Burial"

During mealtime in the house of a leper, a woman breaks in and anoints Jesus from a jar of costly ointment. Some of the guests scold her for this extravagance. Jesus, however, supports her act of devotion, saying,

---

21. Raymond E. Brown, *New Testament Essays* (Garden City: Doubleday, 1968), 314; cited in McKnight, *Jesus*, 114.

22. McKnight, *Jesus*, 128.

23. Ibid.

24. Ibid., 129.

> She has performed a good service for me. For you always have the poor with you, and you can show kindness to them whenever you wish; but you will not always have me. She has done what she could; she has anointed my body beforehand for its burial. Truly I tell you, wherever the good news [or "gospel"] is proclaimed in the whole world, what she has done will be told in remembrance of her. (Mark 14:6-9)

Several features of this story, according to McKnight, offer evidence for its authenticity as an event in the life of Jesus. (1) It occurs in three separate versions (Mark 14:3-9; Luke 7:36-50; and John 12:1-8), which suggests that the event has a historical basis. (2) Believers in the early church would not likely have attributed to Jesus the apparently callous statement he makes about the poor (14:7); they portrayed him as compassionate toward such people. (3) His defense of a marginalized person such as this woman, especially if she was a sinful woman (Luke 7:37), coheres with Jesus' usual way of welcoming and forgiving sinners. (4) Elevating a woman's act of devotion almost to the status of prophecy and dining in the home of a leper represent surprising acts typical of Jesus. Even if verse 9 represents interpretation from a time when the Gentile mission was underway, after the end of Jesus' mission, still verses 7 and 8, along with the others cited so far in this chapter, suggest that Jesus anticipated an early death.[25]

"It Is Impossible for a Prophet to Be Killed Outside of Jerusalem"

The following statement of Jesus in response to a report that Herod was bent on killing him may contain some editing by Luke (indicated by italics), who alone reports it. But it "has much to commend it as historical."[26]

> Go and tell that fox . . . , "Listen, I am casting out demons and performing cures today and tomorrow, and on the third day I finish my work. *Yet* today, tomorrow, and the next day I must be *on my way*, because it is impossible for a prophet to be killed outside of *Jerusalem*." (Luke 13:32-33)

The theme of suffering is typical of the traditions that can be convincingly traced back to Jesus. Given the execution of John the Baptist, would it not be likely that Jesus thought he would suffer a similar death? Is it not also quite

25. Ibid., 130-32.

26. Ibid., 133. McKnight here draws on the study of Kim Huat Tan, *Zion Traditions and the Aims of Jesus*, Society for New Testament Studies Monograph Series 91 (Cambridge: Cambridge University Press, 1997), 57-69.

possible that Jesus thought of Jerusalem as a place where his confrontation with the authorities might end in his death? Jerusalem as a place where prophets had been killed was already a part of the literature of Judaism in the time of Jesus (Jeremiah 26:20-23; 38:4-6; Amos 7:10-17; 2 Chronicles 24:15-22; Josephus, *Antiquities* 10:38; the *Martyrdom and Ascension of Isaiah* 5:1-14; and so forth). Furthermore, the closely positioned time indicators, "today and tomorrow, and on the third day I finish my work" and "Yet today, tomorrow, and the next day," are both hard to harmonize and hard to interpret, which may suggest an Aramaic original that goes back to a time before the final events of Jesus' mission. These verses are characterized by the ambiguity, questioning, and mystery Jesus liked to employ. It was not in the interests of early Christians to make disparaging statements about people such as Herod Antipas either—another bit of evidence that the saying went back to Jesus, who did not hesitate to make such remarks about religious and political authorities. McKnight says that it is this "*attitude* . . . that betrays the authenticity of the tradition."[27]

Finally, these two verses are congruent with "nevertheless, not what I will, but what you will" of Jesus' agonizing prayer in Gethsemane (Mark 14:36). In both of these passages, the conviction emerges that Jesus sees a certain divine necessity in his taking up the cup of deep engagement in the final ordeal. He seems to say, "My prophetic ministry will end, as have the ministries of others, in Jerusalem, but not at the hands of Herod Antipas."[28] Indeed, it is very Jewish to find in the acceptance of God's will the ultimate in human faithfulness (Mishnah, *Avot* 2:1, 4). We turn now to Jesus' saying about drinking and not drinking the cup at the Last Supper.

"I Will Never Again Drink of the Fruit of the Vine until That Day When I Drink It New in the Kingdom of God"

We will look at the Last Supper in general in the next chapter, but here we examine another allusion to Jesus' untimely death called—because it speaks of future celebration in the kingdom of God—the "eschatological prospect": "Truly I tell you, I will never again drink of the fruit of the vine until that day when I drink it new in the kingdom of God" (Mark 14:25).

The Gospel parallels in figure 9.1 below show the eschatological prospect in the Synoptic Gospels. What can we make of this statement? Is it likely to be a genuine statement of Jesus?

27. Ibid., 135.
28. Ibid., 136.

Figure 9.1 The Eschatological Prospect in Three Synoptic Texts
(Boldface type indicates differences in the three accounts.)

Matthew 26:29	Mark 14:25	Luke 22:15-18
		15 He said to them, "I have eagerly desired to eat this Passover with you before I suffer;
		16 for I tell you, I will not eat* it until it is fulfilled in the kingdom of God."
		17 Then he took a cup, and after giving thanks he said, "Take this and divide it among yourselves;
"I tell you, I will never again drink of this fruit of the vine until that day when I drink it new **with you** in **my Father's** kingdom."	"**Truly** I tell you, I will never again drink of the fruit of the vine until that day when I drink it new in the kingdom of God."	18 for I tell you that from now on I will not drink of the fruit of the vine until the kingdom of God **comes**." * Other ancient authorities read [never eat it again].

Matthew, making only stylistic revisions, clearly relies on Mark. As we will discover in chapter 11, for the whole Last Supper narrative, Luke (22:14-20) and Paul (1 Corinthians 11:23-26) have similar wording over against Mark (14:17-26) and Matthew (26:20-30). McKnight believes that the tradition in Mark and Matthew provides a window into the original meal, while Luke works with both Mark and Paul, whose texts are liturgical renderings of the celebration of the Lord's Supper in the early church.[29] Hans Bayer, in contrast, believes the Luke-Paul tradition is the earlier of two separate early traditions, but that, as far as the eschatological prospect is concerned, Mark has the original wording of Jesus' statement.[30] Here again, we note Kenneth Bailey's observation about the preservation of sayings in informal controlled transmission of the Jesus tradition.

Two interpretations have been proposed for the saying, depending on where the interpreter thinks Jesus placed his emphasis. The first half of the pronouncement, "I will never again drink of the fruit of the vine," should be understood as *a vow of abstinence*, if Jesus emphasized the first half of the

29. McKnight, *Jesus,* 262-64. He provides a huge bibliography but bases his decision on the work of Rudolf Pesch, *Das Abendmahl und Jesu Todesverständnis*, Quaestiones disputatae 80 (Freiberg: Herder, 1978), esp. 21-69.

30. Bayer, *Jesus' Predictions,* 35-42.

pronouncement. If he emphasized the second half of the pronouncement, "until that day when I drink it new in the kingdom of God," then the first half should be considered *a promise of death*. If the Last Supper was a Passover Meal and Jesus made the pronouncement in connection with the first cup of wine at the beginning of the meal, it served to introduce his disciples to a temporary ending of the meal's fellowship—a fellowship to be restored after a short time. Thus, the first half of the pronouncement introduces and puts the emphasis on the second half, thus rendering the first half, "I will never again drink of the fruit of the vine," a promise of death rather than a vow of abstinence.[31]

McKnight, who offers a detailed discussion of the Last Supper within the context of the entire scope of the passion narratives, stands, however, for the chronology of John's Gospel. It requires that the Last Supper precede the Passover. While Mark provides the Last Supper with Passover "hues" (14:12, 14, 16), he omits any mention of a Passover lamb, an essential feature of any Passover Meal.[32] McKnight goes on to say, however, that the view of the Last Supper as the Passover Meal could also be true. "Either view of these accounts," he says, "can lead to a meal at which Jesus clearly articulated that his own death was imminent."[33]

Another consideration, not dependent on whether the Last Supper was a Passover Meal, also leads to Bayer's conclusion. Vows of abstinence in the New Testament are conditional demands. For example, Acts 12 reports, "In the morning the Jews joined in a conspiracy and bound themselves by an oath neither to eat nor drink until they had killed Paul" (12:12; see also verses 14 and 21). They were making a conditional demand of themselves. In the case of Mark 14:25, in contrast, Jesus is not saying he will abstain from drinking wine until God brings in the kingdom—as a conditional demand. The whole fabric of Jesus' life and teaching speaks against such an ultimatum presented to God. The pronouncement must therefore be an implicit reference to *the cessation of eating and drinking involved in the death Jesus is to experience*.

The pronouncement also looks forward to a subsequent celebration.[34] Its language reveals that, whereas the death is certain and impending, the future celebration belongs to the indefinite future.[35] Bayer concludes, "the eschatological prospect anticipates a consummation in the Messianic banquet."[36] Though the exact nature of what Jesus expected in the future eludes us, his awareness of his coming death and future participation in a meal of celebration appears certain. Bayer puts it succinctly, "Jesus views his death not as a cul-de-sac but rather as a necessary passage leading eventually to the consummation of the kingdom of God."[37] McKnight, after a lengthy discussion of exactly this saying, concludes,

31. Ibid., 43-44.
32. McKnight, *Jesus,* 272.
33. Ibid.
34. Bayer, *Jesus' Predictions,* 43-44.
35. Ibid., 49.
36. Ibid., 51.
37. Bayer, "Predictions of Jesus' Passion and Resurrection," 631.

"Jesus here predicts not just that he will die and that he will resume fellowship; no, in fact, this saying speaks of the abundance of the final banquet."[38]

The Garden of Gethsemane, already entered above, provides another image that implies Jesus' impending death and resurrection.

"The Hour Has Come!"

In both Mark (14:35 and 41b) and Matthew (26:39 and 45b) Jesus mentions *the hour* in connection with his betrayal "into the hands of sinners" (see figure 9.2). The Gospel of Luke also connects *the hour* with Jesus' betrayal. Luke does not have Jesus use this image in the discourse on the Mount of Olives, Luke's equivalent of the Garden of Gethsemane event. Rather, Luke places it at the end of the betrayal narrative. After he restores a guard's severed ear, in addressing his captors, Jesus says, "When I was with you day after day in the temple, you did not lay hands on me. But this is *your hour*, and the power of darkness!" (22:53).

Figure 9.2 The Cup and the Hour in Matthew and Mark

(Verses in italics from the garden trauma of Jesus stress references to the cup and the hour. Boldface type indicates differences.)

Matthew 26	**Mark 14**
39 And going a little farther, he threw himself on the ground and prayed,	35 And going a little farther, he threw himself on the ground and prayed **that, if it were possible, the *hour* might pass from him**.
"**My** Father, **if it is** possible, let this *cup* pass from me; yet not what I want but what you want."	36 He said, "**Abba**, Father, **for you all things are** possible; remove this *cup* from me; yet, not what I want, but what you want."
45 Then he came **to the disciples** and said to them, "Are you still sleeping and taking your rest? **See**, *the hour **is at hand***, **and** the Son of Man is betrayed into the hands of sinners."	41 He came **a third time** and said to them, "Are you still sleeping and taking your rest? **Enough**! *The hour **has come***; the Son of Man is betrayed into the hands of sinners."

First of all, it is possible to establish the early provenance and probable authenticity of Mark 14:41b, "Enough! *The hour has come*; the Son of Man is betrayed into the hands of sinners." In chapter 10 below, we will see that

38. McKnight, *Jesus*, 331-32.

the enigmatic sayings in Mark 9:31, "The Son of Man is to be betrayed into human hands, and they will kill him, and three days after being killed, he will rise again," and Luke 9:44, "The Son of Man is going to be betrayed into human hands," probably represent pre-Markan and pre-Lukan sayings going back to the Palestinian Jewish Christian community. I will also show that Mark 9:31 is not an elaboration by the later church of an original authentic statement such as Mark 14:41.

If Matthew 26:45-46 turns out to be dependent not on Mark but on a separate tradition, then Mark 14:41b would not be just an abbreviation of Mark 9:31 that Mark inserted at 14:41, but rather Mark's rendering of what Jesus, according to two independent traditions, actually said at this point in the event. Bayer relies on composition criticism in making the following argument. Matthew uses the verb "to draw near" (*engizō*), while Mark has the verb "to come" (*erchomai*). For Matthew to do so surprises careful readers, since both he and Mark use *engizō* in the next verse, and Matthew otherwise shows no preference for *engizō*. Therefore, his use of it in 26:45b cannot be explained as his preference for the term.[39] The verb *engizō* occurs infrequently in Matthew and Mark, and is found mostly in passages taken from their sources. On the other hand, Matthew uses *erchomai* in his Gospel frequently. Why, then, does he have *engizō* in 26:45b? The most plausible conclusion would seem to be that Matthew appeals to his own independent traditional source.[40]

Turning to Luke 22:53b—also in the context of betrayal—we see that Jesus' reference to the hour addresses his adversaries: "this is *your* hour and the power of darkness." This contrast in literary form between Mark and Luke with its accompanying thematic shift suggests Luke's reference to the hour does not depend on Mark's. Thus, the possibility is not excluded that Luke 22:53 adds a pre-Lukan reference to the evidence for "the hour's" stemming from early Christian tradition. Bayer concludes after careful analysis, "No compelling arguments exist which would point against the possibility that Jesus himself referred to this 'hour.'"[41] Now we turn to the question as to what "the hour" meant for Jesus.

In general, the Bible uses the word "hour" as an image of *God's* ordering of time. The image occurs often in John's Gospel. Jesus mentions to his mother at the wedding feast in Cana, "My hour has not yet come" (2:4). In his confrontation with the religious leaders in Jerusalem toward the end of his life, Jesus says, "The hour has come for the Son of Man to be glorified" (12:23). "Hour" can mean a significant time, a ripe time, or a final time. It can mean time is up; it can mean time is now.[42] Gerhard Delling looks at the Greek term for hour (*hōra*) in secular Greek sources, in the Greek translations of the Hebrew scriptures, in intertestamental sources, and throughout the New Testament. In conclusion,

---

39. Bayer, *Jesus' Predictions,* 86.
40. Ibid.
41. Ibid., 87.
42. Ryken, Wilhoit, and Longman, "Cup," 406.

he defines "the hour" in the New Testament as a metaphor for "the time set for something," "the time which is given or appointed for something," and "the time appointed by God."[43]

In the Synoptic Gospels, the hour can refer to the coming or presence (*parousia*) of the Son of Humanity[44] or to the present hour of betrayal. Which meaning is intended in the passages under discussion here is not clear. In Mark 14:41 with its parallels and in Luke 22:53 the hour is *"known* and *at hand,"* so how could it refer to the "final and *unknown* hour of the parousia of the Son of Man?"[45] The introduction in Mark 14:41b, "The hour has come," and its parallel in Matthew 26:45b, "Behold the hour is at hand," are certainly solemn enough. The expression of Jesus' state of mind in Mark 14:35, "And going a little farther, he threw himself on the ground and prayed that, if it were possible, the hour might pass from him," is certainly severe. And the mention of "the power of darkness" in Luke 22:53 is certainly stark enough to suggest that "the hour" has a meaning more vast than merely the time of the betrayal of the Son of Humanity. As Delling puts it, "The hour is defined by the content given to it."[46] So, notice the parallels in Mark 14:35 and 36.

> 35. And going a little farther, he threw himself on the ground and *prayed* that, if it were *possible*, *the hour might pass* from him.
>
> 36. He said, "*Abba, Father,* for you all things are *possible*; remove *this cup* from me; yet, not what I want, but what you want."

In verse 35, "prayed" parallels "Abba, Father" in verse 36; the word "possible" follows in both verses; and "the hour might pass" parallels "remove this cup." The verses are climaxed by the final words of Jesus' prayer, "yet, not what I want, but what you want." This suggests that what we discovered about the cup above provides content for the meaning of the hour in these verses. Can this point to anything other than the hour as a metaphor for "the appointed time of divine judgment of Jesus"?[47] R. S. Barbour, in fact, concludes that "the hour here is analogous to the Johannine hour of humiliation and exaltation."[48] This is the hour as interpreted by Jesus in response to some Greeks who show an interest in seeing him (John 12:23-33). A portion of this passage follows.

> "The hour has come for the Son of Man to be glorified. Very truly, I tell you, unless a grain of wheat falls into the earth and dies, it remains

43. Gerhard Delling, "*Hōra*," in Gerhard Friedrich, ed., *Theological Dictionary of the New Testament*, trans. Geoffrey W. Bromiley, 10 vols. (Grand Rapids: Eerdmans, 1974), 9:677-78.

44. Wright, *Jesus*, 341.

45. Bayer, *Jesus' Predictions,* 87-88.

46. Delling, "*Hōra*," 677.

47. Bayer, *Jesus' Predictions,* 88.

48. R. S. Barbour, "Gethsemane in the Passion Tradition," *New Testament Studies* 16 (1969-70): 233.

> just a single grain; but if it dies, it bears much fruit. . . . Now my soul is troubled. And what should I say—'Father, save me from this hour'? No, it is for this reason that I have come to this hour. Father, glorify your name." Then a voice came from heaven, "I have glorified it, and I will glorify it again. . . . Now is the judgment of this world; now the ruler of this world will be driven out. And I, when I am lifted up from the earth, will draw all people to myself."[49]

Bayer concludes, "The present hour [in Mark 14:41 and Luke 22:53] . . . marks the anxiously anticipated (Lk 12:49f.) and in its full extent accepted (Mk 14:35.36) time of the divine outpouring of wrath and judgment upon Jesus, manifest in the *traditio* [betrayal] of the Son of Man."[50] Thus, the hour joins baptism and the cup as metaphors for the agonizing present crisis that Jesus faces and for the cessation of that crisis in future vindication of the righteous one. Our discussion demonstrates that in these metaphors we find implicit intimations of Jesus' coming death and resurrection. Such a theme not only shows up in Jesus' sayings but in his narrative teaching as well.

"This Is the Heir; Come, Let Us Kill Him"

The parable of the wicked husbandmen (Matthew 21:33-46; Mark 12:1-12; Luke 20:9-19) appears to imply a violent end for Jesus, which is interpreted by a quotation from the Psalms as human rejection and divine vindication. "The stone that the builders rejected has become the chief cornerstone; this is the Lord's doing; it is marvelous in our eyes" (Psalm 118:22-23). The parable represents a possible implicit foreshadowing of Jesus' passion and vindication.

> Then he began to speak to them in parables. "A man planted a vineyard, put a fence around it, dug a pit for the wine press, and built a watchtower; then he leased it to tenants and went to another country. When the season came, he sent a slave to the tenants to collect from them his share of the produce of the vineyard. But they seized him, and beat him, and sent him away empty-handed. And again he sent another slave to them; this one they beat over the head and insulted. Then he sent another, and that one they killed. And so it was with many others; some they beat, and others they killed. He had still one other, a beloved son. Finally he sent him to them, saying, 'They will respect my son.' But those tenants said to one another, 'This is the heir; come, let us kill him, and the inheritance will be ours.' So they seized him, killed him, and threw him out of the vineyard.

49. Other ancient authorities read "all *things* to myself."
50. Bayer, *Jesus' Predictions,* 88.

"What then will the owner of the vineyard do? He will come and destroy the tenants and give the vineyard to others. Have you not read this scripture:

'The stone that the builders rejected
has become the cornerstone [or keystone];
this was the Lord's doing,
and it is amazing in our eyes'?"

When they[51] realized that he had told this parable against them, they wanted to arrest him, but they feared the crowd. So they left him and went away. (Mark 12:1-12)

A parable can be analyzed according to three components: (1) the *scenario* from life used as an analogy; (2) the *substance* of the parable, or truth being illustrated by the analogy; and (3) the *point of comparison* between the scenario and the substance of the parable. The *scenario* of this parable is the tenant system for producing grapes. Its *substance,* or truth being illustrated, is what God will do with those rejecters of his prophet whom he has put in charge of his people. The *point of comparison* is the wicked husbandmen. Among the efforts the owner of the vineyard makes to gain what is owed him is the sending of his own son. He expects the tenant husbandmen to respect his son and to pay him what they owe. The tenants kill the son.[52]

A clue as to the identity of the tenants in the substance turns up in the quotation of Psalm 118:22: "the builders" turns out to be "a well-known *epithet of Jewish leadership* in Rabbinic and Qumran literature."[53] And Bayer considers it "beyond reasonable doubt" that the stone the builders reject can be understood "as a Messianic reference to the rejection of Jesus himself."[54]

Some scholars have relegated this passage to a period later than the time of Jesus because they presuppose that allegorical elements in parables evidence the work of early Christian writers. But at least a dozen factors can be discerned that indicate that the early church did not create this story. The first five draw on the criterion of *dissimilarity*; arguments 6 and 7 represent arguments of *coherence*; and the final one relies on the criterion of *multiple attestation.* (1) No reference is made to the son's resurrection. (2) The parable assumes that Jesus is a prophet rather than the exalted Son of God. (3) It attacks leaders, not the Jews or Israel in general. (4) The response of the owner of the vineyard does not square with the worldview of early Christianity: "He will come and destroy the tenants and give the vineyard to others" (Mark 12:9b). (5) The death of the son here has no overtones of atonement; instead, it fits the paradigm of the slaying of prophets (Jeremiah

51. "They" are presumably the chief priests, scribes, and elders mentioned in Mark 11:27.

52. Bayer, *Jesus' Predictions*, 98-100.

53. Ibid., 102.

54. Ibid., 107. For a detailed discussion of this parable, see N. T. Wright, *The New Testament and the People of God,* Christian Origins and the Question of God 1 (Minneapolis: Fortress, 1992), 74-77.

26:20-23; 38:4-6; Amos 7:10-17; 2 Chronicles 24:15-22; Josephus, *Antiquities* 10.38; *Martyrdom and Ascension of Isaiah* 5:1-14; and so forth).[55] (6) The parable fits in nicely with the often shocking sayings and parables of Jesus (e.g., Luke 15:1-32). (7) Although similar parables can be found in rabbinic literature, they are unlikely to have been borrowed by early Christians, and this parable reveals a vision of "new leaders and a new beginning, both themes being inherent in Jesus' kingdom mission."[56] (8) The scenario of the parable is certainly "historically possible and plausible."[57] (9) The parable is congruent with the contemporary Targum of Isaiah (*Tg. Isaiah* on Isaiah 5:1-7) and represents an indictment of the Temple. (10) The allegorical elements in the parable, according to a source cited by Bayer, were "present from the earliest traceable stages of the parable's development."[58] (11) With the wide range of discourse qualifying as parable (Greek: *parabolē*; Hebrew: *māshal*)—dark sayings, riddles, metaphors, similes, parables, similitudes, allegories, illustrations, fables, proverbs, apocalyptic revelations, symbols, pseudonyms, examples, themes, arguments, apologies, refutations, and jests[59]—how could it be argued that allegorical elements could not be employed by Jesus in a parable? (12) Not only does the parable occur in all three Synoptic Gospels, it has a parallel in the Gospel of Thomas.[60]

Hans Bayer concludes, "[I]t is beyond reasonable doubt that Jesus addressed his opponents . . . prior to his violent death by way of the parable of the Wicked Husbandmen."[61] Scot McKnight connects this parable with Jesus' reaction to the death of John the Baptist, concluding, "We are prepared now to combine Matthew 23:29-32 with Mark 12:1-12 to suggest that Jesus not only saw a connection between John and the fate of Israel's prophets, but placed himself in the same line of rejection."[62] McKnight refers here to a statement of Jesus in Matthew about the killing of the prophets.

> Woe to you, scribes and Pharisees, hypocrites! For you build the tombs of the prophets and decorate the graves of the righteous, and you say, "If we had lived in the days of our ancestors, we would not have taken part with them in shedding the blood of the prophets." Thus you testify against yourselves that you are descendants of those who murdered

55. McKnight, *Jesus*, 152.

56. Ibid., 152-53.

57. Bayer, *Jesus' Predictions,* 91.

58. The quote is from Bayer (*Jesus' Predictions*, 92), but the source is Rudolf Pesch, *Das Markusevangelium*, 2 vols., Herders theologischer Kommentar zum Neuen Testament (Freiburg: Herder, 1976-77), 2:214.

59. Klyne R. Snodgrass, "Parable," in Green, McKnight, and Marshall, *Dictionary of Jesus and the Gospels,* 593.

60. *The Gospel of Thomas: The Hidden Sayings of Jesus,* trans., intro., and ed. Marvin Meyer, with an interpretation by Harold Bloom (New York: HarperSanFrancisco, 1992), 53; see also p. 126 n. 32 above.

61. Bayer, *Jesus' Predictions*, 98.

62. McKnight, *Jesus*, 153.

> the prophets. Fill up, then, the measure of your ancestors. (Matthew 23:29-32)

Thus the parable of the wicked husbandmen qualifies as an implicit prediction of Jesus' suffering and vindication. It fits in also with what the Qur'ān has to say about the slaying of prophets and messengers.

> We gave Moses the Book and followed him up with a succession of Messengers; We gave Jesus, the son of Mary, Clear (Signs) and strengthened him with the Holy Spirit. Is it that whenever there comes to you a Messenger with what ye yourselves desire not, ye are puffed up with pride? Some ye called impostors, and others ye slay! (*Cow* [2]:87)[63]

We have discovered in this chapter that Jesus must have been aware of his impending death as part of the final ordeal connected with the coming of God's kingdom. It can hardly be denied that this awareness goes back to Jesus himself and is embedded in sayings he probably made. I will advance the discussion in the following chapter.

---

63. Several other passages in the Qur'ān refer to the killing of prophets and messengers: *Cow* [2]:91; *Family of Imran* [3]:21, 112, 181; *Women* [4]:155; *Table* [5]:70.

10

"The Son of Humanity Must Be Killed"

Jesus Predicts the End of His Mission

Joel B. Green begins an exhaustive study of the stories of Jesus' suffering and death with the following unequivocal statement, "Jesus of Nazareth was crucified under Pontius Pilate—concerning the facticity of this event, there can be little question."[1] The event is narrated in detail in all four Christian Gospels; various New Testament authors frequently treat it as a historical event; the Latin historian Tacitus (*Annals* 15:44) attests it unmistakably; it was the source of criticism Christians received from their opponents, a stumbling block they had to overcome in order to defend their faith and carry out their mission; and by incorporating the statement "crucified under Pontius Pilate" in their creeds, early Christians bore public witness "to their conviction that the crucifixion of Jesus was an historical fact no one could possibly deny."[2] References in the Talmud and Josephus among other sources from Judaism could be added.[3] With these diverse testimonies, along with the many references to Jesus' death in all the Gospels and the other books of the New Testament, some Christians have made the point that the plethora of reports of the crucifixion of Jesus satisfies the criteria for "recurrent" or "widespread" (*mutawātir*) traditions.

As we saw in chapter 4, Muslim scholars have applied the term *mutawātir* to a report that has come down to the present along so many paths of transmission that forgery of the tradition at any point in its history seems inconceivable. In addition to showing that the reports of Jesus' death do not really satisfy the criteria for "recurrent" reports,[4] al-Qāsimī, whose commentary we followed in some detail in chapter 5, appeals to the following analogy:

1. Joel B. Green, *The Death of Jesus: Tradition and Interpretation in the Passion Narrative*, Wissenschaftliche Untersuchungen zum Neuen Testament, 2. Reihe, 33 (Tübingen: Mohr, 1988), 1.

2. Ibid., 1.

3. For a discussion of these Jewish references to the crucifixion of Jesus, see Robert E. Van Voorst, *Jesus outside the New Testament: An Introduction to the Ancient Evidence*, Studying the Historical Jesus (Grand Rapids: Eerdmans, 2000), chapter 3.

4. Muḥammad Jamāl al-Dīn al-Qāsimī, *Tafsīr al-Qāsimī: al-musammā bi-maḥāsin al-taʾwīl*, ed. Muḥammad Fuʾād ʿAbd al-Bāqī, 17 vols. (Cairo: Dār iḥyāʾ al-kutub al-ʿarabīyah/ʿĪsā al-Bābī al-Halabī wa-shurakāʾ-hu, 1957), 5:1678.

> Suppose we were to put exactly one liter of water in a receptacle and show it to a panel of experts, then—without their knowledge—remove that water and replace it with another exactly measured liter of water. Can the panel, however expert, tell the original water from the substituted water? Only if a difference in the condition of the substitute water can be detected.[5]

According to the Qurʾān commentaries, in this argument, the substitute implied in the phrase *shubbiha la-hum* ("so it was made to appear to them"; *Women* [4]:157) looked as much like Jesus as one liter of water looks like another. In other words, all the items we have cited in our survey of Christian and non-Christian sources could in many Muslim minds affirm a crucifixion of someone *thought to be Jesus*.

Another line of evidence and inference supports the conviction that the person "crucified, dead, and buried" was Jesus and not a substitute. It is my purpose in this chapter to show that Jesus deliberately taught his followers that he was to die and be raised in vindication. This evidence leads to the question, Given the character of Jesus as revealed in the Gospel and the Qurʾān, does it seem possible that Jesus would implicitly and explicitly teach that he must suffer, die, and be raised again and then at the last hour ask for someone else to take his place?[6] In making the case for the authenticity of Jesus' explicit teaching that he was to die, as I did in chapter 9, I cite scholars using historical methods because most of my Muslim readers will not share my confidence in these scriptures as God-inspired and divinely raised up from within Christian communities of faith.

The Gospels of Matthew, Mark, and Luke present Jesus predicting his suffering, death, and resurrection explicitly on three different occasions. These passages reveal a Jesus increasingly aware of an "inescapable mission awaiting him in Jerusalem."[7] We will look at each of these three occasions and comment on how the three Gospel writers deal with each of them.

The Caesarean Prediction Following Peter's Confession

The Gospel according to Mark is the Gospel the majority of interpreters think is the earliest of the three Synoptic Gospels. The question of Jesus' identity dominates it from its "abrupt beginning" to its "enigmatic ending" (1:27; 2:7; 4:41; 6:2; 8:17, 21, 23).[8] A high point in this quest comes at 8:27, where Jesus himself

5. Ibid., 5:1678.

6. Kenneth Cragg, *The Call of the Minaret*, 2nd ed. (Maryknoll, NY: Orbis Books/Ibadan, Nigeria: Daystar, 1985), 267-68.

7. Hans F. Bayer, "Predictions of Jesus' Passion and Resurrection," in Joel B. Green, Scot McKnight, and I. Howard Marshall, eds., *Dictionary of Jesus and the Gospels* (Downers Grove, IL: InterVarsity, 1992), 630.

8. Peter M. Head, "The Self-Offering and Death of Christ as a Sacrifice in the Gospels and the

asks his disciples, "Who do people say that I am?" After Peter answers correctly, "You are the Messiah," Jesus offers his followers the first clear indication of his coming death and resurrection.

Indeed, like the identity of Jesus, his death, as Ernest Best has noted, "broods over the entire Gospel."[9] And thus Mark gives special prominence to three explicit predictions in chapters 8-10. Peter Head points out that these three sets of predictions in this section "provide . . . [its] structural framework."[10] Each prediction has a geographical setting, a misunderstanding, and a teaching, as shown in figure 10.1.

Figure 10.1 Predictions in Mark
The structure of the discourses about Jesus' identity
and mission, showing their symmetry.[11]

Place		Prediction	Misunderstanding	Teaching
Caesarea	8:27	8:31	8:32-33	8:34-37
Galilee	9:30	9:31	9:33-34	9:35-37
Judea	10:1	10:33-34	10:35-41	10:42-45

The Caesarean Prediction in Mark

The structure of these narratives features repeated reminders that Jesus is on "the way" (8:27; 9:33, 34; 10:17, 32, 46, 52). "The way" for Mark recalls "the way of the Lord" proclaimed by Isaiah's herald, whose appearance Mark announces (1:1-3). This way "leads to Jerusalem, but more especially it leads to the fulfillment of the divine purpose."[12]

The first prediction occurs geographically in Caesarea. It occurs structurally in the thematic unit 8:27-33, during this journey in "the way of the Lord."

> Jesus went on with his disciples to the villages of Caesarea Philippi; and on the way he asked his disciples, "Who do people say that I am?" And they answered him, "John the Baptist; and others, Elijah; and still others, one of the prophets." He asked them, "But who do you say that I am?" Peter answered him, "You are the Messiah."

Acts of the Apostles," in Roger Beckwith and Martin J. Selman, eds., *Sacrifice in the Bible* (Carlisle, UK: Paternoster/Grand Rapids: Baker Book House, 1995), 111.

9. Ernest Best, *Mark: The Gospel as Story*, ed. John Riches, Studies of the New Testament World (Edinburgh: T&T Clark, 1983), 66.

10. Head, "Self-Offering," 112.

11. Following Head, "Self Offering," 112.

12. John T. Carroll and Joel B. Green with Robert E. Van Voorst, Joel Marcus, Donald Senior, *The Death of Jesus in Early Christianity* (Peabody, MA: Hendrickson, 1995), 28.

> And he sternly ordered them not to tell anyone about him. Then he began to teach them that the Son of Man must undergo great suffering, and be rejected by the elders, the chief priests, and the scribes, and be killed, and after three days rise again.

It is well known that Mark composed his Gospel by integrating into its structure reports about what Jesus said and did. Peter and other followers of Jesus had passed these stories and other reports on to him. In order to understand this process and to identify Mark's sources, scholars have examined every verse and cluster of verses in his Gospel in detail. They have been able to detect evidence of sources Mark used in his composition as well as the words, phrases, sentences, and paragraphs he employs to integrate this earlier material into his discourse.

In chapter 8, I introduced the methods these scholars use in pursuit of their goals. As I mentioned there, if a unit of the Gospel can be identified as a typical form of discourse with clear evidence of coherence and unity, and if the form can be identified with forms of discourse available for Mark's use, then the likelihood of the unit's being earlier—that is to say, older—than the Gospel of Mark greatly increases.

After this kind of careful analysis, the biblical scholar Hans Bayer confidently identifies verses 8:31-33 above "as one pre-Markan unit." The immediately preceding context of these verses (8:27-30) shows "possible pre-Markan links as well."[13] The prediction of Jesus in verse 31 represents the central instruction in a form commonly used by teachers at the time of Jesus. Therefore, Mark probably received it from his predecessors. Scholars call the form a *didactic discourse*, a discourse consisting of an "introductory dialogue," in this case verses 27-30, a "central instruction" (verse 31), and a "conclusion to the instruction," in this case verses 32-33, not quoted above.[14] Bayer also observes that the Greek of this unit of discourse contains evidence of translation from Hebrew or Aramaic. For this and other reasons, he suggests that Christians from a Jewish background in Palestine provided it for Mark.[15]

This didactic discourse is then followed by an application to those in general who would follow Jesus. They must also take up their own crosses, for "those who want to save their life will lose it, and those who lose their life for my sake, and for the sake of the gospel, will save it" (8:35). We turn now to the parallel passages in Matthew and Luke. Figure 10.2 shows the Caesarean revelation of Jesus' messianic identity, leading up to the Caesarean prediction.

---

13. Hans F. Bayer, *Jesus' Predictions of Vindication and Resurrection: The Provenance, Meaning, and Correlation of the Synoptic Predictions*, ed. Martin Hengel and Otfried Hofius, Wissenschaftliche Untersuchungen zum Neuen Testament, 2. Reihe, 20 (Tübingen: Mohr, 1986), 165.

14. Ibid., 163.

15. Ibid., 166.

Figure 10.2 Revealing Identity of Jesus at Caesarea in Synoptics
(Boldface type indicates distinctive features.)

Matthew 16:13-16	Mark 8:27-29	Luke 9:18-20
13 Now when Jesus came into the district of Caesarea Philippi, he asked his disciples, "Who do people say that **the Son of Man** is?" 14 And they said, "Some say John the Baptist, but others Elijah, and still others **Jeremiah or** one of the prophets." 15 He said to them, "But who do you say that I am?" 16 **And Simon** Peter answered **saying**, "You are the Messiah, **the Son of the living God**."	27 Jesus went on with his disciples to the villages of Caesarea Philippi; and on the way he asked his disciples, "Who do people say that I am?" 28 And they answered him, "John the Baptist; and others, Elijah; and still others, one of the prophets." 29 He asked them, "But who do you say that I am?" Peter answered **him**, "You are the Messiah."	18 **Once when he was praying alone, with only the disciples near him**, he asked them, "Who do **the crowds** say that I am?" 19 They answered, "John the Baptist; but others, Elijah; and still others, **that** one of the **ancient** prophets **has arisen** (*anestē*)." 20 He said to them, "But who do you say that I am?" Peter answered, "The Messiah **of God**."

The Caesarean Prediction in Matthew

Matthew also includes the story of the Caesarean revelation and prediction (16:13-23) with certain additions and revisions. He includes "the Son of Man" in the first question Jesus asks, "Who do people say that the Son of Man is?" (16:13). Matthew includes Jeremiah in the list of popular conceptions of Jesus' identity (16:14). And he adds "the Son of the living God" to Peter's confession (16:16). Matthew, then, has Jesus blessing Peter for his answer and foretelling his future, something Mark does not include. Matthew's verses 17-19 are omitted from figure 10.2 because they have no parallels in Mark or Luke. The blessing and the prophecy are nicely constructed in connection with the confession. I have modified the translation of the passage slightly to indicate (in italics) these parallels:

> *And Simon Peter answered saying*, "*You are* [Greek: *sy ei*] the Messiah, the Son of the living God."
>
> *And Jesus answered saying*, "Blessed *are you* [Greek: *Makarios ei*], Simon son of Jonah! For flesh and blood has not revealed this to you, but my Father in heaven. And I tell you, *you are* [Greek: *sy ei*] Peter [*Petros*], and on this rock [*petra*] I will build my church, and the gates of Hades will not prevail against it. I will give you the keys of the kingdom of heaven, and whatever you bind on earth will be bound in heaven, and whatever you loose on earth will be loosed in heaven."

Matthew uses the phrase "flesh and blood" (16:17) only here in his Gospel. Bayer says it may have a Semitic origin. "My Father in heaven" represents both a Semitic reference to heaven and a statement unusual for a Jew to make, calling God "my Father."[16] Other features indicate that these verses existed together before the composition of Matthew's Gospel. The wordplay indicated by the bracketed Greek words in verse 18 may have stemmed from wordplay in Aramaic. The word translated "church" in verse 18, *ekklēsia*, may not mean "church" as organized after Jesus' resurrection and ascension. If its meaning were restricted to the post-Easter church, then it could be construed as evidence that the post-Easter church placed this prophecy in the mouth of Jesus. But *ekklēsia* here could very well refer to "the people of Israel" or "the elect"—in which case it would fit in with other indications that the passage comes from early Palestinian-Jewish Christianity.

The word translated "prevail against," from the verb *katischyō*, occurs only here in Matthew, which suggests that this prophecy comes from a source Matthew uses, but one not used by Mark or Luke. The terms for "bind" and "loose" in verse 19, as well as the opposition "on earth" and "in heaven," are typical expressions of Matthew. In the context of these expressions, several other elements occur that obviously go back to an earlier Aramaic source. For this reason, the presence of these expressions typical of Matthew does not require us to assume that Matthew added them to Mark. Rather, these additions indicate Matthew has at hand an early source that he uses to supplement Mark's more condensed treatment of the event and that this early source was circulated by Aramaic-speaking early Christians.[17] Although significant voices have dissented from his conclusion, Bayer makes a strong case for Matthew's version's stemming from "strong Palestinian Jewish-Christian roots."[18] He believes Mark condenses his version from a fuller dialogue much like that of Matthew.

Our particular interest, however, rests not only on the "strong Jewish-Christian roots" of the confession but also on the first explicit prediction of Jesus' death and resurrection that follows it—also a close parallel to the first prediction in Mark. The following verses are quoted from Matthew 16:21-23, and can be compared with Mark's and Luke's versions in the figure 10.3.

> From that time on, Jesus began to show his disciples that he must go to Jerusalem and undergo great suffering at the hands of the elders and chief priests and scribes, and be killed, and on the third day be raised.
>
> And Peter took him aside and began to rebuke him, saying, "God forbid it, Lord! This must never happen to you."
>
> But he turned and said to Peter, "Get behind me, Satan! You are a stumbling block to me; for you are setting your mind not on divine things but on human things."

16. Ibid., 183.
17. Ibid., 184.
18. Ibid., 185.

Figure 10.3 The Caesarean Prediction of the Death of Jesus
(Boldface type indicates distinctive features.)

Matthew 16:20-23	Mark 8:30-33	Luke 9:21-22
20 Then he sternly ordered the disciples not to tell anyone **that he was the Messiah**.	30 And he sternly ordered them not to tell anyone **about him**.	21 He sternly ordered **and commanded** them not to tell anyone,
21 **From that time on, Jesus** began to show his disciples that he must **go to Jerusalem** and undergo great suffering at the hands of the elders and chief priests and scribes, and be killed, and on the third day be raised (*egerthēnai*).	31 Then he began to teach them that the Son of Man must undergo great suffering, and be rejected by the elders, the chief priests, and the scribes, and be killed, and **after three** days rise (*anastēnai*) again.	22 saying, "The Son of Man must undergo great suffering, and be rejected by the elders, chief priests, and scribes, and be killed, and on the third day be raised (*egerthēnai*)."
22 And Peter took him aside and began to rebuke him, **saying, "God forbid it, Lord! This must never happen to you."**	32 **He said all this quite openly**. And Peter took him aside and began to rebuke him.	
23 But he turned and said to Peter, "Get behind me, Satan! **You are a stumbling block to me;** for you are setting your mind not on divine things but on human things."	33 But turning and **looking at his disciples, he rebuked** Peter and said, "Get behind me, Satan! For you are setting your mind not on divine things but on human things."	

Matthew's account is again more full than Mark's because of the inclusion of Peter's word of horror and admonition to Jesus, "God forbid it, Lord! This must never happen to you" (16:22). Jesus' response is instructive as to how purposeful he understood his death to be, "Get behind me, Satan! You are a stumbling block to me; for you are setting your mind not on divine things but on human things." Here it becomes clear that God's perspective supports the death of the Messiah!

The scholarly consensus on this passage contends that the only source Matthew had for his version of the unit 16:13-23 was Mark 8:27-33 and that Matthew inserted the fuller dialogue with Peter (16:16-19) into Mark's narrative. Bayer engages in a detailed interaction with the discussion of scholars on this passage. We will, however, consider only some of his reasons for concluding that the predictions in these verses concerning the end of Jesus' mission may have been contained in a unit of narrative Matthew has received from early sources in addition to the Gospel of Mark.[19]

While the essential elements in Matthew 16:21 parallel Mark's account, several differences emerge. Matthew adds "go to Jerusalem" and omits "and be rejected." Matthew uses a form of the Greek verb *egeirō* (*egerthēnai*) for "to be raised," while Mark uses a form of the Greek verb *anistēmi* (*anastēnai*) for "to be raised." Matthew includes a more precise time reference, "on the third day" (16:21).

Furthermore, the "get behind me Satan" episode (16:22-23) exhibits a close connection with the prediction in 16:21. According to Bayer, Peter's "Forbid it, Lord!" (*hileōs soi kyrie*), which Matthew records and Mark omits, is a "Palestinian phrase."[20] Mark says that Jesus rebukes Peter in the presence of his other disciples (8:33), while Matthew mentions no other disciples (16:22-23). Matthew uses the term *skandalon*, "stumbling block." The term is not used in Jewish writings heavily influenced by Greek culture[21] but is closely connected with the conceptual world of the Hebrew scriptures and Jewish religious documents written during the period between the Hebrew scriptures and the New Testament. Luke uses the concept, but not the term. The early church fathers had to define its meaning, which indicates that it was not understood by Greek and Roman readers unfamiliar with Palestinian Jewish culture.

For these reasons, Bayer thinks the second half of Matthew 16:23 comes from a Semitic source earlier than Mark. What Matthew includes, but Mark does not, relates so firmly to its context that Bayer finds it hard to see it as simply Matthew's editorial additions to Mark. Robert H. Gundry attributes it more to the literary activity of Matthew, who "turns Peter's rebuke into a confession of Jesus' lordship."[22]

But even if Bayer's analysis and evaluation prove wrong and the consensus view—represented here by Gundry—proves correct, the passage in Mark still represents an early picture of Jesus' predicting his death and resurrection. Jesus' awareness of his coming death as the will of God for the last days of his mission openly haunts these passages. Mark's "after three days" in 8:31 can hardly be attributed to the early church since it clashes with the resurrection of Jesus "on the third day" as found in Mark 9:31; Matthew 16:21; Luke 9:22; 1 Corinthians 15:4; Acts 10:40; and John 2:19[23]—an application of the criterion of *dissimilarity*.

---

19. Ibid., 187-88.

20. Ibid., 186.

21. Bayer calls these "Hellenistic Jewish writings" (ibid., 187). Some of the Jewish writings, the scriptures, and subsequent writings between the end of the Hebrew scriptures and the beginning of New Testament were translated into Greek, or even composed in Greek, but they were not heavily influenced by Greek culture.

22. Robert H. Gundry, *Matthew: A Commentary on His Handbook for a Mixed Church under Persecution* (Grand Rapids: Eerdmans, 1994), 338.

23. Scot McKnight, *Jesus and His Death: Historiography, Historical Jesus, and Atonement Theory* (Waco, TX: Baylor University Press, 2005), 233.

The Caesarean Prediction in Luke

Luke also includes a parallel (9:18-22) to Jesus' first Caesarean prediction of his passion and resurrection in Mark. It features a streamlining of the material from Mark in order to facilitate a clear presentation of Luke's case.[24] The first part of Luke's account is found in figure 10.2 and verses 21 and 22 in figure 10.3.

> Once when he was praying alone, with only the disciples near him, he asked them, "Who do the crowds say that I am?" They answered, "John the Baptist; but others, Elijah; and still others, that one of the ancient prophets has arisen." He said to them, "But who do you say that I am?" Peter answered, "The Messiah of God."
>
> He sternly ordered and commanded them not to tell anyone, saying, "The Son of Man must undergo great suffering, and be rejected by the elders, chief priests, and scribes, and be killed, and on the third day be raised." Then he said to them all, "If any want to become my followers, let them deny themselves and take up their cross daily and follow me."

Luke, unlike Mark and Matthew, does not identify the geographical location of this event. He alone uses the word "crowds" (*ochloi*) in verse 18 in place of their "people" (*anthrōpoi*) and the expression "one of the ancient prophets has arisen" in verse 19. Bayer says that all three of the opinions about Jesus' identity Luke includes in verse 19 "imply the return to life after death or translation (Elijah)."[25] This provides a link with the prediction of the resurrection in 9:22. By omitting material from Mark and Matthew in 9:20-22, Luke links the confession of Peter more closely with the passion and resurrection of Jesus. The command not to tell anyone applied in 9:21 accentuates the gravity of coming events. Furthermore, omitting the rebuke of Peter makes the call to discipleship in 9:23 follow directly and compactly upon the predictions. Luke also omits the blessing and prophecy in 9:20 that Matthew includes in his version. These omissions do not suggest that Luke works from a source that does not have them, but rather that he shapes his material according to his purposes in writing his Gospel.[26]

In 9:22, Luke seems to rely heavily on Mark 8:31, differing in two significant respects. Like Matthew, he uses a form of *egeirō* for resurrection instead of a form of *anistēmi* and the more precise time reference "on the third day" in place of "after three days." Looking ahead to Jesus' third explicit prediction (18:33, parallel to Mark 10:33; fig. 10.6, page 165), we find Luke *less* dependent on Mark than he is in this first prediction. Yet, in the third prediction Luke surprises us by using Mark's term for resurrection, and not Matthew's term, which he uses in the first prediction. These textual details lead Bayer to ask why Luke does not use Mark's term here at 9:22, especially in light of Luke's use of Mark's term for

24. Bayer, *Jesus' Predictions*, 190.
25. Ibid., 191.
26. Ibid.

resurrection in verse 19, "one of the ancient prophets *has arisen*" (*anistē,* from *anistēmi*).[27]

These and other parallels between Matthew and Luke over against Mark—in spite of some striking similarities between Luke and Mark—"make the interdependency of Luke and Matthew probable."[28] This contributes to Bayer's surmise that possibly Luke and Matthew made use of a different tradition to report this prediction than the one available to them in Mark. This conclusion appears more probable when we recall Bayer's conclusion, mentioned above, that Matthew relies on both Mark's Gospel and another Palestinian Jewish-Christian source.[29] According to this scenario, Luke uses both Mark and the source Matthew uses but omits the "get behind me, Satan" part of Matthew 16:23.[30]

The Galilean Prediction Following the Transfiguration

After Jesus appears in radiant transformation, a voice declares, "This is my Son,[31] the Beloved; listen to him!" (Mark 9:7). In the immediate aftermath of the euphoria generated by this disclosure, Jesus again orders his disciples to keep all this to themselves until the resurrection of the Son of Humanity.

> As they were coming down the mountain, he ordered them to tell no one about what they had seen, until after the Son of Man had risen from the dead. So they kept the matter to themselves, questioning what this rising from the dead could mean. (Mark 9:9-10)

Some commentators have argued that the second half of Mark 9:9, "until after the Son of Man had risen from the dead" (9b), is an editorial addition by Mark, based on Jesus' earlier prediction of the resurrection (8:31). But the fact that Jesus mentions only his resurrection here, while Mark's Gospel normally emphasizes the passion of Jesus, suggests that 9b has not been added by Mark to his source. If 9b were Mark's editorial comment or lifted from the same tradition as 8:31, would he not have put in both the passion and the resurrection?[32] Bayer concludes, "Mk 9:9b constitutes a significant, probably pre-Markan tradition."[33]

When Jesus, Peter, James, and John return from the mountain to the other

---

27. Ibid.

28. Ibid., 192.

29. Ibid.

30. Ibid., 192-93.

31. In Jesus' time, "Son of God," designated the Messiah "as Israel's representative" (see N. T. Wright, *Jesus and the Victory of God*, Christian Origins and the Question of God 2 [Minneapolis: Fortress, 1996], 486).

32. Bayer, *Jesus' Predictions*, 167-68.

33. Ibid., 169.

disciples, they find them and others involved in a turmoil around a failure to heal a boy possessed of an unclean spirit (9:14-24). After Jesus successfully heals the boy, his disciples ask him privately why they had not succeeded. He replies that such power comes only through prayer (9:25-29).[34] From here, Jesus again takes up the instruction of his disciples concerning the role and destiny of the Son of Humanity. This brings us to Jesus' second prediction of his death and resurrection, presented in parallel with Matthew and Luke in figure 10.4.

Figure 10.4 The Galilean Prediction of the Death of Jesus
(Boldface type indicates distinctive features.)

Matthew 17:22-23	Mark 9:30-32	Luke 9:43-45
		43 And all were astounded at the greatness of God. While everyone was amazed at all that he was doing,
22 **As they were gathering in** Galilee,	30 They went on from there and passed through Galilee. **He did not want anyone to know it**;	
Jesus said to them, "The Son of Man is going to be betrayed into human hands,	31 for he **was teaching** his disciples, saying to them, [a] "The Son of Man is to be betrayed (*paradidotai*) into human hands, [b]	he said to his disciples, 44 "**Let these words sink into your ears**: The Son of Man is going to be betrayed into human hands."
23 and they will kill him, and **on the third day** he will be raised (*egerthēsetai*)."	and they will kill him, and three days after being killed, he will rise again (*anastēsetai*)."	
And they were greatly distressed.	32 But they did not understand what he was saying and were afraid to ask him.	45 But they did not understand this saying; **its meaning was concealed from them, so that they could not perceive it**. And they were afraid to ask him about this saying.

34. The later manuscripts add "and fasting," which is clearly not in the original.

The Galilean Prediction in Mark

The prediction in Mark (9:31) falls into two halves: "The Son of Humanity[35] is to be betrayed into human hands" (31a); and "they will kill him, and three days after being killed, he will rise again" (31b). The phrase in verse 31a, "betrayed into hands" (*paradidotai eis cheiros*) appears to be Semitic because "Son of Humanity" and "human hands" constitute a wordplay in Aramaic. The whole saying part of 9:31a could very well be an Aramaic expression "intended to stimulate thought."[36]

The issue of interpretation then turns on the relationship between 9:31a and 9:31b. Is 9:31b also from an early Palestinian Jewish-Christian source? Speaking to his disciples in the Garden of Gethsemane, Jesus uses a phrase in Mark 14:41 that represents a clear parallel with 9:31a, "The hour has come; *the Son of Man is betrayed into the hands* of sinners." This must mean that this dark or riddle-like saying circulated separately from 9:31b, "and they will kill him, and three days after being killed, he will rise again." That is, it was circulated in Jewish-Christian circles in Palestine without being limited to a particular narrative such as the one we are studying. Does this raise a question as to the Palestinian roots of the Galilean prediction? If 9:31b has been added to the preceding half of verse 31 by the later church, then Jesus could have been delivered into human hands, but never killed and crucified.

Bayer agrees that the phrase in 14:41 reinforces the conviction that 9:31a is a "fixed, pre-Markan saying . . . containing strong Palestinian roots."[37] He points out, however, that the phrase in 14:41 is quite possibly itself an "abbreviated saying."[38] That is, Mark does not take the whole of the original saying from the source he is using at 14:41, though he could have.

In addition, internal evidence suggests the inseparability of the two halves of 9:31. Bayer lays out the connections between them. The passive participle, "after being killed" (*apoktantheis*), in the second half of the verse has the same grammatical subject as does the first half of the verse. This participle is also unique in Mark. Furthermore, the Aramaic equivalent that could be behind the Greek verb "to be betrayed" (*paradidotai*) in the first half of the prediction finds an appropriate complementary element in this passive participle. Finally, according to Barnabas Lindars, "three days after being killed, he will rise again" suggests at least a pre-Markan origin.[39] The sentence could then be logically laid

35. I changed "man" (NRSV) here into "humanity" in order to reflect the word play on Son of Humanity in the first half of the verse (*ho huios tou* ***anthrōpou*** *paradidotai eis cheiros* ***anthrōpōn***).

36. Bayer, *Jesus' Predictions*, 169-70. For a detailed defense of this, see p. 170 n. 131. The phrase "saying 'intended to stimulate thought'" translates Bayer's *māshal* (ibid.). Since using "proverb" or "parable" for *māshal* would be misleading, Klyne R. Snodgrass's gloss serves in this context: "A *māshal* is any dark [riddle-like] saying intended to stimulate thought" ("Parable," in Green, McKnight, and Marshall, eds., *Dictionary of Jesus and the Gospels*, 593).

37. Bayer, *Jesus' Predictions*, 170-71.

38. Ibid., 171.

39. Barnabas Lindars, *Jesus Son of Man: A Fresh Examination of the Son-of-Man Sayings*

out in three parts: "betrayed into human hands"; "being killed"; and "rising from the dead," all of which fit and serve to show the unity of the prediction.[40] Now we turn to the parallels in Matthew and Luke.

The Galilean Prediction in Matthew and Luke

The announcement of Jesus' resurrection in Matthew's narrative of the Transfiguration, "Tell no one about the vision until after the Son of Man has been raised from the dead" (17:9), represents a distinct parallel to Mark 9:9, "he ordered them to tell no one about what they had seen, until after the Son of Man had risen from the dead." But Luke's account of the Transfiguration has no parallel prediction or reference to Jesus' resurrection, except within the vision itself where it says, "They appeared in glory and were speaking of his departure (*exodos*), which he was about to accomplish at Jerusalem" (9:31). Neither of the other two Synoptic Gospels contains any conversation among the persons in the vision. Matthew has some unique features, including a word that occurs nowhere else in Matthew, "the vision" (*to horama*) (17:9).[41] Nevertheless, we can safely leave this verse without further comment.

As in Mark, Jesus' second explicit prediction of his passion and resurrection in Matthew (17:22-23) occurs after the Transfiguration and the healing of a young boy with an unclean spirit. It is not clear why Matthew mentions the killing of Jesus (*apokteinō*) only once, "they will kill him, and on the third day he will be raised" (17:23), whereas Mark mentions it twice, "and they will kill him, and three days *after being killed*, he will rise again" (9:31). Matthew could simply have omitted it or taken it from a tradition handed down to him that itself did not have it.[42]

Was Luke's Semitic expression, "Let these words sink into your ears" (9:44a), originally linked with "The Son of Man is going to be betrayed into human hands" (9:44b)? The union of a similar phrase, "So put it in your hearts," with, "do not prepare your defense in advance," in another statement of Jesus recorded by Luke (21:14), suggests that the answer is "Yes." The combination of this Semitic expression with the Semitic betrayal-of-the-Son-of-Humanity expression "suggests that the Son of Man phrase was transmitted at a very early time with themes of rejection."[43] Luke (9:44) shares with Matthew (17:22) the additional word *mellei* ("going to," "is about to," with a following infinitive) in "is *going to be betrayed* into human hands." It could represent an attempt to reproduce in Greek the future sense of an Aramaic participle. Again, putting it in the words of Bayer, "This Lukan parallel to Matthew must be emphasized since it displays a

---

in the Gospels in the Light of Recent Research (London: SPCK, 1983), 63ff.; cited in Bayer, *Jesus' Predictions*, 171.

40. Bayer, *Jesus' Predictions*, 171.
41. Ibid., 188.
42. Ibid.
43. Ibid., 193.

common attempt to render the key-concept of *traditio* in v 44b as faithfully as possible to its Aramaic original. The possibility of a separate tradition common to Matthew and Luke is thus increased."[44] This would support the possibility of a tradition in Aramaic separate from that used by Mark but common to Matthew and Luke. What Luke does is abbreviate the tradition found in Matthew.[45]

> Luke: "Let these words sink into your ears: The Son of Man is going to be betrayed into human hands." (9:44)
>
> Matthew: for he was teaching his disciples, saying to them, "The Son of Man is to be betrayed into human hands, and they will kill him, and three days after being killed, he will rise again." (17:22-23)

The Judean Prediction of Jesus' Passion and Resurrection

Unlike the other two passion and resurrection predictions, this one does not follow a common and significant event. In Mark (10:32-34) it follows Jesus' teaching about divorce, his blessing of little children, his dialogue with a rich man, and his reflection on riches and discipleship with his disciples. These events relate closely to the content of this third explicit prediction.

Matthew's parallel prediction follows the same set of events (19:1-30), but he tucks in the parable of the workers in the vineyard (20:1-16) just before the prediction (20:17-19). The third explicit prediction in Mark (10:35-41) and Matthew (20:20-24) is followed by a teaching of Jesus in response to his disciples' quarreling over places of special privilege next to him in his coming kingdom. This teaching about discipleship in both Gospels contains the important "ransom saying" (Mark 10:45; Matthew 20:28): "For the Son of Man came not to be served but to serve, and to give his life *a ransom for many*."

Luke's parallel (18:15-34), like that of Matthew, follows Mark'S order of events with some modifications. Jesus blesses the children (18:15-17). Then he engages in dialogue with a rich official (18:18-23) and discusses riches and discipleship with his disciples (18:24-30). Luke omits the teaching about divorce that Mark has as well as the long parable of workers in the vineyard featured in Matthew. He also omits the squabble of the disciples over their position in the kingdom and the ransom saying.

The Third Explicit Prediction in Mark

We look first at Mark 10:32-34, again searching for clues about its connection with Markan, pre-Markan, or other early traditions related to the last days of Jesus' mission.

---

44. Ibid.
45. Ibid., 194.

> They were on the road, going up to Jerusalem, and Jesus was walking ahead of them; they were amazed, and those who followed were afraid. He took the twelve aside again and began to tell them what was to happen to him, saying, "See, we are going up to Jerusalem, and the Son of Man will be handed over to the chief priests and the scribes, and they will condemn him to death; then they will hand him over to the Gentiles; they will mock him, and spit upon him, and flog him, and kill him; and after three days he will rise again."

Figure 10.5 Contrasts in Mark's Third Prediction and Passion Narrative

Mark's Third Prediction	Mark's Passion Narrative
33b *paradothēsetai tois archiereusin . . .* (will be betrayed to the chief priests)	14:43f. *para tōn archiereōn* . . . (from the chief priests) *ho paradidous auton* . . . (the one betraying him)
33b *katakrinousin . . . thanatō* (they will condemn . . . to death)	14:64 *katekrinan auton enochon einai thanatou* (condemned him to be liable of death)
33b *paradōsousin . . . tois ethnesin . . .* (will deliver . . . up to the nations)	15:1 *paredōkan Pilatō* (delivered to Pilate)
34 *empaixousin* (they will mock)	15:20, 31 (19-32) *enepaixan*; *empaizontes* (they had mocked him; mocking)
34 *emptousousin* (the will spit at)	14:65, 15:19 *emptyein*; *eneptyon* (to spit; they spit)
34 *mastigōsousin* (will scourge)	15:15 (*phragellōsas*) (flog)
34 *apoktenousin* (they will kill)	15:15, 24 (*staurōthē/staurousin*) (crucify)
34 *anastēsetai* (he will rise again)	16:6 (*egērthē*) (rise)

Several features of Mark 10:32 suggest that Mark presents this third explicit passion and resurrection prediction with a more personal touch than he did in the case of either of the earlier two.[46] "On the road" recalls his "on the way" in both 8:27 and 9:33. This suggests that all three predictions of the end of Jesus'

46. Ibid., 172.

mission came while traveling, and thus were private.[47] When Jesus takes the twelve aside "again" and tells them the things about to happen to him (*ta mellonta autō symbainein*), the disclosure becomes very intimate indeed.

Because the passion prediction is so detailed here, many scholars see it as an addition Mark makes to his sources in the light of events that have already transpired. If this were the case, however, we would expect this prediction to follow Mark's passion narrative more closely than it actually does. My adaptation of Bayer's chart (fig. 10.5) shows how the terminology differs between Mark 10:33-34 and the chapters of Mark's passion narrative. This chart in transliterated Greek with English glosses demonstrates this divergence.

In verse 34, a form of the verb *empaizō*, "mock," *introduces* the insulting behavior directed at Jesus, while it *climaxes* it (15:31) in the passion narrative (15:19-32). Figure 10.5 makes clear that the terms for these acts of disrespect, death, and even resurrection differ. In the passion narrative, both Jews and non-Jews "spit" at and "mock" Jesus (14:65; 15:31), while the prediction suggests the Gentiles will do all the acts of derision. The implication that it is Gentiles alone who humiliate Jesus reflects a Jewish-Christian Palestinian origin of this tradition. Furthermore, the use of a form of *anistēmi* instead of a form of *egeirō* for "he will rise again" in 10:34 "hints at pre-Markan tradition."[48]

This Judean prediction mentions the Son of Humanity while the passion narrative lacks any reference to this title of Jesus. These differences suggest strongly that the passion narrative and this prediction stem from different traditions. The connection of the prediction with the Son of Humanity "supports the probability" that it is the older tradition.[49]

The careful reader will note, however, that, in contrast, Mark 10:32-34 feature connections in both form and content with the previous explicit predictions in Mark: "Son of Humanity" and "after three days he will rise again." The use of the word "again" in verse 32 shows Mark as very conscious of a series of these predictions. This word could be from Mark's editing of the traditions he receives, but it could also be the result of his having used an earlier source, itself containing a repeated explicit prediction of Jesus' impending passion and subsequent resurrection. Bayer thinks the latter is the case, concluding, "Mk 10:32ff constitutes a third major pre-Markan intimation of the passion and resurrection of the Son of Man."[50]

The Judean Prediction in Matthew

Matthew's third explicit prediction passage (20:17-19) appears to rely solely on that of Mark. With the exceptions of Matthew's omission of "spitting" from

47. Ibid., 172 n. 144.
48. Ibid., 173.
49. Ibid., 173, 174.
50. Ibid., 174.

among the acts of derision and his substitution of the more specific term "crucified" for Mark's "killed," the passages are essentially the same.[51]

It therefore looks as though, based on a survey of all three explicit predictions in Matthew, the basic structure of his portrayal of these events is based on Mark's account. The evidence also indicates rather persuasively that Mark consults another source—or sources—with enough Semitic connections to establish a Palestinian Jewish-Christian origin. Bayer says the three prediction sayings represent "traditional *units*,"[52] that is, they are taken from earlier sources Mark uses and earlier sources Matthew uses, essentially in their present form.

The Judean Prediction in Luke

In the case of Luke's rendering of the third teaching of Jesus about his coming passion and resurrection (18:31-33), we find for the first time the same geographical reference featured by Matthew and Mark. In this case, however, the mention of a journey to Jerusalem in 18:31 fits into Luke's own compositional plan.

A major section of Luke begins at 9:51 and extends until 19:44. It represents the Jerusalem journey of Jesus and his disciples, and mixes action and teaching to present the rejection of Jesus by his people and the essential features of a new way of discipleship. Luke includes notes along the way to remind readers of the journey and of its ultimate purpose (9:51; 13:22; 17:11; 18:31; 19:28, 44).[53] In Luke, Jesus asserts a foundation in the Hebrew scriptures for coming events in Jerusalem, "See, we are going up to Jerusalem, and everything that is written about the Son of Man by the prophets will be accomplished" (18:31b).

In contrast with Matthew and Mark, Luke does not include the handing over (*traditio*) of the Son of Humanity to the Jews, limiting his being "handed over" to the Gentiles, a stance typical of his Gospel. Also in itemizing the acts of disrespect Jesus endured, Luke, unlike the other two evangelists, uses the passive voice. The final mention of Jesus' killing and resurrection follow Mark's lead. Bayer concludes that, while Luke could be relying on material special to him, clearly he "generally follows the Markan source."[54]

Looking at the three explicit predictions in Luke, we notice "a minimal amount of interrelationship among them." They all feature the Son of Humanity phrase; but the first and third predictions have only in common the verb "to kill" and a reference to the resurrection "on the third day." Any linkage between the second and third predictions results only from their common verb "hand over" or "betray." But the "linguistic integrity" of each prediction suggests—as Bayer demonstrates—that Luke makes use of a variety of traditional sources.[55] As we

51. Ibid., 188-89.

52. Ibid., 190.

53. Darrell L. Bock, "Luke, Gospel of," in Green, McKnight, and Marshall, eds., *Dictionary of Jesus and the Gospels*, 501.

54. Bayer, *Jesus' Predictions*, 194-95.

55. Ibid., 195.

found out earlier, the second prediction showed evidence that Matthew and Luke made use of Mark, plus separate additional sources. Semitic elements found in Luke's very brief second prediction, especially his introductory "Let these words sink into your ears" (9:44a; parallel Matthew 17:22b-23a), suggest Palestinian Jewish-Christian roots for this tradition.[56]

Figure 10.6 Judean Predictions of the "Handing Over" of Jesus in Synoptics

(Distinctive features in boldface type.
Common *traditio* material is in italics.)

Matthew 20:17-19	Mark 10:32-34	Luke 18:31-33
17 While Jesus was going up to Jerusalem,	32 **They were on the road,** going up to Jerusalem, **and Jesus was walking ahead of them; they were amazed, and those who followed were afraid.**	
he took the twelve disciples aside by themselves, and said to them on the way,	He took the twelve aside again and began to tell them what was to happen to him, 33 saying,	31 Then he took the twelve aside and said to them,
18 "See, we are going up to Jerusalem, and *the Son of Man will be handed over* to the chief priests and scribes, and they will condemn him to death; 19 then they will *hand him over to the Gentiles* to be mocked and flogged and crucified; and on the third day he will be raised (*egerthēsetai*)."	"See, we are going up to Jerusalem, and *the Son of Man will be handed over* to the chief priests and the scribes, and they will condemn him to death; then they will *hand him over to the Gentiles*; 34 they will mock him, and spit upon him, and flog him, and kill him; and after three days he will rise again (*anastēsetai*)."	"See, we are going up to Jerusalem, and **everything that is written about** *the Son of Man* **by the prophets will be accomplished.** 32 **For he** *will be handed over to the Gentiles*; and he will be mocked and insulted and spat upon. 33 After they have flogged him, they will kill him, and on the third day he will rise again (*anastēsetai*)."

56. Ibid., 195-96.

A careful examination of each of these predictions using modern analytic tools shows they are based on earlier traditions. They were not added by those composing the Gospels in Greek, who based them on what they thought happened to Jesus in the last days of his mission. We have seen that two strands of the earliest layer of traditions can be distinguished. These include the formulas in the first two predictions in Mark (8:31 and 9:31) and the separate traditions found in the parallel material common to Matthew (16:21; 27:22-23) and Luke (9:22; 9:44).

Shorter forms of these predictions, particularly those closely integrated into their contexts, reinforce the conviction that the predictions of the passion were recorded often and in a variety of contexts before Mark wrote his Gospel. In addition, intimations of Jesus' resurrection that come up incidentally outside the three sets of explicit predictions also complement this conclusion as far as the resurrection is concerned (Mark 9:9, parallel Matthew 17:9; and Mark 14:28, parallel Matthew 26:32).

The Semitic elements in these passages indicate that the forms of the Caesarean and the Galilean predictions of the end of Jesus' mission were developed at a very early time. The "high probability" of two separately transmitted traditions narrating these events (one by Mark and one by Matthew and Luke) support this conclusion. In other words, the elements common to Mark 8:31 (Matthew 16:21; Luke 9:22) and Mark 9:31 (Matthew 17:22-23) go back to a time before the writing of the Gospels in Greek and "reflect the earliest literary traditions of the resurrection predictions."[57]

Bayer's conclusion that this third prediction also accurately represents Jesus' teaching about the end of his mission proves very helpful indeed. He concludes "with a high degree of certainty" that the explicit predictions Jesus made of how his mission would end are not summaries of the passion narratives (see his chart above, fig. 10.5). They "include rather a didactic statement which may have been brought to present form in the early Palestinian church prior to the development of the pre-Markan passion narrative."[58]

Are the Predictions Too Explicit?

The strongest objection to the case we have made for the authenticity of Jesus' explicit predictions of his death and resurrection can be reduced to this conditional sentence, If Jesus had been this explicit about his betrayal, suffering, death, and resurrection, the disciples would not have been so unprepared for it. Even the constructive Christian expert on the Gospels, Scot McKnight, says about these predictions, "They are explicit enough that, if Jesus said them as

57. Ibid., 214.
58. Ibid.

they now are, the disciples should not have been as confused as they were."[59] An example of the possibility that Matthew turned a hint of suffering in Mark into a passion prediction of Jesus is shown in figure 10.7.

Figure 10.7 Mark and Matthew on Future Suffering of Jesus
(Mark's report can be interpreted as Matthew's prediction.[60])

Mark 14:1	**Matthew 26:2**
It was two days before the Passover and the festival of Unleavened Bread.	"You know that after two days the Passover is coming, and the Son of man will be handed
The chief priests and the scribes were looking for a way to arrest Jesus by stealth and kill him.	over to be crucified."

What the leaders were looking to do, according to Mark, is what Jesus predicts, according to Matthew. In the third explicit prediction, Matthew renders Mark's prediction "to be killed" (10:34) as the more specific "to crucify" (20:19). Having granted the possibility that some of the actions Jesus faced have been touched up or clarified after the events themselves, McKnight goes on to make some other historical observations to support the conclusion that Jesus did in fact predict his death and resurrection. The fully countercultural nature of the lesson Jesus was teaching should also be kept in mind. The Gospels, particularly Mark, again and again provide the reader with a glimpse into the tendency of the Apostles to miss the point of Jesus' message (e.g., Mark 10:35-44). The disciples probably would not have understood the resurrection predictions as specific to Jesus shortly after his death, since they most likely believed in the general resurrection of the righteous before the last judgment, as taught by the Pharisees and supported by Jesus (Mark 12:18-27).[61]

Three versions of Jesus' predictions (Matthew's, Mark's, and Luke's) in three locations (Caesarea, Galilee, and Judea) make nine reports of explicit predictions in the Synoptic Gospels.[62] The three reports of the Judean location are the most detailed. Seven actions against Jesus, such as mocking, spitting, and even crucifying, show up only in this set of reports. The second, or Galilean, set of reports is the least detailed and contains the most common features mentioned in the reports: "The Son of Man is to be betrayed into human hands, and they will

59. McKnight, *Jesus*, 229.

60. Adapted from McKnight, *Jesus*, 259.

61. N. T. Wright, *The Resurrection of the Son of God*, Christian Origins and the Question of God 3 (London: SPCK, 2003), 410.

62. McKnight has twenty-six features of these nine reports charted out (McKnight, *Jesus*, 227).

kill him, and three days after being killed, he will rise again" (Mark 9:31). These three features—*Son of Humanity*, *killed*, and *raised from the dead*—represent the core of what Jesus must have predicted explicitly about the end of his mission.[63]

Of the nine prediction reports, eight employ the designation Son of Humanity. In the Gospels only Jesus uses this designation. Outside the Gospels, the phrase occurs only in Acts 7:56 (Acts 7:56; Revelation 1:3; 14:14). This self-designation for Jesus is never used in Christian creeds. Clearly, Son of Humanity goes back to Jesus' authentic self-understanding. It was not uncommon for people speaking Aramaic to use this designation as a roundabout way of referring to themselves.[64] People in the places where Jesus spoke also understood this phrase, taken from Ezekiel 2:1 and Daniel 7:13-14, as a designation for the expected Messiah. In Jesus' case, it appears to have been both. Seven of the nine instances mention that Jesus will be killed. McKnight finds it "highly unlikely" that Jesus would have predicted his death without assuming along with it his vindication.[65] Already such a hope was assumed in connection with the death of seven martyred brothers at the time of the Maccabees (2 Maccabees 7:13-14, 20-23). Accordingly, of the nine prediction reports, eight mention his resurrection from the dead. In other words, at a minimum, Jesus intimated that he, the Messiah (Matthew 16:13-17; Mark 8:27-30; Luke 9:18-20), would be killed and then vindicated through resurrection.

Another pointer to these predictions as having their source in Jesus himself is the fact that, in spite of the clear teachings of the Apostles after the end of Jesus' mission that Jesus' death atones for the sins of those who trust in him, those who composed the Synoptic Gospels did not insert such a teaching into the predictions Jesus made of his coming death and resurrection. This argument, based on the criterion of *dissimilarity,* shows the fidelity of those who composed the Synoptic Gospels to the essence of what Jesus actually said.[66] This fidelity is congruent with the Qur'ān's positive assessment of Jesus' Apostles (*ḥawāriyūn*) (*Family of Imran* [3]:52; *Table* [5]:111 and 112; and *Lines* [61]:14).

This somewhat detailed discussion of the predictions Jesus makes of his passion and resurrection recorded in the Synoptic Gospels shows that Jesus was set on this outcome of his mission. The foreshadowing of his death in his parables and other sayings laid out in the preceding chapter supports this conclusion. I do not mean to indicate that only those statements of Jesus that can be demonstrated by such criteria as I have identified in chapter 8 are authentic statements. Those criteria help us identify statements that Jesus must have made. Statements and actions that do not survive scrutiny using these criteria cannot

63. Ibid., 229 and 232.

64. Richard A. Burridge in *Four Gospels, One Jesus?* 2nd ed. (Grand Rapids/Cambridge: Eerdmans, 2005), 49.

65. McKnight, *Jesus,* 230.

66. Ibid.

therefore be discarded as inauthentic. The Christian community has generally and consistently held that the Gospels represent authoritative scriptures to guide Christian faith and life.

My purpose in this and the preceding chapter consists of showing that, even from a historical point of view, Jesus envisioned his suffering, death, and resurrection as essential to his mission as God's Messiah. Given the high view of the character of Jesus and his Apostles found in the Qurʾān, I believe it extremely unlikely that he would have finally requested rescue from his destiny or that the Apostles would have promulgated a fabricated narrative of his having gone through with it. In the next two chapters we will examine the most important events in the life of Jesus that some Muslim commentators insist demonstrate the basis for their view that someone was crucified in place of Jesus.

11

"Let This Cup Pass from Me"

The Transfiguration, the Last Supper, and the Garden of Gethsemane

In the last two chapters, we demonstrated that before he was crucified Jesus predicted his suffering and death as well as his victory in resurrection. These predictions—both implied and explicit—occurred on several occasions and contained an awareness that his betrayal, humiliation, and death on a cross represented his expressed purpose as the Messiah and Son of Humanity. If the record of these intimations had been invented and inserted into the story of Jesus by the evangelists after the events themselves, many Muslims would find their interpretation of the last days of Jesus supported. But we discovered telling evidence that these records had already found their way into the sources the evangelists used—the sources of the earliest Jewish Christianity of Palestine. They did not derive from the creative mind of the Apostle Paul or from the sacrifice-oriented Gentile church of the Greco-Roman cultural sphere.

In this chapter I examine a set of events Muslim apologists point to as supporting their case that someone was substituted for Jesus and crucified in his place: the Transfiguration, the Last Supper, and the Garden of Gethsemane.

The Transfiguration

All three of the Synoptic evangelists record the event on a high mountain where Jesus was transformed so that his face shone and his clothes became glistening white (Matthew 17:1-9; Mark 9:2-10; and Luke 9:28-36). While the Gospel according to John does not include this event, in two passages it may be alluding to it. In the prologue John declares, "We have seen his glory . . ." (1:14). And in a short unit announcing Jesus' coming death, a voice from heaven affirms Jesus' glory (12:27-32). These passages suggest that John knows about Jesus' Transfiguration, since they echo its features, especially the features of Luke's portrayal.[1]

Some modern Muslim commentators find in this event evidence that Jesus'

1. Walter L. Liefeld, "Transfiguration," in Joel Green, Scot McKnight, and I. Howard Marshall, eds., *Dictionary of Jesus and the Gospels* (Downers Grove, IL/Leicester: InterVarsity, 1992), 836.

appearance could be transformed. Therefore, God could transform someone else to look like him. And, in spite of its position in the chronology of the Christian Gospels, the Transfiguration represents the occasion on which God took Jesus up to heaven. I know of no classical Muslim commentary dealing with the Transfiguration in quite this way.

Al-Qāsimī, whose commentary we followed closely in chapter 5, and sources he cites deal with the Transfiguration as recorded in Luke 9:28-36. They make three claims about it. First and foremost, they reject the chronology of the Synoptic Gospels and suggest that the Transfiguration actually describes Jesus' experience of being taken up to heaven. Their chronological judgment rests on the contention that the Gospels frequently reveal confusion and inconsistency in such matters. They contend that while the disciples were sleeping (Luke 9:32), Moses and Elijah came and took Jesus to God. As they see it, Jesus surely had the power to change the state of things. He raised the dead, multiplied bread and fish, and healed lepers and the blind. He therefore could simply have been manifesting his spirit in great splendor to Peter, James, and John when they awoke—he himself having already been taken up.[2]

Second, Muslim commentators find significance in the mention of Elijah appearing with Moses on the Mount. Qāsimī and his source, al-Muḥammadī, believe that the Jews had heard Jesus say that Elijah would come.[3] Qāsimī then applies this to his analysis of what went on at the cross. In the Gospel account of the crucifixion, the Jews said, "Call on him so that we can see if Elijah will come and rescue him" (Mark 15:36). Qāsimī attributes this to doubt on their part as to whom they were crucifying. They reasoned, if Elijah should come, they would not raise Jesus on the cross and would know he is the Messiah. But, if Elijah did not come, their hunch that the one crucified was someone other than the Messiah would prove true.[4]

As a third thrust of their approach to this event, Qāsimī and Muḥammadī claim that the Transfiguration could have no other meaningful interpretation than as the occasion of Jesus' being taken up and of a look-alike's being substituted for him. After making a case for his interpretation of the Transfiguration, Muḥammadī states flatly, "If this is not the case, there is no reason for the appearance of these verses."[5] Khayr al-Dīn al-Ālūsī shares in the interpretation of Qāsimī and Muḥammadī, but less confidently. He allows that it might not have been the occasion on which God took Jesus up. But if not, it certainly amounted to a preparation for that event and was designed to strengthen Jesus and familiarize him with what was to come.[6]

First, regarding the chronological issue, can this event reasonably have

---

2. Muḥammad Jamāl al-Dīn al-Qāsimī, *Tafsīr al-Qāsimī: al-musammā bi-maḥāsin al-taʾwīl*, ed. Muḥammad Fuʾād ʿAbd al-Bāqī, 17 vols. (Cairo: Dār iḥyāʾ al-kutub al-ʿArabīyah/ʿĪsā al-Bābī al-Ḥalabī wa-shurakāʾ-hu, 1957), 5:1666.

3. Qāsimī's own discussion is on 5:1662, and he cites ʿIzz al-Dīn al-Muḥammadī on 5:1667.

4. Ibid. Qāsimī cites Muḥammadī in chapter 5 on 5:1667.

5. Ibid.

6. Khayr al-Dīn al-Ālūsī, *Al-jawāb al-faṣīḥ li-mā laffaqa-hu 'Abel al-Masīḥ,* ed. Aḥmad Ḥijāzī al-Saqqā, 2 vols.. (Cairo: Dār al-Bayān al-'Arabī, 1987). Cited in ibid., 5:1676.

occurred around the time of Jesus' arrest? Qāsimī and his two sources state clearly that their view requires a relocation of the event from its place in the Gospels. They think this is entirely possible given the uncertainty about chronology typical of the Gospels. Certainly the Gospel of John rearranges its chronology of events. In the Synoptic Gospels, Jesus goes to Jerusalem only at the end of his ministry, while John portrays most of his ministry as taking place in Jerusalem and Judea. John places the cleansing of the Temple early in his Gospel, while Mark, Matthew, and Luke place it toward the end. John's anointing takes place before the triumphal entry, not afterward as in the Synoptic Gospels. And Jesus and his disciples partake of the Last Supper twenty-four hours before its time according to the Synoptic evangelists.[7]

The three Synoptic accounts of the Transfiguration also exhibit some obvious differences. Matthew and Mark agree on a six-day interval before the event, while Luke makes it eight. Matthew and Luke, using synonyms, agree on the radiance of Jesus' countenance and apparel, while Mark mentions only the brightness of his clothing and adds a comparison with professional bleaching. Matthew alone compares his radiance with the sun. Luke alone adds that Moses and Elijah appeared in glory, and he alone includes the topic of the conversation between the two luminaries. Luke also omits the discussion of Jesus with his disciples about Elijah. Mark and Luke show that the disciples were greatly frightened before the voice from heaven speaks, while in Matthew the frightened and awe-inspired behavior follows the voice. Only Mark tells the reader explicitly that the three disciples were frightened. Only Luke mentions how sleepy they were, that they became fully awake, and that Peter made his proposal to build dwellings "just as they were leaving him."[8]

The similarities of the accounts are also striking, however. They agree on all the participants: Jesus, Peter, James, John, Moses, and Elijah. They agree that Jesus was radiantly transformed, all mentioning specifically his apparel. They all include Peter's clumsy statement about building dwellings. They all mention the cloud, and the voice says almost exactly the same thing in all. The sequence, except for Matthew's location of the disciples' fright, is entirely consistent.

Furthermore, all three Gospels place the Transfiguration in the same literary and chronological context. Peter confesses that Jesus is the Messiah; Jesus commands silence about this; Jesus explicitly predicts his passion and resurrection; Jesus summons everyone to all-out discipleship; Jesus is transfigured; Jesus orders silence until after his resurrection; except in Luke, the disciples discuss the coming of Elijah; Jesus heals a demon-possessed boy; and Jesus again explicitly predicts his death and resurrection.[9]

---

7. Marianne Meye Thompson, "John, Gospel of," in Green, McKnight, and Marshall, eds., *Dictionary of Jesus,* 375. This may be owing to following another calendar (Dale Walker, personal communication).

8. Liefeld, "Transfiguration," 836-37.

9. Ibid., 834.

In addition, the three Synoptic Gospels agree that many events took place between the Transfiguration and the betrayal. Mark, for instance, records the following. Jesus blesses the little children in Judea (10:13-16). At the outset of a journey, Jesus encounters a rich man (10:17-31). On the road to Jerusalem, Jesus predicts his death for the third time (10:32-45). In Jericho Jesus heals a blind man (10:46-52). Jesus enters Jerusalem and curses a fig tree (11:1-14 and 20-26). In the Temple, religious leaders challenge Jesus' authority (11:27-33). Jesus teaches and deals with questions (12:1-44). Jesus, giving signs of the end, predicts the destruction of the Temple and the coming persecution (13:1-36). A woman anoints Jesus (14:3-9). Judas agrees to betray Jesus (14:10-11). Jesus participates in the Passover and eats the Last Supper with his disciples (14:12-31). And Jesus prays in the Garden of Gethsemane (14:32-42). This same interval in Matthew's Gospel takes up nine chapters, and in Luke the interval consists of twelve of his twenty-four chapters!

It clearly amounts to risky analysis to suggest that the Transfiguration, so securely nestled in a common context by three of the evangelists, should be radically relocated to accommodate the Muslim interpretation of the end of Jesus' mission. We found greater discrepancies in the Muslim interpretations of the last days of Jesus' mission than show up in these accounts of the Transfiguration. See the various scenarios identified in chapters 3 and 5.

Second, the connection Qāsimī and his sources make between the mention of Elijah in the Transfiguration event and someone's statement at the crucifixion, "Wait! Let's see if Elijah comes to take him down" (Matthew 27:45-49; Mark 15:34-36), needs attention. For one thing, this statement was made in response to a misunderstanding of the opening words of Jesus' loud shout from the cross, *Eloi, Eloi, lema sabachthani* ("My God, my God, why have you forsaken me?"). *Eloi* sounded like Elijah (*Iliyō*) to some of the bystanders. As our gloss indicates, in reality Jesus was addressing God in Aramaic as *Eloi*, "my God."

For another, if this event were to have been the cause of the Jews' misunderstanding Jesus' cry from the cross, they would have to have overheard the conversation of Jesus with his disciples on the mountain or while coming down from it. None of the evangelists who narrate this event, however, indicates that anyone other than the six identified participants was present on the Mount. Matthew and Mark do relate a conversation about Elijah that the disciples had with Jesus on their way down the mountain after he had commanded them to silence about the Transfiguration event. Of course, if Muslim interpreters want to transfer the Transfiguration arbitrarily to a time close to the arrest of Jesus, then they could also argue that Jews were present and overheard the conversation with Jesus and his disciples about Elijah. But this is nowhere found in the Gospels, and I find this chronological relocation very unlikely.

Third, why do Qāsimī and Muḥammadī think the Transfiguration could only function as an occasion for God's taking Jesus to himself to "cleanse him from the unbelievers" (*Family of Imran* [3]:55)? Is it because alternative functions support what they deny? As it occurs in the record of the Synoptic Gospels, the Transfiguration represents the most graphic and dramatic experience of the identity of Jesus among all the events and lessons Jesus uses to bring his disciples to an understanding of who he is and what he must do. Every event in the sequence of eight composing the common context of the three accounts—four before and four after, as enumerated above—"pertains in some way to who Jesus is and why he came."[10] Possibly when Qāsimī and Muḥammadī select out of the narrative those things that, according to their interpretation of the Qur'ān, are not true, Qāsimī and Muḥammadī can find no other reason for the event than the one they propose.

Not only does Jesus appear in the radiance of his heavenly identity, but Moses and Elijah appear with him. Although, since the time of Origen (d. ca. 254), these two have been seen to symbolize "the Law and the Prophets," which corresponds to two bodies of Jewish scriptural tradition of that time, it is now known that this could not have been its meaning in first-century Judaism.[11] More likely, the two are chosen for this role because they both ended their lives in uncommon ways. God buried Moses and his tomb remained unidentified (Deuteronomy 34:5-6); and a chariot took Elijah to heaven in a whirlwind (2 Kings 2:11). Furthermore, Jewish legend has Moses mysteriously brought to heaven as well. Moses also relates to the future through the prophecy in Deuteronomy 18:18 of a future prophet like him. Malachi presents Elijah as an eschatological figure (4:5-6), a role he obviously plays in the Gospels.

Familiarity with the Muslim proposal for the end of Jesus' mission enables us to see how the presence of Moses and Elijah with Jesus could be cited in support of that proposal—although I have never run across Muslim apologists making this argument. Both of these figures were "taken up" in some way by God himself. According to the Muslim proposal, these figures could be associated with God's cleverly rescuing Jesus from Jewish plotting and taking him up to heaven. This would indeed be a telling argument if isolated from the other considerations in these chapters, especially the chapters dealing with Jesus' predictions of his coming death and resurrection. In the end, according to all three evangelists, Jesus stands alone on the mountain. He is obviously more than one among three!

Furthermore, Luke tells us, Moses and Elijah were discussing the departure Jesus was about to "accomplish" in Jerusalem (9:31). As we shall see below, the Greek word for "departure" here is *exodos*.[12] It is something *Jesus will accomplish*. It will not be a departure done for him or to him by God, as the Muslim proposal requires. Finally, as all three evangelists record, God addresses the company from a cloud, affirming that the sonship of Jesus should be listened to (Matthew 17:5; Mark 9:7; Luke 9:35).

---

10. Ibid.

11. Ibid., 839.

12. The word *exodos* brings to mind Israel's exodus from Egypt. It appears two other times in the New Testament. In Hebrews 11:22, it refers to the Exodus from Egypt in connection with the burial of Joseph. In 2 Peter 1:15 it refers to Peter's death. Here in Luke, therefore, it most likely refers to Jesus' impending death but could refer to "the whole culmination of his earthly life" (ibid., 838).

Luke, whose Gospel Qāsimī relates to primarily, focuses particular attention on the identity and the mission of Jesus in the section of his Gospel that includes the Transfiguration. The outline below shows Luke's arrangement of 9:20-36 in a ring structure that highlights Jesus' identity and mission. A is similar to A', B to B', and C to C':

(A) Peter states Jesus' *identity* in 9:20.
(B) Jesus predicts his *death* in verse 22.
(C) He refers to his future coming in *glory* in verse 26.
(C') The Transfiguration visibly demonstrates his *glory* in verse 29.
(B') Moses and Elijah discuss his *departure* (= death) in verse 31.
(A') The voice from heaven affirms Jesus' *identity* in verse 35.

Some New Testament critics have also questioned whether the Transfiguration took place at this point in Jesus' life. For these scholars, the supernatural brilliance of Jesus' appearance and the audible voice declaring him Son of God do not fit here. They surmise that this story must have been a misplaced resurrection narrative inserted into the account after the event of Jesus' resurrection. N. T. Wright has shown, however, that the Transfiguration has the typical form of a vision narrative: "preparation for a vision, then the vision itself, and then some closing comments about what it might mean." Resurrection narratives are not vision narratives.[13] Responses that have been made to these scholars, offered in support of the event's historicity, may help some Muslim friends and associates recognize its authenticity as well.

For one thing, as we mentioned above, each Synoptic evangelist places the Transfiguration in an identical context featuring a tightly fitted flow of events and teachings. If for reasons of worldview critics cannot accept the possibility of supernatural events, such as those at the beginning and end of the Transfiguration narrative, then they assume the passage is spurious, regardless of literary indications to the contrary. My Muslim readers, however, will have little problem believing that God gifted Jesus with astonishing powers.

In addition, as we have already shown, the event fits well into its context within the story of Jesus' mission. It takes place at a crisis point in his ministry. While his ministry has become amazingly popular, the opposition has grown increasingly foreboding. The Transfiguration clusters with other equally decisive events as part of Jesus' initiation of his disciples into the reality and meaning of his decision to pursue his course to the end, even though it will result in humiliation, dishonor, and death.

While the command from heaven to listen obediently to God's Son would be inappropriate in a later context, it fits well here at or near the outset of the journey to Jerusalem. The Transfiguration narrative never mentions the resurrection as

13. N. T. Wright, *The Resurrection of the Son of God*, Christian Origins and the Question of God 3 (London: SPCK, 2003), 597.

such. If it represented an interpolation after the fact, one would think it would have intimated the resurrection as well as the "departure."[14] The appearance of the radiant Messiah in the narrative may itself represent, however, a foreshadowing of his resurrection.[15]

Motifs in the Transfiguration narrative remind readers of the exodus event. We have already mentioned that Luke uses the Greek word *exodos* itself in verse 31. Moses and Elijah "were speaking of his *departure*, which he was about to accomplish at Jerusalem." The specification "six days later" in Matthew 17:1 and Mark 9:2 recalls Exodus 24:16, where Moses, Aaron, Nadab, and Abihu were surrounded by the glory of God on Mount Sinai. Luke's "about eight days" is compatible with this reference, because the passage in Exodus mentions a seventh day, when the Lord calls to Moses, and the mention of an eighth day could be allowing time for ascending and descending the mountain.[16] The mountain itself, a "high mountain" in Matthew and Mark, could call to mind Mount Sinai for readers. The high mountain also represents a direct quote from the Greek translation of Isaiah 40:9 where those bringing good tidings go up on a "high mountain" (*oros hypsēlon*).[17] The implied readers of the three Synoptic Gospels could not help noticing the motif of the cloud from which the voice affirmed Jesus' identity. It too refers to the exodus event by recalling the cloud that led the released slaves on their journey, that revealed the glory of the Lord, that accompanied the induction of seventy elders, that appeared at the tabernacle, and that marked the *presence of the Lord at Sinai*. The Greek verb *episkiazō* ("to overshadow"; Matthew 17:5; Mark 9:7; and Luke 9:34) translates the Hebrew verb *shākan* in the perfect tense. "The cloud *dwelt* on" the tent of meeting and, along with the glory of the Lord, prohibited Moses from entering the tabernacle in the wilderness (Exodus 40:35). But the cloud motif can also refer to the future, because Daniel 7:13 describes the Son of Humanity coming with the clouds of heaven—a theme Jesus took up in Mark 13:26 and 14:62.[18]

When one realizes that this event took place as part of Jesus' purposeful movement toward Jerusalem—keeping in mind that in Luke it takes place just before Jesus "set his face to go to Jerusalem" (9:51)—one realizes what an elaborate orchestration of action and teaching is related to his mission in that city. Given all this, it is hard to believe that the detailed focus on Jesus' final mission in Jerusalem could be referring to his being rescued by God from death and replaced with someone else. Nevertheless, we turn now to events that take place in and around Jerusalem, first the Last Supper and then the fervent prayer of Jesus in the Garden of Gethsemane.

---

14. Liefeld, "Transfiguration," 835.
15. Ibid., 840.
16. Ibid., 839.
17. Ibid.
18. Ibid.

The Last Supper

Ṭabarī offers his readers the following report from Wahb ibn Munabbih connecting a portion of the Last Supper[19] as reported by the Gospel of John (13:1-20) with the Garden-of-Gethsemane experience, which John does not report.

> When God told Jesus son of Mary . . . that he was to leave the world, he became anxious about death and it grieved him greatly. So he summoned his Apostles, prepared food for them, and said, "Come to me tonight because I have a need you can supply." When they had gathered to him at night, he gave them supper and rose to serve them. When they had finished eating, he began washing their hands to perform *wuḍūʾ* for them, and to wipe their hands with his robe. They were amazed at that and reprimanded him. So he said, "Is there no one who will return to me tonight something of what I do? Then I have nothing to do with him and he has nothing to do with me." They agreed with him so that when he finished with that he said, "As for what I have done for you this night: served you food, washed your hands with my hands, let it be an example for you. You think that I am the best of you so do not act arrogantly among yourselves, rather let one of you pour out himself for another just as I poured out my soul for you.
>
> "What I need from you tonight for which I sought your help is your praying to God for me and that you will put great effort into praying that he will delay my end." But when they applied themselves to prayer and wanted to exert themselves, sleep overtook them so that they could not pray. So he undertook to wake them, saying, "God be blessed! Can you not endure for me one night in which to help me?" Whereupon they said, "By God! We don't know what is the matter with us. We used to keep night vigil, even extending the vigil but [now] we can't stay up the entire night. Whenever we want to pray, something makes it impossible." So he said, "Do away with the shepherd and the sheep are scattered." . . . [Jesus] started speaking along these lines, announcing his death.[20]

In comparison with the treatments of the Last Supper in the Synoptic Gospels, this Muslim reference to part of the event recorded only by John skirts

---

19. Robert H. Stein identifies several designations for this event that are mentioned in the New Testament: "breaking of bread," "eucharist," "table of the Lord," "communion," and "the Lord's Supper"; and two common names for it that are not in the Bible: "mass" and "Last Supper" (Stein, "Last Supper," in Green, McKnight, and Marshall, eds., *Dictionary of Jesus and the Gospels*, 444-50).

20. Abū Jaʿfar Muḥammad ibn Jarīr al-Ṭabarī, *Tafsīr al-Ṭabarī*, ed., Maḥmūd Muḥammad Shākir and Aḥmad Muḥammad Shākir, Turāth al-Islām (Cairo: Dār al-Maʿārif, 1971), 9:368-69 (#10780).

the heart of the event, as does the passage from the Qur'ān (*Table* [5]:112-15). One could not derive from Ṭabarī's account any awareness that very early in the life of the Christian community the Last Supper provided the center of Christian worship. We will now explore this meal in the New Testament looking for the meaning it conveys.

The New Testament contains four accounts of the Last Supper: Matthew 26:26-29; Mark 14:22-25; Luke 22:15-20; and 1 Corinthians 11:23-26. While the probable dates for the writing of the Gospels range from 65 to 90, Paul wrote the first Corinthian letter from Ephesus between 52 and 55.[21] Since the earliest date for the end of Jesus' earthly mission is 30 and the latest 33,[22] the letter's account of the Last Supper dates to about twenty-two years after the supper it reports.

Matthew 26:29 clearly relies on Mark 14:25, making only stylistic revisions. For the whole Last Supper narrative, Luke and Paul have similar wording that differs from Mark and Matthew. Luke and Paul rely on a common earlier tradition.[23] Luke 22:19-20 appears to scholars such as I. Howard Marshall, Joachim Jeremias, and Hans Bayer to be earlier than the version of it Paul has received.[24] For one thing, the version Luke transmits omits the verb *to be*, a typical feature of reports translated from Hebrew or Aramaic into Greek. For another, Luke's tradition does not include the second command to repeat the ritual found in Paul's version. Bayer, after a thorough analysis, concludes: "text critical, literary, linguistic and source critical considerations support the original unity—and priority over 1 Cor 11:23-25—of . . . Luke 22:15-20."[25]

In his Corinthian letters, Paul deals with an array of problems in the church there. Paul's directives regarding the problems related to the celebration of the Last Supper occupy eighteen verses at the end of 1 Corinthians 11. The supper is obviously a full communal meal because Paul says he has heard that people who attend rush to eat the food they have brought, ignoring others who have inadequate food. Thus, one person goes hungry while another gets drunk (verse 21). He suggests they do their eating and drinking in the full sense at home;

21. Scott J. Hafemann, "Corinthians, Letters to the," in Gerald F. Hawthorne, Ralph P. Martin, and Daniel Reid, eds., *Dictionary of Paul and His Letters* (Downers Grove, IL/Leicester: Inter-Varsity, 1993), 177.

22. Joel B. Green, "Death of Jesus," in Green, McKnight, and Marshall, eds., *Dictionary of Jesus and the Gospels*, 148-49.

23. Hans F. Bayer, *Jesus' Predictions of Vindication and Resurrection: The Provenance, Meaning, and Correlation of the Synoptic Predictions,* ed. Martin Hengel and Otfried Hofius, Wissenschaftliche Untersuchungen zum Neuen Testament, 2. Reihe, 20 (Tübingen: Mohr, 1986), 32.

24. I. Howard Marshall, *Last Supper and Lord's Supper* (Exeter: Paternoster, 1980), 40; Joachim Jeremias, *The Eucharistic Words of Jesus*, New Testament Library (London: SCM, 1966), 185, 188; and Bayer, *Jesus' Predictions*, 33.

25. A few ancient manuscripts of Luke omit verses 19b-20, "'which is given for you. Do this in remembrance of me.' And he did the same with the cup after supper, saying, 'This cup that is poured out for you is the new covenant in my blood.'" Bayer demonstrates why he thinks the superior external attestation of these verses should prevail over speculation about the shorter version being more authentic (Bayer, *Jesus' Predictions*, 31).

otherwise they "show contempt for the church of God and humiliate those who have nothing" (verse 22). They should not come to the Lord's Supper hungry if that prevents them from examining themselves before they partake of the bread and the cup (11:28 and 34). The sacredness of the meal itself argues for this self-examination; so Paul summarizes the meal in four verses.

> For I received from the Lord what I also handed on to you, that the Lord Jesus on the night when he was betrayed took a loaf of bread, and when he had given thanks, he broke it and said, "This is my body that is for you. Do this in remembrance of me." In the same way he took the cup also, after supper, saying, "This cup is the new covenant in my blood. Do this, as often as you drink it, in remembrance of me." For as often as you eat this bread and drink the cup, you proclaim the Lord's death until he comes. (11:23-26)

In verse 23 Paul says he has *received* from the Lord and *handed on* to the Corinthians this tradition for the celebration of the Last Supper. These technical terms for passing on oral tradition (cf. Luke 1:12 and 1 Corinthians 15:3) indicate that Paul passes on to the Corinthians what the church has taught him. He *received* this tradition either from the church in Antioch (Acts 11:26) in the mid-40s or from the church at Damascus and, perhaps Jerusalem, in the mid-30s (Acts 9:19; Galatians 1:17).

The tradition Paul has handed on to the community of faith he founded in Corinth was not the only one available to the early Christians for celebrating the Last Supper. The Gospels of Mark (14:22-25) and Matthew (26:26-29) include a similar but separate tradition from the one reported in Luke and 1 Corinthians. The similarities and differences of the four accounts are displayed in figure 11.1 below.

The focal point of the Last Supper is the death of Jesus and its meaning for humanity, and thus a fitting context for telling the passion story. Also Jesus himself asked that the disciples repeat this breaking of bread and partaking of the cup in remembrance of his suffering and death. This repeated telling of the passion story in recollection can account for the modifications that show up in the four accounts laid out in figure 11.1. From the beginning of Christianity, the Supper was integral to the life of the community and provided a "context for assimilating, recounting, and reflecting upon Jesus' death."[26]

---

26. Joel B. Green, *The Death of Jesus: Tradition and Interpretation in the Passion Narrative* (Wissenschaftliche Untersuchungen zum Neuen Testament, 2. Reihe 33; Tübingen: Mohr, 1988), 192. Most scholars consider the tradition of the Last Supper that Mark draws on and Matthew reports earlier than the tradition reflected in Luke and 1 Corinthians (Stein, "Last Supper," 447). Joel Green, however, discerns another early passion narrative that Luke also uses in his account (*Death of Jesus,* 243-44).

Figure 11.1 The Last Supper in the Synoptics and Paul
(Common words are italicized)

Matthew 26	Mark 14	Luke 22	1 Corinthians 11
		15 He said to them, "I have eagerly desired to eat this Passover with you before I suffer;	
26 While they were eating, Jesus *took a loaf of bread*, and after blessing it *he broke it*, gave it to the disciples, and said, "Take, eat; *this is my body*."	22 While they were eating, he *took a loaf of bread*, and after blessing it *he broke it*, gave it to them, and said, "Take; *this is my body*."	16 for I tell you, I will not eat it until it is fulfilled in the kingdom of God."	23 For I received from the Lord what I also handed on to you, that the Lord Jesus on the night when he was betrayed *took a loaf of bread*, 24 and when he had given thanks, *he broke it* and said, "*This is my body* that is for you. Do this in remembrance of me."
27 Then he took a cup, and after giving thanks he gave it to them, saying, "Drink from it, all of you;	23 Then he took a cup, and after giving thanks he gave it to them, and all of them drank from it.	17 Then he took a cup, and after giving thanks he said, "Take this and divide it among yourselves;	25 In the same way he took the cup also, after supper, saying,
28 for this is my blood of the covenant, which is poured out for many for the forgiveness of sins.	24 He said to them, "This is my blood of the covenant, which is poured out for many.		"This cup is the new covenant in my blood. Do this, as often as you drink it, in remembrance of me."
29 I tell you, I will never again drink of this fruit of the vine until that day when I drink it new with you in my Father's kingdom."	25 Truly I tell you, I will never again drink of the fruit of the vine until that day when I drink it new in the kingdom of God."	18 for I tell you that from now on I will not drink of the fruit of the vine until the kingdom of God comes."	

		20 And he did the same with the cup after supper, saying, "This cup that is poured out for you is the new covenant in my blood."	26 For as often as you eat this bread and drink the cup, you proclaim the Lord's death until he comes.

After considerable discussion and analysis, Green affirms the authenticity of the command of Jesus uttered at the Supper, "This is my body, which is given for you. Do this in remembrance of me" (Luke 22:19). In Green's own words,

> At the very least, then, the command to repeat the Supper in "remembrance" of Jesus was implicitly purposed by Jesus himself. Beyond that, it is not unreasonable to believe that the command itself can be traced back to Jesus' own verbal expression of his intention that the Supper be continuously celebrated by his followers.[27]

Joachim Jeremias shows that at the beginning of the Last Supper Jesus

> burns his bridges, forswears feasting and wine, prepares himself with resolute will to drink the bitter cup which the Father offers him. In this renunciation there would thus be already something of the dreadful tension of the struggle at Gethsemane and of the depth of his dereliction on the cross.[28]

We turn now to that garden scene and Jesus' struggle in it, for Qāsimī sees it as evidence of Jesus' great fear of death and earnest request to escape it—a request God honors by rescuing him from his enemies.

The Garden of Gethsemane

The struggle of Jesus in prayer over his destiny while his disciples slept found its way into the Synoptic Gospels in detail. In addition, both the Gospel of John (12:27-29; 17:1-18; 18:1-2, 11) and the Letter to the Hebrews (5:7) refer to this event. This crucial event in the life of Jesus provides subject matter for many paintings and illustrations. The Letter to the Hebrews puts it succinctly.

> In the days of his flesh, Jesus [Greek: "he"] offered up prayers and supplications, with loud cries and tears, to the one who was able to save him from death, and he was heard because of his reverent submission. (5:7)

27. Green, *Death of Jesus,* 199-200.
28. Jeremias, *Eucharistic Words*, 216.

In fact, some Muslim interpreters, since they believe Jesus was exempted from the agony of crucifixion, may interpret the last independent clause, "and he was heard because of his reverent submission" to mean that God answered his prayer by rescuing him from certain death at the hands of the Jews and the Romans! One of Ṭabarī's sources, as we have seen in chapter 3, puts it this way—without, however, mentioning Hebrews 5:7:

> No servant from among the servants of God despised death, according to what has been mentioned to me, to the degree he [Jesus] despised it. None worried about it to the degree he worried about it. God did not permit his request to let it pass from him, until he actually said, according to what they claim, "O God if you will let this cup pass from any one of your creatures, let it pass from me," and until his skin from that agony flowed with blood.[29]

Qāsimī, on whose analysis we relied heavily in chapter 5, considers it impossible that God should answer Jesus' fervent prayer in the negative. He mentions more than once the prayer in the garden in Matthew 26.

> "Oh Father, if it is not possible for you to let this cup pass from me," that is death, "and if it is necessary for me to drink it, then let your will be done."[30]

He, like other Muslim commentators, cannot imagine God ignoring this agonizing prayer and abandoning his precious messenger to the fate he fears at the hands of his enemies. Chapter 9 above dealt with this narrative in connection with three images in it that represent implicit intimations of Jesus' coming death and vindication—thus, a brief consideration here.

First, some Muslim commentators' interpretation of the Gethsemane experience of Jesus shows they have confidence in its historicity—unless they simply use what fits their perspective without reference to any other criteria for distinguishing authentic and inauthentic passages in the Gospels. For Muslim commentators, this passage provides evidence of Jesus' great fear of death.[31]

Second, careful analysis of the passage, using the tools of tradition history that we have found useful in previous chapters, supports its historicity. Hans Bayer studied the history of traditions informing the passage and determined that Matthew and Luke probably base their narratives on two earlier sources: the report Mark uses and another independent tradition that reported the prayer at Gethsemane. He concludes that both reports are genuine and go back to Jesus

29. Ṭabarī, *Tafsīr*, 9:371 (#10785).

30. Qāsimī, *Tafsīr*, 5:1663, 1682-83.

31. Muḥammad Rashīd Riḍā sees the story simply as evidence of contradictions between Christian doctrines and the Gospels such as the Incarnation (*Tafsīr al-manār*, 12 vols. [Beirut, Dār al-Maʿārif, 1970], 6:37).

himself. He bases his conclusion on the traditions' *multiple attestation*, the way they portray Jesus' human weakness (criterion of *dissimilarity*), and indications that both stem from the Palestinian Jewish-Christian community. Although the exact words of Jesus and the exact sequence of events cannot be finally worked out, what Jesus said "includes both a reference to the hour (Mk 14:35) and a reference to the cup which Jesus must drink."[32]

Third, this inclusion of the reference to *the hour* in Matthew 26:35 where Mark has *this cup* makes clear that it metaphorically represents the same purposeful endurance of death that the cup usually represents. And then, in Matthew 26:41 and Mark 14:45, both evangelists report Jesus saying to his disciples, "Are you still sleeping and taking your rest? Enough! *The hour has come*; the Son of Man is betrayed into the hands of sinners." This does not sound like a person who has just been granted an escape from his destiny and then been informed that someone else will be crucified in his place.

Luke's account (22:39-46) is strikingly different from Matthew's and Mark's in too many details to occupy us here. But two things stand out, both coming from Joel Green's careful analysis of every word in Luke's account.[33] For one thing, Luke succinctly presents both the agony of Jesus' prayer and the depth of his submission to the Father's will. For another, Luke could very well be using an earlier source or sources other than Mark's Gospel in constructing his narrative. The combination in verses 43 and 44 of (1) four words unique to the Gospels, and (2) evidence of Luke's own editing support the assumption of another source.[34]

In the case of the Last Supper, examined above, we noticed two strands of tradition going back to Jesus. One reported that Jesus "took a cup, and after giving thanks he gave it to them, and all of them drank from it" and that "he said to them, 'This is my blood of the covenant, which is poured out for many'" (Mark 14:23-24). The other tradition puts it in a slightly different way, "This cup that is poured out for you is the new covenant in my blood" (Luke 22:20). In both cases the cup contains not the wine of God's wrath but the blood of Jesus that is poured out for others. It reminds us of the eschatological pronouncement or prospect given by Jesus before the drinking of the first cup of the Passover Meal: "This is my blood of the covenant, which is poured out for many. Truly I tell you, I will never again drink of the fruit of the vine until that day when I drink it new in the kingdom of God" (Mark 14:25; see also Matthew 16:29; and Luke 22:18).

This cup of wine that Jesus cannot drink symbolizes the blessing poured out on God's people. Yet Jesus must abstain from the cup of blessing because his

---

32. Bayer, *Jesus' Predictions*, 69-70.

33. Green, *Death of Jesus*, 53-58.

34. Ibid., 53-58, 103, 256-57. An alternative position to Luke's having edited verses 43 and 44 has also been proposed: "Although it is probable that these verses were not part of the original Gospel [of Luke] (since important early manuscripts lack these verses), they were known to Christian writers of the second century and reflect tradition from the first century concerning the suffering of Jesus" (Bruce M. Metzger and Roland E. Murphy, eds., *New Oxford Annotated Bible* [Oxford/New York: Oxford University Press, 1991], 118 NT).

cup will be to experience the negative judgment also symbolized in the "cup" image. Jesus confronted this cup in Gethsemane and prayed for release from its prospect, but not at the expense of fulfilling God's will (Mark 14:36).

Throughout the struggle in Gethsemane, readers of the Gospels have been privy to the thoughts and feelings of Jesus and to the actions and attitudes of his disciples. But we have no knowledge of what the Father said to him or communicated to him in the midst of all this. Jesus may even have encountered silence. If the Muslims were correct in their interpretation of the last days of Jesus' mission, however, Jesus would have been assured of his deliverance from the clutches of unbelievers and of his escape to heaven.

For Christians, however, the story goes in a different direction. As the Gospel narratives progress, Jesus undergoes betrayal, arrest, trial, painful humiliation, and agonizing death. Before he leaves the garden, Jesus, in saying "the hour is at hand," appears to have accepted the cup that he had asked the Father to remove from him. He does not embrace an escape that would have been made possible by the arrest, trial, painful humiliation, and agonizing death of someone else; rather, he embraces the very cup he shrank from—the breaking of his body and the pouring out of his blood.

Jesus predicted explicitly and intimated implicitly that his messianic vocation included dying for others. He acted out that servant-messiah role in the Last Supper. He faced this awesome destiny personally and powerfully in the garden. The Gospels testify to all this. For Jesus to go through this only to accept an escape involving a substitute who would die willingly—or unwillingly—seems totally incongruent. For Jesus to have asked for someone else to take his place in confronting the natural results of his prophetic engagement with his people and culture is harder for me to accept than the New Testament's witness to his acceptance of death.

The "hour" that Jesus wrestles to embrace in the garden threatens more than just death. What is this hour and the power of darkness? Chapter 12 looks at Jesus' arrest, trial, and crucifixion.

12

"The Son of Humanity Will Be Handed Over to Be Crucified"

The Arrest, Trial, Crucifixion, and Burial of Jesus

In chapters 3 and 5, I laid out the arguments of the Qurʾān commentators, both classical and modern, on the key verses in *Family of Imran* [3]:55 and *Women* [4]:157-58 that deal with the final events of Jesus' earthly mission. This chapter responds to their arguments related to the betrayal, arrest, trial, and crucifixion of Jesus.

Betrayal and Arrest

In displaying their passion narratives, Qurʾān commentators give elaborate attention to the betrayal and arrest of Jesus, because at the point of the arrest—in most narratives—Jesus is taken up and someone else captured in his place.

Betrayal and Arrest in the Classical Commentaries

The variety of accounts of what transpires to deceive the Jews into thinking they crucified Jesus characterizes the classical commentaries. Three major types of narratives can be distinguished.

In one set, God casts a likeness of Jesus on someone or a group involuntarily. The transaction of substitution generally takes place in a house. The guard comes in and gets someone among the disciples or someone comes out of the house and is nabbed. Or they all come out of the house and one is taken. Another set has Judas becoming the involuntary victim as God casts the likeness of Jesus on him. One report even attributes this view to some Christians.[1] This type becomes more popular among modern exegetes and apologists.

1. Abū Jaʿfar Muḥammad ibn Jarīr al-Ṭabarī, *Tafsīr al-Ṭabarī* (*Jāmiʿ al-bayān ʿan taʾwīl āyy al-Qurʾān*), ed. Maḥmud Muḥammad Shākir and Aḥmad Muḥammad Shākir, 16 vols., Turāth al-Islām (Cairo: Dār al-Maʿārif, 1971), 6:371 (#10785). The report is ambiguous as to whether *one* Christian or *some* Christians sponsored this report.

The third set features Jesus asking for a volunteer to take his place. In some reports he offers no reward, and in others he promises the volunteer a place in Paradise. The identity of the person who volunteers differs in several versions of this scenario. One version leaves the martyr anonymous. In one scenario the volunteer remains anonymous, but Jesus does not recruit him until after all the Apostles have been made to look like Jesus. In one, when a youth volunteers, Jesus twice rejects his offer. But when the youth insists for a third time, Jesus accepts his offer. Individuals identified by name as volunteers include Ṭayṭabūs,[2] Taṭyānūs (Tatian?), Sarkhis, and Sarjis (Sergius). In every case the volunteer is crucified instead of Jesus. The Shīʿī have venerated this volunteer. Perhaps they venerate the martyr because—given the Shīʿī history of suffering and especially the martyrdom of Ḥusayn, the grandson of Muḥammad—they have a special reverence for self-sacrifice.[3]

The commentary of Muḥammad ibn Jarīr al-Ṭabarī represents the culmination of Jane Dammen McAuliffe's "formative period" of Qurʾānic exegesis.[4] Ṭabarī records more than a dozen scenarios of the betrayal and arrest of Jesus. Of these, he considers two of highest value, both transmitted from Wahb ibn Munabbih. The first one runs as follows:

> Jesus and 17 of his Apostles were brought into a house. They [presumably the guard] surrounded them. But when they entered in to them, God transformed all of them into the form of Jesus. So they said to them, "You [pl.] have bewitched us. Let Jesus stand out for us or we will kill you all." So Jesus said to his companions, "Who will purchase Paradise today with himself?" A man among them said, "I"! So he went out to them and said, "I am Jesus." God had transformed him into the form of Jesus. So they took him and killed him and crucified him. And from then on they were deceived (*shubbiha la-hum*)[5] and thus presumed that they had killed Jesus. And the Christians presumed the same—that he was Jesus. God took Jesus up from that day.[6]

The second, Ṭabarī's favorite, amounts to an Islamic passion narrative. We have already quoted the first part in the previous chapter on page 177. The remainder of it takes up the story just after the scene in the Garden of Gethsemane.

---

2. ʿAbd Allāh ibn ʿUmar al-Bayḍāwī (d. 1286?), *Al-tafsīr al-Bayḍāwī, al-musammā Anwār al-tanzīl wa-asrār al-taʾwīl*, ed. Muḥammad Ṣubḥī ibn Ḥasan Ḥallāq and Maḥmūd Aḥmad al-Aṭrash, 3 vols. (Damascus: Dār al-Rashīd/Beirut: Muʾassasat al-Īmān, 2000), 135.

3. Mahmoud M. Ayoub, *Redemptive Suffering in Islam: A Study of the Devotional Aspects of ʿAshūrāʾ in Twelver Shiʿism*, Religion and Society 10 (The Hague: Mouton, 1978).

4. Jane Dammen McAuliffe, *Qurʾānic Christians: An Analysis of Classical and Modern Exegesis* (Cambridge/New York: Cambridge University Press, 1991), 13.

5. The key phrase of *Women* [4]:157, *shubbiha la-hum* ("it/he was made ambiguous to them") is difficult to cast into equivalent English. We examined this in chapter 2 above.

6. Ṭabarī, *Tafsīr*, 6:368 (#10779).

Then . . . [Jesus] said, "In truth, one of you will deny me before the cock crows three times. And one of you will sell me for a few dirhams and surely to consume what he sold me for."

So they went out and dispersed. The Jews were looking for him. They took Simon one of the Apostles and said, "This is one of his companions." But he denied it and said, "I am not one of his companions." So they left him. Then others engaged him and he denied it in the same way. Then the cock's crow was heard so he cried and it grieved him.

When it became morning, one of the Apostles went to the Jews and said, "What will you offer me if I guide you to the Messiah?" They gave him thirty dirhams. He took them and led them to him. Someone was made to look like [Jesus] for them before that.[7] So they apprehended him, secured themselves against him, and bound him with a cord. They began to drive him and to say to him, "You raised the dead, commanded Satan, and healed the possessed, can you not free yourself from this cord?" They spit upon him and put thorns upon him until they brought him to the wood on which they wanted to crucify him.

Then God raised him to himself and they crucified the one who was made to look like him to them. He remained [raised unto God] seven [hours]. Then both his mother and the woman whom Jesus treated so that God freed her from spirit possession came weeping to the place of the crucified one. Then Jesus came to them and said, "Why are you crying?" They said, "For you." So he said, "God raised me to himself and nothing but good has befallen me. Indeed this [corpse] is a thing made confusing to them (*hadhā shayʿ shubbiha la-hum* [*Women* (4):157]). So direct my Apostles to meet me at such and such a place."

Eleven of them met him at that place. The one who had sold him and directed the Jews was missing. He asked his companions about him and they said that he, regretting what he had done, hanged and killed himself. So he said, "If he repented, God forgave him." Then he asked them about a young man who followed them called John. He said, "He is with you. Go your way and it will happen that each person will speak in the language of a people. Let him warn them and let him call them."[8]

---

7. The narrative is ambiguous as to who was made to look like Jesus. The passage I have translated "Someone was made to look like Jesus for them before that" is simply *wa-kāna shubbiha ʿalay-him qabla dhālik*. The reason I translate it as I do is that at the beginning of the next paragraph the report says, "they crucified the one who was made to look like him to them." This transformation of identity happened before the betrayer led them to Jesus, so Wahb must have someone other than Judas in mind here for Jesus' look-alike. This impression finds reinforcement in the final paragraph that explicitly says Judas [although he is not named] experienced remorse and committed suicide.

8. Ṭabarī, *Tafsīr*, 9:368-70 (#10780). ʿIsmāʿīl ʿImād al-Dīn Abī al-Fidāʾ Ibn Kathīr al-Qurayshī al-Dimashqī (d. 1373), *Tafsīr al-Qurʾān al-ʿaẓīm*, 7 vols. (Beirut: Dār al-fikr, 1970), 2:44. This narrative is found in English translation in Neal Robinson, *Christ in Islam and Christianity* (Albany: State University of New York, 1991), 128-30.

Ṭabarī favors these two traditions over the others for a simple and rational reason. The famous exegete and commentator exhibits a high view of the Apostles of Jesus. The Qurʾān mentions the Apostles (*al-ḥawāriyūn*), or disciples, of Jesus four times in three different *sūrahs*: *Family of Imran* [3]:52; *Table* [5]:111 and 112; and *Lines* [61]:14. These passages create the distinct impression that the Apostles of Jesus would not have distorted the message and meaning of Jesus' mission deliberately. The other scenarios preserved in Islamic tradition make explicit that the Apostles saw Jesus taken up and saw someone cast in his image. Neither of the two traditions transmitted by Wahb requires this. In the first, God makes all Jesus' companions look like him. Consequently, no one knows for sure except Jesus who the real Jesus is. When Jesus asks for a volunteer, those who do not volunteer do not know who the volunteer is, and when a "Jesus" is arrested, the remaining "Jesuses" cannot be sure that the volunteer was in fact the volunteer Jesus and not the real Jesus. The second scenario does not really state who gets transformed into a Jesus look-alike. Ṭabarī likes it, however, because it neither states nor assumes that Jesus' other companions witnessed either the transformation of the traitor or the escape and ascension of Jesus.

In the other traditions, Jesus' Apostles witness the entire plot of God to rescue Jesus and to raise him. If any of these dozen or so traditions were true, Ṭabarī reasons, then the Apostles must have engaged in a *deliberate plan of deception*. That is, they made the crucifixion and resurrection of Jesus the centerpiece of their preaching and teaching, knowing full well that neither had taken place! Ṭabarī finds such a scenario unacceptable.[9]

Alternative Suggestions from Modern Qurʾān Exegetes

Some of the problems connected with the bulk of the traditional reports of the betrayal and arrest of Jesus have moved the more modern commentators to emphasize other possibilities. Some proposals referred to by Qāsimī include the following.

In some reports someone other than a human substitute takes Jesus' place. Qāsimī speculates that God may have sent "a satan" in the likeness of Jesus to be crucified instead of him. At the other end of the greater-than-human spectrum, a report similar to Luke 22:43 describes an angel descending to Jesus in order to strengthen him. But this Muslim scenario departs from Luke when the angel then gives his life as a ransom for Jesus.[10]

In one scenario, executioners choose someone else to crucify when Judas gets away. In still another, Judas, feeling remorse for having betrayed Jesus, volunteers to be crucified in his place.[11]

---

9. Ṭabarī, *Tafsīr*, 9:374.

10. From Khayr al-Dīn al-Ālūsī, *Al-jawāb al-faṣīḥ li-mā laffaqa-hu ʿAbd al-Masīḥ* [Ibn Isḥāq al-Kindī], ed. Aḥmad Ḥijāzī al-Saqqā, 2 vols. (Cairo: Dār al-Bayān al-ʿArabī, 1987), cited in Qāsimī, *Tafsīr*, 5:1676.

11. Ālūsī, *Al-jawāb al-faṣīḥ,* cited in Qāsimī, *Tafsīr*, 5:1676.

Some arguments in favor of someone other than Jesus' getting executed do not require a look-alike. These arguments draw on the alleged darkness, confusion, and paucity of witnesses that characterize the arrest and its aftermath.

Burhān al-Dīn al-Biqā'ī raises questions about the trustworthiness of what the Gospels report. He bases his case on the Gospels themselves. According to him, all the Christian Gospels agree that knowledge of the matter of the arrest ends at one person, namely, Judas Iscariot. The other enemies did not know Jesus. And Judas only laid his hand on him and did not say with his tongue that this was Jesus. And the time was night. Furthermore, Jesus himself had said to his Apostles, "All of you will have misgivings about me this night." Finally, all of his disciples fled after the arrest so they had no knowledge after that about what happened to Jesus.[12]

Khayr al-Dīn al-Ālūsī, drawing from the Gospels, also raises questions about the conclusions of Christian scripture. He refers to the question Jesus asks of the Jews two times, "Whom do you seek?" When they answer, "Jesus of Nazareth," he replies, "I am he."[13] Ālūsī thinks it strange that they would have to ask his identity unless it had somehow been altered or they had the wrong person. Ālūsī draws another sign that Jesus' identity somehow confused those sent to arrest him from the fact that they had to bribe Judas to lead them to Jesus and he had to designate Jesus with a kiss. Should not the Jews have been able to identify him themselves, since he had been among them and taught in their Temple?[14]

Qāsimī finds in the Gospel narrative evidence that the Jews would have been familiar with Jesus' looks. He grew up among them, frequently attending their ceremonies, festivals, and places of worship. He preached to them, taught them, and dialogued with them. They registered amazement at his skill and knowledge to such a degree that they exclaimed, "Is this not the son of Joseph? Is his mother not Mary? Are his siblings not among us? From where does he have all this wisdom?" If they knew him so well and yet they needed to have Judas identify him for them, does it not suggest that his countenance had been changed?[15]

Some arguments advanced by Muslim apologists rest on the exact likeness of Jesus and his substitute, while others rest on the differences characterizing them. Ālūsī combines the two emphases. He first notes that the arrest took place at night and that the mistreatment mentioned in the Gospels must have altered the victim's good looks. These circumstances would have caused confusion even if the victim did not look like Jesus. So, given the reports that the victim had been made to look like Jesus, where would the certainty that it was Jesus have come from? And Ālūsī reminds us that the Gospel writers themselves

---

12. Burhān al-Dīn Ibrāhīm ibn ʿUmar al-Biqāʿī, *Maqāsʿid al-naẓar li-al-ʿishrāf ʿalā maqāṣid al-suwar*, ed. ʿAbd al-Sāmiʿ Muḥammad Ahʿmad Ḥasanayn, 3 vols. (al-Riyāḍ: Maktabat al-Maʿārif, 1987). Cited in Qāsimī, *Tafsīr*, 5:1660.

13. Ālūsī, *Al-jawāb al-faṣīḥ*. Cited in Qāsimī, *Tafsīr*, 5:1660.

14. Ibid., 5:1664.

15. Ibid.

included among the Messiah's powers the ability to change from one form to another.[16] Here he takes us back to the substitution scenarios. He suggests that Jesus may have gone off among the group of his followers whom the guards released while the guards busied themselves with the Apostle who volunteered to take Christ's place.[17]

It is also possible, according to Ālūsī, that the guards took a bribe to let Jesus go, just as Judas was bribed to take them to him. The guards then would have taken someone other than Jesus from among those who wanted to sacrifice themselves for Jesus. The fact that the victim never acknowledges that he is the Christ supports this possibility.[18]

The Gospel Accounts of the Betrayal and Trial

Compared to the enormous variety of the accounts as exemplified by Ṭabarī, Qāsimī and their sources, the four accounts of the betrayal and arrest in the Gospels impress us with their consistency and simplicity. (1) A "crowd" comes from the Jewish leadership, led by Judas, the betrayer. (2) Judas identifies Jesus with a kiss. In Matthew and Mark his kiss is delivered; in Luke the delivery of the kiss is assumed; and in John there is no mention of the kiss. (3) Someone cuts off the ear of the priest's slave. This results in the most comment and action: Matthew and John record Jesus' telling the swordsman to put his sword back; Luke shows Jesus healing the slave; and Mark records no comment or reaction to the severing of the ear. Jesus directs a comment to the "crowd" in Matthew, Mark, and Luke, asking why they have to come out against him so heavily armed when he has been with them where he could have been easily arrested in the city. Luke tells his disciples, "No more of this," and heals the slave's ear. Matthew has Jesus saying that if he wanted to he could call a legion of angels to help him. Finally, (4) the crowd/soldiers arrest Jesus: Luke and John mention it after all the above events have transpired, while Matthew and Mark mention the arrest immediately after the kiss and before the lopping off of the slave's ear.

The Gospel of Mark seems to present the bare bones of the betrayal and arrest of Jesus. First of all, "while he [Jesus] was still speaking," the armed crowd arrives, led by Judas. Only Luke fails to mention that it was an armed group; John even goes so far as to describe the crowd as "a detachment of soldiers together with police . . . with lanterns, and torches, and weapons" (John 18:3). Mark says the posse was "from the chief priests, the scribes, and the elders" (14:43), and both Matthew and John say in one way or another that they came from the Jewish leaders (Matthew 26:47 and John 18:3). Luke again omits a description of the crowd's senders (22:47). Just this set of details represents a response to the charge that Jesus was well known to the Jewish leaders. A posse or armed guard *from* the Jewish leaders might not necessarily know who Jesus was or where Jesus was—especially at night.

16. He must here be referring to the Transfiguration.
17. Qāsimī, *Tafsīr*, 5:1665.
18. Ālūsī, *Al-jawāb al-faṣīḥ,* cited in Qāsimī, *Tafsīr*, 5:1665.

In fact, another emphasis in Mark's account represents a common thread in two of the others. Jesus addresses the posse that arrests him, "Have you come out with swords and clubs to arrest me as though I were a bandit? Day after day I was with you in the temple teaching, and you did not arrest me. But let the scriptures be fulfilled" (Mark 14:49). This is not necessarily evidence that the armed posse as individuals had seen him in the Temple teaching, but a recognition that a certain cowardliness was represented by those leaders who had sent the posse because they were afraid to act in this way in broad daylight in the presence of Jesus' many admirers and followers among the common folk (see Luke 22:2).

The differences in the four accounts can easily be discerned as due to the distinctive emphases of each evangelist. John, for example, wishes to show graphically the authority and power of Jesus. He records, therefore, that the posse fell back in awe of him (18:6). Matthew as usual stresses the fulfillment of scripture, "But all this has taken place, so that the scriptures of the prophets may be fulfilled" (26:56). Luke emphasizes the compassion of Jesus by recording that Jesus touched the ear of the priest's slave and healed him (22:51). Mark with his usual penchant for action and eyewitness details alone reports, "A certain young man was following him, wearing nothing but a linen cloth. They caught hold of him, but he left the linen cloth and ran off naked" (14:52).

It is important to all three evangelists, however, to show that Jesus was not weak or helpless, that he could have exercised his power, but in doing so he would have defeated his purpose, not just his enemy. This makes sense in the light of Jesus' crucifixion, a shameful fate at best and at worst a curse. Matthew alone reports Jesus as saying he does not need the weapons of his disciples, since he could call on "twelve legions of angels" to defend him (26:53). Luke suggests something similar by reporting Jesus' final statement to the posse, "But this is your hour, and the power of darkness" (22:53). John comments that Jesus knew "all that was going to happen to him" (18:4). He also supplies an interpretive comment about Jesus' purpose in all this, "This was to fulfill the word that he had spoken, 'I did not lose a single one of those whom you gave me'" (18:9). And in John's account Jesus reveals his supernatural knowledge, "Then Jesus, knowing all that was to happen to him, came forward and asked them, 'For whom are you looking?'" (18:4), reminding readers of what he had said when he washed the Apostles' feet (13:1).

Note how congruent all this is with the Gospel treatment of the Lord's Supper and the struggle in Gethsemane that we dealt with in the previous chapter. Joel Green has this to say about the arrest, "in some way, all of the evangelists witness to the notion that the arrest of Jesus happened as a part of God's plan, and that Jesus allowed his arrest as a corollary to his submission to God's will."[19]

---

19. Joel B. Green, *The Death of Jesus: Tradition and Interpretation in the Passion Narrative*, Wissenschaftliche Untersuchungen zum Neuen Testament, 2. Reihe, 33 (Tübingen: Mohr, 1988), 266.

Mark alone includes a brief sentence that some Muslim interpreters of the Gospels pick up on, "All of them deserted him and fled" (14:50). For them, this indicates both the confusion that afflicted the followers of Jesus and the absence of eyewitnesses to what would happen after they had absconded. The touch also has the ring of authenticity about it, since one can hardly imagine the disciples making something like this up about themselves.[20] And if they transmit such things about themselves, does it not suggest they have not fabricated the essence of the whole story?

Evaluation of the Muslim Interpretations of the Arrest of Jesus

The quality of the traditions Ṭabarī records appears to be such that he can decide about the most reliable of them based on a criterion other than the quality of their *isnād* or supporting chain of transmitters. He chooses the two reports from Wahb ibn Munabbih because they do not require that the Apostles of Jesus deliberately falsified the events at the end of Jesus' mission.

Ṭabarī, thus, limits the reports we must deal with—from him at least—to two. Of these two the briefer one rests on the assertion that all of Jesus' companions took on his form and countenance. God made them all look alike. If this were true, it would have been a departure from the usual flow of events on the magnitude of the resurrection of Jesus from the dead. If an event of this magnitude had in fact transpired, is it reasonable to conclude that the reports of such an event should turn out to be as surprisingly diverse as the Muslim reports turned out to be? Clearly it is not. This leaves just one report, then, that does not require the Apostles of Jesus to have deliberately misled all subsequent believers in their reports, building the Christian movement on deliberate falsehood.

But what then of the longer tradition from Wahb? For one thing, of the many reports recorded for us by Ṭabarī, it is the one most similar to the story line of the Gospel accounts. For another, as we have seen, the tradition remains ambiguous about who was made to look like Jesus. But the major problem with Wahb's narrative does not occur in connection with the arrest, but at the point of meetings with the women and his Apostles during Jesus' temporary return to earth, after his initial assumption to heaven. Jesus says to the women who weep for him at the grave of his look-alike, "God raised me to himself and nothing but good has befallen me. Indeed this [corpse] is a thing made confusing to them. So direct my Apostles to meet me at such and such a place." He meets his Apostles and, after asking them about Judas and a young man named John (Mark 14:52?), commissions them to warn and call all peoples.

We may ask some questions about this part of the narrative. When the women directed the Apostles to meet Jesus "at such and such a place," what did they tell the Apostles? Did the women tell what Jesus had told them: that the corpse was of someone else; that Jesus had not been crucified? Or did the

20. Ibid., 268-69.

women say nothing about what had transpired? The narrative does not answer these questions.

Did Jesus tell his Apostles what he had told the women? In the narrative he merely commissioned them to warn and invite the people to whom they were sent. If neither the women nor Jesus told them that Jesus had not been crucified, then, as Ṭabarī maintain, the Apostles did not knowingly distort the truth. Is it reasonable to assume that neither Jesus nor the women told the Apostles what he told the women? Can one imagine that Jesus would send out his Apostles to proclaim the truth without telling them what it was? If he had done such a thing, should Jesus himself not be held responsible for the false gospel his Apostles proclaimed? Surely this is not the case.

The modern commentators offer a variety of other solutions to the apparent discrepancy between the Qur᾿ānic witness and the Gospel witness to the arrest. First, they supply an array of options, such as a satan or an angel could have been the look-alike; the guards could have been bribed to let Jesus go; the guards could have grabbed someone else; Judas could have gotten away; or Judas could even have felt such remorse for the betrayal that he volunteered to be crucified in Jesus' place. They also suggest that the guards could have been confused by the darkness or by the battered appearance of Jesus, and taken the wrong person. The report that the Jews needed a guide to direct them to Jesus when Jesus was so well known suggests that he looked different.

When contrasted with the four reports of the arrest in the canonical Gospels, these views appear to be mere guesses to support a conviction drawn interpretations of the Qur᾿ān that someone else was crucified and Jesus was not. When taken together, the reports from classical commentaries and the reports from more modern ones are far more diverse in their central features than the four reports from Matthew, Mark, Luke, and John. The common core of the Islamic reports is that Jesus was not crucified and did not die. The common core of the Gospel reports is that Jesus was arrested at night by a host of people sent by the Jews; that he not only did not resist arrest, but he resisted resisting arrest; that he saw the arrest as a part of the fulfillment of his purpose, a purpose he had previously taught his followers to expect and exemplify in their own lives of service to others. "If any want to become my followers, let them deny themselves and take up their cross and follow me" (Mark 10:45).

Trial

We look now at the two trials of Jesus in a Muslim interpretation and in the light of the Gospels.

The Trial before the Chief Priest

Qāsimī finds the silence of Jesus before the chief priest particularly indicative that the one being tried was not Jesus. This is especially true, he maintains, when, according to Matthew 26:63, the chief priest puts the person on trial under oath before God to answer truthfully, "Tell us if you are the Messiah, the Son of God." When the accused does not answer that he is the Messiah, but merely replies, "You have said," Qāsimī becomes suspicious. Would the Messiah not have said "Yes," under oath?[21] This contrasts tellingly with Jesus' answer to the posse that sought him out in the garden across the Kidron valley. When Jesus asked them for whom they were looking and they answered, "Jesus of Nazareth," he replied, "I am he" (John 18:4-5). In the garden Jesus answered forthrightly; at the trial before the chief priest, Jesus' look-alike under oath equivocated.

But Qāsimī also uses his material selectively. For example, he draws on Luke 22:66-68 to reinforce what he has said about the silence of the person accused at the trial before the Jewish leaders. They demand, "If you are the Messiah, tell us." Whereas the accused replies, "If I tell you, you will not believe; and if I question you, you will not answer."[22]

The Trial before the Chief Priest in the Gospels

In addition to the incongruity between the probable mental state of a Jesus look-alike and the tone of command the accused assumes in Luke 22:66-68, the following verse makes it clear that Jesus is the one on trial: "But from now on the Son of Man will be seated at the right hand of the power of God" (Luke 22:69). Does this sound like the words of a person conscripted and brought to trial for his life? If the substitute—whether Judas or someone else taken involuntarily—was coerced into standing trial, the answer is obviously no. He would take every opportunity to declare that he was not the Messiah. If the substitute were a volunteer who knew that Jesus had been safely taken up to heaven, why should he hesitate to declare his innocence and get acquitted? He had done his part in enabling Jesus to escape.

The remainder of the passage follows.

> All of them asked, "Are you, then, the Son of God?" He said to them, "You say that I am." Then they said, "What further testimony do we need? We have heard it ourselves from his lips." (Luke 22:69-71)

Obviously the leaders interpret his answer as affirming that he is the Son of God. Would a stand-in take this radical position when acknowledging who he is?

The Trial before Pontius Pilate

Basing his argument on Ernst Rénan's *The Life of Jesus*, Qāsimī maintains that Pilate, the Roman governor over Palestine, despised the Jews "as he would

21. Qāsimī, *Tafsīr*, 5:1661.
22. Ibid., 5:1682.

have despised being thrown in a fire." Pilate exhibited little concern for the complaints, arguments, and opposition of the Jews. Whenever the government introduced some project to improve the life of the people, the rabbis would reject it on the basis of a Torah interpretation. Thus they, in the more colorful words of Qāsimī's paraphrase of Rénan, "slammed the door of improvement and change shut in Pilate's face." He consequently treated them arrogantly and harshly and ignored their requests. The hostility of the governed toward Pilate eventually reached a point where the Roman leadership had to remove him from his position.[23] As is clear from the Gospel, reports Rénan,[24] Jesus was aided by the wife of Pilate, who said, "Have nothing to do with that innocent man, for today I have suffered a great deal because of a dream about him." Qāsimī concludes with Rénan that Pilate liked Jesus and exhausted his power in an attempt to free him.[25]

Clearly Pilate would like to have saved Jesus from the fate being sought by his accusers. So Qāsimī stresses the point that, since the accused person did not answer in a situation that would clearly have helped him, somebody else must have taken Jesus' place.

The Trial before Pilate in the Gospels

Qāsimī and the sources he cites challenge the content of the Gospel accounts of the trials before the chief priest and the Roman governor only at one point. They claim that Jesus' look-alike was the one on trial. The silence the accused maintained and the ambiguity of his answers indicate he was not Jesus.

Jesus did remain largely silent and evasive at points where he could have been more precise. It does look as though he was trying to get on with his condemnation and death. Indeed, his responses harmonize with what he spent his last journey to Jerusalem teaching his followers: the necessity of his suffering and death, followed by his vindication in resurrection (Mark 8:31; 9:30-32; 10:32-34).

Crucifixion

Qāsimī, finding support from his analysis of the crucifixion narratives, makes three main points: (1) Things that the crucified one says on the cross are not congruent with Jesus as the victim; (2) incongruities and discrepancies in the narratives lessen their credibility; and (3) the paucity of witnesses and other features of the narratives suggest the reports were forged.

---

23. Ibid., 5:1694. Ernst Rénan, *The Life of Jesus* (London: M. Lévy Frères/Paris: Trübner, 1867), 276.

24. Matthew 27:19. Here Qāsimī (*Tafsīr*, 5:1694) continues to follow Rénan (*Life of Jesus*, 277).

25. Qāsimī, *Tafsīr*, 5:1695-96; Rénan, *Life of Jesus*, 277.

Evidence from the Crucifixion Scenarios

When the one to be crucified was raised up on the cross, bystanders said, "Wait, let us see whether Elijah will come to take him down" (Matthew 27:49; Mark 15:36). Qāsimī interprets this as an expression of uncertainty on their part. That is, if Elijah should answer his call, it would indicate that he is the Messiah. On the other hand, if Elijah did not come, then the victim was someone else, as they had surmised.[26] Obviously, Elijah did not come, because both Mark and Matthew record that Jesus immediately dies (Matthew 27:50; Mark 15:37).

The problem with this piece of evidence is that it ignores the context of this statement by the bystanders. Their caution, "Wait, let us see whether Elijah will come to take him down," results from their misunderstanding what Jesus has just said in Aramaic, "*Eli, Eli, lema sabachthani*," "My God, my God, why have you forsaken me?" (Matthew 27:46; Mark 15:34). *Eli*, "my God," evidently sounded to them like "Elijah" and so they became apprehensive that maybe Elijah would come to their victim's rescue. The fact that the uninvited Elijah did not come has no bearing on who was being crucified.

This statement in its actual meaning also serves Qāsimī as evidence that someone other than Jesus was the one whose crucifixion is described in the Gospels. "My God, my God, why have you forsaken me?" evidences dissatisfaction with destiny as well as reluctance to submit to God's will. Since Jesus would never express such dissatisfaction and would certainly submit to the will of God, the victim who cried out must have been someone else.[27]

Qāsimī has no problem with Jesus son of Mary cringing from death in the Garden of Gethsemane. Indeed, one of the reports recorded in the commentaries says Jesus was the most apprehensive of death of any of the messengers of God. If one of the "tenacious" among the messengers can shrink from death and ask God to rescue him from it, why would one expect such a person to find the pain and sense of abandonment of the cross something to experience joyfully? Furthermore, it is clear from the consistent content of the Gospel passion narrative up to this point that Jesus in fact saw this suffering, humiliation, and shameful way of dying as precisely the destiny and will of God. Part of it was the sense of abandonment that Jesus expresses in one of the last statements he makes before he dies, "My God, my God, why have you forsaken me?" The reader of the Gospel who knows the world of Judaism at the time of Jesus recognizes in this cry of agony the first verse of Psalm 22. R. G. Hamerton-Kelly, of Stanford University and a participant in the first Princeton Symposium on Judaism and Christian Origins, speaks to precisely this issue. He says that this cry of Jesus expresses a "rejection of the way of violent self-assertion

---

26. Qāsimī, *Tafsīr*, 5:1662. Qāsimī inserts this piece of evidence from the crucifixion narrative as a parenthetical remark in his discussion of the Transfiguration where Moses and Elijah meet with Jesus.

27. Ibid., 5:1667-68.

in favor of trust in God to vindicate him in the future."[28] In other words, this agonizing cry of dereliction on the cross embodies a testimony to Jesus' way of understanding his role as Israel's Messiah.

In the Gospel according to John, one of the last things Jesus says is, "I am thirsty" (19:28). Qāsimī follows ʿIzz al-Dīn al-Muḥammadī, author of *The Distinguisher between Truth and Falsehood*, who cites this as evidence that it was not Jesus who was crucified, since Jesus had once fasted for forty days (Luke 4:1-13) and announced, "I have food to eat you know not of" (John 4:32). Would Jesus, "the elite of the prophets," with this measure of self-discipline and this source of supply, have been thirsty during the brief time of crucifixion?[29]

Aside from the fact that the accounts of Jesus' forty-day desert period of fasting, initiation, and temptation say nothing about being deprived of water—thirst being always a greater problem for fasting than hunger, it would seem that Muḥammadī has no firsthand knowledge of the effects of crucifixion. Although what remains of antiquity preserves no full descriptions of crucifixion, we have some inkling of the agony involved from brief references to this cruel method of execution. Seneca (d. 65), who flourished at the time of Paul, gives some sense of the prolonged agony of crucifixion. In a letter to Lucius,[30] he criticizes a man who uses the agonies of crucifixion in a poem to make the point that he wants to stay alive even under crucifixion agony. Seneca responds by depicting such agony.

> Can anyone be found who would prefer wasting away in pain dying limb by limb, or letting out his life drop by drop, rather than expiring once for all? Can any man be found willing to be fastened to the accursed tree (*ad illud infelix lignum*),[31] long sickly, already deformed, swelling with ugly tumours on shoulders and chest, and draw the breath of life amid long-drawn-out agony? I think he would have many excuses for dying even before mounting the cross![32]

In reflecting upon this passage, Martin Hengel extends the description of crucifixion.

> In Roman times not only was it the rule to nail the victim by both hands and feet, but that the flogging which was a stereotyped part of

28. R. G. Hamerton-Kelly, "Sacred Violence and the Messiah: The Markan Passion Narrative as a Redefinition of Messianology," in James H. Charlesworth, ed., *The Messiah: Developments in Earliest Judaism and Christianity*, First Princeton Symposium on Judaism and Christian Origins (Minneapolis: Augsburg Fortress, 1992), 492.

29. Qāsimī, *Tafsīr*, 5:1667.

30. Seneca, *Ad Lucilium: Epistulae Morales*, trans. Ricard M. Gummere, 3 vols.; Loeb Classical Library, Seneca in 10 vols., 6 (London: Heinemann/Cambridge, MA: Harvard University Press, 1971), 3:165-67.

31. The translator supplies this note: "*Infelix lignum* (or arbor) is the cross" (ibid., 167).

32. Cited in Martin Hengel, *Crucifixion in the Ancient World and the Folly of the Message of the Cross*, trans. John Bowden (London: SCM/Philadelphia: Fortress, 1977), 30-31.

> the punishment would make the blood flow in streams. Binding the victim to the cross only with bonds remained an exception. Presumably Jesus was so weakened by loss of blood that he was unable to carry the beam of the cross to the place of execution; this is the best explanation of his relatively speedy death. The "ugly weals [welts] on shoulders and chest" in Seneca's macabre description are probably a reference to the consequences of flogging.[33]

Jesus' crucifixion cannot be compared even with his heroic desert fast. We turn now to look at the narratives of the crucifixion through the eyes of our Muslim exegetes.

The Crucifixion Narratives Could Have Been Forged

At the outset of chapter 10, I mentioned the Christian contention that references to the crucifixion of Jesus abound enough to qualify as "recurrent" (*mutawātir*), that is, passed down by so many during the first three generations of transmitters that the possibility of fabrication is excluded.[34] Qāsimī insists that the reports of the crucifixion of Jesus do not satisfy this requirement. For one thing, out of fear for their lives, the Apostles abandoned Jesus, which would exclude them as firsthand witnesses to the crucifixion.[35] Furthermore, the opponents of Jesus who could have observed the event of the crucifixion included only the armed guard and the ruler's minor officials, a small group—two, three, or the like, small enough to have agreed on a false report. In addition, the generality of the people attending the crucifixion saw on the cross between two crucified bandits a person whose countenance and features had changed as a result of his arrest and suffering.[36] Finally, the fact that the chief priests and scribes in their council had to ask their victim, "If you are the Messiah, then tell us" (Luke 22:67), indicates that the elders of the Jews themselves did not recognize him. For these reasons, the reports—necessarily based on speculation and conjecture—lack historical significance.[37]

Qāsimī himself moves into the realm of speculation and conjecture when he gives reasons why, even if a large number of opponents did witness the crucifixion and perceive it correctly, the elders still could have agreed together to forge their report. The elders, even though they realize their prisoner is not Jesus, decide to kill him anyway. They will spread it round that he is Jesus, hoping the people will cease following him as their Messiah and will give up

---

33. Hengel, *Crucifixion*, 31-32.
34. See chapter 4 above.
35. Qāsimī, *Tafsīr*, 5:1680.
36. Ibid., 5:1680-81.
37. Ibid., 5:1682. In making this final point, Qāsimī cites the author of *Shaming the Gospels,* whom I have not been able to identify.

taking him to be a prophet. If and when they do locate Jesus, they can do to him what they have done to his substitute.[38]

Next, Qāsimī calls on Taqī al-Dīn Ibn Taymīyah (d. 1328), who suspects reports about the crucifixion of Jesus for the same reason he questions the reliability of the story of Moses. God could not have given either report to either messenger since they would have been dead. Ibn Taymīyah assumes here that both received a scripture in the way Muḥammad received the Qurʾān—as sent down.[39]

Ibn Taymīyah, however, exonerates followers of Jesus who believe he was crucified. Supposing Jesus was crucified represents no defect in their faith as long as they affirm him as servant, Messenger, and word of God, and a spirit from God. After all, the children of Israel had killed many of the prophets, and God said to the believers, "Muḥammad is only a messenger of whom many messengers have passed away before him. If he dies or is killed are you going to turn on your heels?" (*Family of Imran* [3]:143).[40]

To sum up, according to Qāsimī, no disciples were present at the crucifixion; the Jews likely spread a rumor that they crucified Jesus and not one of his companions; and the altered appearance of the crucified one, born of his flogging and the other agonies of the process, made the crowds susceptible to false information about who was being crucified. All this resulted in inconsistent and contradictory reports of the death of the one crucified.

A Christian Response

Although I pointed in chapters 7 and 10 to a variety of independent witnesses to the crucifixion of Jesus, I have based my case for the authenticity of reports of that event primarily on the authenticity of the predictions Jesus made of his death and resurrection. Furthermore, in connection with the multiple scenarios of the arrest presented by Muslim interpreters and exegetes, I stressed, following Ṭabarī, the reliability of the Apostles, especially in light of the way they are viewed in the Qurʾān. As Ibn Taymīyah has claimed, the Apostles could have been both authentic believers and wrong about the crucifixion of Jesus, but only if they had not *knowingly* promulgated a false narrative of the end of Jesus' mission.

Of the two narratives that satisfied Ṭabarī's criterion of integrity, one was so astounding a departure from the normal course of events that it could not

38. Ibid.

39. Ibid., 5:1703.

40. Cited in ibid., 5:1707-8. It is worth noting here again that these arguments do not exhaust the attitudes and positions of Muslims on the matter of Jesus' last days. For example, the Brethren of Purity of Basra, tenth-century Shīʿī of the Ismaʿīlī variety, in their *Letters*, summarize Jesus' life and describe his crucifixion. They state, "his body (*nāsūt-hu*) was crucified and his hands were nailed to the wood of the cross" (*Rasāil ikhwān al-ṣafāʾ wa-khullān al-wafāʾ*, 4 vols. [Beirut: Dār Bayrūt/Dār Ṣādir, 1957], 4:28-32). See Neal Robinson, *Christ in Islam and Christianity* (Albany: State University of New York Press, 1991), 55-57; and Lootfy Levonian, "The Ikhwān al-Ṣafāʾ and Christ," *The Muslim World* 35 (1945): 27-31.

have been compatible with the variety of reports that have circulated among Muslims about the event. Surely the multiple transformations it reports would itself have been the good news the Apostles would have spread—as astounding as the resurrection of Jesus from the dead.

A final scenario in the other narrative Ṭabarī favors has Jesus commissioning his Apostles to call people from all nations in their own languages to the faith. To what faith did he call them: to faith in his crucifixion and resurrection or to faith in his divine rescue through a human substitute? If, on the one hand, he commissioned them to spread the truth of divine rescue, then the Apostles were guilty of propagating a deliberate falsehood because they spread the news that he was crucified and resurrected—something incongruent with what we know of them from both the Qur᾿ān and Christian tradition. If, on the other hand, Jesus commissioned them to spread the false message of his death and resurrection, then Jesus himself was guilty of propagating a deliberate falsehood—something incongruent with the Islamic picture of Jesus' impeccable character.

The Gospel Narratives of the Crucifixion: Comparison and Contrast

As further evidence that Jesus was not killed, Qāsimī mentions structural, semantic, and intentional differences in the passion narratives.[41] We must look, then, at the narratives of the crucifixion to see wherein they agree and wherein they differ across the four Gospels (Matthew 27:32-56; Mark 15:21-41; Luke 23:26-49; John 19:16b-37). Are the differences contradictions, alternatives, or added details?

Essential Agreements of the Four Gospel Narratives. We will start with those aspects of the crucifixion narrative on which all four Gospels demonstrate essential agreement.

1. All locate the crucifixion at the Place of the Skull. Three Gospels (Matthew 27:33; Mark 15:22; John 19:17b) provide the Aramaic (called "Hebrew" in the Greek text) name *Golgotha* for the place name.
2. All four state explicitly, "they crucified him," although Luke replaces "him" with "Jesus."
3. They all agree that others were crucified with him, but they indicate this at different points in the unfolding of events. Luke (23:33b) and John (19:18) mention that two were crucified with him immediately after stating that they crucified him. Matthew and Mark mention those crucified with him after going over the derision of the passers-by and of the Jewish leaders; Matthew (27:44) calls them "bandits," and Mark simply refers to "those crucified with him" (15:32b). Matthew and Mark both mention them in connection with the crowd's derision of Jesus. Luke mentions this also

41. Ibid., 5:1663.

at the same point in the flow of events and gives details of the interaction between Jesus and the two "criminals" (23:39-43).

4. The inscription on the cross at the crucifixion represents a fourth area where all four Gospels are in essential agreement (Matthew 27:37; Mark 15:26; Luke 23:38; John 19:19). All record that it said, "The King of the Jews." John clarifies by adding "Jesus of Nazareth" before "the King of the Jews" and appends a discussion about the inscription between "the chief priests of the Jews" and Pilate (19:21). Matthew notes that it represented "the charge against him" and that it was placed "over his head." Luke says it was "over him." John attributes it to the command of Pilate.
5. All four mention the moment when Jesus dies (Matthew 27:50; Mark 15:37; Luke 23:46; John 19:30). The three Synoptic Gospels mention that Jesus "breathed his last"; John alone uses, "gave up his spirit."
6. Casting lots occurs in some form in all four accounts, though not at the same point. Matthew (27:35), Mark (15:24), and Luke (23:34) all state, "they"[42] divided his clothes by casting lots. John, who gives more detail, places the episode after the discussion of the inscription over Jesus (19:23-25a). Like the other evangelists, John has distribution by lot, but only of Jesus' seamless garment.
7. The Synoptic Gospels find a way of saying that Jesus' last breath was preceded by a loud cry. All four Gospels include something Jesus says at the end. Three different sayings, however, are recorded: "My God, my God, why have you forsaken me?" (Matthew 27:46 and Mark 15:34); "Father, into your hand I commend my spirit" (Luke 23:46); and "It is finished" (John 19:30).
8. Another feature of all four narratives is the offering of sour wine to Jesus. In the case of Matthew (27:48), Mark (15:36), and John (19:29), it occurs at the very end of Jesus' crucifixion as he is about to expire. But Luke treats it before his mention of the inscription in connection with the soldiers mocking Jesus (23:36). Matthew says it was one of the bystanders who offered the wine and Mark attributes the act to "someone." Both actors accompany the offer of wine with the taunt, "Wait, let us see whether Elijah will come to take him down." John simply uses the pronoun "they" to refer to those who offer Jesus the drink, probably referring to "the soldiers," mentioned in verse 25.
9. Finally, all four Gospels mention certain women connected with the cross. Matthew (27:55-56), Mark (15:40-41), and Luke (23:49) mention women watching from a distance. Matthew and Luke mention women who had followed Jesus from Galilee. Mark enlarges on this connection after identifying the names of the women. Matthew says the women were

42. "They" refers to "the soldiers of the governor" (Matthew 27:27) or "the soldiers" (Mark 15:16); Luke provides no clear antecedent for the pronoun.

many, and Luke places them in the context of "all his acquaintances."[43] Matthew and Mark mention Mary Magdalene and Mary the mother of James and Joseph; Matthew, in addition, names the mother of the sons of Zebedee, while Mark adds Salome (Matthew 27:56; Mark 15:40).[44] Luke omits the names of the women in 23:49, while John connects with the three Synoptic evangelists by mentioning them (19:25b). John includes either the women's names or their relationship to Jesus: his mother, his mother's sister, Mary the wife of Clopas, and Mary Magdalene. These women appear earlier in John's passion story than they do in those of the other three evangelists; and they stand "near" the cross rather then "looking on from a distance."

Essential Agreements of Three of the Gospel Narratives

Next, we look at features of the crucifixion event agreed upon substantially by three of the Gospels.

1. Simon of Cyrene carries Jesus' cross (Matthew 27:32; Mark 15:23; Luke 23:26). Mark notes that Simon was the father of Alexander and Rufus (15:21). John says simply that Jesus carried his cross "by himself" (19:17).
2. One of those crucified with him (Luke 23:39) or both of them (Matthew 27:44; Mark 15:32b) taunt Jesus.
3. Darkness engulfs the land at noon (Matthew 27:45; Mark 15:33; Luke 23:44).
4. The Temple curtain tears (Matthew 27:51; Mark 15:38; Luke 23:45).
5. The centurian (Mark 15:39; Luke 23:47) and those with him (Matthew 27:54) testify to Jesus' integrity.

Agreements of Two Gospel Narratives

Only two events are shared by two Gospels:

1. An early offer of wine (Matthew 17:34; Mark 15:23)
2. Jesus' cry, "My God, my God, why have you forsaken me?" and its misinterpretation by bystanders (Matthew 27:46-47; Mark 15:34-35).

---

43. This probably includes his Apostles, "whose whereabouts have been unknown since the arrest" (Joel B. Green, *The Gospel of Luke*, New International Commentary on the New Testament [Grand Rapids: Eerdmans, 1997], 823).

44. See also Mark 15:47, where Salome is not mentioned, and 16:1. Salome is not the mother of the sons of Zebedee (Richard Bauckham, "Salome the Sister of Jesus, Salome the Disciple of Jesus, and the Secret Gospel of Mark," *Novum Testamentum* 33, no. 3 [1991]: 255). Forty-seven percent of the Jewish women whose names have been recorded for the period 330 BCE to 200 CE were either Mary (Maria and Miryam) or Salome (ibid.).

Items Restricted to One Gospel Narrative

Now we turn to matters of substance that are found in only one of the Gospels (without discussing in detail minor differences in the narrative). Luke has five such passages, John four, and Matthew one. All of Mark's material has some parallel in the other Gospels.

1. Immediately after introducing the procession in which Simon is commandeered to carry Jesus' cross, Luke introduces a group of women among the great mob of people who follow in procession and lament his circumstances. Jesus responds by warning them of what they as women of Jerusalem can expect in the future from violent revolutionaries (23:27-31).
2. According to Luke alone, just before the dividing up of his clothes, Jesus says, "Father, forgive them; for they do not know what they are doing" (23:34).
3. Only Luke reports a transaction between Jesus and those crucified alongside him. One derides him, and the other upbraids the derision and asks Jesus to remember him when he comes into his kingdom. Jesus assures him, "today, you will be with me in Paradise" (23:40-43).
4. Jesus' last statement in Luke is also unique, "Father, into your hands I commend my spirit" (23:46).
5. Luke includes a reaction of the crowds gathered at the cross, "they returned home, beating their breasts" (23:48), reminding readers of the procession to the Place of the Skull where the women beat their breasts and wailed at the prospect of Jesus' cruel death (23:27) and of Jesus' response to them (23:28-31). Both components of this *inclusio* are unique to Luke.
6. John's portrayal of Jesus' last words occurs only in his narrative: "I am thirsty." This saying brings on the sour wine. After receiving the wine he says, "It is finished," and dies (19:28 and 30).
7. Just before these words, John includes a scenario in which Jesus commends his mother to the care of "the disciple whom he loved" (19:26-27).
8. John alone includes a report narrating the Jews' request that the death of the victims be expedited by breaking their legs out of respect for the Sabbath. The soldiers carry this out in the case of the two victims alongside Jesus; but, since Jesus has already expired, they need not break his legs. They put a spear in his side instead. After a parenthetical testimony that the writer was an eyewitness of these events, he adds that scripture foretells that none of his bones would be broken (Exodus 12:46; Numbers 9:12, passages that refer to the Passover Lamb) and that his side would be pierced (Zechariah 12:10) (John 19:31-37).
9. Finally, Matthew alone mentions the earth-shaking and grave-cleaving events that accompany the end of the agonizing death of Jesus. Mark

(15:38) and Luke (23:45) share with Matthew (27:51) the mention of the tearing in two of the curtain of the Temple. Matthew, however, adds a shaking of the earth, accompanied by splitting of rocks, and the raising of saints from their tombs (27:51b-53).

Analysis

The features common to all four Gospels I will refer to as "the Structure" because it supplies the architecture or skeleton of the event of crucifixion. The Structure provides the specific place; the type of execution; those sharing Jesus' fate; an inscription defining the charge; the fact that Jesus died; and identifiable witnesses to the event. Some additional details of the process also show up in all four Gospels: lots were cast for Jesus' clothing; he was offered sour wine to drink; and he died with a last cry or word.

The parts of the narratives found in the three Synoptic Gospels bring out the important role played by Mark's account. It should not be assumed, however, that the other three Gospel writers merely elaborate on Mark. With the possible exception of John, they probably use Mark as one of their sources. In some cases the wording of the Synoptic Gospels is virtually the same (e.g., Matthew 27:45; Mark 15:33; Luke 23:44; and Matthew 27:55; Mark 15:40; Luke 23:49). Enough differences occur, however—especially in Luke—to indicate that other sources were at hand to draw on (e.g., Matthew 27:44; Mark 15:32b; Luke 23:39). Luke follows a different order than Mark and Matthew at several important points. All Mark's material finds some echo in another Gospel, except for details such as the names of Simon of Cyrene's children (Mark 15:21), the inclusion of Salome among the women viewing the crucifixion from afar (Mark 15:40), and the comment at the end of Mark's narrative about the women accompanying Jesus and providing for him in Galilee (Mark 15:41). John, in contrast, has little other than the Structure he shares with the Synoptic Gospels and the material unique to him, analyzed in the following paragraph.

The items occurring in only one Gospel narrative add color and detail to the Structure. Jesus' last words are among these unique features. Matthew (27:45-49) and Mark (15:33-36) include Jesus' cry of dereliction from Psalm 22, "My God, my God, why have you forsaken me?" along with the response to it from bystanders. Luke and John do not have a hint of this, in spite of the fact that John focuses on aspects of the crucifixion that fulfill scripture (19:24b, 28, 36, 37). Luke provides the final statement, "Father, into your hands I commend my spirit" (23:46). John contributes, in addition to Jesus' statement commending his mother to the care of one of his disciples, the final two statements: "I am thirsty" (19:28) and "It is finished" (19:30). In addition, Matthew, Luke, and John allow the reader to zoom in on details not covered in the Structure itself. The commendation of Jesus' mother to the care of John is one of these. John also introduces us to some behind-the-scenes conversations with Jewish leaders about the inscription over Jesus' head and about the breaking of the victims' legs, along with the consequences of that procedure (19:31-34). Luke provides a similar graphic detail in bringing out an interaction between Jesus and the two criminals crucified with him that both fits in with the forgiveness theme and supports the reader's awareness of Jesus as one of the suffering righteous (23:39-43).[45] The breast-beating scenes at the beginning (23:27-31) and end (23:48-49) of Luke's narrative focus on the opening procession and the closing dispersion, and provide a context for recording Jesus' prophetic statement,

> "Daughters of Jerusalem, do not weep for me, but weep for yourselves and for your children. For the days are surely coming when they will say, 'Blessed are the barren, and the wombs that never bore, and the breasts that never nursed.' Then they will begin to say to the mountains, 'Fall on us'; and to the hills, 'Cover us.' For if they do this when the wood is green, what will happen when it is dry?" (Luke 23:28-31)

The breast-beating in the aftermath of Jesus' demise belongs with this prophecy because it reminds the reader through the repetition of the "breast-beating" that Jesus had said this earlier. As mentioned above, this *inclusio* enables Jesus to speak again even after death.

Enough evidence has been presented to show that a core Structure can be discerned with largely noncontradictory additions. Two possibly contradictory statements appear across all four narratives. In one, John states flatly that Jesus carries his cross "by himself," whereas the Synoptic Gospels have Simon of Cyrene carrying it for him. In the other, John has Jesus' mother, her sister, Mary the wife of Clopas, and Mary Magdalene standing *near* the cross (19:25), while the Synoptic Gospels locate the women observing from, or standing at, a distance (Matthew 27:55; Mark 15:40; Luke 23:49). Of course, the event in John is earlier and connected with something Jesus says to his mother from the cross, while the corresponding part in the Synoptic narratives comes at the very end when Jesus has passed away.

As I stressed in chapter 8, unlike the Qurʾān, which comes down from above by means of an angel or by direct divine inspiration, the scriptures of the New Testament arise under the inspiration of the Holy Spirit from the Christian communities of faith. As such, each of the four Gospels displays unique characteristics. But, by virtue of their very diversity, they also present a united witness to that which they collectively affirm—to what I have called the Structure. This reminder will prepare us for exploring the resurrection.

---

45. Joel Green shows how Jesus represents a "righteous sufferer" identified especially in the Psalms; see *Death of Jesus*, 317.

13

"And after Three Days Rise Again"

The Resurrection of Jesus

Most Muslims believe in the resurrection of the dead before the final judgment in much the same way as did Paul and other Pharisees at the time of Jesus. As the Qur᾽ān makes clear, traditional Arabian polytheists found this belief in a future resurrection of the body hard to believe. The Qur᾽ān tells Muḥammad to affirm this truth:

> And they used to say, "What! When we die and become dust and bones, shall we then indeed be raised up again? We and our fathers of old? Say: 'Yea, those of old and those of later times, all will certainly be gathered for the meeting appointed for a Day well-known.'" (*Event* [56]:47-50)

And the power of God supports this conviction, "Does man think that We cannot assemble his bones?" (*Resurrection* [75]:3).

The worldview of most Muslims, therefore, would not exclude the resurrection of Jesus as a harbinger of universal resurrection. Their belief, however, that Jesus escaped death and the cross leaves no room for a resurrection. Some Muslims, however, do not believe Jesus escaped the cross and burial in a tomb. The crucial sentence from the Qur᾽ān, "they killed him not, nor crucified him, but so it was made to appear to them" (*Women* [4]:157), fits with their conviction that Jesus did not die on the cross but passed out. He then revived in the tomb and walked away from it.

Did Jesus Really Die on the Cross?

A set of nineteenth-century Western rationalists whose worldview did exclude a resurrection from death speculated that Jesus did not die on the cross but swooned and was later revived by medication and the cool environment of his tomb. Modern historians, however, no longer take this hypothesis seriously. For example, Gerd Lüdemann, who rejects the bodily resurrection of Jesus entirely,[1]

---

1. Gerd Lüdemann, *The Resurrection of Jesus: History, Experience, Theology,* trans. John Bowden (London: SCM, 1994), 180.

also rejects this swoon theory with no less conviction. Mentioning it only in two footnotes, he concludes, "The fact of Jesus' death as a consequence of crucifixion is indisputable."[2] N. T. Wright, who argues for the historicity of the resurrection of Jesus in a book of more than eight hundred pages, gives only seven lines and a footnote to the swoon theory—in short, "Roman soldiers after all, were rather good at killing people, and when given a rebel leader to practise on they would have had several motives for making sure the job was done properly."[3] This may, in fact, be the best response to the whole theory that Jesus was not dead when they took him down from the cross and laid him in a tomb. Nevertheless, some Muslims have appealed to this theory.

The Ahmadiyyah movement, a marginal sect claiming to be Islamic, rejects the more standard view that Jesus was taken up in rescue from being crucified and will return in the end times.[4] The members of the movement believe that Jesus revived in the tomb and made his way to Kashmir "to give his message to the Lost Tribes of Israel who lived in those parts."[5] The death of Jesus is supported, according to them, by *Family of Imran* [3]:144. They translate a portion of this verse as follows: "Muḥammad is no more than an Apostle. Verily, *all* messengers have passed away before him (*qad khalat min qabli-hi al-rusul*)." Abu Bakr in the aftermath of Muḥammad's death quotes this verse to demonstrate to all that Muḥammad had in fact died and had not been taken directly up to heaven. If the verse does not mean that all the messengers before Muḥammad had died, it would not have been convincing that Muḥammad had died.[6]

Since the 1970s, Ahmad Deedat has been popularizing the resuscitation theory.[7] More recently, a Muslimah, Ruqaiyyah Waris Maqsood, devotes twenty pages to it in her book *The Mysteries of Jesus*. She allows that *Family of Imran* [3]:55 may indicate that Jesus died, but not that he was overcome by death. She mentions the position of the Ahmadiyyah sect we have just summarized, and, although she does not accept their tradition that Jesus journeyed to Kashmir where he married and had children, she makes a case for Jesus' being "miraculously saved" from dying on the cross. She mixes genuine historical details, such as a Latin inscription of an edict of the Emperor Claudius (41-54) demonstrating the Roman reverence for entombed individuals, with reinterpretations, such as Jesus' use of the three days of Jonah in the great fish as a reference to his rescue from the

---

2. Ibid., 39, 193 n. 71, 203 n. 170.

3. N. T. Wright, *The Resurrection of the Son of God*, Christian Origins and the Question of God 3 (London: SPCK, 2003), 709 and 709 n. 70. In Wright's *Who Was Jesus?* (Grand Rapids: Eerdmans, 1992), 19-36, he contends with a similar theory of Barbara Thiering (*Jesus the Man: A New Interpretation from the Dead Sea Scrolls* [New York: Doubleday, 1992]).

4. Ghulam Farid, [notes to] *The Holy Qurʾān: Arabic Text with English Translation and Short Commentary*, ed. Malik Ghulam Farid (Tilford, Surrey, U.K.: Islam International Publications, 1994), 142 n. 424.

5. Ibid., 138 n. 415. See also Farid's comment on *Believers* [23]:50 (51 in the Ahmadiyyah recension [*qirāʾah*]), 742-43 n. 2000.

6. Ibid., 166 n. 494. Verse 144 is verse 145 in the recension used by the Ahmadiyyah.

7. See page 61 and n. 10 in chapter 5 above.

grave. After all, Jonah came out *alive*, not dead. Although she indicates serious research in some areas, in others she simply makes claims. Her work, therefore, has the appearance of careful research but lacks the consistent substance of it. She even calls forth a prophetic foreshadowing of Jesus' "human body being overcome by death":

> Come, and let us return to the Lord; for it is he who has torn, and he will heal us; he has struck down, and he will bind us up. After two days he will revive us; in the third day he will raise us up, that we may live before him. (Hosea 6:1-2)

Maqsood mentions a variety of factors best explained by assuming Jesus was not dead when placed in the tomb: Jesus was on the cross for a shorter time than was normally true of crucifixions; the disciples expected no resurrection; the Jews expected only a resurrection at the time of the final judgment; the disciples suspected at first that the body was stolen; he appeared only to his followers; they rejoiced when they saw him, assuming he was fully alive, could eat, and that his wounds could be touched; and Paul's letters indicate a belief in his resurrection within twenty years after the event of the crucifixion.

Maqsood takes her reader on a journey through the discovery of the Shroud of Turin and Veronica's handkerchief, along with a detailed analysis of what the tomb would have been like, to demonstrate that Jesus had to have been alive in the tomb. She accepts the theories that the Shroud, kept in a golden grille[8] with the *keramion* (protective tile) placed over the top, was the burial cloth of Jesus. He wiped the blood and sweat from his face with Veronica's handkerchief. She adduces evidence to show that the stains on these two relics were from the bodily fluids of a live and not a dead person.[9]

Suppose the shroud and the handkerchief do go back to the first century CE; suppose they do indicate that the person whose corporal fluids have stained them was alive; how do we know that it was in fact Jesus of Nazareth who was the person contained in these cloths? Maqsood herself states it might have been Barabbas. Maybe it was one of the thieves crucified next to Jesus. Even a bone box (ossuary) with the name "James, son of Joseph, brother of Jesus" engraved on it and dated to the first century has been controversial as to whether this was in fact the brother of Jesus of Nazareth.[10] How can relics such as the Shroud of Turin and Veronica's Veil be substantial enough evidence to place beside the testimony of the New Testament so as to deny their most central teaching?

Maqsood does not interact with critics of the resuscitation theory, such as

---

8. Maqsood connects this with the word "grail" and suggests that this receptacle was the Holy Grail. See n. 9 below.

9. Ruqaiyyah Waris Maqsood, *The Mysteries of Jesus: A Muslim Study of the Origins and Doctrines of the Christian Church* (Oxford: Sakina Books, 2000), 171-91.

10. On this issue, see Hershel Shanks and Ben Witherington III, *The Brother of Jesus: The Dramatic Story and Meaning of the First Archeological Link to Jesus and His Family* (New York: HarperSanFrancisco, 2003).

C. F. D. Moule who offers two main reasons why the survival of Jesus after appearing to have died on the cross is unlikely to be true. (1) It requires for its presentation details from the Gospels that would not have survived had the resuscitation theory been true. If the followers of Jesus were either propagating a falsehood or had been hoodwinked by the surviving Jesus, they would not have preserved the very details that the resuscitation theory needs for its cogency: the rapidity of Jesus' death; the fact that some victims of crucifixion in antiquity did not die from it; the effect of the cool atmosphere in a spacious tomb and the aromatic spices applied to the body for burial. Would these details have been provided by writers wishing to exchange the scenario that Jesus was raised from the dead for the historical fact that he survived death in a resuscitating tomb? Maqsood, for example, relies on testimonies in the narratives that the disciples who went to the tomb did not expect to find Jesus missing. If they were intending to press a spurious case for the resurrection of Jesus, would they have included this detail? If Jesus had been the type of person who would press a falsehood such as would be necessary for Maqsood's theory to work, would the narratives even have existed? Or put another way, would a pure romance such as the one necessary to support such a blatant fraud culminate in the Gospels—the kind of narratives Maqsood requires for the materials to formulate her case?

(2) A resuscitated Jesus could not have launched the church that Jesus launched. The Gospel presentation of the response of the disciples to the appearances of Jesus represents the polar opposite of the response to someone who had nearly died on the cross and had only recently regained consciousness and emerged from the grave. They were joyous, enthusiastic, and confident. Under the circumstances required by the resuscitation theory, they would have expressed sympathy, pity, and helpfulness. If Jesus survived the cross, he had to die at some time in the future. Could his death have escaped the notice of the church? Is there any evidence other than a tomb in Kashmir of his actual death?

Maqsood takes the Ahmadiyyah to task for their conviction that the tomb in Kashmir contains the body of Jesus. "The subcontinent is full of tombs of Middle Eastern saints and prophets who never went within a thousand miles of India," she writes. "The region contains several thousand 'tombs' of Shaykh Abd al-Qadir al-Jilani alone."[11] She does not, however, provide an alternative explanation for the eventual death of Jesus, after which God raised him up (*Family of Imran* [3]:55). If his disciples had been with Jesus until his final demise, would they not have had the same candor about narrating that event as they had when they reported their own scattering and their denial of the master on the eve of his crucifixion?[12]

If Jesus' disciples thought he had died and Jesus knew he had not died; if Jesus knew that the false belief in his resurrection was causing the joy and

11. Maqsood, *Mysteries*, 262 n. 4 in chapter 20.

12. C. F. D. Moule, *The Phenomenon of the New Testament: An Inquiry into the Implications of Certain Features of the New Testament*, Studies in Biblical Theology, Second Series 1 (London: SCM, 1967), 7.

worship he observed among them; if he further discerned that the delusion they were entertaining would be their primary message to their widening world, would the Jesus we know from the Gospels or the Qurʾān have allowed them to continue in jubilant error?

Obviously no historian of the Bible can make a totally convincing case for the resurrection. Events in history that are unique can hardly be treated scientifically or historically. They have to be transmitted by witnesses. When it comes to the New Testament, however, no doubt can remain that its writers believe in the resurrection of the body. The certitude about the resurrection of the body found in the New Testament represents a reflection on the teachings of Jesus and on his resurrection. What should be kept in mind, however, is that both New Testament writers and the Pharisees of the New Testament period believed bodily resurrection would take place in the coming messianic age, or world to come, when justice and peace would prevail. The resurrection of the dead, therefore, was always seen as a collective event inaugurating God's new day, not something that happened to one person while the rest of life and history went on untransformed.[13] Thus, even for those who believe in the resurrection of the body, the resurrection of Jesus represented an innovation of the highest order.

The Resurrection of Jesus

The Apostle Paul contributes the earliest written records to the New Testament. According to N. T. Wright, Paul's letters reveal that "the resurrection of Jesus is not just a single, detached article of faith." By the time of Paul's earliest letters, Jesus' resurrection has already woven its way into the "structure of Christian life and thought, informing (among other things) baptism, justification, ethics, and the future hope both for humans and for the cosmos."[14]

The Letters of Paul

Paul never argues as follows, "If Christ had not been raised, there would be no resurrection."[15] That is, he never argues that the resurrection of Jesus is proof that there will be a general resurrection. Rather, he writes to the Corinthian believers: "If there is no resurrection of the dead, then Christ has not been raised" (1 Corinthians 15:13). This passage, written in the year 56, only twenty-three years after the end of Jesus' mission, assumes that the believers to whom he writes already believe in the resurrection of Jesus; what they seem to be questioning is the general resurrection.

---

13. Ibid., 114.

14. N. T. Wright, *The Challenge of Jesus* (London: SPCK, 2000), 94.

15. J. A. T. Robinson, "Resurrection in the NT," in George A. Buttrick et al., eds., *The Interpreter's Dictionary of the Bible*, 4 vols. (Nashville: Abingdon, 1962), 4:43.

Earlier on, in Paul's first Letter to the Thessalonians, written from Corinth in 50, the Apostle deals with a very serious question about deceased relatives: What will happen to those who have already died when the Messiah returns? The Apostle answers in part as follows:

> Since we believe that Jesus died and rose again, even so, through Jesus, God will bring with him those who have died [Greek: "fallen asleep"]. For this we declare to you by the word of the Lord, that we who are alive, who are left until the coming of the Lord, will by no means precede those who have died [Greek: "fallen asleep"]. (4:13-15)

His argument is *based on* their belief in the death and resurrection of Jesus. He is not urging them to believe in the resurrection. Like the Corinthian Christians, they have already come to that conviction.

Early in this letter the resurrection had already been mentioned. Here again the resurrection of Jesus is a belief the Thessalonian Christians had settled on when Paul visited them previously. Paul recalls the felicitous welcome he had received from them as they "turned to God from idols, to serve a living and true God, and to wait for his Son from heaven, whom he raised from the dead" (1:10).

Paul opens his letter to the believers in Galatia, written about the same time[16] as 1 Thessalonians, by insisting that he is an Apostle "through Jesus Christ and God the Father, who raised him from the dead" (Galatians 1:1). The letter addresses the fact that Christian leaders who think all believers should be required to observe the Jewish Law and ceremonial traditions have followed Paul to Galatia and tried to get those who had believed in Jesus there through Paul's labors to be or become observant Jews (Acts 13-14; ca. the year 48). Here again, the issue is not the crucifixion or resurrection of Jesus, but rather the observation of particularly Jewish religious practices. In other words, these people, like their fellow religionists in Thessalonica and Corinth, had come to believe in the resurrection already on Paul's earlier journeys.

Only five years later Paul reminds the church at Corinth that on an earlier visit he had "handed on to them" a creed he had "in turn received," including that Jesus was raised on the third day and appeared to Peter, to the twelve disciples of Jesus, to an unidentified group of five hundred, to Jesus' brother James, and to all the Apostles (1 Corinthians 15:1-11). The creed, according to Cambridge University New Testament historian Markus Bockmuehl, "may well date from the first decade after the crucifixion."[17] At issue in the letter, however, is not the resurrection of Christ, but the resurrection of the body for all.

> Now if Christ is proclaimed as raised from the dead, how can some of you say there is no resurrection of the dead? If there is no resurrection

16. Markus Bockmuehl, "Resurrection," in Markus Bockmuehl, ed., *The Cambridge Companion to Jesus* (Cambridge: Cambridge University Press, 2001), 102.

17. Ibid.

> of the dead, then Christ has not been raised; and if Christ has not been raised, then our proclamation has been in vain and your faith has been in vain. (1 Corinthians 15:12-14)

In other words, you believe Christ has been raised from the dead. Then you argue that there is no resurrection of the dead, which would mean no resurrection of the dead for all at the end of time. You are inconsistent. You should believe in both resurrections or in none.

As this passage moves on we see how fundamental the resurrection was for the first Christians: "We are even found to be misrepresenting God," the Apostle insists, "because we testified of God that he raised Christ—whom he did not raise if it is true that the dead are not raised" (15:15). His argument makes no sense unless we recognize that the people he writes to already have settled on believing in the resurrection of Jesus. According to N. T. Wright, in this resurrection story, "we are . . . in touch with the earliest Christian tradition, with something that was being said two decades or more before Paul wrote his letter,"[18] a story shared not only with "all the other apostles,"[19] but "by all early Christians actually known to us."[20]

I stated above that a unique event of the magnitude of Jesus' resurrection cannot be demonstrated as historically true. It can only be witnessed and reported. But, as Bockmuehl himself points out, "It is a matter of historical record that *something* happened—and that this changed the course of world history. . . ."[21] Can history be accounted for without it?

The Uniqueness of the Resurrection of Jesus

The resurrection of Jesus was of a different order from his raising others from the dead (Matthew 11:5; John 11:38-44). For one thing, all those raised by Jesus or by his Apostles (Matthew 10:8) will eventually die again. In these cases the raising of the dead occupies a position somewhere between resuscitation and resurrection. But God raised Jesus from the dead permanently, for later he ascended to heaven (Acts 2:33).[22] Furthermore, and even more decisively for the resurrection of Jesus, it is the resurrection of the Messiah. The earliest preaching of the gospel points to the resurrection as that which designates Jesus as the Messiah[23] (Acts 2:31-36). When Jesus is resurrected, his reign as Messiah, as Lord over the new age of glory, begins. John A. T. Robinson puts it this way, "At the hour when Jesus is glorified (Luke 24:26; John 12:23; Acts 3:13; Rom. 6:4; 1 Pet.

18. Wright, *Resurrection*, 319.
19. Ibid.
20. N. T. Wright, *Jesus and the Victory of God,* Christian Origins and the Question of God 2 (London: SPCK, 1996), 658.
21. Bockmuehl, "Resurrection," 103.
22. Robinson, "Resurrection," 4:44.
23. *Christos* (Greek) means the same as *māshîaḥ* (Hebrew, "Messiah").

1:21, etc.), God's messianic act is complete, and the age to come has begun to supersede this one."[24]

The Resurrection of Jesus and the Kingdom of God

In a number of recent publications, N. T. Wright has set the resurrection in the context of the Judaism of Jesus' time, showing the relationship between his death and resurrection and the expectations of God's people at that time.[25]

Two corollaries of the conviction that Israel's God was the only and universal God (Psalm 22:28; 24:7-10; 47:2; Isaiah 44:6; Jeremiah 10:7, 10-15; Daniel 2:20-22; 4:35; Malachi 1:14b) and that Israel was his chosen people (Isaiah 43:15; Jeremiah 10:16; Daniel 2:23) were that God would eventually come to their rescue and show his favor to them (Deuteronomy 10:12-22; Ezekiel 16:1-14; Isaiah 35; 61; Micah 4:6; Zephaniah 3:15) and that this blessing would come to the whole of humanity through them (Daniel 2:44). If God were not specially related to them, they could not hope necessarily to be liberated from suffering and oppression by God. If their Lord were just a tribal deity, they could not necessarily expect him to act for other peoples as well—although they also hoped for vindication through the defeat of the oppressor (Isaiah 66:6; Jeremiah 48:15; 51:57). But since the Lord is both Israel's God and the God of all, Israel's destiny would be tied up with the destiny of all (Daniel 7:27; Zechariah 14:16-19).

When Jesus came on the scene, Israel was suffering under the heavy hand of imperial Rome. His people's belief in God, however, helped them to conclude that their suffering must be temporary. They understood that their oppressive situation was the result of their disobedience and infidelity to God. All this had political repercussions. Naturally, individuals or groups presented themselves as saviors and liberators; so Rome kept as tight a lid as possible on the rise of leaders who might proclaim themselves a messiah or lead an unconventional war of resistance.

There were two events or complexes of events that provided images for Israel to understand its oppressive situation and the possibility of freedom from foreign domination. One was the period of exile in Babylon. This exile from their land and Temple that began for the Northern Kingdom in 722 BCE and for the Southern Kingdom in 586 BCE served the people of Israel as a model for suffering under oppression. (It should be noted that the "deportation to Babylon" figures significantly in the genealogy of Jesus in Matthew 1:1-17.) It had been justified as a punishment for the sin of God's people (Jeremiah 8:19). Because they were still under oppression, the people of Israel of Jesus' time considered that their exile had not ended. The end of their Babylonian exile and the return

24. Robinson, "Resurrection," 4:44.

25. Wright, *Jesus and the Victory of God*, 109-11, 127-28, 131, 255-56, 659; and idem, *Resurrection*, esp. chapter 4. Some of Wright's shorter summaries of this material include *Challenge of Jesus*, 52-113; and Marcus J. Borg and N. T. Wright, *The Meaning of Jesus: Two Visions* (San Francisco: HarperSanFrancisco, 1999), 31-52, 93-127.

of Israel to its own land also provided the Jews of Jesus' time with an image of what restoration would mean. It would mean restoration of the land to its people and the rebuilding of their Temple. The exodus from Egypt much earlier in their history also served as an image of liberation from bondage. Israel expected liberation and vindication from God.

It was difficult for Israelites to grasp why God was waiting so long to do what had been promised. When was God going to vindicate and liberate God's people and establish God's righteous kingdom throughout the world? Isaiah stressed this identity of God with God's own people (33:22) and anticipated the joy of the good news of God's deliverance (52:7-9). The poet of Psalm 145 connected God's acts of deliverance with the spread of the divine kingdom to all peoples (verses 10-13); and Zechariah stated plainly and briefly, "the LORD will become king over all the earth; on that day the LORD will be one and his name one" (14:9). Many of the Jewish people of Jesus' time connected this longing or hope with what they expected of the coming anointed one, or Messiah.

Although the Jews of Jesus' time had more than one concept of the Messiah's identity and vocation, in general the following dimensions of their conception can be stressed. The Messiah would be a type of king, for that is what Messiah means—an "anointed one" or king (1 Samuel 24:10). He would also be a type of priest (or associated with a priest), because priests were also anointed (Exodus 28:41), as well as a type of prophet, because anointing can also be associated with prophets (1 Kings 19:16). The Jews of Jesus' time expected Elijah as a forerunner (Malachi 4:5-6; Mark 8:28), and, based on a passage in Deuteronomy, they anticipated the Messiah to be a prophet like Moses (Deuteronomy 18:15, 18; Matthew 17:5; Mark 8:28; 9:7b; Luke 7:16-17; 9:12-17, 31; John 6:14).[26]

In any case, the Messiah was the focus of Israel's hope for vindication by the defeat of Israel's enemies, and for universal rule with Israel as an instrument of the new universal order or covenant—the longing for the Lord to return to his holy hill, Zion. Generally his vocation would be to "restore the Temple and to fight the decisive battle against the enemy."[27] David was the image of this vocation. David's first act after his anointing (1 Samuel 10:1) was to defeat the enemy in the form of Goliath (1 Samuel 17:19-51), and his last act was to announce his vision for the Temple (2 Samuel 7:1-29).

Similarly, Judas Maccabeus (d. 161 BCE) defeated the Seleucid armies and liberated the Temple (166-164 BCE) (1 Maccabees 4:36-61); King Herod (d. 4 BCE) also rebuilt the Temple, having been victorious over the Parthians; and Simeon ben Kosiba (d. 135 CE), whom Rabbi Akiba named "Bar Kochba" ("Son of the Star," a reference to Numbers 24:17), designating him as the Messiah, set out to defeat the Romans and to re-establish the Temple destroyed in 70 CE.

---

26. J. D. G. Dunn, "Messianic Ideas and Their Influence on the Jesus of History," in James H. Charlesworth, ed., *The Messiah: Developments in Earliest Judaism and Christianity*, First Princeton Seminar on Jewish Christian Origins (Minneapolis: Fortress, 1992), 367-69.

27. Wright, *Challenge of Jesus,* 53.

Messiahs fight wars of liberation and restore Temples. Did Jesus set out to do either of these tasks? At first glance the answer appears to be no.

Yet Jesus did consider himself the Messiah. He certainly made the kingdom of God an important theme in his teaching and prophetic action (as will be seen below). And he was both explicit and implicit in identifying himself as the Messiah. Clearly, in his response to a delegation from the imprisoned John the Baptist who wanted to know whether he was in fact the Messiah or not, Jesus laid claim to being the Messiah (Matthew 11:2-9). In Mark 8:27-33 (Matthew 16:13-20; Luke 9:18-20), Jesus accepts Peter's confession that he is the Messiah. Jesus in his own way "cleansed the Temple," as Judas Maccabeus had done (Matthew 21:12-17; Mark 11:15-17; Luke 19:45-48; John 2:13-17), asserting his messianic connection with, and authority over, the Temple.

His warfare also was clear, but it was defined by his conception of the kingdom of God. Jesus' understanding of the kingdom of God was connected with the good news stressed in Isaiah 40-55. Here is the epitome of it.

> How lovely upon the mountains are the feet of the one
> who brings good news, who publishes salvation, who says to Zion,
> "Your God reigns!"
> Listen! Your watchmen lift up their voices and shout for joy,
> because in plain sight they see YHWH returning to Zion.
> YHWH has bared his holy arm in the sight of all the nations, and
> all the ends of the world shall see the salvation of our God.
>
> Depart, depart, go out thence, touch no unclean thing . . .
> for YHWH
> will go before you, and the God of Israel will be your rearguard.
> (Isaiah 52:7-12)[28]

When Jesus answered the delegation from John the Baptist (Matthew 11:2-9), he was working within this good news understanding of the kingdom of God. None of this good news had happened in Jesus' day. In fact, in the whole of the Second Temple period no one stated that the Lord had come to reside in the Temple. By stressing the good news passages from Isaiah, Jesus was saying that a new day was dawning. A new understanding of the messianic mission was afoot in the land. The return from exile had begun; the defeat of evil was imminent; and the Lord would return to Zion. Israel's story was reaching its climax in Jesus. This was the clear sense of mission Jesus had. It was a messianic mission in which the war was against evil both within and without Israel and the Temple was about to be replaced by the Messiah himself.[29]

The rule of God was surely political, but it did not depend on political control. Rather, it was seen to be present when a widow gave a small but costly

28. Translation by N. T. Wright in Borg and Wright, *Meaning of Jesus*, 34.
29. Borg and Wright, *Meaning of Jesus*, 35.

offering at the Temple, when people went the second mile in helping others—even their oppressors; when people loved God and their neighbors; when people even loved their enemies. God's rule was often undetected; but when located, it was precious beyond measure; God's rule could start small, but it could also grow; it was an expression of God's generosity and love; it was God meeting peoples' needs; it involved healing, helping, liberating, and even proclaiming the good news.[30] Jesus' call to Israel was to accept this kind of kingdom and to be the salt and the light for the world, to live out a different image of the kingdom of God. Accordingly he had a perspective on the Messiah that was congruent with his view of the kingdom.

John the Baptist was waiting for the traditional activities of the Messiah, especially the defeat of enemies and the renewal of Israel's spiritual life. When the delegation he sent asked Jesus in essence if he was the Messiah, Jesus answered, "Go and tell John what you hear and see: the blind receive their sight, the lame walk, the lepers are cleansed, and the deaf hear, the dead are raised, and the poor have good news brought to them. And blessed is anyone who takes no offense at me" (Matthew 11:4-6). He refers here to Isaiah 35:5, 6.

> The eyes of the blind shall be opened,
> and the ears of the deaf unstopped;
> then the lame shall leap like a deer,
> and the tongue of the speechless sing for joy.

Perhaps John also had in mind the previous verse (4), to which Jesus did not allude:

> Say to those who are of a fearful heart,
> "Be strong, do not fear!
> Here is your God. He will come with a vengeance,
> with terrible recompense.
> He will come and save you." (35:4)

Jesus made a similar omission when he read from Isaiah in his home synagogue at Nazareth.

> The Spirit of the Lord is upon me,
> because he has anointed me to bring good news to the poor.
> He has sent me to proclaim release to the captives
> and recovery of sight to the blind,

---

30. In the following passages, the kingdom, rule, or reign of God (=kingdom of heaven) is mentioned: Matthew 5:3, 10, 19, 20; 7:21; 10:7; 12:28; 13:11-52 (Mark 4:26-32; Luke 13:18-21); 18:3 (Mark 9:33-37; Luke 9:46-48); 20:1-16; Mark 9:47; 10:14-15 (Luke 18:17-18), 23-25; 12:34; Luke 4:43; 6:20; 8:1; 9:2; 10:1-12; 11:20; 17:20, 21; and John 3:3-5. Many other passages could be cited, some mentioning the kingdom of God and some merely implying or illustrating it.

to let the oppressed go free,
to proclaim the year of the Lord's favor.
(Isaiah 61:1-2a; Luke 4:18-19)

At this point, he rolled up the scroll, handed it to the attendant, and said, "Today this scripture has been fulfilled in your hearing" (4:20-21). He had closed the scroll before finishing verse 2. It is as though he deliberately refused to read, "and the day of vengeance of our God" (Isaiah 61:2b).

His view of the Messiah combined one who identified with the suffering righteous—minus their hostility toward their enemies (4:24-28)—with the suffering servant of Isaiah 40-55, the one by whose stripes Israel would be healed. To his disciples he presented himself as the New Temple[31] and his family of followers as the New Israel. He saw in his own acceptance of the sentence of suffering and death placed on him by both Romans and Jews, a vicarious role played for Israel and all people that would provide them with forgiveness—forgiveness that would release them from their bondage and exile and enable them to follow the rule of God as he had taught and lived it himself.[32] In the words of N. T. Wright, "Jesus died the death that awaited others, in order that they might not die it."[33] Jesus chose this way to fight the final battle against the Enemy behind the enemy. In this way he would build the real Temple. This victory would be his true messianic work, transforming the coming kingdom into a present reality.

But he also discerned that he would be raised on the third day. God would demonstrate that what Jesus revealed of the kingdom of God was truly God's own vision, God's own priorities, God's own program for his Messiah and for his people—his new family.

Jesus himself labored to get across to his disciples the purpose of his mission: to suffer, die, and be raised from the dead (Mark 8:31-33; 9:30-32; 10:32-34; and parallels). In a telling passage connecting his resurrection with his crucifixion and with the purpose of his mission, Jesus responds to a warning from the Pharisees that Herod wants to kill him, "Go and tell that fox for me, 'Listen, I am casting out demons and performing cures today and tomorrow, and on the third day I am perfected (*teleiomai*)" (Luke 13:32-35).[34] Let us now look at a case that can be made for the resurrection of Jesus.

---

31. Harold W. Turner has shown very thoroughly that New Testament writers have applied the images and features associated with sacred space, especially temples, to Jesus himself (*From Temple to Meeting House: The Phenomenology and Theology of Places of Worship*, Religion and Society 16 (The Hague/New York: Mouton, 1979).

32. Borg and Wright, *Meaning of Jesus,* 36.

33. Ibid., 98. The whole of chapter 6 helps readers understand why and how Jesus met his death.

34. The translation departs slightly from the NRSV and reflects the literal meaning of *teleiomai*.

The Historicity of the Resurrection: The Empty Tomb, the Appearances of Jesus, and the Experience of the Resurrected Lord

A strong case can be made for the resurrection of Jesus, son of Mary and Messiah, as a fact of history. John A. T. Robinson contributed a surprising article on the resurrection to the *Interpreter's Dictionary of the Bible*, published in 1962.[35] It was surprising because only shortly after the appearance of the article he placed on the market a book challenging the traditional biblical and Christian understanding of God. At any rate, the article discusses the resurrection under three main topics: the empty tomb, the appearances, and the experience of the living Christ.

The Empty Tomb

Ironically, Robinson starts his discussion of the empty tomb by talking about the full tomb, about the burial of Jesus. Normally, victims of crucifixion were given an ignominious burial in a lime pit or left to decay. The Jews were sometimes permitted to bury their victims in a collective grave. With Jesus, however, the report that he was buried in a tomb occurs in all four Gospels (Matthew 27:57-61; Mark 15:42-47; Luke 23:50-56; and John 19:38-42). With minor differences of detail, the Gospels tell that Joseph of Arimathea successfully requested from Herod the body of Jesus. He buried the body in a tomb in his garden—after, of course, it was prepared for burial in the traditional Jewish way. Robinson remarks that this consistent testimony to the burial "must be accepted as one of the most firmly grounded facts of Jesus' life."[36]

Some have argued that the reason the body of Jesus could not be produced by those wanting proof that he was not resurrected is that it would have been subject to rapid decay in the traditional lime pit or in some other way. This consistent testimony to the burial in Joseph's tomb shows why this argument remains weak. Even though the earliest testimonies to the end of Jesus' mission do not specifically mention an empty tomb (1 Corinthians 15:4; Acts 2:31; Acts 13:29-30), it is implied in all of them. For example, "he was not abandoned to Hades, nor did his flesh see corruption" (Acts 2:31). In any case, these references surely refer to a bodily resurrection because no other form of resurrection was conceivable in the Jewish context of the earliest witnesses to the events at the end of Jesus' mission.[37]

When it comes to the witness of the Gospels to the empty tomb, critics have overdone an emphasis on the differences in detail of their stories. One solid feature of these stories is their substantial unanimity that the tomb was empty. Robinson identifies six features about which the narratives of the discovery of

35. Robinson, "Resurrection," 4:43-53.
36. Ibid., 4:45.
37. Ibid., 4:46. See Wright's discussion of 1 Corinthians 15:4a (*Resurrection*, 321).

the empty tomb differ. Differences show up in (1) the number of women who visit the tomb; (2) the degree of darkness when they arrive; (3) the purpose for which they came; (4) the description of the figure or figures at the tomb; (5) what these figures said; and (6) how the women responded.[38]

One would expect an event of this kind to generate some such set of distinctive features. The discrepancies help support the conviction that none of these four Gospel writers conspired together to fabricate the stories so as to create the impression that a resurrection had occurred. On the other hand, the narratives do not require skepticism regarding the historicity of *what they agree upon*. On the conviction that the tomb was empty and on several other features of the event, these narratives prove "extraordinarily unanimous."[39] A summary of their unanimous testimony follows:

> Through the good offices of Joseph of Arimathea the body of Jesus, swathed in linen, was given hurried burial outside Jerusalem on the Friday night in a rock tomb which was subsequently closed by a large stone. After the rest imposed by the sabbath, the women came at dawn on Sunday, to find the stone rolled away from the tomb and the body gone. The natural supposition was that the grave had been disturbed by human agents: "*They* have taken the Lord out of the tomb, and we do not know where they have laid him" (John 20:2).[40]

Matthew, Mark, and Luke have the figures at the tomb insisting that Jesus arose. In John, Jesus himself delivers this message; Matthew says both Jesus and the figures at the tomb convey the message; and Luke says that when the women gave the message to the disciples, "these words seemed to them an idle tale, and they did not believe them" (24:11).

The only reference to *belief* in these tomb scenarios arises in connection with the beloved disciple who "saw and believed" (John 20:8). Otherwise, the empty tomb proved only a source of bewilderment and confusion. In fact, when the tomb was found empty, the first reaction was an attempt to locate the body (John 20:2). The question of what happened to the body is perplexing. If the Jews were correct in charging the disciples with stealing it (Matthew 28:13-15), then the whole early Christian preaching of the cross and resurrection rested on "a conscious fraud." Robinson says that a deception this blatant "is . . . psychologically improbable."[41]

The Qurʾānic exegete Ṭabarī, as we have mentioned before, rejects the bulk of the substitution traditions he preserves because they require that Christianity resulted from a deliberate deception by the Apostles. But the fact that the theory of the disciples' stealing the body of Jesus arose at all demonstrates two important

38. Robinson, "Resurrection," 4:46.
39. Ibid.
40. Ibid. Italics in the original.
41. Ibid., 4:46.

historical points: (1) the tomb was empty; and (2) the authorities could not produce the body. What reason would some unidentified grave robbers have had to rob the body of Jesus? This charge ought to be rejected out of hand. Robinson insists that the other two possible explanations (other than the explanation given in the scriptures themselves) "have failed to command any serious measure of support." These two unsuccessful solutions include (1) that the women visited the wrong grave and (2) that Jesus was not really dead, but, having swooned and been revived by the coolness of the grave, made his way out of the tomb.[42]

No evidence can be adduced for any preaching of the gospel earlier than that recorded in the Acts of the Apostles and the New Testament letters. Both of these earliest sources contain testimony to both the crucifixion of Jesus and to his bodily resurrection. If we assume that a substitute was crucified in Jesus' place, where was he buried? What other historical circumstances might we imagine than the ones recorded in the Gospels? Was there no tomb at all and was Jesus/or his substitute thrown into a pit, or buried in a collective grave? Did the women not come to the tomb and find it empty? Or did they come to the tomb and find Jesus or a substitute there? Or could they not roll away the stone? If any of these scenarios had actually transpired, would the resultant accounts have been as alike as those of the Gospels or have had the kinds of differences that show up in them?

Robinson states with characteristic scholarly caution, "Many, in fact, will continue to find it easier to believe that the empty tomb produced the disciples' faith than that the disciples' faith produced the empty tomb."[43] But, since an empty tomb does not equal a resurrection from the dead, we turn, as the Apostles and other followers of Jesus did, to the appearances of the risen Jesus.

The Appearances

The appearances of Jesus convinced the followers of Jesus that he had been raised from the dead. Paul shows that they were an essential part of the earliest witness of the Apostles and others as well. In his first letter to the church at Corinth, Paul provides his readers with a list of those to whom the risen Jesus appeared. He writes that Jesus

> appeared to Cephas, then to the twelve. Then he appeared to more than five hundred brothers and sisters at one time, most of whom are still alive, though some have died. Then he appeared to James, then to all the apostles. (15:5-7)

Paul prefaces this with the following,

42. Ibid.

43. Ibid., 4:47. Wright points out that both an empty tomb and appearances of the resurrected Messiah account for the conviction that Jesus was raised from the dead (*Resurrection*, 686-87).

> For I handed on to you as of first importance what I in turn had received: that Christ died for our sins in accordance with the scriptures and that he was buried, and that he was raised on the third day in accordance with the scriptures. (15:3-4)

He hands on to them what he has already received from others. We dealt with the early testimonies to the resurrection above. Here we will simply add what N. T. Wright has to say about the subject. He first mentions the fact that, while other movements of failed messiahs either ended or regrouped around a new leader, the Jesus movement found a new lease on life following Jesus' execution. Then he states that, "Within weeks," the Jesus movement "was *announcing* that he was indeed the messiah; within a year or two it was proclaiming him to pagans as their rightful Lord." Finally, Wright asks, "How can a historian explain this astonishing transformation?"[44] Could it have been the appearances of the risen Jesus?

Examining the New Testament, including 1 Corinthians 15, the four Gospels, and the book of Acts, we can identify eleven different appearances, not including the one to Paul on the Damascus road (1 Corinthians 15:8; Acts 9:3-8; 22:6-11; 26:12-18).[45] These appearances of the risen Christ are listed below.

1. to the women (Matthew 28:9-10)
2. to Mary Magdalene (John 20:11-18)
3. to Peter (1 Corinthians 15:5; Luke 24:34; Mark 16:7?)
4. to two disciples on the road to Emmaus (Luke 24:13-31)

5-8. to the eleven and other disciples
   5. (Luke 24:36-49; John 20:19-23 [= 1 Corinthians 15:5?])
   6. (John 20:24-29)
   7. (Matthew 28:16-20 [Mark 16:7?])
   8. (Acts 1:6-9 [= Luke 24:50-51?])

9. to seven disciples (John 21:1-14)
10. to more than five hundred brethren (1 Corinthians 15:6)
11. to James (1 Corinthians 15:7).[46]

In the cases where a location is provided for the appearances, the place is either Jerusalem and environs or Galilee. Matthew and Mark seem to follow a tradition of appearances in Galilee, while John's appearances all occur in Jerusalem. Even though these appearances cannot be fully harmonized, it remains possible that appearances did occur in both places.[47]

---

44. Borg and Wright, *Meaning of Jesus*, 111.

45. Paul, of course, included his experience of Jesus on the road to Damascus as one of the appearances of the risen Christ even though it occurred after the ascension, but he indicated that it was the last of its kind (Borg and Wright, *Meaning of Jesus,* 119).

46. Adapted from Robinson, "Resurrection," 4:47.

47. Ibid.

Given the fact that the Gospel of Mark led the way in recording Jesus' own explicit and implicit predictions of his coming death and resurrection, the first surprise that confronts us in the case of resurrection narratives is that the earliest manuscripts of Mark's Gospel end without narrating any resurrection appearances at all! Based on available manuscripts of Mark, five different possible endings present themselves. Basing their choice on the principle that the simplest and most difficult reading should be preferred—assuming it has adequate manuscript support—scholars have determined that Mark originally ended at 16:8, as is the case in some of the best manuscripts. Thus, Mark ends with two of Jesus' women disciples encountering an empty tomb where a young man in white tells them that Jesus has been raised. The young man wants them to tell his disciples and Peter that he will meet them in Galilee. But the two women go out too frightened to utter a word.

Although ending Mark's Gospel at 16:8 may seem unsatisfactory, giving rise to the several options for bringing closure offered by other manuscripts, many contemporary interpreters work with the assumption that Mark intended to end at what is now verse 8. Did Mark want the reader to take up the responsibility the women were too frightened to fulfill? But given the failure of Jesus' male disciples even to show up at the grave, and given the women's inability to obey the directive of the young man in white to tell the disciples of Jesus' plans, is it reasonable to expect the reader to have the courage to go and tell about the resurrected Lord? A careful reading of these last eight verses reveals an important clue to Mark's purpose. The young man says, "go tell his disciples and Peter that he is going ahead of you to Galilee, there you will see him, just as he told you" (16:7). Does the closure the reader needs from this the shortest of the Gospels reside in the promise of Jesus?

Recalling Jesus' several explicit predictions of his death and resurrection in Mark, the reader might receive the first eight verses of Mark 16 as evidence that his promises have been fulfilled—his tomb is empty! According to this interpretation, resurrection discipleship of Jesus rests not on superior obedience and courage but on the faithfulness of the resurrected Lord to his promise: "he is going ahead of you to Galilee, there you will see him, *just as he told you*."[48] All three of the other Gospels contain accounts of Jesus' post-resurrection appearances.

Matthew tells of Mary Magdalene and another Mary's encounter with an angel who descends in an earthquake, rolls back the stone, shows them the empty tomb, and tells them that Jesus has risen and that he will meet them in Galilee. On their way from the tomb, however, Jesus himself meets them and gives them the same charge as the angel had given them (see number 1 in the list of appearances). Then comes the report about the Jewish priests paying off the tomb guards to be silent about the event. Finally, Jesus meets his disciples on

48. This discussion is based on Donald H. Juel, *The Gospel of Mark*, Interpreting Biblical Texts (Nashville: Abingdon, 1999), 167-76. Wright thinks that Mark intended to produce a longer ending, although one cannot say for sure what that ending was (*Resurrection*, 617-24).

a mountain in Galilee (see number 7) and commissions them to make disciples from among all peoples, teaching them his message and baptizing them in the name of the Father, the Son, and the Holy Spirit.

In Luke, the disciples discount as an "idle tale" the report of the women who have encountered two angels at the tomb. Peter himself follows this up with a visit to the tomb, and Jesus encounters two discouraged pilgrims returning from Jerusalem (number 4). He explains to them that Jesus was to have been raised from the dead according to the scripture. They eat together, and only then do they recognize who he is. The couple returns with the exciting news to the other disciples and learns of an appearance to Peter (number 3). Then Jesus himself again comes on the scene, assuring the disciples of his live physical presence by eating fish (number 5). He then commissions them on the Mount of Olives (number 8), and is finally taken up to heaven.

John reports that Peter and the Beloved Disciple respond to Mary Magdalene's news of the risen savior by rushing to the tomb. But there they find only the linen grave cloths. The Beloved Disciple believes because of this evidence. Mary meets Jesus in the garden but thinks he is the gardener (number 2). Jesus then appears to the disciples behind closed doors (number 5). When he shows them his wounds, they believe. They then report their discovery to Thomas, who also believes when Jesus appears and shows his wounds (number 6). The last chapter of John, a kind of appendix, gives one more appearance of Jesus: the disciples catch fish and eat together with Jesus, who makes Simon Peter the pastor of his flock (number 9). Paul mentions appearances 10 and 11 in 1 Corinthians.

In the Acts of the Apostles, Jesus appears among his disciples over a period of forty days. A sketch of his last meeting with them occurs in Acts 1:6-9 (number 8). Jesus responds to their question about the restoration of the kingdom to Israel by saying it is not for them to know; rather, they should be his witnesses in Jerusalem, Judea, Samaria, and worldwide—after they have been baptized with the Holy Spirit.

At least one feature holds true for all the appearances—and this is implied even in Mark who reports no appearances: Jesus appeared only to those who already followed him. In other words, Jesus did not reveal himself to compel faith on the part of those who had not believed in him. See Acts 10:40-41.

Some scholars have been drawn to establishing a progression of appearances from the most spiritual to the most physical. They base that, however, on a commitment to a worldview that affords more weight of probability to spiritual appearances than to physical appearances. Paul says nothing about this type of appearance and marvels that his own experience of the risen Messiah was included among the others (1 Corinthians 15:8-11).

It does not take a natural skeptic to notice the differences between and within these narratives. Paul's witness to the resurrection mentions no women and no empty tomb. He does mention, however, appearances not recorded in any of the Gospels. Furthermore, he suggests that his own encounter with Jesus was one of the resurrection appearances, even though it presumably came after the ascension. Nevertheless, as N. T. Wright points out, no one reading Paul can doubt that he believes Jesus was raised bodily, that no body was left in the tomb when he arose.[49]

Most people will find hard to escape the obvious testimony of the sources that the appearances of the risen Messiah transformed those to whom he appeared. Did the appearances create the belief or did the belief create the appearances?[50] This takes us back again to the question that motivated Ṭabarī's decision about the reliability of the reports he adduces in his commentary. He chose the two traditions he did because the others require that the Apostles of Jesus had spread a deliberate falsehood. It is possible, of course, that the ones to whom Jesus "appeared" were simply deluded. This explanation may satisfy some, but a mass delusion on this scale seems almost as improbable as the resurrection itself. And of astonishing proportions is the fact that Jews such as Paul came away from these experiences convinced that Jesus was more than a human Messiah approved by God; rather, in some way, he was a participant along with the Holy Spirit in the identity of God (2 Corinthians 13:13).

N. T. Wright points out that two modern historians of the New Testament period who do not appear to believe in the resurrection themselves take it very seriously and historically. The first, Geza Vermes, comes to the same conclusion as Robinson that the tomb was empty and that the disciples of Jesus did not steal his body.[51] The other, E. P. Sanders, says that Jesus' life and work culminated in "the resurrection and the foundation of a movement which endured."[52] Wright gives more details from Sanders and goes on to say,

> Both Vermes and Sanders thus bear witness, as historians of first-century Judaism, to the great difficulty faced by any attempt to say that on the one hand nothing happened to the body of Jesus but that on the other hand Christianity began very soon after his death, and began as precisely a resurrection movement.[53]

According to Markus Bockmuehl, while the New Testament never describes or clearly defines the resurrection, its "writings unanimously agree on one thing: in some sense that was both inexplicable and yet unmistakable, Jesus was seen alive in personal encounters with his disciples soon after his death."[54]

The Experience of the Living Christ

If the appearances had been merely psychic phenomena, Robinson asks, would they not have faded as time went on? In contrast, even people who had not seen

---

49. Borg and Wright, *Meaning of Jesus,* 119.

50. Robinson, "Resurrection," 4:48.

51. Geza Vermes, *Jesus the Jew: A Historian's Reading of the Gospels* (London: Collins, 1973), 37-41; cited in Wright, *Challenge of Jesus*, 97.

52. E. P. Sanders, *Jesus and Judaism* (London and Philadelphia: SCM and Fortress, 1985), 340; cited in Wright, *Challenge of Jesus*, 97.

53. Ibid.

54. Bockmuehl, "Resurrection," 102.

the risen Lord but who came to believe in him spread the faith with enthusiasm and persistence, amid great odds and sometimes even under persecution leading to martyrdom.

If we take Paul as an example, we can find a clue to this phenomenon. Even though Paul established his identity as an Apostle and thus his authority among the early Christians partly by means of the risen Messiah's appearance to him (1 Corinthians 9:1; 15:8, 9), he does not point to that appearance as the basis for his current faith. Rather, the foundation of his faith is the Messiah who died for him and who lives within him (Galatians 2:20). He wants to continue knowing the Messiah in the "power of his resurrection" and in the "sharing of his suffering" (Philippians 3:10). Surely this must have been true of others. Here is Robinson's succinct conclusion:

> This abiding and transforming experience, grounded, not on the reports of others, but on the firsthand awareness of the living Christ, is what made and sustained the Christian church.[55]

Because of this ongoing reality of the experience of the living Messiah among them, the church itself provides evidence for the reality of the bodily resurrection of Jesus. The resurrection in the New Testament, however, comes up again and again *as an event* and not primarily *as an experience*. The designation "witness of the resurrection" was reserved for those who had seen the risen Messiah with their own eyes. It was not offered to those who had experienced the power of the risen Messiah but had not witnessed him as resurrected (Acts 1:21-22; cf. 10:41; 13:31).

None of this proves the reality of the resurrection, but it does put some of the burden of proof on those who want to reconstruct the records so as to present them in conformity with their own worldview. It is congruent, however, with the explicit predictions of Jesus that he would suffer, be killed, and be vindicated through resurrection, something his followers fully realized only after having experienced the risen Messiah.

The Problem of Women Witnesses

Qāsimī, with whose commentary I have interacted extensively, notes that the only original witnesses to the empty tomb and the resurrected Messiah were women—less reliable witnesses than men.

> The ones who conveyed the message that the angel said he had risen from the dead were merely women who were at the tomb at a great distance. The women did not know the angel from others. And circumstances like

55. Robinson, "Resurrection," 4:49. See also Wright, *Resurrection*, 607-8.

> that are useful only for speculation. The verses that resulted, assuming their soundness, do not compel us to recognize their veracity.[56]

If the Apostles had fabricated these narratives, why would they have made so much depend on the testimony of women? Their contemporaries, like Qāsimī, also thought women's testimonies were less reliable than those of men.

Pinchas Lapide, a Jew of the school of the Pharisees and a New Testament scholar, sets out to discover "traces of authentic Jewish experience" in the narratives of the resurrection. The first thing he notices has to do with the women witnesses.

> According to all four Gospels, women are the first ones to find the tomb of Jesus open and empty. In a purely fictional narrative one would have avoided making women the crown witnesses of the resurrection since they were considered in rabbinic Judaism as incapable of giving valid testimony (compare Luke 24:11).[57]

The second thing he notices also has to do with women. The women at the empty tomb trembled and were amazed. They even ran away at first. They could not speak because of fear. Mary Magdalene "from whom seven demons had gone out" (Luke 8:2) was hardly a person whose accuracy as a witness was guaranteed! The report that the women came to the tomb ready to anoint his dead body soon after his burial indicates they were not expecting anything like a resurrection. Nobody believed their reports either. In other words, because these details were included in spite of their immediate negative implications in a Jewish context, "the total picture of the Gospels also gains in trustworthiness."[58]

---

56. Muḥammad Jamāl al-Dīn al-Qāsimī, *Tafsīr al-Qāsimī: al-musammā bi-maḥāsin al-taʾwīl*, ed. Muḥammad Fuʾād ʿAbd al-Bāqī, 17 vols. (Cairo: Dār iḥyāʾ al-kutub al-ʿAarabīyah/ʿĪsā al-Bābī al-Ḥalabī wa-shurakāʾ-hu, 1957), 5:1660.

57. Pinchas Lapide, *The Resurrection of Jesus: A Jewish Perspective* (Minneapolis: Augsburg, 1983), 95.

58. Ibid., 97.

14

"The Son of Humanity Came . . . to Give His Life a Ransom for Many"

The End of Jesus' Mission and the Forgiveness of Sins

Since this book hovers around the subject of whether or not the crucifixion of Jesus occurred at all, we have not yet focused on the Muslim theological objections to the Christian conviction that Jesus died for others. Most Muslims do not believe that Jesus died for others. Consequently, in giving a reason for my hope (1 Peter 3:15), I must respond not only to the Muslim interpretation of the end of Jesus' mission in the sense of its *final events*, but also—in a common-ground way—to Muslim discomfort with Christian convictions about the end of Jesus' mission in the sense of its *final purpose*. Accordingly, in this chapter, we will take a closer look and find a wider perspective on the Christian doctrines of original sin and the atonement, Jesus' death for others.

Original Sin: A Closer Look and a Wider Perspective

Two convictions most Muslims hold appear to render the cross of Christ—as taught by Christians—both theologically unnecessary and morally offensive. They believe all of us have come into the world pure, and they believe we alone bear full responsibility for our own sins. No one can pay the price for another's sin.

People Are Responsible for Their Own Sins

The Qur'ān makes clear that people are responsible for their own sins: "No bearer of burdens can bear the burden of another; . . . man can have nothing but what he strives for; . . . (the fruit of) his striving will soon come in sight; then will he be rewarded with a reward complete; . . . to thy Lord is the final Goal" (*Star* [53]:38-42).

The Hebrew scriptures agree. Ezekiel, the prophet and priest of Israel, is especially known for making this point. The entire eighteenth chapter of Ezekiel consists of a word from the Lord critiquing a popular proverb that says that children receive the consequences of their parents' sin: "The parents have eaten sour grapes, and the children's teeth are set on edge" (Ezekiel 18:2). God tells Ezekiel, "Know that all lives are mine; the life of the parent as well as the life of the child is mine: it is only the person who sins that shall die" (18:4). If a father does evil and his son does good, then the father will die; but his son will live (18:14-18).

Baher Foad, a Muslim who agrees with this conviction, has this to say about human responsibility.

> Everything will be taken into account. Any mitigating circumstances will be considered, for God is the most just. We cannot hide anything, and our deeds that are recorded by angels who never fail in their duties, will speak for or against us. Our faculties will bear witness against us. Nothing escapes God. . . .[1]

Ezekiel would agree. The problem that really troubles him, however, is that, with the *possible* exception of some of the years in the desert wanderings following the exodus from Egypt, there appears to have been no time in Israel's history when they were not rebellious and guilty of sin. True, each person bears responsibility for his or her own sins. But what about the fact that *no one is innocent*? The exhortations Ezekiel has been sent to proclaim have largely been ignored. God shows Ezekiel that in the future Israel's people will be gathered from the Diaspora to the land of Israel where, says the Lord, "I will give them one heart, and put a new spirit within them; I will remove the heart of stone from their flesh and give them a heart of flesh. . . . Then they shall be my people, and I will be their God" (Ezekiel 11:19-20; cf. 36:26-27). The remedy will come from God.

Ezekiel also presents God as intimately related to Israel and irrevocably committed to its well-being. The Lord speaks metaphorically as a husband to Israel; though she has been wayward, "I passed by you again and looked on you; you were at the age for love. I spread the edge of my cloak over you, and covered your nakedness: I pledged myself to you and entered into a covenant with you, says the Lord God, and you became mine" (16:8). The prophets Jeremiah and Isaiah share this theme of divine intimacy with Ezekiel.[2]

The problem then is not that God does not treat all persons fairly and

---

1. Baher Foad, *Islamic Concepts: Evidence from the Qur'an* (Cincinnati: Zakat and Research Foundation, 1989), 43. See *Prophets* [21]:47 and *Earthquake* [99]:7, 8.

2. Christopher T. Begg, "Ezekiel, Book of," in Bruce M. Metzger and Michael D. Coogan, eds., *The Oxford Companion to the Bible* (New York and Oxford: Oxford University Press, 1993), 217-19.

judge them for their sin and reward them for their virtue; the problem is that an intimate relationship has been marred by a disobedience that simple, even dramatic, exhortation cannot remedy. While humans may remain satisfied with a distant relationship with God or no relationship at all, God's project of building relationships with human individuals and communities of faith fails without some solution to the problem of human disobedience and resistance to God's grace. While Muslims do not object to the Apostle Paul's conviction that "all have sinned and fall short of the glory of God" (Romans 3:23), they do reject the Christian doctrine called "original sin."

Human Beings Are Not Guilty Because of Original Sin

Muslims also object to the claim of many Christians that all humans are guilty because of the transgression of Adam and Eve. Imam Mohamad Jawad Chirri (d. 1994), a Shīʿī and the late leader of a Muslim community in Michigan, represents most Muslims, including Sunnīs, in rejecting this doctrine.

> Islam disagrees with Christianity on the Doctrine of Redemption. The Doctrine of Redemption is based on the Doctrine of Original Sin: that mankind had been condemned by God because of the sin of Adam and Eve which was consequently inherited by their children. Islam denies the whole Doctrine of Original Sin; God did not condemn mankind because a sin was committed by a couple at the beginning of time.[3]

Again, two arguments convince Muslims that no atonement effected by the death of the Messiah is necessary: no one can pay for another's sin, and no one can be held guilty for the sin of another. Common ground turns up here also.

Common Ground on the Human Condition

Dialogues with Muslims have contributed to my wider perspective on the human condition. A closer look at original sin reveals more common ground on our understanding of the human condition, and also some distinctive features. First, the common ground.

The Qurʾān itself presents a composite picture of human nature that looks very much like Ezekiel's description of the human condition. Humankind is described as *hasty*: "The prayer that man should make for good, he maketh for evil; for man is given to hasty (deeds)" (*Night Journey* [17]:11); *fickle*: "When some trouble toucheth man, he crieth unto his Lord, turning to Him in repentance: but when He bestoweth a favour upon him as from Himself, (man) doth forget what he cried and prayed for before, and he doth set up rivals unto Allah. . . ." (*Throngs* [39]:8);

3. Imam Mohamad Jawad Chirri (1913-1994), *Inquiries about Islam*, 4th ed. rev. (Detroit: Islamic Center of America, 1996), 69.

unjust and *foolish*: "We did indeed offer the Trust to the Heavens and the Earth and the Mountains; but they refused to undertake it, being afraid thereof: but man undertook it; he was indeed unjust and foolish" (*Parties* [33]:72); *perverse* and *thankless*: "Verily, man is given up to injustice and ingratitude" (*Abraham* [14]:34); *contentious*: "man is, in most things, contentious" (*Cave* [18]:54); and *rebellious*: "Nay, but man doth transgress all bounds (*kallā inna al-insāna la-taṭghā*)" (*Clot* [96]:6). Even the righteous Joseph, asserting his innocence of misbehaving with his master's wife, qualifies his self-defense as follows, "Nor do I absolve my own self (of blame): the (human) soul is certainly prone to evil (*inna al-nafsa la-ammāratun bi-al-sūʾ*), unless my lord do bestow His Mercy: but surely my Lord is Oft-Forgiving, Most Merciful" (*Joseph* [12]:53). Finally, "If Allah were to punish men for their wrong-doing, He would not leave, on the (earth), a single living creature: but He gives them respite for a stated Term . . ." (*Bee* [16]:61).[4]

According to Christian theology, in disobeying God, Adam and Eve represent us humans—all of us. The first couple, confronted with the choice between obeying God and pursuing their own desires, planted "the seeds of separation between God and humanity."[5] This does not land far from where Muslim theology stands. Muslims, according to Imam Chirri, believe that Adam disobeyed God (*Ṭāʾ Hāʾ* [20]:121; *Heights* [7]:22; *Cow* [2]:36) but insist that God forgave him (*Ṭāʾ Hāʾ* [20]:122), and his sin affected no one else, although God required Adam and Eve to leave paradise (*Ṭāʾ Hāʾ* [20]:123; *Heights* [7]:24; *Cow* [2]:36).[6] But in answering the question "If Adam was forgiven, why was he expelled from the paradise of God?" Chirri, in spite of his conviction that "the fall of Adam from paradise, is not necessarily a punishment for a sin," comes close to a Christian position:

> It may be a necessary result of the change of his status. At the beginning, Adam was worthy of communicating with God at any time, and this was his blessing and paradise. By acting improperly, he became susceptible to slip again; that is, he had lost his immunity for impropriety. So . . . he was no longer in such a high position that enables him to communicate with his Lord at any time. Now he is able to do so only at the time of his firm purity. His firm purity, of course, is no longer permanent as it was before he slipped. . . .[7]

Does this change in status resulting from Adam and Eve's forgiven disobedience affect only them or does it affect their offspring? Is the new context

---

4. See Chawkat Moucarry, *The Prophet and the Messiah: An Arab Christian's Perspective on Islam and Christianity* (Downers Grove, IL: InterVarsity, 2001), 97.

5. Clayton N. Jefford, "Sin," in David Noel Freedman, Allen C. Myers, and Astrid B. Beck, eds., *Eerdmans' Dictionary of the Bible* (Grand Rapids: Eerdmans, 2000), 1225.

6. Jacques Jomier offers a good discussion of these passages in *The Great Themes of the Qurʾan*, trans. Zoe Hersov (London: SCM, 1997 [1978]), 37-51.

7. Chirri, *Inquiries*, 74.

of Adam's existence a permanent one for humankind or not? I am not inclined to dispute that Adam was forgiven by God, but it seems clear that *the results of the sins of Adam and Eve changed the circumstances faced by the human community thereafter*. The offspring of Adam and Eve were no longer in paradise. Like Adam and Eve, they also made choices to disobey. Although God did not forsake them, and although they did not determine human sinning, Adam and Eve were the initial sinners. From their experience we learn that sin separates us from God and—unless forgiven—can destroy the intimacy God designed for the divine-human relationship. "Then learnt Adam from his Lord words of inspiration, and his Lord turned towards him, for He is Oft-Returning, Most Merciful" (*Cow* [2]:37).[8]

Imam Chirri says that since the expulsion from the garden, Adam and his progeny can now communicate with God only at times of "firm purity." That is, according to his take on Islam, humans must be symbolically made pure in body when they pray and the place where they pray must be symbolically pure as well. In other words, Adam and Eve's sin affected all humankind. Purity becomes a major theme in Islamic life and thought, possibly because communication with God remains very important now that we are out of the garden.

Mahmoud Ayoub points out that Adam was made for the earth and that when God placed him on earth as a vicegerent (*Cow* [2]:30), "the battle between good and evil begins."[9] Ayoub understands the expulsion from the garden not as a punishment for disobedience but as a fulfillment of the promise God made to the angels in *Cow* [2]:30: "I will create a vicegerent [*khalīfah*] on the earth." But this promise occurs before God tells Adam and his wife to "settle down in the garden," to "eat freely of it," and to avoid "this tree" lest they become transgressors. This all takes place before Satan makes the couple stumble and God tells them to leave the garden (*Cow* [2]:35-36).

At any rate, the distance between where Muslims stand and where Christians stand on the common ground of our needy human condition seems to be a matter of how the need is defined and how the need is met. Clayton N. Jefford, associate professor of sacred scripture at St. Meinrad's Seminary in Indiana, writes that sin is "a reality signifying the broken relationship between God and humanity."[10] The Christian Bible, including the portions identical in content with the Hebrew scriptures, can be conceived of as a story about occasions when that relationship breaks, about calls to recognize the rupture, and about the means of mending it. We have already seen how this works out for Ezekiel.

For mainstream Islam, according to the late Ismail Ragi al-Faruqi (d. 1986), one of Islam's towering representatives, the covenant between God

---

8. Thomas Irving translates this verse into English, interpreting the two pronouns for "he" differently: "he [i.e., Adam] turned toward Him [i.e., his Lord]." A. Yusuf Ali makes God the subject of "he turned toward him" (*tāba ʿalay-hi*), because God is referred to at the end of the verse as *al-Tawwāb*, "Oft-Returning," from the same root as, "he turned."

9. Mahmoud A. Ayoub, *A Muslim View of Christianity: Essays on Dialogue*, ed. Irfan A. Omar, Faith Meets Faith (Maryknoll, NY: Orbis Books, 2007), 93-94.

10. Jefford, "Sin," 1224.

and humankind is “a purely ethical contract, unequivocally binding upon man and God.”[11] For him, sin breaches the contract. Sin does not disturb a potential relationship between God and the sinner.

Christians see the intimacy that God demonstrates with his people Israel to be an instance of the intimacy he wishes to share with all people. Precisely *this* intimacy appears to be universally compromised by human behavior. Ezekiel’s picture of God’s, the lover’s, broken relationship with Israel fits well the situation of all humankind before God. As the Apostle Paul puts it, “All have sinned and fall short of the glory of God” (Romans 3:23).

The wider perspective that comes from a biblical look at original sin in the light of the dialogue with Islam finalized for me a conviction that people are not guilty because Adam sinned; rather, they gain *solidarity* with Adam by sinning. Thus, the Apostle Paul can say, “As in Adam all die; so in Christ shall all be made alive” (1 Corinthians 15:22) and “the wages of sin is death” (Romans 6:23). But Paul also says: “sin came into the world through one man, and death came through sin, and so death spread to all because all have sinned” (Romans 5:12). The fact of original sin is not that everybody is guilty because of Adam’s sin. Rather, since Adam and Eve, everybody comes into a fallen world, into a human community already subject to alienation from God and in which it appears that people inevitably sin. Original sin—not, after all, a biblical term—points to what all humans are up against, namely, *the pervasiveness and persistence of sin*. True, we are also born into a world that God created and continues to create, where God’s love is manifest everywhere, and where resources exist for penitent, thankful, and obedient response. Both the Qurʾān and the Bible affirm this fact too.

How far does Chirri’s position deviate from what Christians mean when we follow Paul in saying, “in Adam all die”? Paul also says, “death spread to all because *all have sinned*” (Romans 5:12). Chirri uses the image of interrupted communication to describe the results of the fall and expulsion. Christian scripture employs the image of death because Christians understand the changed circumstances resulting from the expulsion more radically. Christian understanding of God includes an awareness of the divine passion for involvement and close relationship with each person God loves. The loss of this intimacy through disobedience remains tragic. Death appropriately symbolizes this loss of divine intimacy.

Muslims I have interacted with believe all babies are born *ʿalā al-fiṭrah*, “in their pure nature” and in natural submission (*islām*) to God. The Qurʾān comes very close to making this explicit, “Set thou thy face steadily and truly to the Faith: Allah’s handiwork according to the pattern (*ʿalā al-fiṭrah*) on which He has made mankind: no change in the work of Allah: that is the standard Religion . . .” (*Byzantium* [30]:30). In fact, the Prophet Muḥammad is believed to have said, “Every child is born in this natural disposition; it is only his parents that later

11. Ismail Ragi al-Faruqi, “A Comparison of Islamic and Christian Approaches to Hebrew Scripture,” *Journal of Bible and Religion* 31, no. 4 (October 1963): 288.

turn him into a 'Jew,' a 'Christian,' or a 'Magian.'" Muḥammad Asad comments, "These three religious formulations, best known to the contemporaries of the Prophet, are thus contrasted with the 'natural disposition' which, by definition, consists in man's instinctive cognition of God and self-surrender (*islām*) to Him."[12] That is, all people would naturally obey God if they were not socialized by their family and their society to follow their own passions and thus deviate from God's way. That does not mean they are born perfect, because all people are subject to fallibility, frailty, fickleness, and finitude. But they are certainly not prone to disobey and act selfishly.

At a dialogue I participated in, after listening to an eloquent and persuasive lecture on the unity of God and the Islamic theory of government, I naively asked the question, "Where in history has this form of government prevailed?" A silence followed, broken at long last by a Muslim graduate student. "We are hoping," she said, "it will happen under Imam Khomeini." That was in 1982 when the Iranian revolution was in its infancy. I do not find anyone now pointing to Iran as the ideal Islamic state. Indeed, the fact that all legislation has to be approved by a council of clerics in Iran suggests they believe that even a nation of people who have been born Muslim, raised by Muslims, educated by Muslims, and governed by Muslims still needs a strong check on the laws it promulgates. It may be, however, that they do believe outside influences have indeed dominated their society, even though it is predominantly Muslim.

What the Qurʾān supports, what I believe, and what Imam Chirri regards as a break in communication, Christian scripture refers to as the pervasiveness of sin and death in all human experience—the very problem that required the solution God offered through the prophets in the form a new covenant.

At any rate, the reality is that sin is pervasive and persistent and separates people from God. It violates God's standards of behavior and brings harm to one's self and to others. It contributes to the breakdown of community. All people struggle with this reality, including Christians and Muslims. Muslims struggle with obedience and consistency in piety. Christian experience of sin and forgiveness has relevance to Muslim experience. Christians in turn can learn from the Muslim commitment to being and doing good.

But viewed more widely, original sin does not mean people are condemned because of what Adam and Eve did. The circumstances of human existence have changed—we are no longer in the garden—but people are responsible for their own sins, not those of their forebears. Even in this wider sense, however, the human condition pointed to by the Bible and the Qurʾān appears to require a serious remedy. We turn now to look more closely at the doctrine of atonement in the light of Muslim objections to it. Can someone die for the sins of others?

---

12. In a comment on *Byzantium* [30]:30, Muḥammad Asad, from whom I took this prophetic tradition and comment, defines the term *fiṭrah* as "natural disposition," his translation of *ʿalā al-fiṭrah* in this verse. He says it "connotes . . . man's inborn, intuitive ability to discern between right and wrong, true and false, and, thus, to sense God's existence and oneness" (Asad, trans. and commentator, *The Message of the Qurʾān* [Gibraltar: Dar al-Andalus, 1980], 621.

Atonement and the Cross: A Closer Look and a Wider Perspective

Because of the pervasiveness and persistence of sin, the Bible shows that even prophetic figures have sinned. Abraham lied about his wife to protect himself (Genesis 20:1-7); Moses murdered an Egyptian who threatened his kinsman (Exodus 2:11-15); Aaron helped construct an idol for impatient Israelites (Exodus 32:1-6); and David got Bathsheba's husband killed so he could have her for himself (2 Samuel 11:14-27). According to many Muslims, however, the prophets represent a higher category of sanctity than other Muslims, and some of them are even beyond experiencing death through persecution.[13]

Jesus Was a Special High-ranking Messenger Whom God Rescued

According to these Muslims, God would never have let Jesus be killed by his enemies—especially not by the shame-laden means called crucifixion. Because, ideologically, most Muslims do not see sin as affecting everyone, they can support their conviction that some persons in God's economy are beyond sin. The prophets from Adam to Muḥammad are believed to have been sinless. In addition, some of the messengers—Abraham, Moses, Jesus, and Muḥammad—represent people of such high holiness that God has exempted them even from suffering death at the hands of their enemies. These messengers of God, designated by the attribute of "tenacity" (*ūlūl ʿazm*), cannot finally be defeated.[14] Abraham was rescued from the fire (*Prophets* [21]:69-70; *Ranks* [37]:98-99); Moses, from Pharaoh (*Smoke* [44]:24-30); Jesus, from the Jews (*Family of Imran* [3]:54-55; *Women* [4]:157-58); and Muḥammad, from the polytheists (*Repentance* [9]:40).

Both Islam and Christianity hold that Jesus never sinned.[15] According to Islamic tradition, his purity exempts him from suffering a death such as crucifixion. According to Christianity, his unique freedom from sin qualifies him to represent others in death and resurrection (Hebrews 4:15-5:10).

In one sense, Christians agree with the Muslim conviction that God vindicated Jesus, along with other "Tenacious Messengers." While Abraham, Moses, and Muḥammad were vindicated by being rescued from the evil plans

---

13. Kenneth E. Nolin translates the response of a Muslim scholar, ʿAbd al-Karīm al-Khaṭīb, who, taking up Nolin's challenge of reading the Bible, finds the accusation that Aaron had a hand in the idolatrous production of the Golden Calf preposterous, since Aaron is a Qurʾānic prophet ("Christ in the Qurʾān, the Taurāt, and the Injīl: A Continuing Dialogue," *The Muslim World* 61, no. 2 [1971]: 90-101).

14. See Muḥammad ʿAbd al-Munʿim al-Jammāl, *Al-tafsīr al-farīd li-al-Qurʾān al-majīd*, 4 vols. (1973), 1:468; and Sayyid Abū al-Aʿlāʾ al-Mawdūdī, *Towards Understanding the Qurʾān*, 7 vols., trans. Zafar Ishaq Ansari (London: Islamic Foundation, 1989), 1:260.

15. Mahmoud M. Ayoub, "Towards an Islamic Christology: II: The Death of Jesus: Reality or Delusion," *The Muslim World* 70, no. 2 (1980): 93; Irfan A. Omar, ed., *A Muslim View of Christianity: Essays on Dialogue by Mahmoud Ayoub*, Faith Meets Faith (Maryknoll, NY: Orbis Books, 2007), 158.

of their enemies, Jesus was vindicated by his resurrection from the dead (Mark 8:31; 9:31; 10:33-34). God had promised that he "would not let his holy one experience corruption" (Psalm 16:10, as quoted in Acts 13:35). Paul quoted this Psalm as he addressed the Jews of Antioch in Pisidia: "he whom God raised up experienced no corruption" (Acts 13:37). Other Tenacious Messengers were protected from death. Jesus triumphed over it.

Thus, resurrection remains inseparable from the crucifixion of Jesus. In enduring the death of crucifixion, Jesus triumphed over death. This victory testifies to his ability to liberate others from the fear of death and Satan, who holds the power of death. The Messiah, according to one early Christian leader, "has abolished death and brought life and immortality to light through the gospel" (2 Timothy 1:10). And another writes, "through death" Jesus destroyed "the one who has the power of death, that is, the devil" and frees "those who all their lives were held in slavery by the fear of death" (Hebrews 2:14-15).

Jesus is the "one who has become a priest, not through a legal requirement concerning physical descent, but through the power of an indestructible life" (Hebrews 7:16). Modern Muslims believe in the Qurʾānic conviction that all humans will be resurrected bodily in the last days—most of them in very much the same way as the Apostle Paul taught. We look now more directly at the atonement in conversation with a Muslim objection.

God Does Not Need the Sacrifice of a Sinless Person to Forgive Sins

Imam Chirri expresses another typical Muslim objection to the Christian understanding of the end of Jesus' mission. We are now in a position to respond to his concern, expressed in the following passage from his book *Inquiries about Islam*.

> To forgive mankind their original sin, God does not need a sinless person, such as Jesus, to be crucified. He can forgive the human race without causing an innocent person to suffer. To say that God does not forgive mankind unless mankind crucifies Jesus, is to put Him in the position of a ruler who was disobeyed by his own subjects. When the children asked the ruler to forgive the sin of their father, he refused to do so unless they kill one of his beloved ones. If they commit such a terrible crime, he will forgive them; otherwise, he will not. . . . God, the Most Just and Merciful, does not condemn people because of their ancestor's sin. He may forgive them their own sins without requiring them to commit a bigger one.[16]

Chirri's objection differs very little in meaning from an objection to the Christian view of the death of Christ put forth by some Christian feminist theologians: the dominant theology of the cross amounts to divine child abuse,

16. Chirri, *Inquiries*, 69.

or “the abuse of the one perfect child.”[17] Imam Chirri’s critique of the doctrine of the cross, like that of some feminists, represents a critique of *one theory* of the atonement—albeit the dominant one in evangelical Christian circles, the circles I have mainly moved in. The theory has been labeled “penal satisfaction.”

A Closer Look at the Penal Satisfaction Theory

The roots of the penal satisfaction theory of the atonement have been traced back to Anselm of Canterbury (d. 1109). According to him, rather than responding to God in obedient acts of faithfulness and service—their true vocation as God’s creatures—humans responded in disobedient acts of unfaithfulness and rebellion. This human response represented an attack on God’s honor. Since humans are responsible for this dishonoring of God, the responsibility for making the relationship right lies with them. Humans, however, lack the requisite innocence to make things right. Only God possesses this requirement. So, in grace, Jesus the Messiah became the divine-human instrument for restoring God’s honor, repairing the chasm separating God and humankind.

Joel B. Green and Mark D. Baker point out that Anselm’s theory of what Jesus accomplished on the cross was an attempt to speak relevantly to the people of his time, employing metaphors upholding the feudal system of lords, vassals, honor, and obligation.[18]

A more modern version of Anselm’s doctrine of the cross has so captured the loyalty of many Christians that to challenge it amounts in their eyes to challenging the Bible and the classical Christian worldview. The reason for its popularity and the consensus that it is both biblical and the only true understanding of the cross again relate to culture, according to Green and Baker. The metaphors that communicate meaning in Western culture today connect believers with themes of guilt, innocence, and personal experience. The Western view of justice orients people toward guilt and innocence. In the courtrooms of the Western world the key issue turns on whether an individual person is guilty or innocent.

This legal perspective spills over into everyday life. If people turn out to be destitute, Westerners tend to attribute it to some flaw in their character such as laziness or poor financial management. In other words, people in difficulty must have features of their personal stories that render them guilty. Just as the judge in a court of law determines punishments appropriate to the guilt and the law, so Westerners view poverty as a kind of punishment for the flaws of the individuals who are poor. In Western culture, individual guilt and innocence has become a clue for understanding “the way the world works” or “the way the world was

---

17. Rita Nakashima Brock, “And a Little Child Will Lead Us: Christology and Child Abuse,” in *Christianity, Patriarchy, and Abuse: A Feminist Critique*, ed. Joanne Carlson Brown and Carole R. Bohn (New York: Pilgrim, 1989), 52-53; cited in Joel B. Green and Mark D. Baker, *Recovering the Scandal of the Cross: Atonement in New Testament and Contemporary Contexts* (Downers Grove, IL: InterVarsity, 2000), 91.

18. Green and Baker, *Recovering*, 21-23.

made by God."[19] For cultural reasons, the remaking of Anselm's honor-based theory—once relevant to feudalism—into a theory based on the guilt and innocence of individuals comes to modern Westerners as uniquely meaningful because of their cultural worldview.

While the penal satisfaction theory fits Western culture nicely, it has flaws. For one thing, it still has features that Westerners find difficult to accept. It is hard for people to understand why the things they have done deserve a kind of punishment they cannot pay. Thus, Westerners tend to ask, "Why are the wages of sin death?" Even people who believe strongly in capital punishment for "capital crimes" such as murder and kidnapping find it difficult to accept that sins committed by people who try very hard to live according to God's standards deserve punishment by death. Thus they tend to ask, "Why is a death necessary?"

Another flaw in the theory relates to its being too easily accepted by modern Western people. Green and Baker point out that "this theory gives us permission to disregard the *suffering* of Jesus."[20] Because many Western Christians, and their disciples elsewhere, have come to see Jesus' crucifixion almost exclusively as taking the suffering and pain that we deserve as punishment for our sins, Jesus' cross loses much of its power as exemplary for our discipleship. It is as though "he suffered so severely . . . so we would not have to."[21] Truth lies in this statement, but it can also be misleading. Jesus said, "If any want to become my followers, let them deny themselves and take up their cross and follow me" (Mark 8:34).

In chapters 9 and 10 above we dealt with Jesus' own interpretation of the cross and its meaning revealed in his explicit and implicit predictions recorded in the Gospels. Jesus says and implies much more about the cross as a model for his followers (Mark 8:34-38; 9:33-50; and 10:17-31, 38-45) than about its role as atonement for their sins (Mark 10:45). Even in the ransom verse, "For the Son of Man did not come to be served but to serve, and to give his life a ransom for many" (Mark 10:45), Jesus offers his disciples a model for their own way of life. They too must be ready to serve and to give their lives, if need be, for others.

To say that Jesus died for our sins reflects the clear teaching of four passages of the New Testament (1 Corinthians 15:3; Galatians 1:4; 1 John 2:2; 4:10). But that teaching about the cross should not obscure the causal connection between Jesus' death and his life and teachings. Jesus was crucified in large part because he lived out the values of the kingdom of God.

Again, the passages of scripture we studied carefully in chapter 10 led to the conclusion that the perspective Jesus reveals in the teachings and deeds accompanying his journey from Caesarea, through Galilee, to Judea represents God's perspective or the values of God's reign. This connection is stated boldly by God in the story of the Transfiguration embedded within the narrative of this

19. Ibid., 24-25.
20. Ibid., 25. Emphasis added.
21. Ibid., 26.

journey, "This is my Son, the beloved, *listen* to him" (Mark 9:7). The simple truth that Jesus "died for our sins" should not obscure the many different ways the meaning of the cross is presented in the New Testament.

A Wider Perspective on the Meaning of the Cross

The Acts of the Apostles, the book of Revelation, and most of the New Testament letters deal with the death and resurrection of Jesus, showing the many-faceted interpretations possible for these great events. Green and Baker identify five "constellations of images" employed by New Testament writers to interpret the meaning of the cross. One constellation containing words such as "justification" (e.g., Romans 3:23) borrows from the courts of law prevailing in the Mediterranean environment of New Testament writers. Another, containing such metaphors as "redemption" (e.g., the very next verse, Romans 3:24), draws from the marketplace. A third constellation draws such images as "reconciliation" (2 Corinthians 5:18) from the sphere of personal relationships in the Greco-Roman world. Worship familiar to the Jews and the non-Jews to whom New Testament writers wrote supplies a fourth constellation of images such as "sacrifice" (Hebrews 7:27). Finally, the field of battle provides a set of images such as "triumph over evil" (Colossians 2:15). Green and Baker conclude "that the significance of Jesus' death could not be represented without remainder by any one concept or theory of metaphor."[22]

New Testament writers represented the crucified Jesus by a number of images and concepts: Passover Lamb (1 Corinthians 5:7; Revelation 5:12); suffering servant of Isaiah 53 (Mark 10:45); one of the suffering righteous of Psalms 22 and 69 (Matthew 27:46); alternative to the Temple sacrifices (Hebrews 4:14); and one of the prophets who suffered rejection from their people (Matthew 23:29-39).[23] Jesus brought to the Apostle Paul's mind the son whom Abraham was ready to sacrifice—only this time God provided no ram as a substitute (Romans 8:32).[24] Mark remembered that Jesus said his death would be like a ransom payment for the release of a prisoner or a slave (Mark 10:45). John detected in him an exemplar of the Greco-Roman ideal of a friend who lays down his life for his friends (John 15:13).[25] And Luke saw Jesus' death as a new covenant sacrifice that God used to constitute his new covenant community in fulfillment of Jeremiah 31:31-34 (Luke 22:21). [26]

---

22. Ibid., 23.

23. Karl Olav Sandnes ("The Death of Jesus for Human Sins: The Historical Basis for a Theological Concept," *Themelius* 20, no. 1 [October 1994]: 20) calls this line "the deuteronomistic pattern of the prophetic ministry." The concept of rejection of prophets finds a prominent place in the Qurʾān, e.g., *Cow* [2]:87.

24. Martin Hengel, *The Cross of the Son of God: Containing the Son of God, Crucifixion, and the Atonement* (London: SCM, 1986), 223.

25. See C. S. Keener, "Friendship," in Craig A. Evans and Stanley E. Porter, eds., *Dictionary of the New Testament Background* (Downers Grove, IL: InterVarsity, 2000), 380-88.

26. Peter M. Head, "The Self-Offering and Death of Christ as a Sacrifice in the Gospels and the

If this plethora of meanings in the New Testament makes understanding Christ's death and resurrection difficult,[27] two considerations may be helpful: (1) if the events of the end of Jesus' mission turn out to be as significant as Christians hold them to be, then it makes sense that their ramifications multiply; and (2) one of these ramifications may have special relevance to Muslim readers. This factor, I suggest, is the connection between Jesus' death and his faithfulness to his prophetic mission.

The Cross and the Message of Jesus

Consider, by way of example, the experience of some Iranian poets for whom the cross served as a significant symbol. Their conclusions cohere with the interpretation I have made in chapter 10 above of Jesus' predictions of his death and resurrection (Mark 8:27-10:52 with its parallels in Matthew and Luke). For these Iranian poets, according to Sorour S. Soroudi, the New Testament Jesus represents a spiritual shepherd who is publicly responsible. His deeds and words, including his embracing of his crucifixion, aim at saving others. Here is a selection from one of them, Ahmad Shamlu (born 1925), who identifies openly with the symbol of the cross:

> Lo, there am I, having traversed all my bewilderments,
> Up to this Golgotha.
> There am I, standing on the inverted cross
> A statue as tall as a cry.
> There am I
> Having plucked the cross-nails out of the palms with my teeth.[28]

One major problem with the very popular interpretation of the death of Jesus as penal satisfaction is that it obscures the causes of his crucifixion, which originate in his implementation of God's perspective and agenda. Because God's values crossed purposes radically with both the order of the Roman Empire and that of the Jewish establishment, Jesus' faithfulness had its cost. Precisely this

---

Acts of the Apostles," in Roger T. Beckwith and Martin J. Selman, eds., *Sacrifice in the Bible* (Grand Rapids: Baker Book House, 1995), 119. This paragraph is based on Sandnes ("The Death of Jesus," 20), although I modified it and added scripture references.

27. Marston Speight, "Al-Ghazālī on the Divine Name, *Al-MUQĪṬ*: An Opening for Muslim-Christian Dialogue," *Recueil d'articles offert à Maurice Borrmans par ses collègues et amis* (Rome: Pontifico Istituto di Studi Arabie d'Islamistica, 1996), 227. See also the six ways of grasping the meaning of the end of Jesus' mission offered by William J. Wolf in "Atonement: Christian Concepts," in Mircea Eliade et al., eds., *Encyclopedia of Religion*, 16 vols. (Chicago: Macmillan, 1987), 1:495; on the theories of the meaning and effect of the cross and resurrection, see Wolf, "Atonement," 1:497-98.

28. Sorour S. Soroudi, "On Jesus' Image in Modern Persian Poetry," *The Muslim World* 69 (1979): 224.

faithfulness to ideals made him attractive to the Iranian poets. They too paid a price for their devotion to principle and ideal. They identified with the suffering that resulted from Jesus' authentic faithfulness.

This opposition of Jesus to both the Roman and the Jewish ideals of his day becomes most clear in the passages of the Synoptic Gospels studied in chapters 9-13 above. Jesus speaks of his impending death both explicitly and implicitly again and again in these Gospels. He speaks of his death in terms of dying for others, however, in only two verses, both "ransom sayings."

One climaxes the long section of Mark's Gospel featuring Jesus' three explicit predictions of death and resurrection (8:22-10:52): "For the Son of Man also came not to be served but to serve, and to give his life as a ransom for many" (Mark 10:45; Matthew 20:28). The other, Jesus uttered at the Last Supper, "This is my blood of the covenant which is poured out for many" (Mark 14:24; Matthew 26:28; Luke 22:19-20). Both sayings occur in narratives characterized by concerns about power and position typical of those prevailing in the Roman imperial view of the world. Both sayings occur in settings rich in images and promises from the Hebrew scriptures.

The Roman Empire supported a network of roles of dominance and subservience. This patronage system made Caesar subservient only to the gods who supported and guaranteed the legitimacy of his rule. Under him stretched a descending web of patrons and clients. Slaves served their masters. Sons obeyed their fathers. Even clients themselves served as patrons to those in client relationship to them. Such a hierarchy of authority was assumed in the Greco-Roman culture of Jesus' time and place. Jesus' values and priorities laid bare those of God's kingdom. But his loyalty to those values set him in uncompromising opposition to the imperial order of Rome.

It was his disciples' unreflective espousing of the values of Caesar's rule that shows itself again and again in the sections of the Synoptic Gospels that culminate in Mark's and Matthew's ransom saying. While the disciples dickered over their respective positions in the hierarchy of Jesus' anticipated coming kingdom, Jesus made clear that the greatest in God's kingdom would be a little child, "the least impressive inhabitants of the Roman social world."[29] Furthermore, the one who would be first (read "patron") in God's kingdom must be servant of all (Mark 9:33-37; 10:13-16, 35-45).

This exaltation of the lowliest person and most menial role represents Jesus' radical commitment to the value of each and every person. Jesus committed himself to this perspective publicly and lived it out consistently—despite the consequences to himself. In doing so he challenged the foundation of the prevailing social order. Because he attracted a significant following, he endangered Rome's political control over the people in its territories. His death was the price he paid for revealing God's order and acting consistently with it.

God's order as revealed in and by Jesus also put him in grave tension with the Jewish establishment. Put very simply, he ate with unclean people. Wherever

29. Green and Baker, *Recovering*, 41.

Jesus went, people celebrated—festive meals must have abounded. N. T. Wright summarizes this practice very briefly when he says "that Jesus welcomed all and sundry is one of the most securely established features of almost all recent scholarly portraits."[30] It was not so much his partying with "all and sundry," however, that troubled the religious establishment, but "that he was doing so *as a prophet of the kingdom*."[31] And he was making these parties with their inclusive table fellowship a central plank in his platform. They were part of his radical agenda of acceptance and forgiveness for all. The establishment limited forgiveness to those who sought it through the Temple in Jerusalem, which they controlled. Jesus was offering forgiveness on his own authority without any necessary connection with the Temple (Matthew 9:2-8).

Jesus was announcing the possibility of "a way of life, a way of forgiveness and prayer, a way of jubilee, which they [ordinary people] could practice in their own villages, right where they were."[32] The hostility of the established Temple leadership reached its climax when Jesus challenged the Temple itself—"the symbolic heart of Judaism" and "the power base of the priestly elite who, along with the Herodian house, ran second-temple Judaism at this time" (Mark 11:15-19; Matthew 21:12-16; Luke 19:45-48; John 2:13-16).[33]

Jesus' cleansing the Temple of money-changers amounted to a prophetic action that symbolized God's judgment on Israel for abandoning its divinely ordered vocation of mission—internally to the poor and externally to the nations. Instead, "the temple had become the focal point for the nationalists in their eagerness for revolt against Rome, as well as for the rich and powerful in their oppression of the rest of the nation."[34]

Jesus put himself in grave danger, then, in that he confronted the religious establishment, the revolutionary nationalists, and the wealthy elite. His death was partly a function of his faithfulness to his messianic and prophetic vocation to reveal and abide by the values of God's kingdom. The Last Supper found Jesus living out both his radical table fellowship and his free offer of forgiveness.

Thus, both of his "for others" sayings recorded in the Synoptic Gospels occur in contexts where Jesus challenges the Roman and Jewish cultural perceptions of his day. The Iranian poets discerned correctly that Jesus died living out his vocation in faithfulness. And we might add with Green and Baker, his "death demonstrates the distance between God's ways and the ways typical of human communities."[35]

What, then, is the connection between Jesus' crucifixion and the forgiveness of sins that the Christian communities of faith celebrate in the Lord's Supper?

---

30. N. T. Wright, *The Challenge of Jesus: Rediscovering Who Jesus Was and Is* (Downers Grove, IL: InterVarsity, 1999), 45.

31. Ibid. Italics in the original.

32. Ibid., 46.

33. N. T. Wright, "The Mission and Message of Jesus," in Marcus J. Borg and N. T. Wright, *The Meaning of Jesus: Two Visions* (San Francisco: HarperSanFrancisco, 1999), 44.

34. Ibid., 45. The quote is from 254f. n. 22.

35. Green and Baker, *Recovering*, 41.

Jesus must have seen more significance in his death than the inevitable result of the faithfulness to conviction that the Iranian poets celebrated. Ben Meyer in *The Aims of Jesus* helps us see the connection between Jesus' crucifixion as a result of his faithfulness to his vision and its meaning. "Jesus did not aim to be repudiated and killed; he aimed to charge with meaning his being repudiated and killed."[36]

Jesus could draw from much in the Jewish sources of his day to illumine his vocation to suffer, die, and be raised. For one thing, he inherited from scripture a tradition pointing to the suffering of the prophets (Nehemiah 9:26 and Jeremiah 2:30). For another, the Bible itself has a tradition that the suffering of the righteous can be for others.

Biblical writers answer the question, Why do the righteous suffer? in at least three ways. Job, aided by divine disclosure, resigns himself to the mystery of God's wisdom (Job 42:2-3). One Psalmist feels free to "assail God violently for neglecting his people" and calls on God to redeem them (Psalm 44:9-26). Another rests finally in the conviction that God will vindicate the righteous who suffer unjustly (Psalm 22:19-31) and punish those who oppress them (Psalm 35:8-10). This became extended to the Day of the Lord when in the end perfect justice would be meted out (Daniel 12:1). In the period just before the coming of Jesus, Jewish writers promised divine recompense in the next life for those who suffer unjustly (e.g., Wisdom of Solomon 3:1-4). But the question of why even God's prophets suffered came to be answered by the strong conviction that the servant of God in solidarity with God's people would in suffering take on even their sins redemptively (Isaiah 53:2-12).[37] Green and Baker suggest it is not by chance "that the Synoptic Gospels portray the death of Jesus in terms reflecting the influence of the pattern of the suffering righteous one," nor is it by chance "that this pattern was itself shaped under the influence of Isaiah's portrayal of the suffering servant."[38]

N. T. Wright, Scot McKnight, and Green and Baker emphasize that at the time of Jesus the expectation that Israel's reconciliation to God and deliverance from the yoke of occupation would be achieved through great suffering.[39] Wright makes clear that just as Jesus' symbolic act of cleansing the Temple points to his replacement of the Temple's system of purity and sacrifice, so the Last Supper, shared with his disciples, points to Jesus' own teaching that what the Temple had been he was and what its sacrificial system offered was present in his death.[40] By taking up their own crosses in faith, believers could participate through his death and resurrection in God's forgiveness and love.

---

36. Ben F. Meyer, *The Aims of Jesus* (London: SCM, 1979), 218.

37. Otto A. Piper, "Suffering and Evil," *Interpreter's Dictionary of the Bible*, 4 vols. (Nashville: Abingdon, 1962), 4:452.

38. Green and Baker, *Recovering*, 44.

39. Ibid., 45. See Borg and Wright, *The Meaning of Jesus*, 97; and Scot McKnight, *Jesus and His Death: Historiography, the Historical Jesus and Atonement Theory* (Waco: Baylor University Press, 2005), 337-38.

40. Wright, *Challenge of Jesus*, 83-85.

Also, the resurrection tells us that what Jesus taught about his authority to forgive sins is true. When Jesus symbolically demonstrated that the Temple cult of atonement for sin would be replaced (Mark 11:15-19), the resurrection assures us that it is replaced with his sacrificial death.

Furthermore, Jesus' resurrection appearances demonstrate the cross's power of forgiveness because Jesus restores his disciples to intimate fellowship even though they have forsaken him. "These post-Easter encounters were a decisive factor in assuring" Jesus' disciples, says Karl Olav Sandnes, "of the result of his death being one of atonement for sins."[41] In 1 Corinthians 15:5 Paul says of the resurrection of Jesus, "He appeared to Cephas (Peter), then to the twelve." Does this not suggest that the chief of deniers was singled out for forgiveness?[42] Poor Judas, if he had only known what the cross and resurrection reveal, he too could have been added to Paul's sentence—perhaps ahead of Peter!

The explicit predictions Jesus made of his passion and vindication, analyzed in chapter 10, were structured in a narrative climaxing in Jesus' statement, "For the Son of Man came not to be served but to serve, and to give his life as *a ransom for many*" (Mark 10:45; Matthew 20:28).

The Greek word *lytron* ("ransom") literally refers to ransom from prison or slavery rather than forgiveness of sins. Peter Head, however, who has explored the matter thoroughly, says we should not make too much out of what is not said in the brief text.[43] Since it is clear that Jesus' death deals with the forgiveness of sins, it makes sense that in this explanation of the meaning of his death, Jesus points to sin as making people prisoners and slaves.

Jesus serves as the focal point of God's sovereign mercy. He ransoms us from the slavery of sin. Just as Jesus' crucifixion assured the Iranian poets of his faithfulness and authenticity, just so is he the one "in whom we know God as forgiving and ourselves as forgiven. The assurance his active mercy allows us is not presumption. For it is God who in Christ leaves no room for doubt."[44]

Mahmoud Ayoub, to whom I have referred many times, has made a serious and disciplined attempt to grasp the essence and meaning of Christianity. He has identified two basic interpretations of redemption in Christianity: one, dominant in Western Christianity, I have just elaborated on; it focuses on the cross as sacrifice. In this interpretation, Jesus' death on the cross takes the place of the Temple's sacrifical system and offers believers forgiveness. The other interpretation, dominant in Eastern Christianity, focuses on redemption as victory: through dying and rising Jesus gains victory over death.[45]

But Ayoub brings in two additional types of redemption from the Islamic tradition. One type involves people dealing with their own sin through repentance,

---

41. Sandnes, "Death of Jesus," 23. Martin Hengel covers this same ground (*The Atonement: Origins of the Doctrine in the New Testament* [Philadelphia: Fortress, 1981], 67ff.).

42. Sandnes, "Death of Jesus," 23.

43. Head, "Self-Offering," 114.

44. Kenneth Cragg, *Call of the Minaret*, 2nd ed. (Maryknoll, NY: Orbis Books/Ibadan, Nigeria: Daystar, 1985), 265.

45. Ayoub, *Muslim View,* 91-92.

fasting, prayer, and giving to the needy. Intercession in its several forms represents the other Islamic type of redemption. Although this second Islamic type of redemption focuses greatly on Muḥammad as intercessor, intercession need not be limited to him. Successful redemption can even involve ordinary believers praying for one another.[46]

I understand all four of Ayoub's types of redemption as involved in the process of redemption, although I would not use his words exactly: "redemption is what men and women do with their own sin through repentance and through expiation through prayers, fasts, sharing their wealth with the poor, and so on."[47] Redemption requires that believers participate in their own salvation through the very kinds of things Ayoub lists. I mentioned above several images or themes, including sacrifice-forgiveness and victory over sin and death. And just as divine involvement in redemption is written all over the Christian understanding of the cross and resurrection, so human engagement in the form of obedience, prayer, fasting, almsgiving, and other forms of spiritual formation, as well as intercession, is crucial for its full realization (Luke 6:28; 22:32; Acts 8:15; 2 Corinthians 13:9; Colossians 1:9; James 5:16). Again, Jesus requires believers to take up their own crosses and to follow him (Mark 8:34-38). One of the main problems of the very popular penal satisfaction doctrine of redemption is that it tends to overlook this human engagement both individually and collectively in the "working out" of salvation (Romans 2:6, 7; 1 Corinthians 15:1, 2; Philippians 2:13; James 1:12, 13).

In this chapter we have considered the human condition and the atonement of Christ in the light of a common-ground dialogue with Muslims. This has required of us a closer look and has given us a broader perspective. While I may not have established agreement with my Muslim readers, and we still may be standing apart, we are standing apart on common ground. In the final analysis, Anglican Bishop Kenneth Cragg of Oxford, probably the most prominent living Christian interpreter to Muslims, offers a straightforward condensation of what this chapter has delved into. In any case, I hope that this chapter bears witness "to the fact of the power of Christ crucified in transforming human souls, breaking the entail of wrong and emancipating formerly selfish lives into the service of God and humanity."[48] Could a better depiction of the meaning of "ransom" be conceived? This is what Jesus, Prophet and Messiah, can do and does. But more of the story still beckons us. In the last chapter we examine the end of Jesus' mission as revelation of the nature and purposes of God.

---

46. Ibid., 92-94.
47. Ibid., 94.
48. Cragg, *Call of the Minaret*, 269.

15

"In Plain Sight They See the Return of the Lord to Zion"

The End of Jesus' Mission and the Nature of God

This book opened with a response to the call of Sheikh Fawzī al-Zafzāf for a Christian-Muslim dialogue that emphasized common ground. In that opening chapter, I briefly defended the thesis that we both believe in the same and only God. The search for common ground with Muslim friends and dialogue partners has helped me discover a deeper and broader meaning for the Christian conviction that Jesus died for others. These conversations have enriched my understanding also of the meaning of the last days of Jesus' mission for understanding the nature of the God in whom both Muslims and Christians believe. The most profound thing I can say in this last chapter is that the end of Jesus' mission as reported in the Gospels represents the most dramatic and climactic chapter in the unfolding of *God's self-revelation.* Now we turn to our common ground in belief about God, a very important place to begin—and end.

Common Ground in the Beautiful Names of God

In chapter 1, I cited David W. Shenk's statement in dialogue with Badru D. Kateregga that Christians can agree with all the ninety-nine names for God celebrated by Muslims. This is especially true for the ones Kateregga mentions: God is One, Creator, the Merciful, the All-powerful, All-wise, All-knowing, and the Eternal. It has become an important ritual practice in Islam to recite God's ninety-nine Beautiful Names (*al-asmā' al-ḥusnā*) from memory, using a *misbāḥah*, a kind of "rosary" of thirty-three beads. Obviously, these names are important.

Shenk accepts them as compatible with the Christian understanding of God. Some of these Beautiful Names, in fact, appear strikingly compatible with a Christian view of God. *Al-Ḥāfiẓ* means "the vigilant Guardian," who knows us intimately; *al-Raqīb* is close to *al-Ḥāfiẓ*, and adds the sense of jealousy, "the jealous vigilant Guardian"; *al-Mujīb*, "the One who answers [our prayers]," anticipating and meeting our needs; *al-Wadūd* signifies God as "the Very Loving," "who loves the well-being of his creatures";[1] *al-Wakīl* means "the Trustee," who takes care of the well-being of his creatures; and *al-Walī* means "the Friend," in the sense of "helper and defender."[2] The Qurʾān and the Islamic Tradition make room for a wide understanding of God's attributes. As a Christian, I find much common ground here.

Divine Intimacy in the Qurʾān

God expresses divine will and works out divine love, guardianship, friendship, and love by sending messengers (*rusul*; sing. *rasūl*), including prophets (*anbiyāʾ*; sing. *nabī*), and scriptures. Messengers are human agents sent to a people with a message in their own language (*Abraham* [14]:4). The message they bring is essentially the same: shun false gods; act justly and generously; and worship only the one true and living God (*Bee* [16]:36).

Muḥammad, the model and final Messenger and Prophet (*Parties* [33]:21, 40), brought a complete message for all humanity, while God sent earlier messengers to a particular people. Most of the Qurʾānic stories of earlier messengers exhibit a remarkably similar structure: the messenger proclaims his message; his people then refuse to accept the message and reject him; God rescues him along with his faithful followers; and God uses some calamity to punish those who reject the messenger. This is essentially the same story that Muḥammad participated in at Mecca, except that no natural calamity fell on those who rejected him. These stories must have been a great comfort to Muḥammad and his group of followers. They represented a warning to his opponents also.

Stories of seven messengers: Noah, Hūd, Ṣāliḥ, Lot, Shuʿayb, Abraham, and Moses appear—among other *sūrah*s—in *Poets* [26]:10-191. The narratives each end with the refrain, "Surely in this there is a sign; yet most of them do not believe. Your Lord is the mighty one, the merciful" (e.g., verses 67 and 68).[3] "The mighty one, the merciful": obvious common ground exists here with the Bible; God is clearly both ultimate and intimate. One name among the many in the Qurʾān stands out as particularly helpful in interpreting how these two attributes come together. It is the name *al-Ḥalīm,* "forbearing, ever-forbearing, or most forbearing."

The word *ḥalīm* appears fifteen times in the Qurʾān. Once it is attributed to the son of Abraham, whose name is not mentioned, but who will be obedient to his father's intent to sacrifice him. In his translation of the verse, A. Yusuf

1. Louis Gardet, "al-Asmāʾ al-Ḥusnā," in *The Encyclopaedia of Islam*, ed. C. E. Bosworth, 16 vols., 2nd ed. (Leiden: Brill, 1960-2003), 1:716.

2. Ibid., 1:714-17. It is quite a treat to examine carefully the article in the second edition of the *Encyclopaedia of Islam* by Louis Gardet on the Beautiful Names, cited in note 1. He gives a brief explanation for each name along with identifying several other names not among the ninety-nine. It demonstrates a lot of common ground.

3. A. H. Mathias Zahniser, "Messenger," in *The Encyclopaedia of the Qurʾān*, ed. Jane Dammen McAuliffe, 6 vols. (Leiden: Brill, 2006), 3:380-83.

Ali renders the one word as "suffer and forbear" (*Ranks* [37]:101). It occurs twice as an attribute of Abraham (*Repentance* [9]:114; *Hood* [11]:75), and once the Qur'ān applies it to Shu'ayb (*Hood* [11]:87). The remaining eleven times it describes God (*Cow* [2]:225, 235, 263; *Family of Imran* [3]:155; *Women* [4]:12; *Table* [5]:101; *Journey* [17]:44; *Pilgrimage* [22]:59; *Parties* [33]:51; *Creator* [35]:41; *Loss and Gain* [64]:17). In all fifteen instances the word occurs in the rhyme phrase at the end of its verse. When it contains a name or attribute of God, a single rhyme phrase often provides a commentary on its verse or verse group from the divine perspective. And together, such rhyme phrases in a thematic unit of the Qur'ān provide a theological and ethical frame for the content of that unit. Readers can observe this by reading *Joseph* [12].[4]

The procedure then for getting at a more fruitful range of meaning for *Ḥalīm* as a divine name would be to examine it in all of the verses and thematic units in which it appears, as well as in the general cultural and religious world at the time of the Qur'ān. This is, in fact, what the Japanese scholar Toshihiko Izutsu does in his widely acclaimed book *God and Man in the Koran*.[5]

A person in ancient Arabia who was designated *ḥalīm* was the polar opposite of hot-blooded, impetuous individuals who surrender to whatever their violent passions may dictate. Persons who are *ḥalīm* can stop such outbursts and loss of control. They are characterized by calmness, balanced judgment, and self-control. This quality characterized the ideal ruler. Leaders described as *ḥalīm* have the power to do "all kinds of violence when provoked and yet . . . [possess] at the same time, the power to restrain [themselves] from being violent." Leaders who possess this quality forgive their enemies. They are "forbearing of faults" in those they could punish. A. Yusuf Ali uses these words to translate *ḥalīm* as attributed to Abraham (*Hood* [11]:75). As Izutsu puts it, they show "gentleness from above," that is, from the position of a superior.[6] The Qur'ān reveals that certain individuals yielded to Satan and turned their backs at the Battle of Uḥud. But, says the Qur'ān, "God has blotted out (their fault); God is Oft-forgiving, Most Forbearing" (*ghafūr ḥalīm*; *Family of Imran* [3]:155). In six of the eleven instances where the Qur'ān attributes *ḥalīm* to God, the name is combined with "Oft-forgiving" (*ghafūr*). That is, God is in complete control and has the unfettered freedom to forgive whomever he pleases. But God is friend, trustee, loving, and guardian, but always from a position of superior strength.

In my experience, Muslims have tended to emphasize the ultimacy of God at the expense of divine intimacy. I have heard several young Muslim men make a statement similar to this one made by an engineer working in Chicago,

---

4. Angelika Neuwirth, "Zur Struktur der *Yūsuf*-Sure," in Werner Diem and Stefan Wild, eds., *Studien aus Arabistik und Semitistik: Anton Spitaler zum siebzigsten Geburtstag von seinen Schülern überreicht* (Wiesbaden: Harrossowitz, 1980), 148-52.

5. Toshihiko Izutsu, *God and Man in the Koran: Semantics of the Koranic Weltanschauung*, Studies in the Humanities and Social Relations 5 (Tokyo: Keio Institute of Cultural and Linguistic Studies, 1964).

6. Ibid., 207-8.

"Everybody could reject God and he would not care." It was important to him that God be invulnerable.

In a dialogue I attended at a mosque in Chicago, I made an unexpected mistake in my perception of Islam. I said, "As is well known, you Muslims believe God is revealed in the Qurʾān, your holy book; whereas we Christians believe God is revealed in Jesus, the Messiah." In what amounted to almost a chorus, the Muslims replied, "No! the Qurʾān does not reveal God; it reveals God's will. God does not self-reveal. We cannot know God."

This view of God is similar to the more sophisticated position of a scholar such as the late Ismail al-Faruqi who insists that Islamic "revelation is ideational and only ideational." He contrasts this with Christian revelation in *deed and person*. He knows that Christians believe that, in Christ, God is revealed. He goes on to say, "in Islam, God does not reveal Himself. Being transcendent, He can never become the object of knowledge."[7] Thus, according to al-Faruqi, God reveals guidance only. We learn only God's will. The covenant between God and Israel or between God and humankind as Islam sees it is simply, "if man obeys God and does the good, he would be blessed."[8]

But this is not the whole story. I once presented this issue to a devout Muslim friend. I said, "Some Muslims tell me it is not possible to know God; yet I have known Muslims who seem to me like people who know God (I actually had him in mind). Is it possible to know God?" He thought about my question for what seemed like a long time, finally replying, "It is impossible to possess true religion without knowing God."

As Professor al-Faruqi reports, Christians do believe in divine self-revelation in Jesus. And the cross amounts to a crucial dimension of that self-revelation. To grasp this understanding we need to see the whole story of God's relationship with Israel his people as one of engagement and involvement.

The Cross and the Involvement of God

It was this issue of knowing God that led me to explain one aspect of the nature of God to Muslims in the hope of helping them understand my faith, or, to put it more biblically, to give an explanation of the inner conviction that provides hope for the near and distant future (1 Peter 3:15)—exactly my purpose in this book.

I recall an engagement with Muslim men during a visit my students and I

---

7. Ismail Ragi al-Faruqi, "A Comparison of Islamic and Christian Approaches to Hebrew Scripture," *Journal of Bible and Religion* 31, no. 4 (October 1963): 286. Mahmoud Ayoub of Temple University advocates a very different understanding of revelation in Islam; see "Divine Revelation and the Person of Jesus Christ," *Newsletter of Christian-Muslim Concerns: Interfaith Relations* 43 (July 1990): 1-5. He believes it includes both personal and scriptural revelation. This should caution us again that Islam is not one thing. Islam features a variety of thinkers and a variety of conclusions about the matters we are discussing.

8. Al-Faruqi, "A Comparison," 287.

made to the Islamic Society of North America in Plainfield, Indiana. Ali,[9] one of the men at a table where I and two of my students were seated, asked me right in the middle of a discussion about how Christians pray, "What do you mean when you say that Jesus is the Son of God?" In the course of our discussion stimulated by Ali's question, I tried to connect the cross of Jesus with a Christian understanding of God's nature and purpose. This approach generated interest on the part of the Muslims at our table until the call to prayer interrupted us. We never got back to the conversation. Some of the things I said in response to his question follow, with some editing for clarity and brevity:

> When we say Jesus is the Son of God, we mean Jesus participates in who God is, and that in him God participates in being human. We do not worship a human being, Jesus, and thus treat him like a god. That would be idolatry. Rather, we believe God wants to relate intimately with us humans. In working out this purpose, God fully participated in being human in Jesus. To worship a human being would be idolatry, but if God chose to participate in being human that would seem legitmate. We believe as you do that God is not restricted, other than by choice.
>
> It is like what you believe about the Qur'ān. In the Qur'ān God chose to speak a word to human beings to reveal the right path so they can live harmoniously and well on earth and enjoy paradise in the hereafter. When Muslims came into contact with Greek philosophy, they had to decide whether the Qur'ān, as God's speech, was created or uncreated. This is the same problem Christians had earlier, not with the Bible, but with Jesus. Was Jesus, the word of God, eternal with God or was he created?

At this point Ali responded, "But it is different with the Qur'ān. The Qur'ān is God's *speech*. As long as God exists he speaks and expresses himself. It would not be the same with Jesus." I continued:

> I think it is parallel here too because, according to the Torah, God has always come down to self-reveal and to act for the freeing of his people. God spoke to Moses in the Torah, "I have seen your people's suffering, I have heard their cry and I have come down to rescue them." What God did in releasing the children of Israel from Egypt, God has always done: expressing this divine involvement with people, rescuing them from difficulty and revealing in the process loving care for them.[10] The Qur'ān and the Gospel speak of Jesus as the Word: Jesus is God's self-expression. Just as you believe, that even though there are many true and excellent writings about God, there is only one Qur'ān, we also believe, that even though you can see God at work in many people and events,

9. This is not the individual's actual name.

10. And God's engagement with peoples does not stop with Israel (Amos 9:7).

> only one final and perfect self-expression of God exists: Jesus. That is one thing we mean by Jesus' being God's son. I think it is interesting that you Muslims believe the Qurʾān cannot be understood without the way of life and the teachings of Muḥammad [Ali nodded approval] because we believe that Jesus is God's revelation and the New Testament is the indispensable commentary on that revelation in Jesus.

Ali then asked, "Why did Jesus die? Why did that have to happen?" I replied,

> That is part of what I mean by God participating in what it means to be human. A Muslim friend of mine was complaining to me that the Gospels teach that Jesus said on the cross, "My God, my God, why have you forsaken me?" He felt God would never forsake a prophet. I pointed out to him that here Jesus is quoting from Psalm 22. In that Psalm David expresses the pain of his own sense of separation from God. In fact, the Psalm ends on a note of hope. By quoting the Psalm, Jesus gives further evidence that in him God is experiencing all that is fully human—the worst that can happen to humans—the sense of God's absence, of being abandoned. We Christians believe God participates in what it means to be human. Participation is a key word for us.[11]
>
> Because God wants to participate with us and because we have been disobedient, God needed to make us friends again before a relationship with us could be achieved.

Ali vigorously agreed with me that a relationship with God would require transformation. I would have liked to have gone on to discuss the relationship between God's suffering in Jesus and removing the alienation that exists between God and human beings because of disobedience, but the discussion was terminated by the call to prayer. After prayer the schedule led to other things and to our departure. But I will never forget the degree of engagement and interest that this interaction elicited. It led me to believe that the differences in the way Christians and Muslims conceive of God could in fact be communicated in a common-ground dialogue. The common ground in this case was a mutual desire, born of our visit and their unparalleled hospitality, to understand each other.

> O humankind! We created you from a male and a female, and made you into peoples and tribes, in order for you to know each other (*li-taʿārafū*). (*Chambers* [49]:13; author's translation)

In chapter 10 above we traced through the Gospel of Mark Jesus' repetitive teaching of his disciples about the way he understood his role as Israel's Messiah. This teaching climaxed in the following declaration, "the Son of Man

11. I had in mind the *koinōnia* of the Holy Spirit (2 Corinthians 13:13).

has come, not to be served, but to serve, and to give his life a ransom for many" (Mark 10:45). Here Jesus indicates that God sent him to be the suffering servant portrayed by the prophet Isaiah.

> Surely he has borne our infirmities
>   and carried our diseases;
> yet we accounted him stricken,
>   struck down by God, and afflicted.
> But he was wounded for our transgressions,
>   crushed for our iniquities;
> upon him was the punishment that made us whole,
>   and by his bruises we are healed.
> All we like sheep have gone astray;
>   we have all turned to our own way,
> and the LORD has laid on him
>   the iniquity of us all. (Isaiah 53:4-6)

One valid interpretation of Isaiah's suffering servant insists that it constituted a personification of God's chosen people, Israel (Isaiah 41:8-10; 42:18-20; 43:10; 44:2, 21; 49:3). Israel was called to this vocation: suffering for the liberation of others and mediating to others the kingdom of the God who had chosen them. They were to be a light to the nations (42:6; 49:6). Israel's suffering was to be redemptive for others. But this had not fully happened. Isaiah's beautiful hope had not been fulfilled:

> How beautiful upon the mountains are the feet of the messenger who
>   announces peace,
> who brings good news, who announces salvation, who says to Zion,
>   "Your God reigns."
> Listen! Your sentinels lift up their voices, together they sing for joy;
>   for in plain sight they see the return of the Lord to Zion.
> Break forth together into singing, you ruins of Jerusalem;
>   for the Lord has comforted his people, he has redeemed Jerusalem.
> The Lord has bared his holy arm before the eyes of all the nations;
>   and all the ends of the earth shall see the salvation of our God.
> (Isaiah 52:7-10)

Israel had returned to Jerusalem, but God had not yet returned to Zion. The salvation of the Lord had not been seen by all the nations. In intimate relationship with God (Luke 10:21-23), Jesus came to understand that he was to do for Israel what Israel had not done for itself. He would be the suffering servant. He would provide the new exodus for his people; he would pay the price for the sin that kept them in exile. He would create a new exodus people who would be the salt of the earth and the light of the world (Matthew 5:13-14). In him the Lord would return to Zion!

In a sense the people of Israel were still locked in a kind of Babylonian exile. They had returned to their land—at least many of them had. They had been restored to their land, but their land had not been restored to them. They were in bondage to Rome on land that should have been their own. Their Temple was being rebuilt, but the Lord had not returned to it. God's kingdom had not come; God's will was not being done. Furthermore, they understood their plight to be a function of their sins. If they could be forgiven and reclaimed, they could be restored. They expected a Messiah to be sent to effect this transformation and liberation.[12] Jesus was sent to be this Messiah. It was his calling, but what it meant to be the Messiah came as a surprise to almost everybody.

Many, especially the followers of John the Baptist, were certain that Jesus was the expected one. As I laid out in chapter 13, when John was in prison, he sent a delegation of his followers to Jesus with a very penetrating question: "Are you the one or shall we wait for another?" The radical way Jesus understood his mission as Messiah can be discerned from his reply:

> Go and tell John the things you see and hear: the blind receive their sight, and the lame walk, the lepers are cleansed, and the deaf hear, and the dead are raised up, and the poor have the good news preached to them. And blessed is he who shall find no occasion of stumbling in me. (Matthew 11:4-6)

These three verses contain an allusion to Isaiah 35:5 and 6: "Then shall the eyes of the blind be opened and the ears of the deaf unstopped. Then the lame man shall leap like a hart and the tongue of the dumb shall sing." The verses in Matthew also allude to the text Jesus chose for announcing his identity and mission at the synagogue in Nazareth:

> The spirit of the Lord is upon me, because he anointed me to preach good news to the poor: he sent me to proclaim release to the captive, and recovery of sight to the blind, to set at liberty them that are abused, to proclaim the acceptable year of the Lord. (Luke 4:18-19)

Here Jesus read directly from Isaiah 61:1-2. It should be noted, however, that he stops and closes the scroll just before the text says, "and the day of vengeance of our God" (Isaiah 61:2b). He intentionally leaves the vengeance part out. In the allusion to Isaiah he makes in responding to John the Baptist's delegation, he also leaves out the references to the stern features of the Day of the Lord. The verse just before the ones he alludes to in Isaiah 35 says, "Say to them that are of

12. The New Testament historian N. T. Wright has fleshed this out in a number of places. He nicely summarizes it in his dialogue with Marcus Borg; see Marcus Borg and N. T. Wright, *The Meaning of Jesus: Two Visions* (San Francisco: HarperSanFrancisco, 1999), 31-35.

a fearful heart, be strong, fear not: behold your God will come with vengeance, with the recompense of God he will come and save you" (Isaiah 35:4).

Jesus made no bones about being the Messiah; these passages make that clear. But the way he understood the role of the Messiah represented something new. While it drew from the traditions familiar to the Judaism of his time, it appeared so unexpected that even his disciples had a hard time getting it, as we saw in chapter 10. His messianic role was not simply to deliver them from their current exile. He also called them to be the true Israel, to be the "returned-from-exile people of God."[13]

This did not mean just to be good people, pure, and holy in a timeless ethical sense. It meant to be the people of the kingdom that was coming into the world with Jesus; to be salt and light; to reveal God's nature and purposes to the world. This meant they had to abandon their dreams of nationalist revolution. Jesus warned them that this dream would only lead to their destruction; if they persisted in ethnocentric self-preservation and hatred of their enemies, their Zion would again be destroyed. Furthermore, he ate with sinners, claimed lordship over the Sabbath, and took authority over the Temple. The returned-from-exile people of God would be a community of forgiven sinners who could forgive their oppressors and love their enemies (Matthew 5:44; 6:15). He in fact demonstrated through forgiveness that even sinners could be constituted members of his kingdom. For the Judaism of his time, particularly its leaders, forgiveness flowed from the sacrificial system of the Temple. Jesus mediated forgiveness himself, bypassing the Temple (Matthew 9:2; Mark 2:5; Luke 5:20). As N. T. Wright puts it, "Jesus was offering forgiveness to all and sundry, out there on the street, without requiring that they go through the normal channels. That was his real offense."[14]

The people of this newly constituted Israel had to accept the challenge of Jesus to take up their crosses, "a call to follow Jesus into political danger and likely death, in the faith that by this means Israel's God would bring Israel through its present tribulations and out into the new day that would dawn."[15] It would be a new day, not only for Israel, through her ransom and restoration, but for the entire Gentile world as well. In his cleansing of the Temple, this messianic vision for the nations emerges. While overturning the tables of the money-changers and the seats of those who sold doves, he quotes scripture, "My house shall be called a house of prayer for all the nations; but you have made it a den of robbers" (Isaiah 56:7; Jeremiah 7:11; Mark 11:17). Why was Jesus so insistent on this way of being the returned-from-exile people of God? The answer turns out to be rather simple: *It is God's way.*

God, in the belief of Judaism at the time of Jesus, engaged with the people of Israel. The story they lived in was a story of creation, covenant, exodus, and

13. Ibid., 37.
14. Ibid., 39.
15. Ibid.

return. The God of creation was the only Lord; this covenant Lord had chosen Israel to be God's special people, had made promises to Abraham, Isaac, and Jacob; God had saved Israel from Egyptian bondage and established them in the land of promise; and, even when the people's sins occasioned their exile from this land into captivity again in Babylon, God had brought them back once more and would eventually liberate them from their current bondage to Rome. The earliest Christians believed that "what had happened in Jesus was the unique and personal action of the one God of Israel."[16] Paul summed up the meaning of the end of Jesus' mission in the following brief phrase, "in Christ God was reconciling the world to himself" (2 Corinthians 5:19). The mission of Jesus the Messiah was an extension of God's action in the world. Jesus' mission was the mission of God. Jesus carried out his mission in God's way. God's forgiven people, the new Israel of God, were to take the way of the cross *because it is God's way.*

In fact, Jesus and his way so agreed with themes in Jewish monotheism that the early Christians' understanding of what Jesus had said and done led them to expand their understanding of the one God to include Jesus and the Spirit. It was not the miracles he did, or the fact that he referred to himself as the Son of Humanity, or even his resurrection from the dead that led them to believe this, but rather "resurrection pointed to messiahship; messiahship, to the task performed on the cross; that task, to the God who had promised to accomplish it himself."[17] They derived this from Jesus himself who not only spoke of God's kingdom; but also enacted and embodied it himself.[18] In his triumphal entry, cleansing of the Temple, agony in Gethsemane, Last Supper with his disciples, crucifixion, and resurrection, Jesus was coming to Zion and doing what the Lord had promised to do (Isaiah 52:8). Of special significance in Jesus' way being the way of God is Jesus' own conviction that he was "called to do and be in relation to Israel what, in Scripture and Jewish belief, the Temple was and did."[19] Just as the Temple embodied the presence of God and the sacrificial system by which sins could be forgiven, so Jesus embodied the very presence of God and provided a sacrifice that would be the means of forgiveness for the people of the kingdom.

While this book is not about the deity of Jesus, we cannot escape the subject as a facet of the meaning of the cross. The cross speaks of the nature and purposes of God. In chapter 14 we spoke of the cross itself in relation to sin and forgiveness. Here I want to speak about what it reveals about God. Going back to my explanation of Christianity to the group of young men in an Indianapolis mosque above, I repeat, if my readers want to understand Christianity, they need to realize that Christians believe God wants to be involved, to be engaged, and

16. Ibid., 162.

17. Ibid., 164.

18. Ibid. See also N. T. Wright, *Jesus and the Victory of God*, Christian Origins and the Question of God 2 (Minneapolis: Fortress, 1996), 615-29.

19. N. T. Wright, *The Challenge of Jesus: Rediscovering Who Jesus Was and Is* (Downers Grove, IL: InterVarsity, 1999), 111.

to participate in the human story. In the cross, God engaged most intimately and most fully in the human experience. In doing so, God both demonstrated love and forgiveness and enabled that forgiveness and transformation for those, who—trusting in God—live according to the model Jesus set for his followers. This is what it means to take up one's cross and to follow Jesus (Mark 8:34).

As a result of the cross, we know God identifies with us—even to the extent of sharing our sense of abandonment by God. We know that in Jesus God identified with the worst we can experience. Our concern in chapter 8 above with Christian scripture as *raised up*, as opposed to being *sent down*, can now be seen in light of the Christian understanding of God as engaged and involved in the human story.

Christian Scripture and Divine Engagement

What do we make of a holy scripture that arises out of the community of faith the way the New Testament does? What do we make out of authoritative scripture humans have composed? For one thing, this mode of divine revelation suggests that God is engaged in the life of the communities of faith from which revelation emerged. God did not "send down" the Gospels, that is true; but the Holy Spirit participated in the communities of Christian faith, guiding and facilitating the writing of the Gospels.

As we have just seen, the crucifixion and resurrection of Jesus can be understood as the climactic events in the history of God's involvement in the human story—of God's engagement with persons and communities. The cross speaks as much about divine engagement as it does about human salvation. Christian scripture can be understood as arising out of this divine engagement with individuals and communities. Christian scripture shows that God is still engaged in the human story in the aftermath of Jesus' resurrection.

As we mentioned above, the Qurʾān presents a series of prophets and messengers who are sent to their respective communities to guide them back to the belief in, and obedience to, the one true God. The Torah and the Gospel—in their widest sense, comprising the whole of the Bible—show God's engagement with the people of Israel and other peoples through patriarchs, matriarchs, prophets, judges, priests, kings, pastors, teachers, preachers, apostles, deacons, elders, ordinary people, Jesus, the Messiah, and the Holy Spirit.

The Bible provides a continuous narrative of God's engagement with leaders whose own humanity is revealed along with the nature and purposes of God for them and their people. In the process, the communities of faith represented in the Bible—and by the Bible's readers—learn more and more about the nature of the God who journeys with them and woos them.

Above, we picked a word descriptive of the nature of God in relation to his people as depicted in the Qurʾān. The word was *al-Ḥalīm,* with connotations of clemency and forbearance, but clemency and forbearance flowing from strength under control. Some Qurʾānic names for God, such as *al-Wudūd,* point in the direction of God's intimate concern for humankind. Such an understanding of God is compatible with the name *al-Ḥalīm.*

The Hebrew scriptures also feature stories about God and names for God that support divine intimacy. Among the names is *ha-ʿŌzer*, "the Helper": "You have been the helper of the orphan" (Psalm 10:14); "O Lord, be my helper" (Psalm 30:10); and "But surely God is my helper" (Psalm 54:4). In the Gospel, a related term is rich in meaning: *ho paraklētos*, "the Helper, the Advocate, the Mediator," is used for the Holy Spirit in John 14:26. The same term is used for Jesus in 1 John 2:1. What Jesus taught about the Father coheres with this concept. God is certainly the Ultimate Reality; but God is also the Intimate Reality.

By means of the Holy Spirit of God, the startling divine engagement accomplished in Jesus could be continued in and among all believers in God as revealed by Jesus. The longing of Moses, "Would that all the Lord's people were prophets, and that the Lord would put his spirit on them" (Numbers 11:29), found its fulfillment in Jesus and his followers. All members of the communities of faith in Jesus as the Messiah could now be empowered by the Spirit of God in and among them to offer their gifts to the community. The Apostle Paul laid out this new situation in more than one of his letters (Romans 12:3-8; 1 Corinthians 1:5-7; 12:1-14:40; Ephesians 4:1-16): the community of faith, gifted and empowered by the Spirit, represents the body of Christ in the world.

> There is one body and one Spirit, just as you were called to the one hope of your calling, one Lord, one faith, one baptism, one God and Father of all, who is above all and through all and in all. But each of us was given grace according to the measure of Christ's gift. . . . The gifts he gave were that some would be apostles, some prophets, some evangelists, some pastors and teachers, to equip the saints for the work of ministry, for building up the body of Christ. . . . (Ephesians 4:4-12)

This does not mean that God merely adds the Spirit to the body of Christ as a helper, as though Christ established the church and then added the Spirit. The Spirit gave birth to the church, just as the Spirit conceived Jesus in the womb of Mary. The Spirit empowers the church for ministry and mission, just as the Spirit empowered Jesus for mission in baptism. And as Jesus did, so must the community of his disciples do. It "must live not out of its own resources, but by the power of the indwelling Spirit, which breathes, strengthens, inspires and guides."[20]

In other words, God does not only send down instructions for faith and life. God comes among the believers to strengthen, inspire, and guide them in the Spirit just as in Jesus God "became flesh and lived among us" (John 1:14).

Rather than being sent down as guidance, the Bible emerges from the Spirit-indwelt community of faith called the church. One could say of the Bible, "God

20. Clark H. Pinnock, *Flame of Love: A Theology of the Holy Spirit* (Downers Grove, IL: InterVarsity, 1996), 115.

raised it up!" God used human writers from within the communities of faith that grew up in the aftermath of the end of Jesus' mission to bring conviction, to offer guidance, to provide comfort, and to reveal truth and divine mysteries. Thus, the Gospels—and other books of the Bible—testify to the Word-become-flesh. They chronicle the life of the Spirit in the church. They arise out of the forge of the church wherein the fire and the hammer of the Spirit have shaped them out of the experience of the humanity of faithful disciples in service to the world. Ultimately they exist to bear witness to God's self-revelation in Jesus. The Spirit inspired them; the Spirit preserves them; the Spirit aids in interpreting them for every generation of believers in space and time. Scripture is a gift of "the grace of the Lord Jesus Christ, the love of God, and the communion of the Holy Spirit" (2 Corinthians 13:13).[21] In the light of God's radical engagement with the world, Christian scripture makes sense *as it is*—not sent down but raised up. In that same light, the last days of Jesus' mission on earth make sense *as they are* portrayed in the Gospels. Jesus, the one sent down, was also raised up—on a cross and from the grave.

I have shown in chapter 2 that the Qurʾān did not unequivocally rule out the Christian conviction that Jesus' mission ended in crucifixion. Chapters 3, 4, and 5 laid out the Muslim case in classical and modern Qurʾān commentary for the dominant Islamic view that Jesus was taken up before his crucifixion and someone else crucified in his place. Chapters 11, 12, and 13 responded to the Muslim interpretation of significant events at the end of Jesus' mission as recorded in the Gospels. In chapter 6, I reinforced the conviction of some Muslims that the Gospel of Barnabas does not meet the criteria for a genuine portrayal of the life of Jesus and his mission. Chapter 7 laid out the conviction of the earliest Christian communities that Jesus was crucified and resurrected.

Nevertheless, the heart of the argument for the crucifixion of Jesus remains chapters 8, 9, and 10: Given the nature of Christian scripture as divinely raised up from communities of faith in God through Jesus, I used historical analysis to show that Jesus predicted his death and resurrection. I argued that Jesus would not have predicted his death and resurrection and understood it as essential to his messianic vocation and then, at the end of his mission, managed an escape from that destiny. This was also based on a kind of common ground: how could a person with the integrity both Muslims and Christians believe Jesus exhibited allow someone else to die for him—to die in his place—when he had made it clear that his death was certain and would be vindicated (Mark 9:31; Luke 9:44; Matthew 17:22)? And how could Jesus or his Apostles, the *ḥawārīyūn*, so highly regarded in Qurʾānic revelation themselves, have ignored the true story of Jesus'

21. The word translated "communion" in 2 Corinthians 13:13 is *koinōnia*. It can also be translated, according to context, "fellowship," "a close mutual relationship"; "sharing in," "partnership"; and "contribution," "gift"; see Barclay M. Newman, Jr., *Greek-English Dictionary of the New Testament* (Stuttgart: United Bible Societies, 1971), 101.

rescue from the unbelievers, in order to spread a story of his ignominious death and miraculous resurrection?

Finally, of utmost importance in the discussion of the cross will always be what it reveals about God. It testifies profoundly to the way God returned to Zion. It testifies clearly to the depth of God's identification with his human creation. And when viewed in the light of the resurrection, it eloquently brings together the intimacy and ultimacy of God. In the final analysis, the end of Jesus' mission in both the sense of its *final days* and the sense of its *ultimate purpose* represents an unexpected but liberating divine self-disclosure.

Index

ʿAbduh, Muḥammad, 59, 63
Abū Bakr: on death of Muḥammad, 207
Abū Hurayrah, 35, 36, 48, 51, 52, 56, 57
Abū Zahra: and Gospel of Barnabas, 80
Acts of the Apostles, speeches in: and death of Jesus, 107
Acts of Barnabas, 82
affirmation verse
 classical commentaries on, 34-36
 context of, 28-31
 reconciliation with denial verse, 24, 25
 and resurrection, 24
 and spiritual journey, 36
Aḥbar, Kaʿb, al-: on interpretation of affirmation verse, 35
Ahmadiyyah movement: on death of Jesus, 61, 207, 209
Aʿlā Mawdūdī, Abū, al-: on death and raising of Jesus, 60
Alexandria, church in, 112-14
 and belief in death and resurrection, 113, 114
 and Gospel of Mark, 112, 113
 Jewish roots of church, 112, 113
Ali, A. Yusuf: on *ḥalīm,* 246, 247
Ālūsī, Khayr al-Dīn, al-
 on betrayal and arrest of Jesus, 189, 190
 on God's casting a likeness of Jesus on someone, 70, 71
 on Muslim interpretation of Gospel events, 64, 65, 66
 and substitution hypothesis, 68
 on Transfiguration, 171
angel: as substitute for Jesus, 188, 193
Anselm of Canterbury: and theory of penal satisfaction, 236, 237
Antichrist, 56, 57
Antioch, church in, 108-9
 and Gospel of Matthew, 108
apologetic, principles for dialogical, 10-12
appearances (of risen Jesus), 220-24
Asad, Muḥammad: on human condition, 233
atonement: and the cross, 234-39
Attridge, Harold W.: and Gospel of Truth, 103
authority, chains of, 45, 48, 49, 50, 51, 192
 and arrest of Jesus, 192
 and descent-of-Jesus traditions, 50, 51, 52, 57
Ayoub, Mahmoud A.
 on Christian-Muslim dialogue, 11
 on human condition, 231
 on interpretation of affirmation verse, 26, 27, 28, 34
 on Muslim commentators and Gospel of Barnabas, 61
 on al-Rāzī's interpretation of denial verse, 42
 on redemption in Christian and Islamic traditions, 243, 244
 on Sunni scholarship on death of Christ, 59
 on types of dialogue, 2n5

Bailey, Kenneth E.: on transmission of Gospel tradition, 122-24, 131
Baker, Mark D.
 and Anselm's penal satisfaction theory, 236, 237
 and meaning of the cross, 238
 on reconciliation through suffering, 242
baptism: as metaphor for suffering, 132, 133
Bāqī, Muḥammad Fuʾād ʿAbd, al-, 48
Barbour, R. S.: on "the hour," 143
Bardaisan (Bardesanes): and end of Jesus mission, 99, 100
Barnabas. *See* Gospel of Barnabas
Basilides, 102, 104, 105, 113
Bayer, Hans F.
 on Caesarean prediction, 151, 153
 on eschatological prospect, 139, 140

Bayer, Hans F. (*continued*)
on Galilean prediction, 157
on Garden of Gethsemane scene, 182, 183
and "the hour," 142, 144
on Judean prediction, 163, 164, 166
on Last Supper, 178
on metaphor of baptism, 133
on metaphor of cup, 135
and rejection of Jesus, 145, 146
Best, Eugene: on death of Jesus in the Gospels, 150
betrayal and arrest (of Jesus)
in classical Qurʾān commentaries, 185-88
Gospel narrative of, 190-92
in modern Qurʾān commentators, 188-90, 193
Bible and Qurʾān
common moral values of, 10
significant figures common to, 10
biographies of Muḥammad: absence of descent-of-Jesus traditions in, 56-57
Biqāʿī, Burhān al-Dīn, al-
on betrayal and arrest of Jesus, 189
on confusion about identity of Jesus, 64
Bockmuehl, Markus, 211, 212, 224
Bogiani, Franco: on Tatian as a Gnostic, 99
Brown, Raymond E.: on churches in Antioch and Rome, 108, 110, 111
Bukhārī, Abū ʿAbd Allāh Muḥammad ibn Ismāʿīl, al-: and *Ṣaḥīḥ* tradition, 47
Bultmann, Rudolf
and methodology in study of Gospels, 121
and transmission of oral tradition, 122

Carpocrates: teachings of, 105-6
Carpocratians, 105, 106
Cerinthians: and someone substituted for Jesus at crucifixion, 96
Cerinthus: and crucifixion of Jesus, 97, 98
Charinus (Carinus), Leucius: on someone substituted for Jesus at crucifixion, 101
Chirri, Mohamed Jawad
critique of doctrine of the cross, 235, 236
on original sin and redemption, 229, 230, 231, 232
Christianity and Islam
building relationships, 12
common elements, 1-10
disagreements between, 2, 10
Cirillo, Luigi: on Gospel of Barnabas, 81
Claudius, Emperor, 207
Clement of Alexandria, 104
coherence: as criterion for authenticity of sayings of Jesus, 125, 145
collective-casting narrative, 39, 40, 41
companions of Jesus: made to look like Jesus, 188
Companions of the Prophet: and interpretation of the Qurʾān, 57
composition criticism, 126-27
Cragg, Kenneth
on Christian use of the Qurʾān, 4
on multiple Gospels, 5
on origin of the Gospels, 119
on witness to Jesus in the Gospels, 117
Cramer, J. F.: and Gospel of Barnabas, 80
cross
and atonement, 234-39
and involvement of God, 250-55
meaning of, 238-39
and message of Jesus, 239-44
crucifixion
belief in: in Christianity before Paul, 106-14
Christian response to Muslim interpretation, 199-205
denied by Christians in Egypt and Syria, 95
as forged narratives, 198-99
and the Gospels, 76-77, 200-205
lack of Christian consensus on, 77
as metaphorical, 78
Muslim interpretation of, 77, 195-99
not foretold by God, 68, 69
of someone other than Jesus, 196
Cumming, Joseph: on interpretation of denial verse, 16, 17
cup
as metaphor for divine judgment, 134-36
as symbol, 183, 184

Ḍaḥḥāk, al-, 56
Daniélou, Jean: on Elkesaism, 100
Darrat, Suleiman
on *aḥādī* status of *ḥadīth*, 57
on Qurʾān and Gospels, 5
Darwazah, Muḥammad ʿIzzat, 69
on denial of crucifixion, 96
death of Jesus. *See* Jesus: death of
Deedat, Ahmad: and resuscitation theory, 61, 207
Delling, Gerhard: on "the hour," 142, 143
denial verse
Christian interpretation of, 20
classical commentaries on, 37-42
commentary of Qasimi on, 63
context of, 17-23
interpretation of, 16-17
passive construction in, 16
Shīʿīte commentators on substitutionist solution to, 44
substitutionist solution to, 37-44
and "those who differ," 17
descent of ʿĪsā: in *Ṣaḥīḥ* Muslim, 47-49
Dhu Khulasa, 62
dialogue, Christian-Muslim: common ground in, 1-2, 10, 245-257
Diatessaron, 98, 99, 119
Didache: and church in Antioch, 108
didactic discourse, 151
disciples of Jesus, Muslim respect for, 8-10
dissimilarity: as criterion for authenticity of sayings of Jesus, 125, 133, 145, 155, 168
double dissimilarity: as criterion for authenticity of sayings of Jesus, 125, 136
double standards: in Christian-Muslim dialogue, 10, 11
drunkenness: as image, 135

Ebion: and death of Jesus, 98
Ebionites
and crucifixion of Jesus, 97, 98
See also Gospel of the Ebionites
Ehrman, Bart: on Ebionite understanding of God and Jesus, 98
Elder, E. E.: on denial verse, 20, 25
Elkesaism, 100
empty tomb, 218-20
engagement, divine, 255-57
Ephrem Syrus, 100
Epistle of Barnabas: and Alexandrian church, 113, 114
eschatological prospect, 138-41
Eugène of Savoy, Count: and Gospel of Barnabas, 80
Eusebius: and church in Alexandria, 112

Family of Imran (*sūrah*)
occasion for revelation of, 34
structure and narrative, 29, 30
Faruqi, Ismail Ragi, al-
on revelation, 248
on sin and human condition, 231, 232
form criticism, 120-21
Frémaux, Michel: on Gospel of Barnabas, 81

Gabriel (angel): as Holy Spirit, 43
Garden of Gethsemane scene, 181-84
Gelasian Decrees: and Gospel of Barnabas, 81, 82
Gerhardsson, Birger: on Gospel tradition, 122
Glassé, Cyril: on Gospel of Barnabas as medieval forgery, 82, 94
Gnosticism: in Antioch and Egypt, 102-6
God
attributes of: in the Qurʾān, 4, 246-48
beliefs shared by Christianity and Islam, 3-4
as *al-Ḥalīm,* 246, 247
Hebrew names for, 256
involvement with cross of Jesus, 250-55
Muslim names for, 245-46
oneness of, 3
revelation of, in Islam, 247, 248
Goddard, Hugh: on double standards in Christian-Muslim dialogue, 10, 11, 54
Gospel
and four Gospels, 117
Qurʾānic view of, 115
Gospel of Barnabas, 77
geographical errors in, 86
historical anachronisms in, 86, 87

Gospel of Barnabas (*continued*)
history of, 79, 80
and knowledge of canon of scripture, 89
lack of citation of, in Prophet's *Sunnah*, 93-94
on last days of Jesus, 83-85
as medieval forgery, 86
and the Qurʾān, 90-93
Gospel of the Ebionites, 98
Gospel of Mark: problematic ending of, 222
Gospel of Philip, 102
Gospel of Truth, 102, 103, 104
Gospels
and authenticity of words of Jesus, 127-29
canonical: knowledge of, and Gospel of Barnabas, 89
composition and canonization of, 117-19
and contradictions about Jesus' last days, 72
contrast with Qurʾān, 5, 116, 117
and the crucifixion, 76-77
development of, 77
illegitimacy of four, 77
methodology in study of, 120-27
Muslim understanding of, 5, 6
and Prophetic Tradition, 117
as "raised up," 118
and reliability of oral transmission, 123, 124
and support for Qurʾānic interpretation of, 64-69
Green, Joel B.
and Anselm's penal satisfaction theory, 236, 237
on arrest of Jesus, 191
on death of Jesus, 148
on Last Supper, 179, 181
and meaning of the cross, 238
on reconciliation through suffering, 242
Guillaume, Alfred, 56
Gundry, Robert H.: on Caesarean prediction, 155

ḥadīth, 45, 46
collections of, 47
and descent-of-Jesus traditions, 52-55
qudsī ("Sacred Tradition"), 117
See also Prophetic Tradition
Ḥalīm, al-: as name of God, 246, 247, 255
Hamerton-Kelly, R. G.: on Jesus' cry on the cross, 196, 197
Hengel, Martin: on crucifixion, 197, 198
Hippolytus, 97
Holy Spirit: angel Gabriel as, 43
"hour, the," 141-44
human beings, sinless, 234
human condition: Qurʾānic and Christian views of, 229-33

Ibn ʿAbbās, 56
on affirmation verse, 24, 34
on *mutawaffī-ka,* 50
Ibn Antarah, Hārūn: on substitutionist solution to denial verse, 39, 40
Ibn Āshūr
on interpretation of denial verse, 61, 62
on use of tradition in interpreting the Qurʾān, 57
Ibn Isḥāq, 56, 57
on someone made to look like Jesus, 39
Ibn Kathīr: on substitutionist solution to denial verse, 41
Ibn Maʿqil, ʿAbd al-Ṣamad: on interpretation of denial verse, 40, 41
Ibn Munabbih, Wahb
on affirmation verse, 24, 34
on arrest of Jesus, 186, 188, 192
on denial verse, 37, 38, 39, 40, 41
on Last Supper of Jesus, 177
on *mutawaffī-ka,* 50
Ibn Shihāb al-Zuhrī, 56
Ibn Taymīyah, Taqī al-Dīn: on crucifixion, 199
Ibn ʿUqbah, Mūsā, 56
Ibn al-Zubayr, Abd Allāh: on affirmation verse, 35
Ībūn: on lack of knowledge of Jesus' end, 96, 97
Ignatius of Antioch: and cross of Christ, 109
implausibility: as criterion for authenticity of sayings of Jesus, 126
incoherence: as criterion for authenticity of sayings of Jesus, 126

infants/children: natural condition of, 232, 233
injīl. See Gospel; Gospels
intimacy, divine, 228, 232, 246-48, 256
Irenaeus, 97, 98, 104, 105, 106
ʿĪsā: name of Jesus in Qurʾān, 7
isnād. See authority, chains of
Izutsu, Toshihiko: on *Ḥalīm* as divine name, 247

Jalālayn Commentary, 62, 63
Jamiʿ of al-Tirmidhī, 47
Jammāl, Muḥammad ʿAbd al-Munʿim, al-: and Gospel of Barnabas, 61
Jefford, Clayton N.: on sin and human condition, 231
Jeremias, Joachim: on Last Supper, 178, 181
Jerusalem: as place for death of prophet, 137-38
Jerusalem believers, 106-7
Jeshu bar Nagara, 62
Jesus
- affirmation of death in Qurʾān, 23-25
- anointing for burial, 136-37
- anticipation of early death, 130-47
- ascension of, 60, 61, 71
- betrayal and arrest, 65, 141-44, 185-93
- claim of Jews to have killed, 17-20
- confusion about identity, 64
- crucifixion of, 66, 76, 77, 200-205. *See also* cross; crucifixion
- death and resurrection: and Antioch church, 108, 109; in speeches of Acts, 107
- death of, 206-10; and ambiguity of Qurʾān, 32; attested in Talmud and Josephus, 148
- and death of John the Baptist, 131, 132
- disciples of: Muslim respect for, 8-10
- fear of death by, 39
- final days of: in Gospel of Barnabas, 83-85; in modern Qurʾān commentary, 59-78
- and "the hour," 142-44
- likeness of, cast on someone, 185, 188
- and meaning of the cross, 239-44
- as Messenger and Confirmer in Qurʾān, 30
- as Messiah, 213, 214, 215, 216
- and monotheism, 254
- and Muslim belief in oneness of God, 3
- Muslim identification with suffering of, 239, 240, 241, 242
- Muslim reverence for, 7-8
- necessity for someone to die in his place, 72
- opposition to: by Romans and Jews, 240, 241, 242
- and parable of wicked husbandmen, 144-47
- prayer in Garden of Gethsemane, 181, 182
- predictions of death, 148-69
- predictions of suffering and vindication, 144-47
- Qurʾān's treatment of, 2n4
- request for volunteer replacement at death, 186, 188
- resurrection appearances of, 220-24
- resurrection of, in New Testament, 210-18
- return of, 35, 36, 46; in Muslim tradition, 45
- role in Gospel of Barnabas, 93
- sayings of: criteria for authenticity, 125, 126
- as sinless: in Islam and Christianity, 234, 235
- someone made to look like, 16, 17, 38
- as Son of God, 249, 250
- as Son of Humanity, 143, 157, 158, 159, 163, 164, 168, 170, 176, 254
- spiritual journey of, 36
- substitution for, 16, 17, 27, 32, 35, 37
- as suffering servant, 251
- in teachings of Mani, 101
- and thirsting on the cross, 69
- traditions about descent of, 46, 47-49, 50, 51, 52-55
- Transfiguration of, 65, 71
- trial of, 65
- words of, authenticity of, 127-29

Jews
- charges against, in Qurʾān, 18
- and claim to have killed Jesus, 17-20

John the Baptist
- and Gospel of Barnabas, 84, 85, 93

John the Baptist (*continued*)
premature death of, 131
view of Messiah, 215, 216, 252
Judas
hanging of, 64
likeness of Jesus cast upon, 185
as substitute for Jesus, 32, 39, 40, 188, 193
Justin Martyr, 98, 102, 119

Kateregga, Badru D.
on dialogue between Christians and Muslims, 3-4, 245
on Muslim respect for disciples of Jesus, 8
on Muslim reverence for Jesus, 7, 8
on names for God, 245-46
Khan, Sayyid Ahmad: on crucifixion of Jesus, 61
kingdom of God, 212-16

Lapide, Pinchas: on women witnesses to the resurrection, 226
Last Supper, 177-81
Lindars, Barnabas: on Galilean prediction, 159
Lüdemann, Gerd: on death and resurrection of Jesus, 206, 207

MacRae, George W., S.J.: and Gospel of Truth, 103
Mahdī, al-, 25
Mani: teachings of, 100, 101
Maqsood, Ruqaiyyah Waris
and authenticity of Gospel of Barnabas, 61
on lack of identity between Jesus of New Testament and ʿĪsā of Qurʾān, 62
and resuscitation theory, 61, 207, 208, 209
Marāghī, al-: on raising of Jesus, 61
Marcion: and belief in crucifixion, 99
Mark. *See* Gospel of Mark
Marshall, I. H.: on Last Supper, 178
Mary: as sister of Aaron, 27, 28
Mawdūdī, Abū al-Aʿlā, 66, 75
and descent-of-Jesus tradition, 68
McAuliffe, Jane Dammen, 186
on contemporary relevance of al-Ṭabarī in Muslim world, 13
McElwain, Thomas, 11, 12
McKnight, Scot
on Jesus' predictions of death, 166, 167, 168
on Jesus' understanding of his death, 130-47
on reconciliation through suffering, 242
Meier, John P.: on church in Antioch, 108, 109
Menander of Samaria, 104
messengers
of God, 55, 196, 246
Tenacious Messengers, 234, 235
Messiah
experienced by the church as living, 224, 225
Jesus as, 213, 214, 215, 216, 250, 252, 253
Jewish concept of, 213
John the Baptist, view of, 215, 216, 252
messianic figures, 213, 214
methodology: in study of Gospels, 120-27
Meyer, Ben F.: on faithfulness of Jesus and crucifixion, 242
monotheism: and understanding of Jesus, 254
Moucarry, Chawkat: on al-Rāzī's interpretation of denial verse, 42
Moule, C. F. D.: critique of resuscitation theory, 209
Muḥammad
and authenticity of descent-of-Jesus traditions, 52-55
biographies of, 56, 57
dispute with Christians from Najrān, 33, 34
as God's final messenger, 246
messiahship of: in Gospel of Barnabas, 90-92
obedience/disobedience to, 46
Muḥammadī, ʿIzz al-Dīn, al-
on crucifixion of Jesus, 197
on last days of Jesus, 68, 69
on Transfiguration, 171, 173, 174
multiple attestation, 125, 133, 145
Musnad of Ahmad ibn Ḥanbal, 47, 52
Musnad of al-Dārimī, 52

mutawaffī-ka, 24, 30, 34, 35, 36, 50, 69
*Muwaṭṭā*ʾ of Mālik ibn Anas, 52

names: of God, 245-46, 256
Nisābūrī, Muslim ibn al-Ḥajjāj al-Qushayrī, al-, and *Ṣaḥīḥ* tradition, 46, 47
Nolin, Kenneth
 on affirmation and denial verses, 20, 25, 26
 on Christian reading of the Qurʾān, 25

original sin, 227-33
 and human guilt, 229

Parrinder, Geoffrey: on denial verse, 20, 25
Paul (apostle)
 and church in Rome, 111, 112
 and crucifixion as metaphorical, 78
penal satisfaction theory, 236-38
People of the Book
 and corruption of scripture, 7
 Jews and Christians as, 4
 reprimand by the Qurʾān, 7
persons, primacy of: in Christian-Muslim dialogue, 11, 12
Philip. *See* Gospel of Philip
Photius: and someone substituted for Jesus at crucifixion, 96, 101
Pines, Shlomo: on Gospel of Barnabas, 81
predictions of death of Jesus
 Caesarean, 149-57
 Galilean, 157-61
 Judean, 161-66
 problem of explicitness, 166-69
Prophetic Tradition, 45-47
 authority of, 46
 and Gospels, 117
prophets
 Muslim belief in, 8
 as sinless, 234
Ptolemy, 103

Qadhdhāfī, Muʿammar, 79
Qāsim ibn abī Bazzah, al-: on likeness of Jesus cast upon someone, 38
Qāsimī, Jamāl al-Dīn, al-
 on betrayal and arrest of Jesus, 188, 189
 and case of the wavering Christian, 73-75
 on crucifixion, 195-99
 on death of someone made to look like Jesus, 148, 149
 on denial of crucifixion by Christians, 95, 96
 on Gospel of Barnabas, 82-83
 interpretation of Garden of Gethsemane scene, 181, 182
 on Jesus' escape from death, 32
 on last days of Jesus, 63-78
 on Qurʾānic interpretation supported by Gospels, 67
 response to Christian claims, 69-72
 and substitution hypothesis, 68
 and substitution of Satan for Jesus, 68
 on Transfiguration, 171, 172, 173, 174, 175
 on trial of Jesus, 193-95
 on women witnesses to the resurrection, 225-26
Qatādah, 35, 56
 on likeness of Jesus cast upon someone, 38, 39
Quadragesima: and dating of Gospel of Barnabas, 88
Qurʾān
 affirmation verse, 23-31
 and attributes of God, 3-4
 authoritative text of, 116
 and Bible: significant figures common to, 10
 on Christians, Jews, and Muslims and "those who differ," 17
 commentaries on: and final days of Jesus, 15
 contradicted by Gospel of Barnabas, 90-93
 contrast with Gospels, 5, 116, 117
 on death of Jesus, 27
 denial verse, 15-23
 descent-of-Jesus traditions absent in, 55
 and divine intimacy, 246-48
 on human condition, 229, 230
 interpretation of, 57
 on Jesus as Messenger and Confirmer, 30

Qurʾān (*continued*)
on last days of Jesus as triumph of God, 31
memorization and recitation of, 122
on mutual understanding, 1
on obedience/disobedience to God, 46
origin of, 116
and personal responsibility for sin, 227
positive attitude toward Christian scripture, 6, 7
reprimand of People of the Book, 7
treatment of Jesus, 2n4
on universal resurrection, 206
Quṭb, Sayyid
on death and ascension of Jesus, 60
and descent-of-Jesus tradition, 68
and Gospel of Barnabas, 61
on *tawḥid,* 28, 29
Qurṭubī, Muḥammad ibn Ahmad, al-: on eschatological traditions about Jesus, 36

Ragg, Laura: and Gospel of Barnabas, 80, 81, 83, 87, 88, 89
Ragg, Lonsdale: and Gospel of Barnabas, 80, 81, 83, 87, 88, 89
Rahman, Fazlur: on attributes of God, 3-4
al-Rāzī, Fakhr al-Dīn
on affirmation verse, 27, 35
on necessity for someone to die in place of Jesus, 72
objections to substitutionist solution to denial verse, 42-43
redaction criticism. *See* composition criticism
redemption: in Christian and Islamic traditions, 243, 244
Rénan, Ernst, 194, 195
resurrection
bodily, 210
universal: Muslim belief in, 206
resurrection of Jesus
in affirmation verse, 24
historicity, 218-25
and the kingdom of God, 212-16
in letters of Paul, 210-12
in New Testament accounts, 210-18
uniqueness of, 212-13
resuscitation theory, critique of, 209
revelation: "sent down," 115, 255
Riḍā, Muḥammad Rashīd, 69
on belief in the crucifixion, 59, 60
and descent-of-Jesus tradition, 68
on Ebion and death of Jesus, 98
and Gospel of Barnabas, 61
on someone substituted for Jesus at crucifixion, 96, 101
Riesenfeld, Harald
on Gospel tradition, 122
on importance of four Gospels, 117
Robinson, John A. T.: on resurrection, 212, 213, 218-22, 224-25
Rome
church in, 109, 109-12; and belief in death and resurrection of Jesus, 111, 112
expulsion of Jews from, 110
Jewish roots of church in, 110, 111
Rowland, Christopher: on speeches in Acts, 107

Saʿādah, Khalīl: and Arabic translation of Gospel of Barnabas, 80
Sabzawārī, ʿAbd al-Aʿlā, al-
and descent-of-Jesus tradition, 68
on necessity for someone to die in place of Jesus, 72
Sacred Tradition, 117
Ṣaḥīḥ Muslim, 46, 47
Sale, George: and Gospel of Barnabas, 79, 80
Salibi, Kamal S.: on lack of identity between Jesus of New Testament and ʿĪsā of Qurʾān, 62
Sanders, E. P.: and the resurrection, 224
Sandnes, Karl Olav: on atonement, 243
satan/Satan
likeness of Jesus cast upon, 68
as substitute for Jesus, 188, 193
Saturninus (Satornilus): teachings of, 103, 104
Sayous, Eduard: on Simon of Cyrene substituting for Jesus at crucifixion, 96
Schäferdiek, Knut, 101, 102
Schirrmacher, Christine, 59
Schweidweiler, Felix, 98

scripture
  common ground between Christians and Muslims, 4-7
  corruption of: by People of the Book, 7
Seneca: on agony of crucifixion, 197
Sergius: as the one made to look like Jesus, 39
Shaltūt, Maḥmūd: on truth of God, 29
Shamlu, Ahmad: and cross of Jesus, 239
Shenk, David W.
  on dialogue between Christians and Muslims, 3-5, 245
  on Muslim respect for disciples of Jesus, 8
  on Muslim reverence for Jesus, 7, 8
  on names for God, 245-46
Shroud of Turin, 208
shubbiha la-hum, 16, 20, 38, 40, 61, 73, 149, 186, 187
Siddiqi, Muhammad Zubayr: on principles for criticism of traditions, 49
Simon of Cyrene: as substitute for Jesus at crucifixion, 96, 104
sin
  human beings without, 234
  responsibility for: in Hebrew scriptures, 228; in Muslim perspective, 227-33
Sīrah of Ibn Isḥāq, 56
Six Books, 46, 47
Slee, Michelle: on the *Didache,* 108-9
Slomp, Jan: on dating of Gospel of Barnabas, 87, 88
Son of Humanity. *See* Jesus: as Son of Humanity
Soroudi, Sorour S., 239
source criticism, 124-26
Sox, David: and Gospel of Barnabas, 79, 87
spiritual journey
  and affirmation verse, 36
  of Jesus, 36
Strecker, Georg: and Gospel of the Ebionites, 98
substitution hypothesis: Qurʾānic interpretation supported by Gospels, 66, 67
Suddī, al-: on someone substituting for Jesus, 38, 39
Suetonius: and expulsion of Jews from Rome, 110
suffering
  positive view of, 27
  of the righteous, 242
Sunan of Abū Dāʾūd, 47
Sunan of Ibn Mājah, 47, 52
Sunnah of the Prophet, 46

Ṭabarī, Muḥammad ibn Jarīr, al-
  on affirmation verse, 24, 34, 35
  and authencity of eschatological tradition, 55-58
  on betrayal and arrest of Jesus, 186, 187, 188, 192
  on denial verse, 37, 38, 39, 40, 41, 42
  and descent-of-Jesus tradition, 51
  and empty tomb, 219, 220
  interpretation of Garden of Gethsemane scene, 182
  on last days of Jesus, 69
  on Last Supper of Jesus, 177, 178
  and Muḥammad's dispute with Christians from Najrān, 34
  on reliability of resurrection reports, 224
  on return of Jesus, 35, 36
  and *Ṣaḥīḥ* traditions about end of Jesus' mission, 46, 47
  on someone made to look like Jesus, 50
  on substitution for Jesus, 35
  on tradition and ambiguity of affirmation and denial verses, 46
  view of Jesus' disciples, 199, 200
Ṭabāṭabāʾī, al-, on substitutionist solution to denial verse, 44
Tacitus: and death of Jesus, 148
Tatian
  and the *Diatessaron,* 119, 129
  and end of Jesus' mission, 98, 99
tawḥīd, 28, 29
Tenacious Messengers. *See under* messengers
Timothy I (Nestorian patriarch): on the affirmation verse, 25, 26
Toland, John: and Gospel of Barnabas, 80
Tradition/tradition(s)
  aḥādī, 49, 57, 69
  authenticity of, 49
  formal/informal controlled/uncontrolled models, 122, 123

Tradition/tradition(s) (*continued*)
- *mashhūr*, 49
- *mutawātir,* 49, 50, 52, 57, 148
- oral, 121, 122, 123, 124
- "raised up," 115, 129, 255
- reliability of Bukhārī and Muslim, 49

Transfiguration, 170-76
- and *exodos*, 174, 176
- as misplaced resurrection narrative, 175, 176
- as support for substitution hypothesis, 170, 171

trial of Jesus
- Gospel interpretation, 194, 195
- Muslim interpretation, 193-95

Ṭūsī, Muḥammad ibn al-Ḥasan, al-, on substitutionist solution to denial verse, 44
Two-Ways teaching, 113

ʿUthman, Caliph, 116

Valentinus, 113
- teachings of, 102-3

Vermes, Geza: and the resurrection, 224
Veronica's Veil (handkerchief), 208
Vielhauer, Phillip: and Gospel of the Ebionites, 98
volunteer: as replacement for Jesus at death, 186

Wāḥidī, al-: on Qurʾānic revelations, 33
Walton, Steve
- on composition of Gospels, 118, 119
- on interpretation and source criticism, 124

Wansbrough, John: on disputation between Christians and Muslims, 31
Warrāq, Maṭar, al-: on affirmation verse, 35
Watt, W. Montgomery: on denial verse, 20
Way of the Prophet, 46
Wenham, David
- on composition of Gospels, 118, 119
- on interpretation and source criticism, 124

White, Joseph: and Gospel of Barnabas, 80
wicked husbandmen, parable of, 144-47
witnesses to resurrection, 220-24
- problem of women witnesses, 225-26

Women (*sūrah*), 15, 17, 20, 21, 23
Word of Witness, 46
Wright, N. T.
- on death and resurrection of Jesus, 207, 217
- on Jesus and forgiveness, 253
- and meals of Jesus, 241
- on reconciliation through suffering, 242
- and resurrection of Jesus, 210, 212, 221, 223, 224; and kingdom of God, 212
- on Transfiguration, 175

Zafzāf, Fawzī, al-, on dialogue between Christianity and Islam, 1-2, 10, 245
Zahlawi, Father Iliyas: on Gospel of Barnabas, 83, 84

Other Titles in the Faith Meets Faith Series

Toward a Universal Theology of Religion, Leonard Swidler, editor
The Myth of Christian Uniqueness, John Hick and Paul F. Knitter, editors
An Asian Theology of Liberation, Aloysius Pieris, S.J.
The Dialogical Imperative, David Lochhead
Love Meets Wisdom, Aloysius Pieris, S.J.
Many Paths, Eugene Hillman, C.S.Sp.
The Silence of God, Raimundo Panikkar
The Challenge of the Scriptures, Groupe de Recherches Islamo-Chrétien
The Meaning of Christ, John P. Keenan
Hindu-Christian Dialogue, Harold Coward, editor
The Emptying God, John B. Cobb, Jr., and Christopher Ives, editors
Christianity through Non-Christian Eyes, Paul J. Griffiths, editor
Christian Uniqueness Reconsidered, Gavin D'Costa, editor
Women Speaking, Women Listening, Maura O'Neill
Bursting the Bonds?, Leonard Swidler, Lewis John Eron, Gerard Sloyan, and Lester Dean, editors
One Christ—Many Religions, Stanley J. Samartha
The New Universalism, David J. Krieger
Jesus Christ at the Encounter of World Religions, Jacques Dupuis, S.J.
After Patriarchy, Paula M. Cooey, William R. Eakin, and Jay B. McDaniel, editors
An Apology for Apologetics, Paul J. Griffiths
World Religions and Human Liberation, Dan Cohn-Sherbok, editor
Uniqueness, Gabriel Moran
Leave the Temple, Felix Wilfred, editor
The Buddha and the Christ, Leo D. Lefebure
The Divine Matrix, Joseph A. Bracken, S.J.
The Gospel of Mark: A Māhayāna Reading, John P. Keenan
Revelation, History and the Dialogue of Religions, David A. Carpenter
Salvations, S. Mark Heim
The Intercultural Challenge of Raimon Panikkar, Joseph Prabhu, editor
Fire and Water: Women, Society, and Spirituality in Buddhism and Christianity, Aloysius Pieris, S.J.
Piety and Power: Muslims and Christians in West Africa, Lamin Sanneh
Life after Death in World Religions, Harold Coward, editor
The Uniqueness of Jesus, Paul Mojzes and Leonard Swidler, editors
A Pilgrim in Chinese Culture, Judith A. Berling
West African Religious Traditions, Robert B. Fisher, S.V.D.
Hindu Wisdom for All God's Children, Francis X. Clooney, S.J.
Imagining the Sacred, Vernon Ruland, S.J.
Christian-Muslim Relations, Ovey N. Mohammed, S.J.
John Paul II and Interreligious Dialogue, Byron L. Sherwin and Harold Kasimow, editors
Transforming Christianity and the World, John B. Cobb, Jr.
The Divine Deli, John H. Berthrong
Experiencing Scripture in World Religions, Harold Coward, editor
The Meeting of Religions and the Trinity, Gavin D'Costa

Subverting Hatred: The Challenge of Nonviolence in Religious Traditions, Daniel L. Smith-Christopher, editor

Christianity and Buddhism: A Multi-Cultural History of Their Dialogue, Whalen Lai and Michael von Brück

Islam, Christianity, and the West: A Troubled History, Rollin Armour, Sr.

Many Mansions? Multiple Religious Belonging, Catherine Cornille, editor

No God But God: A Path to Muslim-Christian Dialogue on the Nature of God, A. Christian van Gorder

Understanding Other Religious Worlds: A Guide for Interreligious Education, Judith Berling

Buddhists and Christians: Toward Solidarity through Comparative Theology, James L. Fredericks

Christophany: The Fullness of Man, Raimon Panikkar

Experiencing Buddhism: Ways of Wisdom and Compassion, Ruben L. F. Habito

Gandhi's Hope: Learning from Others as a Way to Peace, Jay B. McDaniel

Still Believing: Muslim, Christian, and Jewish Women Affirm Their Faith, Victoria Erickson and Susan A. Farrell, editors

The Concept of God in Global Dialogue, Werner G. Jeanrond and Aasulv Lande, editors

The Myth of Religious Superiority: A Multifaith Exploration, Paul F. Knitter, editor

A Muslim Looks at Christianity: Essays by Mahmoud Ayoub, Irfan Omar, editor

Mending a Torn World: Women in Interreligious Dialogue, Maura O'Neill

Hospitality and the Other: Pentecost, Christian Practices, and the Neighbor, Amos Yong